The Qualities of Time

ASA Monographs

ISSN 0066-9679

The Qualities of Time

Anthropological Approaches

Edited by
Wendy James and David Mills

Oxford • New York

First published in 2005 by

Berg

Editorial offices:

1st Floor, Angel Court, 81 St Clements Street, Oxford OX4 1AW, UK

175 Fifth Avenue, New York, NY 10010, USA

© Wendy James and David Mills 2005

Berg is the imprint of Oxford International Publishers Ltd.

Library of Congress Cataloging-in-Publication Data

A catalog record for this book is available from the Library of Congress.

British Library Cataloguing-in-Publication Data

A catalogue record for this book is available from the British Library.

ISBN 1 84520 045 4 (Cloth)
1 84520 074 8 (Paper)

Typeset by JS Typesetting Ltd, Wellingborough, Northants.
Printed in the United Kingdom by Biddles Ltd, King's Lynn.

www.bergpublishers.com

Contents

Contents

Contents

Preface

Since its foundation in 1946, the Association of Social Anthropologists has always welcomed members from the Commonwealth who have attended many of the annual and decennial conferences it has held in the United Kingdom since 1963. Every year since then one or more volumes have been published from these conferences, each devoted to a thematic issue at the forefront of anthropological theory. Thanks to their consistent excellence, the 'ASA Monograph Series' has become recognized world-wide as a leading-edge forum for the advancement of social anthropology.

However, it was not until 1997 that the ASA held its first annual conference outside the UK in Harare, Zimbabwe. The intention was that a Commonwealth conference should be held every five years, so in 2002 the Association was especially grateful to Wendy James and David Mills for arranging that our meeting took place in the superb surroundings of Arusha, Tanzania. Planning for a further Commonwealth conference is in hand for 2007, and the Association remains committed to consolidating the international character of its activities.

ASA Monographs now also enter a new phase as we forge a partnership with Berg, a publisher with exemplary commitment to the discipline of anthropology. We look forward to deepening this association over the coming years. With a new Millennium recently upon us, it seems appropriate that we embark on this phase in the Association's life with a collection of essays exploring the role played by time in the way that we work out our lives together as social animals.

Chair of ASA, on behalf of the Committee

Illustrations

The Contributors

Maggie Bolton currently has an ESRC funded research fellowship in the Department of Social Anthropology at the University of Manchester. She has conducted fieldwork in the Andean region, in the southwest of Bolivia, principally with llama-herders and miners. Her current research interests include science, technology and modernity; power and knowledge; colonialism; ethnicity; and anthropology and history. She is currently researching the impact of discourses of science and technology on a Bolivian herding community. Maggie.Bolton@man. ac.uk

Jasper Chalcraft is completing his PhD on UNESCO's World Heritage, and rock art sites in both central Tanzania and the Italian Alps. He lectures occasionally on cultural heritage issues at the University of East Anglia and the University of Teramo, Italy. He is also involved with a research project aimed at the documentation and international legal protection of rock art sites in war zones (Western Sahara). j.chalcraft@uea.ac.uk

Roy Dilley is Senior Lecturer in the Department of Social Anthropology, University of St Andrews, Scotland. He has conducted extensive fieldwork in Senegal on hereditary craftsmen, and his most recent publication on this topic is entitled *Between Mosque and Termite Mound: Islamic and Caste Knowledge Practices among Haalpulaaren* (International Africa Institute, London, 2004). His latest research is on the life and work of French colonial officers in Senegal. rmd:st-and.ac.uk

Richard Fardon is Professor of West African Anthropology at the School of Oriental and African Studies. His current research concerns the historic material culture of the Middle Belt of Cameroon and Nigeria. A co-authored book on Chamba statuary is in press, and a comparative account of middle-belt masquerade is nearing completion. His paper in this volume derives from a project on the development of Chamba ceremonial. rf@soas.ac.uk

Monica Heintz, Research Fellow, Max Planck Institute for Social Anthropology (Halle, Germany). Her current research project bears on religious moral education in Romania and the Republic of Moldova. Her PhD (Cambridge, 2002) was on 'Changes in Work Ethic in Postsocialist Romania'. heintz@eth.mpg

Contributors

Elisabeth Hsu, University Lecturer at the Institute of Social and Cultural Anthropology and Fellow of Green College, University of Oxford. Research interests centre on Chinese medicine, and other non-Western medicines; fieldwork has been carried out in the People's Republic of China and East Africa. Recent publications include: *The Transmission of Chinese Medicine*, CUP, 1999, *Innovation in Chinese Medicine* (ed), CUP, 2001, and *Countervailing Creativity: Patient Agency in the Globalisation of Asian Medicines* (co-ed), Special Issue, *Anthropology and Medicine*, 2002. Elisabeth.Hsu@anthro.ox.ac.uk

Andrew Irving is a Research Fellow in the Dept. of Psychiatry and Behavioural Sciences, University College London and Royal Free Hospital and works on perception, art and death. He is particularly interested in how the world appears to persons close to death and documenting those moments where time and death emerge into everyday life. His award winning PhD is entitled 'Life Made Strange; A Comparative Study of How HIV/AIDS Affects Perception of Time, Existence and Otherness' and was completed at the School of Oriental and African Studies in 2002. andrew.irving4@virgin.net

Wendy James is Professor of Social Anthropology in the University of Oxford, and a Fellow of St. Cross College. She has carried out research over many years in the Sudan, Ethiopia, and East Africa, and has a special interest in the relations between anthropology and history. Her best-known ethnography is *The Listening Ebony: Moral Knowledge, Religion and Power among the Uduk of Sudan* (reissued by OUP in 1999) and she has recently published a general book, *The Ceremonial Animal: A New Portrait of Anthropology* (OUP, 2003). wendy.james@anthro.ox.ac.uk

Aneesa Kassam, Ph.D., is an honorary Research Fellow in the Department of Anthropology, University of Durham. She has published and co-authored a number of papers on the Borana, Gabra and Waata groups of northern Kenya and southern Ethiopia, as well as on change and development in the Oromia region of Ethiopia. She is currently working on a monograph of the Gabra. Aneesa.Kassam@durham.ac.uk

Paul Lane is an archaeologist who specializes in African archaeology. He has taught at the University of Dar es Salaam and University of Botswana, and helped establish archaeology programmes at both institutions. For his PhD research at Cambridge, he spent 16 months with the Dogon of Mali, studying their attitudes to time and the use and organization of dwelling space. His more recent work has encompassed archaeological studies of Tswana responses to European colonialism and the conversion to Christianity, the historical archaeology of Luo settlement in

Nyanza Province, Kenya, and the history of soil erosion in the Kondoa region, northern Tanzania. He is currently Director of the British Institute in Eastern Africa. pjlane@insightkenya.com

Gemetchu Megerssa, Ph.D., is a lecturer in the Department of Social Anthropology, University of Addis Ababa. Between 1985 and 1990, Borana historians initiated him into the traditional knowledge system. He has published and co-authored a number of papers on the Borana of southern Ethiopia. Currently, he has been seconded to the Ministry of Education. Hundee@telecom.net.et

David Mills is Lecturer and Anthropology Co-ordinator at the Centre for learning and teaching Sociology, Anthropology and Politics (C-SAP) at the University of Birmingham. After doing PhD research on education and gender politics in Uganda, he has carried out research into the political history of social anthropology and on contemporary higher education. d.mills@bham.ac.uk

Martin A. Mills lectures in religious studies, social anthropology and politics at the University of Aberdeen, Scotland. Author of *Identity, Ritual and State in Tibetan Buddhism*, he specializes in the study of religious and political authority. m.a.mills@abdn.ac.uk

Anne-Marie Peatrik is senior researcher at the CNRS, attached to the 'Laboratoire d'ethnologie et de sociologie comparative' founded in 1967 at the University Paris X-Nanterre by the late Pr Eric de Dampierre. Her recent publications include *La vie à pas contés. Génération, âge et société dans les hautes terres du Kenya (Meru Tigania-Igembe)* (1999, Nanterre, Société d'ethnologie); *Passages à l'âge d'homme* (special issue of *L'Homme* 2003). peatrik@mae.u-paris10.fr

Julia Powles is a Lecturer in Human Sciences at St. Catherine's College, University of Oxford. She has carried out extensive fieldwork in a refugee settlement in Zambia. Her research interests include experiences of displacement and repatriation, life history and narrative, witchcraft and religion in Africa. Email: julia.powles@stcatz.ox.ac.uk

Mary Rack currently works as a teacher for Gateshead Council's Ethnic Minority and Traveller Achievement Service. She has published papers on place and nationalism in China and is currently completing a monograph entitled *Ethnic Distinctions, Local Meanings: Negotiating Cultural Identities in China* to be published by Pluto Press. Email: maryrack@aol.co.uk

Trevor Stack is a Lecturer in Hispanic Studies at the University of Aberdeen. He did research in the 1990s on talk and writing about history in Mexican towns and he is preparing a monograph entitled 'Places That Have History: The Public

Knowledge of Mexican Towns'. He is also developing a project that focuses on the citizenship of towns and cities as opposed to nations. Email: t.stack@abdn.ac.uk

Bilinda Straight is Assistant Professor of Anthropology at Western Michigan University. She works with Samburu pastoralists in northern Kenya on issues relating to cosmology and consciousness, gender, narrative, and material culture. Her work has appeared in various books and journals, including *American Anthropologist*. She is currently completing a book entitled *Elusive Souls: Samburu at the Edges of Transformation*. Email: Bilinda.Straight@wmich.edu

Wolde Gossa Tadesse took his MSc and PhD in Anthropology at the London School of Economics. He is affiliated to the Max Planck Institute for Social Anthropology where he was a member of the research staff from 2000–2003. Currently he is with the Christensen Fund in California. wolde@christensenfund.org

Richard Vokes received his D.Phil in social anthropology from the University of Oxford in 2003. He currently holds an ESRC funded Post-doctoral Fellowship at the Institute of Social and Cultural Anthropology, Oxford, and is a Lecturer in Social Anthropology at St. Hugh's College. He is completing a book on the Kanungu fire. richard.vokes@wolfson.ox.ac.uk

Ian Watts obtained his PhD in anthropology from the University of London (University College) in 1998. His only institutional attachment is as Honorary Research Associate with the University of Cape Town, Department of Archaeology. His current research interests are Middle Stone Age pigment use and Khoisan cosmology. ochrewatts@hotmail.com

David Wengrow is lecturer in archaeology at the Institute of Archaeology, University College London. David's research addresses the nature of early social transformations in ancient Egypt and Iraq, and the role of the remote past in the formation of modern political identities. david.wengrow@chch.ox.ac.uk

Chris Wingfield is Curator of Human History (Ethnography) at the Birmingham Museum and Art Gallery. Since completing an M.Phil in Material Anthropology and Museum Ethnography at Oxford in 2002, he has worked on a project documenting the history of the collections of the Pitt Rivers Museum, and one relating to a museum collection from remote north Australia. His continuing research interests are in the history of exchange systems in sub-Saharan Africa and the early history of anthropology and ethnographic collecting. wingfieldchris@hotmail.com

Acknowledgements

This volume is the first in a newly relaunched series of the Association of Social Anthropologists of the UK and the Commonwealth. All collectively-made and international books like this are the fruit of intensive work among networks of colleagues and feats of complicated communication and logistics on the part of a wide range of their advisers, friends, and even family. As volume editors, we can list but a few of these: and express our gratitude to all those who remain un-named. First of all, we would like to thank all of the participants at the 2002 ASA conference held in Arusha, Tanzania, for their papers, contributions and stamina. More than seventy-five papers were delivered over the course of the five days, on the theme 'Time and Society: Perspectives from Anthropology and History'. A particular strength of the conference was the way it brought together anthropologists, sociologists, archaeologists and historians, from a wide range of institutions in eastern Africa as well as Europe and the USA. Contributors had a fresh chance of opening up a valuable set of interdisciplinary conversations. We were ably assisted by our panel chairs and by an expert local advisory panel. The organizational complexities of the conference were more than matched by the deft administrative skills of Rohan Jackson and his indomitable lap-top. Many thanks to him, and to all the staff at MS-TCDC for making their centre into the consummate conference venue.

This conference could not have taken place without the financial support we were offered. Generous grants from the Ford Foundation and OSSREA (Organization for Social Science Research in Eastern Africa) enabled the participation of almost forty African-based scholars from Ethiopia, Eritrea, Sudan, Kenya, Tanzania, South Africa, Zimbabwe, Nigeria and Uganda. A British Academy grant supported the travel of sixteen participants from Britain to Tanzania, and two others were assisted by the Oxford University Swan Fund. A grant from the Royal Anthropological Institute went towards the travel of two of the conference's four key-note speakers – all of whom delivered provocative and stimulating lectures. Particular thanks go to Professor Johannes Fabian, Dr Christine Obbo, Professor Richard Fardon and Dr Paul Abungu. Thanks are also due to the ASA for providing a grant to support the travel and subsistence of ASA members and scholars from the region.

The chapters in this book all derive from the conference, but all have been extensively revised in line with our key theme of seeking an articulation between

Acknowledgements

anthropological approaches to time and the undeniably quirky course of history. Frances Kennett has provided sterling assistance on the editorial side, helping us create a coherent and accessible volume, and Ahrum Pilendiram has helped with the illustrations. We are delighted to be opening the newly-relaunched ASA series with Berg Publishers, who have an outstanding track-record in the support of anthropology worldwide.

We would also like to mention here that a number of other publications have arisen from the Arusha conference. These include a special issue of the journal *Africa* (Vol. 74, 1, 2004) entitled: 'Grandparents and Grandchildren', edited by Wenzel Geissler, Erdmute Alber and Susan Whyte. Richard Reid and Uoldelul Chelati are in discussion with the British Institute in Eastern Africa over the publication of an edited volume on the histories of nationalisms and regional identities in Eastern Africa. Preparations are also in hand for a volume to be published by CODESRIA (Council for the Development of Social Science Research in Africa), entitled 'African Anthropologies: History, Practice, Critique' and edited by David Mills, Mustafa Babiker, and Mwenda Ntarangwi.

WJ, DM

Introduction: From Representation to Action in the Flow of Time

Wendy James and *David Mills*

Anthropological writings on time tend to be ahistorical in their approach. They have often been explicitly concerned to emphasize cultural conventions of measurement and the symbolic structuring and representation of time; but have also focused on the linked issue of the making of social time as an ongoing dimension of social practice. The question of historical time has entered mainly as a projection of 'present-day' representation, including the representations built in to evolutionary and world-historical schemes. Arguably, however, there is still scope for exploring some of the convergences between 'time' as patterned in ongoing representations and social practice, on the one hand, and the way that events are produced, as they happen – often unexpectedly – on the other; the kind of events that historians may later come to see as marking change.

Abstract time-markers can provoke potentially 'historical' events: as no doubt a minor example, we can mention here that among the events marking the recent millennium were two anthropological conferences devoted to the topic of time. While the Association of Social Anthropologists of the UK and the Commonwealth was planning its Arusha meeting on 'Time and Society: Perspectives from Anthropology and History', the Wenner-Gren Foundation was mounting an international symposium in Spain on 'Time and Temporalities in the Anthropological Record'. This resulted in a special issue of *Current Anthropology,* entitled 'Repertoires of timekeeping in anthropology', and including studies of the patterns of temporality in social practice, including language, gendered inter-action over family history, landscape and ritual in historical contexts (Gingrich, Ochos, and Swedlund, 2002). The projects of the ASA and Wenner-Gren overlapped in time, but they have been developed and published quite independently, and have resulted in collections that complement each other in interesting ways. In particular, our present volume seeks to move some distance from timekeeping as cultural representation, even from everyday practice as a temporally patterned process, to the relevance of these 'anthropological' concerns to history in the social, or even political, historian's sense. How do embedded ideas and practices marking time affect the way we act, even the production of collective events? Some of our contributors downplay representation altogether, attempting to contextualize the disparate origin of those very 'signs and symbols' which resonate together in the human imagination of time (cf. Warnock 1994).

In the present volume, we have brought some archaeologists and historians together with anthropologists in order to develop a fresh chapter in our academic conversation about the anthropology of time. We have, moreover, sought to bring together the classic anthropological interest in 'symbolic' theories of time's rhythms with a view of the actualities of human life as lived, both in 'the present' and 'the past'. The present is of course a convention, a sort of symbolic fiction, in itself. (Does it extend to last week, yesterday, or just the last half-hour? Does it include what we are *about to say* in reply to what has just been said?) It is surely better for anthropologists to recognize that the notion of the present is itself a representation, and to seek the articulation of this idea itself within the flow of action, the flow of life. Such a shift would make it easier for us to encompass the idea of the past as more than a representation, but part of an extended flow of human action. R. G. Collingwood (1993) famously insisted that history should be a study of *things done*, not simply things said, and similarly Alfred Gell has insisted not only in *The Anthropology of Time* (1992) but also in his later work *Art and Agency* (1998) that anthropology should focus on *what is done* by people in real time, rather than the way they represent things. All contributors to the present volume aim to bring aspects of the way the world is represented into relationship with that continuing chain of human action which constitutes the flow of history; some within the span of a life, others with reference to longer periods. Representation and the patterns of action are not always congruent. Several chapters identify irregularities, opportunism, and ideological currents which shift the representation and ceremonial enactment of time; its special occasions in themselves often provide space in which expectation can provoke political action, even violence. It is not always remembered that action is not a phenomenon simply of 'the present'; it is part of an anticipated flow leading into 'the future'. Even almost completely habitual actions (at least of the British) such as putting on the kettle implicitly anticipate a cup of tea. History is always 'in the making' in this sense, and on an admittedly bigger scale, the expectations generated by the conventional time structures of shared social life can shape major events (riots around religious festivals, transport strikes around Bank Holidays, millenialism generally). Events may follow conventional representations of time, but reciprocally, representations – including unorthodox expectation – can precipitate events.

Some Anthropologies of Time: a Recapitulation

While our collaborative effort is thus to find a fresh way of bringing *the timing of how things are done* into the foreground of anthropological analysis, nothing of course is totally new, and we are indebted to much that has been said before.

Introduction

In attempting to bring back in the question of history, we have drawn from the various but overlapping approaches to time in anthropology identified above. First are those who broadly favour an emphasis on the culturally-embedded ways in which time is lived and marked. The Durkheimian vision of time as something emanating from the social experience of regularity in gatherings and festivals can be traced back to the early twentieth century, among other things to a 1905 essay of Henri Hubert, prepared in collaboration with Mauss (Hubert 1999) – a work whose insights are still fruitful, as we explain below – and to the better-known 1907 essay of Robert Hertz on death, in *Death and the Right Hand* (1960). These studies have much in common with Arnold van Gennep's classic 1909 model of the marking of stages in the life of persons and groups, in which he drew attention to the patterned resemblances between those rituals which mark out our lives through baptism, initiations, marriages and funerals, not to mention the celebration of seasons or passage of phases in the life of kingdoms or nations. Such 'rites of passage', which he compared to movements in space from one defined zone to another, such as moving across the threshold of a house or across political borders, resembled each other not only within the life of a given human community, but across the world. They were the foundation of all more sophisticated notions about time. With reference to the human life span, classic anthropology has been particularly emphatic about the cyclical character of rites, linking birth, marriage, and death in a self-referential closed system. Robert Hertz wrote of birth that 'it accomplishes, for the collective consciousness, the same transformations as death but the other way round. The individual leaves the invisible and mysterious world that his soul has inhabited, and he enters the society of the living ... the body of the newborn child is no less sacred than the corpse' (1960: 80–81).

These ideas were later taken up by Edmund Leach, and drawn on in his well-known writings on time in *Rethinking Anthropology* (1961), as well as being developed by Victor Turner (e.g. 1969) and in more recent works such as Bloch and Parry's *Death and the Regeneration of Life* (1982). Leach did propose a rather mechanical contrast between the modern imagining of 'linear' time and the festival-markers of collective social life, arguing that the latter are not so much cyclical as zig-zag turning points of 'sacred' or liminal time in between stretches of the 'profane' or ordinary. The formal way in which rites of passage can signal 'time passing' was shown by Rodney Needham typically to include – perhaps universally – coded percussion sounds: bells, striking clocks, guns, drums, cymbals and so on (1967). We may ponder, in anticipation of further discussion below, the way that sound is, intriguingly, a phenomenon 'of the moment', an experiential *now*, appropriate for marking the present but inescapably sequential too, flowing in a rhythmic direction recognized as significant by participants.

The participant's perspective is given pride of place by the second group of philosophically-inclined anthropologists who have written specifically on time:

these have sought to escape 'relativism' by the application of rough common sense, on its own or combined with rationalist philosophical argument about the necessarily common experiential foundations of the category 'time'. A distinguished example is Gell's work, mentioned above. He takes to task those anthropologists who have been too preoccupied with 'Durkheimian' approaches, as though each community lived in its own culturally-constructed time-world. He insists 'There is no fairyland where people experience time in a way that is markedly unlike the way in which we do ourselves, where there is no past, present and future, where time stands still, or chases its own tail, or swings back and forth like a pendulum... Only a minimalist approach to "time as such" is consistent with the fundamental project of subsuming the diversity of "what there is" under general explanatory categories' (1992: 315–17). Gell's approach is not 'sociocentric' but rather intellectualist, from the viewpoint of the individual as an experiencing actor. The early French-language writers and their successors emphasized the formative impact of social practice upon individual experience. Gell, however, favours the clean, clear, we could say 'culture-free' metaphysical categories of Kant, and the 'action-frame' of reference within which real people carry out their more or less time-conscious and time-labelling activities. He insists that time is an asymmetrical category and we all face it in the same way in our practical lives. The ethnographer should not, at least initially, seek out 'concepts of time', but plot what choices people make in the morning about how they will spend their day, or the next few days, in the light of the 'opportunity-costs' facing them. We could respond, however, that this seems too narrowly a modern 'Protestant ethic' motif. It might tell us a lot about the pragmatic priorities of people in a productive economy geared to manipulating prices or at least meeting survival targets (Weber 1958). But how far in reality will it do justice to people's multiple 'notions of time' even in these circumstances, let alone helping us with, say, hunters and gatherers – where Sahlins pointed to the total lack of a puritan attitude to time in dubbing them the 'original affluent society' (1974)?

Gell admits towards the end of his book that he has not considered 'historical time' in his study. He concentrates on the view from the present, from the here-and-now, the 'phenomenology' of the time experience. However 'the present' itself can only be experienced in specific historical and social circumstances. Those circumstances include the 'cultural construction' of attitudes to the future, immediate and long-term, that constitute part of the shared framework within which individual action formulates its reasons, and its feelings. There is no such thing as one person's time. Even the most personal experience and individual intellectual referents of time come alive mainly through the rhythms and exchanges, expectations and actual events of shared life (Davis 1991). Here we could cite also the influence of Nancy Munn's view of time 'as a symbolic process continually being produced in everyday practices' (1992: 116).

Locating the Present

Sometimes the timings of human life are compared to those of the physical and organic worlds – to geometric movements or those of the life-cycle of seasons, plants, and animals. Yet there is a distinctive aspect to the significance of 'timing' in the flow of human action; images of time in social life may counterpoint the ubiquitous rhythms of physical or organic nature but are not reducible to them. In some sense, and here we fully acknowledge Gell's key point, there is always a one-way movement, in personal life or in the flow of history, despite symbolic and religious denials (1992: 314–17). But to help ourselves along we have an interesting habit of invoking shape, regularity, and rhythm as we speak of, and enact, the 'timings' of the actions and events we take part in, or learn of from others. Our languages are full of such idioms of regularity, from grammar and vocabulary to the stories we tell of the past and future, not to mention the ceremonial occasions which mark our shared sense of time, and these cultural conventions thus help us to locate ourselves in a more or less predictable and comfortably knowable 'present'. Our sense of timing is imbued with a sense of where we are in relation to patterns of the proper whole, a sense which can affect the unexpected events of personal life as well as those of collective action, not only as they are remembered but also indeed as they happen. Timing in social affairs can be ill-judged as well as skilled; irregularity, rude interruption and unlucky accident are as frequent in practice as carefully planned co-incidence.

It was common in the earlier anthropological literature to identify social time as 'modern linear' or 'traditional cyclical', but nowhere is any such robotic society found. This book is not so much about 'concepts of time' as objects of culture, but rather about the way in which we *create significance in the timing of our actions* as they shape and colour the things we do and the things we make, frame our interpretations of events around us, underlie the way we read evidences of the past, and act with reference to the future. Enactment, labouring, even specific projects of production, are basic to any way in which we can imagine time; and yet, especially for the past, this has often been rendered invisible in the thinking of the social sciences. There is a profound tendency to 'presentism' in anthropology, as Richard Fardon suggests below, a view which rests on a synchronic combination and recombination of signs but ignores the past human labours which have produced some of those very signs. It is difficult for history itself to escape the strong colouring of *present* ideas in the way we envisage the past, as Wengrow's chapter shows with reference to the ways that post-revolutionary France discovered for itself significance in the residues of ancient Egypt. The way we rewrite or retell history, as it 'proceeds', has its own rhythms not unconnected to those of the phenomenological present. However, as both Lane and Wingfield demonstrate, if the evidences of the past are properly read as part of the chain of concrete human labouring activity we can perhaps get beyond presentism. The real challenge is to distance ourselves intellectually from our current, and perhaps local, sense of the shapes of time, including our current ideas of 'modernity', and to place these alongside other senses of the shapes of time which have informed human life, action, and experience. In doing this we may recognize some less conscious features of our own time-frames; we may not be as 'modern' as we think.

This book is devoted to an exploration of the claim that 'significant timing' in human affairs, including our making of and response to historical events, is basic to sociality. Our starting point is the Durkheimian insight that our consciousness and intellectualization of time is at root a social phenomenon, arising from the experience of co-ordinated rhythm in action that permeates language and our everyday practice as social persons. We attempt, however, to go beyond this sociological insight to accommodate 'history': the essentially one-way flow of productive activity, at its most evident cumulative in unexpected ways, perhaps especially of social differentiation; the resulting clashes of expectation, political aspects of the 'competing calendars' present in any real-world situation, the dissonances of timing in personal experience, and the build-up of new large-scale rhythms in great events. The various chapters offer insights into the way that the classic anthropological apprehension of 'pattern' in human affairs, specifically here the shared imagination of time, through an examination of how time's patterned qualities affect *action* can be brought to bear on the making and subsequent interpretation of history.

Questions from History: From 'Concepts Of' to 'Actions In' Time

Johannes Fabian has convincingly shown how anthropology itself, along with popular historical attitudes, has tended to operate within a very imperialistic set of assumptions about time. Drawing on the disjunction between the researcher's conception of time during field research and that communicated in ethnographic writings, Fabian argues that anthropological accounts suppress the simultaneity and 'coevalness' of the anthropological encounter (Fabian 1983: 1991). For Fabian, anthropology's 'allochronism' continues to influence the discipline, a situation that he sees only resolvable by reinventing anthropological practice as a more inter-subjective and dialogical activity. His critique has been an important one, and has encouraged careful attention to the use of tense and person in ethnographic writings, a technique that can help historicize the practice of ethnography itself (cf. Davis 1992).

Social anthropologists have often discussed history in their work, but in doing so have each taken rather different positions on the nature of historical time and its constitutive role in the present. Mauss set an early precedent with his broad comparative use of historical material (James 1998). If Radcliffe-Brown, distancing the nascent discipline from evolutionist thinking, rejected historical explanations, Evans-Pritchard later repudiated the suggestion that societies could be understood without reference to their past (Radcliffe-Brown 1952, Evans-Pritchard 1950). In doing so, he drew upon Collingwood's philosophical, and reflexive, rather than empirical conception of historical process. The anthropological anxiety over speculative reconstructions of the past continued, and a concern with ensuring reliable data tended to overshadow the potential for using historical sources. To this day, and despite the increasing historicization of the discipline, anthropologists tend towards a 'presentist' view of history; perhaps this is linked with assumptions integral to the 'modern' age we live in, as argued by Fardon below (not to mention its 'post-' varieties); but as Elisabeth Hsu, Monica Heintz and several other contributors point out, what counts as 'modern' in the way we live and act in time is by no means without ambiguity.

Reconsidering Hubert: History and the Qualities of Time

In finding ways to bring together the insights of a range of writers who have taken different approaches to the 'timing' of action in social life, and indeed in history, the essay by Henri Hubert already mentioned offers a starting point and some inspiration. Recently translated into English, this study is explicitly about the representation of time in religion and magic. However, its relevance is more general. Hubert reminds us that the religious notion of time 'has presided over the development of calendars' (1999: 44). He proposes as a principle that 'time is a necessary condition of magical and religious acts and representations', and that rites are carried out in conditions of time which 'contribute to the definition of their specific environment' – helping, in fact, to define secular contexts. Myths are also situated with respect to such chronologies, constituting 'a prehistory of humanity, of the tribe or nation', partly because (in our own words here) while they are set outside 'the present', they are continually evoked in relation to the everyday normal time we know (ibid: 46). They can be 'rejuvenated' in their specific reference at successive festivals, such as ritual combats which are given different historical associations on different occasions of performance. The anniversaries of parish churches in French villages are grafted upon ancient agrarian festivals and seem to repeat themselves; but in practice, patron saints can supplant one another, so their festivals 'instead of commemorating a mythical fact, going back to the beginning of time ... commemorate a historical fact'. The memory of previous periods is obliterated, or 'a new and more efficacious consecration of the chosen date is imagined' (ibid: 47).

Calendars constitute ways of notating time through a sequence of dates and durations; but according to Hubert, 'the object of a calendar is not to measure time but to endow it with rhythm.' There is a periodicity to religious and mythic durations; the various millenarianisms 'are proof of this' (ibid: 49). We might point out here that 'secular time' is also coloured by ideas about the qualitative and relational properties of periods of duration and dates. Our idea of time is not one of 'pure quantity', but rather 'the properties of the parts of time are deduced from their relations with the concrete durations that they frame', that is within the calendar, or within a succession of critical dates (ibid: 51). People devote great mental effort to reconciling events with the proper rhythms of the calendar. The same dates are expected to 'bring back the same events'; 'Every year, every seven years, every nine years, on the same date as the original catastrophe, the town revives, the bells ring, the lady of the chateau leaves her seclusion, the treasury is opened...' (ibid: 58). Astrology and much ancient and popular science is founded on this principle. Moreover there are repeating and echoing rhythms within the patterns of time; Sunday is to the week what Easter is to the year. There are 'active qualities' to the subdivisions of time, in addition to their dimension and relative position (ibid: 61). The relative value of durations will depend not only upon their extent but partly upon 'the nature and intensity of their qualities' (ibid: 62). Hubert writes of bringing to light 'the qualitative nature attributed to time', to its parts, such as the individuality of the various days or months, or to 'time in general', as something endowed with, or capable of having, qualities (ibid: 62–3).

Hubert develops Bergson's image of the presence of different rhythms in the individual consciousness, to admit that these are in tension, and that in 'the play of ideas' the mind works constantly to adjust the given conventions of calendrical period, duration, and date to a succession of new 'representations', and, we might add, to productive actions and events. The struggle to adjust between rhythmic expectation and actual event, in Hubert's argument, is more than a matter of individual psychology but of social activity. 'In work, poetry and song, rhythm was the sign of collectivity activity, becoming more strongly marked as social collaboration spread and intensified'; and it is therefore legitimate to suppose that 'the rhythm of time does not necessarily model itself on the natural periodicities established by experience, but that societies contain within themselves the need and the means of instituting it' (ibid: 70–71).

In several respects Hubert's essay goes far beyond the somewhat static and circular model of social time that later commentators have attributed to the Durkheimian school (for example, Leach 1961, Gell 1992 as discussed above). He sees that there is tension between individual and collective perceptions of time, and that intellectual effort is always being made to reconcile them. He recognizes that time-scales and rhythms may exist in the plural, that they are sometimes in competition, and that something always remains of 'dead calendars'. He emphasizes the role of expectation in the making of events. By distinguishing mythical from historical time, a contrast not easy to find in all writings of the school or in later writings by anthropology, Hubert in fact is validating the very category of 'history' while showing how it is partly shaped by what he calls the 'religious and magical' qualities of time. This insight into the relations between 'anthropology and history', we believe, can help us tackle some old problems in a new way.

The contributions to this volume all seek to find connection between the conventional representations of time and the way that things are actually done, whether through productive work or symbolic rhetoric and ritual, in the profile of personal life or the wider historical process. All explore ways in which the socially-anchored and currently-present rhythms of 'significant timing' in representations and actions both influence, and are influenced by, those events which become a part of remembered history. What all the studies in the present volume draw attention to, in addition, is the fact that plurality in time-scales, and tension in the way that they have to be revised or adjusted to in the light of the unexpected, is 'normal' rather than anomic in human history. There is no such thing as 'social time' except *in time*, and as a part of what we usually mean by history.

Case Studies

We have organized the chapters which follow into several groups, but each contributor explores aspects of our common unfolding theme, and there are internal correspondences and echoes throughout the book. We open with three studies of how varieties of presentism in the way that people view the past can obscure the actual processes of the past, and indeed ongoing processes in the present. Paul Lane seeks previously neglected evidence of the lives of women in the past of Dogon villages, a past which is obscured by the standard views of Dogon themselves about the continuity of patrilineages as represented by important and still-surviving house structures. The material residue of women's lives, by contrast, consists of personal possessions now scattered between different houses where they have lived, and where their inheriting daughters have later lived. The former lived realities of Dogon families can be filled in by the proper reading of this evidence, 'invisible' to local theories of the past. Jasper Chalcraft outlines a particularly dramatic, and ironic, case where present-day national and international definitions of 'cultural heritage' quite obscure the lived realities of a place today, and arguably of the past too. A group of Stone Age rock paintings at Kondoa in central Tanzania is in the process of being nominated as a UN World Heritage site. This is likely to lead to unwelcome local transformations of the site, which is at present actively revered by local peoples not for the paintings as such, but for the ritual significance of the site within a wider landscape of sacred geography (though UN definitions of 'cultural landscape' are still very far from local ones). Trevor Stack mounts a critical enquiry into the presentist conceptions of history current among people living in two towns in West Mexico, showing how evidences of complex and interactional factors in the rise of the towns are overlaid by modern stereotyped associations of ethnicity with place.

Richard Fardon's chapter is a comprehensive enquiry into the 'presentism' underlying modern ethnography and social anthropology, and the Malinowskian-style figure of the 'observer' who glosses over the processes of the past. He identifies this presentism lucidly in the analytical vision of Franz Steiner, and then proceeds to show how a theory of the interrelatedness of signs as such cannot provide an account of the figure of a tiger represented in a Cameroon palace. He argues that only a labour-theory of value can reveal the piecemeal character of the way that traders, craftsmen, ritual specialists, photographers and so on at different times of history and for different reasons have assembled the appearance of a grand royal unity.

In view of the very great relevance to our theme of the ambitious theories of Chris Knight and his collaborators over the crucial role of symbolic time structures in the evolutionary establishment of early human society (Knight 1991, Dunbar, Knight and Power 1999), we invited Ian Watts to contribute an overview of the argument and the evidence from southern Africa, where he has himself worked. He outlines what constitutes in essence a new kind of a-temporal structuralism, offered as a glimpse into our common symbolic heritage of social time itself, but anchored in the specific ethnography of southern Africa. There are clearly world-wide resonances in this system linking the moon's cycle with the ecology of hunting, with sexuality, with myth and religion, with exchange and with collective social action. These resonances, which can perhaps be detected in several chapters of our collection, justify serious attention to this theory of a deep source of time-patterning in human sociality. However, we have invited Chris Wingfield to provide a critique of Watts's chapter, on more orthodox historical and ethnographic grounds. Wingfield, like many other critics of structuralism and post-structuralism, is sceptical of the value of imagining sign-systems as wholes without seeking to set their parts back in the pragmatic context whence they have come – in some cases, like that of ostrich-eggshell beads – where they were actually made by human labour. David Wengrow's chapter shows how post-revolutionary France found great significance, at its particular time, in the remains of long-dead Egyptian civilization, and how popular were the Parisian exhibitions of crumbling remains and unwrapped mummies. Theories of 'divine kingship' have themselves shifted over the history of anthropology too, up to the pragmatic co-optation of Shilluk rulers by the Anglo-Egyptian government of the Sudan and their ethnographer-administrators. Far from being a mere spectacle, a couple of generations earlier, we know that kings of the Shilluk kind were truly awesome to their people and rarely 'observed' by anyone.

Following these efforts to contextualize anthropology's presentism, we have placed two studies which reflect on the uncertainties of 'modern' time, modernity, and the idea of sequence and measurement which pervade this concept. Elisabeth Hsu follows local Tanzanian practice in distinguishing between traditional, advanced-traditional, modern-traditional, and modern medical practice, including the practice of Chinese medical specialists who are currently popular in East Africa. By using spatial analogues of medical consultation practice, she shows how the modern medical procedure whereby diagnosis precedes treatment (and corresponds to Gell's assumption that there is always a 'before versus an after') to which we relate as conscious subject (1992: 157) turns out to be elusive. Not only do some 'traditional' procedures obviously conflate these supposedly distinct steps, but so do many 'modern' ones too. Monica Heintz describes vividly the emptiness of 'modern' working time in the post-socialist state of Romania, contextualizing what is supposedly the accepted puritan ethic of Western industrial society, but at the same time implicitly pointing to its partial character there.

Perhaps in other places too the overarching national or religious schemes of social time are subverted by people and their local interests. Maggie Bolton, Mary Rack and Tadesse Wolde focus on the way that provincial ritual occasions which are on one level part of a national ceremonial structure can open up spaces for redefinition of the relations between a locality and the state – respectively, in these chapters, Bolivia, China, and Ethiopia. That redefinition can become an open political contest, or it can remain implicit in the unspoken politics of ceremony, a memorial of past change and possibly a pointer to future change. Roy Dilley's contribution highlights the hidden, even potentially subversive, ways in which musicians and blacksmiths among the Haalpulaaren of Senegal can evoke present spiritual entities which 'collapse time', as against the over-arching genealogies of power claimed by the Muslim leading families who place themselves in formal historical time through descent lines reaching back to early Islam. Each of our chapters demonstrates how perceived trajectories of history can be at once invoked and countered at particular ceremonial moments. Historians have shown how ceremonies and traditions can be 'invented' as a part of political processes in a context of conventional historical time (Hobsbawm and Ranger 1983). But ceremonies can also be the vehicle of quite subtle, and layered, understandings in themselves which invoke contrasting time shapes in the understanding of past and present.

Among the strictest systems for structuring time, in both the social and cosmological senses, are the traditional age and generation systems of Eastern Africa. A classic example, the case of the Borana Oromo, is offered here by Aneesa Kassam and Gemetchu Megerssa, in which they combine earlier published ethnography (see especially Legesse 1973) with their own recent field enquiries. They are able to provide a few points at which the system has been used in recent times to predict events. The system of the neighbouring Samburu is recalled by Bilinda Straight, as it is by her informants, many of them women who use beads to signify personal and social memory. The Samburu know very well that the rivalries built in to age systems can provoke conflict, and Anne-Marie Peatrik shows how deeply such tensions may lie even where the traditional system may seem to have been left behind. Her analysis of the history of a section of the Meru people in central Kenya suggests that the basic principles of the succession of age grades remains in theory the way that local social relations work, and that colonial and post-colonial governments have never understood this. However, a mass invasion of a girls' dormitory by schoolboys in 1991, leaving many raped and dead, was at least in part a violent reaction to what the boys had seen as violations of their standing within the age system by the (male) girls' teachers. More explosive as an event shaped partly by the logic of time structures was the series of mass deaths in south-western Uganda following closely on the achievement of the Millennium. Richard Vokes portrays the lead up to the Kanungu fire as a story with many beginnings, but one given a real boost by the millenarian literature that found its way into this extreme corner of Uganda where Marian cults were already flourishing. This illuminates perhaps, even more than in many other parts of the book, Hubert's identification of 'critical moments' as themselves produced by our calendrical systems, but potentially turning points for history too.

Many of our case-studies, like the last chapters mentioned, include events of disruption and even violence linked to the 'real history' of the working out of time structures. The implications for personal life, for memory and expectation, are obviously profound. Rhythm and timing are essential to the way that processes of birth and death, not to mention sex, are managed by human beings. But the biological life-course is not always predictable; departures from the norm again provide an emotional stimulus and opening for moral reflection when expectations are confounded, life can be foreshortened by illness or death, or extraordinarily lengthened. Our last group of studies are all concerned with the question of individual lives, memories, and adjustments as normal expectations change, through a knowledge of terminal illness, through complete displacement in space – which can also be a dislodging in expected time patterns; or through the individual process of adjusting personal experiential life to a complex and rigid religious time-formula. Andrew Irving finds parallels between the experiences of AIDS sufferers in the USA and in Africa; Julia Powles points to the connection between the spatial disruption experienced by Angolan refugees in Zambia and their sense of the disruption in the expected 'normal' shape of their lifetime, as they remember the rich riverlands and delightful fishing of their youth, stranded on the dry highlands, but still deeply affected by songs, dances and proverbs which recall the fertile rivers and their fruit. Will they ever return? Will their children ever know these delights of their own childhood? Martin Mills's study draws together a wide range of the themes which run through our book as a whole, and we have therefore placed it as a concluding chapter. He finds great personal complexity in people's lives in Buddhist Ladakh, where individuals – and particularly women – have to weave their way through a sophisticated religious calendar of purity and impurity in time, all the while coping with the ordinary businesses of bodily life, providing food and raising a family. The private and the public shapes of time are here always in tension, rather than in harmony. But then in many of the cases considered in this book, individual expectations of the 'normal' course of life have been interrupted. Mills aptly quotes from Shakespeare, 'the time is out of joint'; people have to manage their lives through calendars which specify pollution, people die too early, live too long, remember as a part of themselves places and activities to which they are no longer connected. Mills describes the moments when people and societies step out of time, arguing from his ethnography of Tibetan Buddhist ritual practice that anthropologists should not privilege calendrical or astrological systems as models for action. Rather we should look to the way in which people's relationship to time ideologies is constituted through social bodies and embodied in ritual and material practice.

Conclusion

We too easily forget that the 'abstract' nature of time measurement itself is partly an artefact of changing technology, and that even in the 'scientific West' has often been spurred on by deeply symbolic and religious imperatives. In the medieval monasteries, handbells were rung at the hours of prayer, and monks had to be detailed to stay awake in order to perform this duty in the night and early morning. The invention of a mechanical clock, with a rachet and a weight, which could ring bells automatically at these times was a breakthrough, and spread extremely fast throughout Europe, helping fuel the work ethic in early modern businesses, and no doubt also philosophical speculations on the nature of time and the moral significance we have given to it. Time is not homogeneous, but full of markers on different scales – not only sounding bells, alarms, and ceremonial guns, but changes in the weather, rising and falling levels on the stockmarket, organic life and death itself, none of these necessarily working in harmony.

The advance of technology by no means removes the 'qualititative' aspects of time. David Harvey's concept of 'space-time' compression within the modern world system and its effects on 'how we represent the world to ourselves' (1989: 240) is an influential one. The realm of time is not agreed even by the specialist physical scientists and philosophers to be one thing, one field (Butterfield 1999). As lay people we are conscious that even our most seemingly basic modes of reckoning time are arbitrary and do not fit the world, hence our leap-years and occasional adjustment of milliseconds at the turn of the year. Since Einsteinian relativity we have gradually accepted that time is not uniform and undifferentiated.

Together with space, one tries to understand from popular scientific debate that it is *shaped* in a curve, and it is perfectly acceptable to speculate about unique events, beginnings and endings. Time 'exists' for academic discussion, speculation, and comparison, only in the interplay of idioms we provide or invent for it through our languages, ceremonies, 'cultural' codes and technical inventions. These rest in a range of ways on shapes and rhythms which become resources for us to draw on when the unexpected happens. Moreover, it is fruitful for anthropologists to speculate on the way that the scholar's own sense of time changes during and after fieldwork (cf. Dresch and James 2000). The plain 'minimalist' approach to time recommended by Gell fails to capture the rhythm and time-shapes of events; like the plain historical chronology of one-damn-thing-after-another it fails to recognize the collusion of people in the making of material life and events through significant timing. There is still a need to rescue an 'anthropology of time' which can engage with history and the work of historians, and the present volume is offered in this spirit.

References

Bloch, M. and J. Parry (eds), (1982), *Death and the Regeneration of Life*, Cambridge: Cambridge University Press.

Butterfield, J. (ed.), (1999), *The Arguments of Time*, Oxford/New York: Oxford University Press for the British Academy.

Collingwood, R.G., (1993 [1946]) *The Idea of History*, W. J. v. d. Dussen (ed.), (revised edition with additional material), Oxford: Clarendon Press.

Davis, J. (1991). *Times and Identities* (Inaugural Lecture). Oxford: Oxford University Press.

——(1992) 'Tense in ethnography: some practical considerations', in Judith Okely and Helen Callaway (eds), *Anthropology and Autobiography*, ASA Monograph 29, London and New York: Routledge.

Dresch, P. and W. James (2000), 'Introduction: Fieldwork and the Passage of Time'. In P. Dresch, W. James and D. Parkin (eds), *Anthropologists in a Wider World: Essays on Field Research,* Oxford/New York: Berghahn.

Dunbar, R., C. Knight and C. Power (eds), (1999), *The Evolution of Culture,* Edinburgh: Edinburgh University Press.

Fabian, J. (1983), *Time and the Other: How Anthropology Makes its Object,* New York: Columbia University Press.

——(1991), *Time and the Work of Anthropology: Critical Essays*, Reading: Harwood Academic Publishers.

Evans-Pritchard, E.E. (1950), 'Social anthropology: past and present', the Marett Lecture (reprinted in his *Essays in Social Anthropology*), London: Faber, 1962.

Gell, A. (1992), *The Anthropology of Time: Cultural Constructions of Temporal Maps and Images*, Oxford: Berg.

——(1998), *Art and Agency: An Anthropological Theory*, Oxford: Oxford University Press.

Gingrich, A., E. Ochs and A. Swedlund (eds), (2002), 'Repertoires of timekeeping in anthropology', Special Issue, supplement to *Current Anthropology* 43.

Harvey, D. (1989), *The Condition of Postmodernity: An Enquiry into the Origins of Cultural Change,* Oxford: Blackwell.

Hertz, R. (1960 [1907]), 'A contribution to the study of the collective representation of death', in his *Death and the Right Hand,* trs. R. and C. Needham, London: Cohen & West.

Hobsbawm, E. and T.O. Ranger, (eds), (1983), *The Invention of Tradition,* Cambridge: Cambridge University Press.

Hubert, H. (1999 [1905]), *Essay on Time: A Brief Study of the Representation of Time in Religion and Magic*, trs. R. Parkin and J. Redding, Oxford: Berghahn.

James, W. (1998), 'Mauss in Africa: On Time, History and Politics', in W. James and N.J. Allen (eds), *Marcel Mauss: A Centenary Tribute,* Oxford: Berghahn.

Knight, C.D. (1991), *Blood Relations: Menstruation and the Origins of Culture,* New Haven, CN: Yale University Press.

Leach, E.R. (1961). *Rethinking Anthropology,* London: Athlone.

Legesse, Asmarom (1973), *Gada: Three Approaches to the the Study of African Society,* New York: Free Press.

Munn, N. (1992), 'The cultural anthropology of time', *Annual Review of Anthropology* 21: 93–123.

Needham, R. (1967). 'Percussion and transition', *Man* 2: 606–25.

Radcliffe-Brown, A.R. (1952), *Structure and Function in Primitive Society,* London: Cohen and West.

Sahlins, M. (1974), 'The original affluent society', Chapter One in *Stone Age Economics*, London: Tavistock.

Turner, V.W. (1969), *The Ritual Process: Structure and Anti-Structure*, Chicago: Aldine.

Van Gennep, A. (1960 [1909]), *The Rites of Passage,* London: Routledge & Kegan Paul.

Warnock, M. (1994), *Imagination and Time,* Oxford: Blackwell.

Weber, M. (1958 [1904]), *The Protestant Ethic and the Spirit of Capitalism,* New York: Charles Scribner.

Part I
Objects and Places as Signs of the Past

–1–

The Material Culture of Memory
Paul Lane

The real name of the city was erased from memory by the conquerors, and this is
why – say the taletellers – the place is now known only by the name of its own
destruction. The pile of stones thus marks both an act of deliberate remembrance,
and an act of deliberate forgetting. They're fond of paradox in that region.

Margaret Atwood, The Blind Assassin

Early on a Sunday morning in February 1983, a group of Dogon men, from the
village of Banani Sirou at the foot of the Bandiagra escarpment in east central
Mali, began assembling on a broad ledge partway up the escarpment face. Over the
next few hours, these men proceeded systematically to dismantle an old building,
known as the village *binu ginu*, that was built of puddled mud, stone blocks,
wooden beams and brushwood. Work then began on constructing a new building
on exactly the same spot, using the same range of raw materials (and in some cases
re-using materials from the recently demolished structure), employing identical
building techniques. This building work continued for several days, beginning
with the construction of the walls of a rectangular stone structure, followed by
the addition of wooden roof beams and a covering of brushwood to form the roof,
and culminating in the coating of the roof and walls with fresh layers of puddled
mud mixed with dung and millet chaff. The final result was a small, single-roomed
structure that differed little from the building that had stood on the same spot just a
few days before. Rather similar events took place a few weeks later in the adjacent
village of Banani Kokoro, whose inhabitants are regarded as being structurally
junior to those of Banani Sirou, but nevertheless related to them through principles
of lineage segmentation. In this instance, however, the villagers only replaced
the roof and some of the walls of their *binu ginu*. What was most striking about
these events was that when interviewed about their respective *binu ginu* after
reconstruction, villagers from both Banani Kokoro and Banani Sirou insisted that
this was 'the oldest building in the village'.

Although the paradox in this case is the direct opposite of that described by
Atwood's character, both the Dogon and Margaret Atwood seem to have identified
something curious about the relationships between remembering, forgetting and

the material traces of the past. Specifically, how is it that in some societies, such as the Dogon, a building can be literally torn down and rebuilt and yet still be regarded conceptually as the *oldest* building in the community, while in other societies or contexts, a building or object can be deliberately destroyed in an effort to erase the past only for its memory to survive as a consequence of this means of forgetting?

To explore this question, in this chapter I draw on a range of case studies mostly but not exclusively from African contexts, that deal with some of the ways in which different societies use the material remains of their own past and that of others in order to reach a better understanding of how historical values and meanings can be attached to ancient material culture. There is, of course, a detailed and sophisticated system of such understanding that began to emerge in Western thought in the 1850s (Daniel 1950). Known as 'Archaeology', this knowledge system has been exported to and adopted in most parts of the world, and is widely recognized and supported by national governments and the international scholarly community. Much less well understood is whether there exist similar, non-Western practices and modes of thought, and if so, how non-Western societies utilize historical and archaeological remains in their own (re)constructions of their past. Moreover, those studies which have been conducted on such issues (e.g. Layton 1989a, 1989b; Robertshaw and Kamuhangire 1996), all tend to characterize indigenous uses of ancient sites and remains as being driven by present day sectional, political, or religious ends which stand in marked contrast to the kind of 'objective' history and archaeology that is produced by the scholarly community.

This neglect of the manner in which historical objects are mobilized by different contemporary societies to construct a 'past' is especially ironic, given the efforts within the discipline of Archaeology since at least the 1960s to make it more *anthropological* (*vide* Binford's 1962 rally to arms for 'Archaeology as Anthropology'). Although this resulted in the birth of a sub-field known as 'ethnoarchaeology' and led to numerous archaeologists conducting their own 'anthropological' research on the material culture, settlement structure and discard practices of contemporary societies, the era of the New Archaeology also encouraged, rather perversely, a deep suspicion toward Anthropology's most fundamental premiss. Namely, that it is concerned primarily with grasping 'the native's point of view' and her or his 'vision of the world' (Malinowski 1922: 25). In other words, with the articulation of indigenous knowledge and beliefs in everyday practice and the reproduction of social structures.

An alternative and more etymologically correct type of 'ethnoarchaeology', however, would be one concerned with precisely these 'indigenous' archaeologies; that is, with how different societies ascribe historical values and meanings to the physical world and employ these material traces in their construction of individual and collective memory, and the creation and representation of the past (Lane 1996). Improving understanding of the range and conceptual basis of non-Western modes of doing archaeology, would have a number of potential consequences. First, at a practical level, understanding how contemporary peoples draw on the physical remains that surround them to construct a past for themselves could help redress some of the tensions that exist in many parts of the world between 'disciplinary' archaeology and local historiographic traditions. In other words, just as efforts have been made to create intellectual space for indigenous knowledge and practices within such fields as tropical agriculture and forestry, wildlife conservation, conflict resolution and even biomedicine (Sillitoe 1998), so too scope exists for integrating indigenous 'archaeological' epistemologies into mainstream archaeological practice. By doing so, archaeologists may well dissipate some of the excesses of what Foucault (1979) describes as 'governmentality' that pervade current archaeological resource-management policies and their implementation in many parts of the non-Western world, especially Africa.

The insights afforded by the way non-Western peoples practise 'archaeology', also have potential implications for how the remains of past societies are interpreted and how the observed patterning of these remains may have arisen. For instance, archaeological research has shown that at various times in the past, communities have re-used older monuments, buildings and/or artefacts. Sometimes, as for instance in the re-use of Bronze Age burial mounds as cemeteries during the Anglo-Saxon period in Britain (e.g. Semple 1998; Williams 1998), such re-use has been for seemingly similar purposes. At other times and in other contexts, the re-use has resulted in a change in function of earlier objects or structures – for instance, in the incorporation of Neolithic settlement remains into Bronze Age burial mounds in parts of south Wales (Lane 1986a). Conventional interpretations of these sites tended to regard the evidence for re-use (and also that of abandonment and/or deliberate destruction) purely in terms of functional expediency. More recent interpretations, on the other hand, have argued that such phenomena cannot be so simply explained away, and that instead they also represent evidence of ways in which social memory was constructed *by people in the past* from the physical remains that were visible to them in the landscape, or which they encountered in the earth. As such, these traces not only provide insights into the role of the past in the past, but also, as a form of 'archaeological practice' *in the past*, they influenced what sites, monuments and physical objects were preserved and which were dismissed as having no historical value. In other words, a complex set of recursive relationships would appear to exist between how societies use ancient remains to construct their past *and* the form and processes by which such ancient remains are passed on to future generations. If this is so, then it would appear that archaeology has enormous potential to illustrate the operation and relative significance of different concepts and attitudes to time over the course of human history. To achieve this goal, however, better understanding is needed of how these recursive relationships operate in the present, and in particular those that link memory, practice and material culture.

Memory Practices

In his discussion of how social memory is achieved, Paul Connerton has identified two broad categories of practices, which he has termed 'incorporation' and 'inscription'. The former is an internal process whereby social practices are remembered through bodily enactment (Connerton 1989). Another way of describing incorporation is habit, or, habituated practice (Bourdieu 1977). Habit, as Connerton explains, 'is a knowledge and a remembering in the hands and in the body; and in the cultivation of habit it is our body which "understands"' (1989: 95). Inscribing practices, on the other hand, are external (ibid.: 73), and so typically involve the manipulation of the physical world, such as through building monuments, erecting memorials or by writing texts. In so doing, such practices can leave more durable traces, which often have the potential to outlive the individuals who produced them. By surviving their authors and the moment of their production, these traces can acquire representational significance, and so come to stand for the actions and identities of those individuals and the social groups to which they belonged. Although Connerton sought to draw a distinction between societies which rely on inscriptive practices for the maintenance of social memory and those in which this is achieved through incorporeal practices, it is clear that both categories coexist within any society.

Thus, the manufacture of artefacts and the construction of buildings and settlements involve the mobilization of incorporeal memory, in the form of the bodily practices employed in the shaping and forming processes. As recent work on technological styles has illustrated, these practices are open-ended, such that the ultimate selection of one form out of many possible similar forms is a product of a wide range of factors. The decisions leading up to the final product are nevertheless potentially knowable through the reconstruction of the relevant *chaînes opératoires* involved, by which is meant the sequence of culturally-informed technical and mechanical steps taken during the manufacture of the object (Lemonnier 1986). Once made, however, completed objects can also become vehicles of inscriptive memory, and begin to acquire their own histories and 'social lives' (Appadurai 1986), as they are utilized for successive sets of social practices. Objects, from at least the moment of their manufacture, begin to acquire historical value, which actors can deploy as part of their strategies, but also to which actors refer in making decisions about the object's future. A classic and well known example is that of the stone axes and shell ornaments which circulate as part of the '*kula* ring' exchange system in the western Pacific.

Annette Weiner and others have documented how, as these objects pass from one custodian to another, they acquire a history of associations with their previous owners, whose fame and reputation within their community results in some *kula* axes and ornaments becoming more desirable than others (Weiner 1992).

The preservation and circulation of 'holy relics' (Geary 1986), and the creation and disposal of family heirlooms (Lillios 1999) are other obvious examples of the mnemonic power of objects. 'Burials, caches and storehouses', as Hendon has recently observed, can also be considered integral aspects to the process of creating social memory, as can body ornamentation and other methods of inscribing identity (2000: 49). Similarly, the development of writing technologies in the Near East and elsewhere, which mark a transition in emphasis from incorporation to inscription, also entailed widespread use of material objects, such as 'jetons' (small, stone or chipped sherd disks), or stamps and seals, as types of mnemonic devices (e.g. Costello 2000). However, it is important to recognize that cultural understanding and assessments of the historical value of objects, places and structures also have a bearing on the life histories of even the most mundane items of material culture (e.g. Chevalier 1996; Roberts and Roberts 1996; Hoskins 1998; Marcoux 2001), and pervade a range of routine decisions regarding their repair, modification, replacement, curation, preservation or disposal (Lane 1987, 1994; Rowlands 1993). These points will now be illustrated by various examples from different parts of Africa, and the implication these knowledge systems have for our own understanding of archaeological materials discussed.

Dogon and Haya Archaeologies

The first example is drawn from my fieldwork in the early 1980s among the Dogon of Mali, with particular reference to communities living along the foot of the Bandiagara escarpment. At the time of this study, the Dogon were predominantly small-scale subsistence farmers with limited involvement in the production of crops or other products for the market economy. Descent was traced patrilineally, and the preferred pattern of post-marital residence was patrilocal. Settlement was mostly concentrated in villages that ranged in size from just a few hundred inhabitants to those containing several thousand. The main unit of production and consumption was the minimal lineage – an agnatic descent group typically composed of between three to four generations and headed by the eldest living male member. Such descent groups are referred to as '*ginna*', and the same term is also used to refer to the compound and place of residence of the lineage head, who is known as the *ginu bana* (Lane 1986b).

Whereas in many other West African societies members of the same minimal or minor lineage occupy a single, spatially extensive compound (e.g. Brasseur 1968;

Denyer 1978), among the Dogon, members of the same lineage reside in several spatially separate compounds that are dispersed throughout the village. Each minor lineage is able to name the individuals believed to have built various compounds belonging to it, and by relating this information to lineage genealogies, it is thus possible to build up a kind of relative chronology for the development of lineage house building. With the exception of the lineage head's compound, known as the *ginu na* or *ginna*, all other lineage-owned compounds can be used, as circumstances demand, for a variety of different residential and cohabiting groups. They may also fall out of use and into disrepair when not required. Each lineage's *ginna*, on the other hand, is selectively maintained and curated for use by future generations of lineage heads. Significantly, the *ginna* is always regarded as being the oldest extant compound belonging to the lineage, and the event of its construction is taken to represent the birth of the lineage. Since this compound also functions as the main context for the storage, processing and collective consumption of food obtained from lineage fields through the labour of lineage members, its selective maintenance provides a tangible symbol of the lineage's own continuity through time (Lane 1994). In this way, each *ginna* thus becomes a 'historical monument' within the contemporary landscape and so provides an 'archaeological trace' from which individual lineages can construct their history.

The historic value invested in such compounds, however, has a number of consequences for the spatial patterning of material culture which go beyond the selective preservation of particular structures. In the first place, the symbolic valorization of the *ginna* as the legitimate locale for a variety of tasks and activities (such as the storage and processing of crops, the preparation and cooking of food, the performance of lineage-based rituals, and the maintenance of ancestral shrines and other material symbols of the lineage), results in the generation of a fairly restricted range of material residues and micromorphological signatures.[1] In other types of lineage compound, on the other hand, even though many of these same activities may also be performed, the changing residential composition of these compounds and the lack of long-term task repetition results in a much lower density and/or greater diversity of material traces, and a greater 'smearing and blending' (*pace* Stevenson 1991) of activity areas.

As physical symbols, *ginna* compounds serve as an archaeological trace that lineage elders draw on in the construction of their history. However, these histories are very much in a male idiom, and the *ginna*, in particular, is a means of inscribing the history of the *patri*lineage. Although female members of the lineage are remembered in genealogies and are accorded their own individual memorials within the collective ancestral shrines, houses and other physical structures are regarded very much as male property. Partly as a consequence of this, and partly also because of the spatio-temporal trajectory that women follow as they move from one residence to another during the course of their lives (see Lane 1986b,

1994 for details), women invest considerable time and effort in amassing large inventories of household possessions. Thus, the houses of older women, and especially elderly widows, typically contain large quantities of objects, many of which are no longer used and may even be broken or damaged in some way (Fig. 1). There is far less evidence for such deliberate curation of personal possessions among men (Fig. 2), partly because of the range of social practices open to them for securing memory of their identity. In contrast, the objects that a woman accumulates during her lifetime are her main means of ensuring social recollection of her identity, through their public display at her funeral and their subsequent transmission to her female agnates as heirlooms (see Lane 1986b). Given the preference for post-marital patrilocal residence and lineage exogamy, most women tend to spend most of their married adult lives living in villages of their affines, rather than in their natal settlement. One consequence of this pattern of inheritance is that objects made by a woman or acquired from her post-marital place of residence are dispersed to many other villages on her death. This in turn results in a blurring of the boundaries of artefact style zones (compare Bedaux 1986: 244).

A contrasting example can be drawn from recent work by Brad Weiss among the Haya of north-western Tanzania (Weiss 1996, 1997). The Haya, like the Dogon, are mostly subsistence farmers, although they rely on bananas rather than millet

Figure 1 Interior of a Dogon widow's house. Photo: Paul Lane

Figure 2 Interior of a Dogon widower's house. Photo: Paul Lane

as their staple crop, and as a consequence their villages are much more dispersed than most Dogon settlements. Unlike the Dogon, who use stone as their primary building material, Haya houses are typically built from puddled mud and thatch on a wooden frame. There is an even more important contrast, in that instead of preserving houses for future generations the Haya, at least in the remembered past, would normally demolish the house of a recently deceased household head by removing the centre-post and scattering the hearthstones (Weiss 1997). Other personal possessions belonging to the deceased, such as beer gourds, spoons, pots and other household utensils were also destroyed. The Haya described these actions as ways of 'forgetting the dead'. Yet, as Weiss observes, they are perhaps better understood as a way of 'casting out death' by means of removing the deceased's possessions from circulation. Rather paradoxically, then, destroying these objects 'worked to render them *inalienable* from the person who once had possessed them' (ibid.: 170, emphasis in the original), and in so doing laid the foundations for the memorialization of the deceased. In other words, what was destroyed was 'death', not the memory of the person. Although such practices have changed in the recent past, so that objects formerly destroyed are now inherited, the process of inheritance, Weiss argues, acts in a rather similar way to transform these objects from alienable personal wealth into inalienable family heirlooms.[2]

Remembering and Forgetting the Past

No doubt such issues as utility and least-effort came into play in the decision-making of people in the past, just as they do today. However, as the examples discussed above illustrate, other factors that relate to the life histories of individuals and objects can be equally important. For example, what made it important for Dogon women to invest so much of themselves in their material possessions, was that, unlike men, the 'official' histories as represented by lineage genealogies provided little scope for the memory of their individual identities. Whereas the names of the female members for the last two or three generations of a particular patrilineage could generally be recalled, beyond this, memory of the names of wives, sisters and daughters of the male lineage ancestors was much more selective. This contrasted with the situation for male patrilineal ancestors, whose names and even accomplishments were commonly sustained through lineage genealogies. Equally, despite their close practical association with houses and compounds, women had and still have no legal claim on domestic space and throughout the course of their lives women are moved from one such space to another in response to male strategies. Men, on the other hand, follow a trajectory through space-time which has as its logical conclusion residence in their lineage's *ginna* compound. As explained above, this compound, as a result of its selective maintenance and curation, is a powerful symbol of lineage continuity. Men can be said to move *into* its space during their lives, whereas women are moved *through* it (see Lane 1987, 1994). Moreover, compounds generally, and the houses they contain, are perceived as male spaces, and the sequence in which individual compounds belonging to a lineage were added and the names of their builders can often be recalled going back several generations. The durability of domestic architecture thus ensures that there will be tangible traces to a man's identity long after his death.

The use that the Dogon make of material objects to create personal and collective histories is by no means unique. Andrew Smith, for instance, has noted the use by a Ju/'hoan man in NE Namibia of the fragments of a Mbukushu pot originally obtained through trade, as an heirloom that had become an important means of recalling his family's history (Smith 1999: 6). Likewise, in her discussion of witchcraft and domestic relations among the Mura in Cameroon, Diane Lyons (1998) recounts a representation of women as 'impermanent' and men as 'permanent', and the manipulation of the built environment in ways that reinforce this ideology. Such sentiments and uses of material possessions have also been recorded in non-African contexts. They are particularly well illustrated by Amanda Vickery's conclusion to her study of the meanings invested in the household goods belonging to an eighteenth-century Lancashire gentlewoman, Elizabeth Shackleton:

Denied access to the professions and public office, women could not pass on the invisible mysteries of institutional power or professional expertise to their descendants. A gentlewoman's skills were characteristically *embodied* in that 'unskilled' arena, the household. Small wonder if, in consequence, she turned to personal and household artefacts to create a world of meanings and ultimately to transmit her history. (1993: 294, emphasis added)

Equally, examples of the deliberate destruction of a recently deceased's possessions and buildings (or reliance on their relative susceptibility to the natural process of decay) have been noted in a variety of contexts. A well-known example from East Africa concerns the *vigango*, or carved and painted wooden memorial posts that are erected by most of the nine groups of Mijikenda on the Kenya and Tanzania coasts, as a way of commemorating members of the *Gohu* secret society (Brown 1980). These are not erected immediately after death, but instead are installed only after the ancestor has appeared to a spiritual leader in a dream expressing a wish to be 'brought home out of the cold' (Parsons 2001: 57). These posts are held to be like humans and should be of human height. They are buried so that the lower half of the 'body' and the legs are below ground while the upper torso and head are visible. Thus, their spatial relationship with the earth mimics that of the ancestor being commemorated, encompassing both that of the living and the spirits. Like humans, *vigango* are said to have a single life and so no effort is made to preserve them. Over time they succumb to natural weathering processes, eventually rotting away entirely. At this point, they may be replaced by a smaller, uncarved figurative post known as *kibao*, but this practice is not always followed. Parallel processes have been recorded in some detail for Malangan carvings from New Ireland (Papua New Guinea) (Küchler 1987), which after their use in death rituals were traditionally thrown out into the surrounding forest, the smell of the rotting wood serving as a sign of the object's symbolic death.

As discussed above with regard to the respect taken by the Haya towards remembering their dead, these types of practices would have quite different consequences for the formation of the 'residues of the past' among the Dogon. A similar kind of contrast has been noted by Rowlands (1993), and following Küchler he has suggested that societies that habitually employ practices of deliberate destruction of buildings and possessions should be distinguished from those which place greater emphasis on the preservation of objects as a means of cultural transmission. In the latter types of society, Rowlands argues, the acts of artefact curation and inheritance should result in material styles being rather conservative over time since older objects are continually available for future generations to copy. In societies where the emphasis is on the physical destruction of cultural material, on the other hand, there is inevitably greater reliance on the recollection of the images of objects seen in the past, and hence a greater potential for stylistic change. Time, in these contexts, survives not as a visible, physical trace, but only through the 'remembrance of things past', that is, as images.

The Haya example also demonstrates that remembering is intimately linked with forgetting. For this reason, as Margaret Atwood clearly recognizes, in the words at the beginning of this chapter, many practices which generate archaeological traces may be about 'casting out' the past rather than retrieving it. Diane Mines, for example, has described how Tamil communities in southern India perceive past actions as having the potential to 'endure or "stick" ... as material traces to the bodies and selves of actors and their descendants' (1997: 174). Such material traces have the potential to affect a person's capabilities, and Tamil consequently use objects to detach a person's misfortune and other kinds of unpleasant past experience from his or her body. These objects are subsequently discarded. Although in the Tamil case the objects used are normally of a non-durable type, such as eggs and vegetable matter, the process is closely linked to much broader concepts of cleanliness and purity that may influence a wide range of mundane activities such as refuse disposal and house cleaning, both of which leave quite clear archaeological traces. There may be even further distinctions to be drawn between these different kinds of society, such as their attitudes to time, duration, and the maintenance of 'tradition'. Exactly how all such differences are manifested archaeologically, if at all, remains unclear, although elements such as deliberate destruction and curation are certainly potentially recognizable. How such practices, especially with respect to domestic assemblages, correlate with evidence for such aspects as monumentalization, ritual practices, stylistic variability and the temporality of settlement has yet to be established (for a recent attempt using examples from European prehistory, however, see Bradley 2002). Such issues clearly offer fruitful ground for future ethnoarchaeological studies. Equally important, there needs to be much wider recognition within the discipline that practices such as artefact disposal, curation and maintenance, and the repair, recycling and abandonment of buildings, do not just concern matters of utility but also provide rich clues as to how past societies understood, for themselves, the 'archaeology of things'.

Conclusion

Various studies have shown that the scholarly community may well generate a different reading of the past of a particular geographical locality than that held by the local populace. In recent years the trend in archaeology has been to encourage acknowledgement of such different interpretations and to accord respect for local narratives. Thus different 'pasts' are allowed to co-exist, and in some cases efforts may be made to understand the epistemological basis on which indigenous models are constructed. Although well intentioned, such strategies have nevertheless encouraged an implicit evaluation of the different accounts whereby the 'local' is contrasted unfavourably with the 'universal' as being more partial and selective, even though there is widespread recognition that 'scientific' archaeology is far from being objective and free from interpretative bias. At times, more confrontational stances have been adopted – as has been the case regarding the archaeological treatment of human remains and debates over the rights of various groups to claim such remains for reburial. In such cases, those opposed to reburial argue that the practice not only infringes academic freedom and prohibits future research through the application of new techniques, but also curtails understanding of universal aspects of human behaviour, genetic heritage and physiology in favour of local, partisan interests (for an overview of such debates, see Fforde et al. 2002).

Regardless of whether antagonistic or accommodating positions are adopted, neither strategy can be regarded as sufficient. As Friedman has observed, since 'the attribution of meaning and construction of cultural models is a motivated practice, our own purported truth-value vision of history and ethnography must be understood in terms of the way in which it is produced, if we are to place it alongside the way other people produce their own visions' (1992: 855). One way of doing this is to examine each for their specific combination of what Trouillot refers to as history's 'mentions' and 'silences' (1995). As he explains, these occur at multiple levels of historical production that encompass: 'the moment of fact creation (the making of *sources*); the moment of fact assembly (the making of *archives*); the moment of fact retrieval (the making of *narratives*); and the moment of retrospective significance (the making of *history* in the final instance)' (1995: 26, original emphasis).

Unravelling the different layers of 'silences' and 'mentions', whether in archaeological discourses or in those produced by the indigenous inhabitants of an area, is by no means an easy task (for an excellent attempt, see Stahl 2001). Thus, to take the case of historical production among the Dogon, the selective preservation of the houses occupied by lineage heads ensures their long-term survival as sources of settlement history. These physical 'mentions' of the historical presence of male elders are further reinforced by the 'mentions' of named male elders in lineage genealogies, some of whom resurface in the various clan and village-scale oral histories. Just as houses are cleared of women's objects, thereby 'silencing' them from this element of the archaeological record of Dogon practice, so their names are typically absent from genealogies and oral histories. In turn, the primacy given to principles of patrilineal descent and primogeniture structure the way in which these sources are assembled as archives of Dogon history, and in so doing not only silence women but also junior men. In constructing narratives of family, lineage and village history, Dogon typically draw on these different archives, usually in a selective fashion creating yet further 'silences' and 'mentions', in a pattern of what I have called recursive relationships over time, which in turn imposes constraints on the type of history that both they and outsiders can provide from other sources.

The manner in which history is produced in any society can involve the selective conservation and destruction of physical traces. This not only creates the conditions for certain 'silences' and 'mentions' in the present, but also has the potential to reproduce the same pattern of 'silences' and 'mentions' in the future. For instance, discard and site abandonment practices among the Dogon ensure that most artefacts (and recall here, that it is Dogon women more than men who invest their personal histories in artefacts as opposed to buildings) are likely to be deposited away from areas of habitation, such as in the various fields that border the foot of the Bandiagara escarpment, where fragments of pottery, household sweepings and other categories of 'refuse' are ultimately scattered as manure. Such localities are conventionally overlooked by archaeologists, or given only minimal attention, and so, hypothetically, the material testimony to their presence in Dogon history that Dogon women seek to preserve is once again 'silenced' – in this case as a result of the dominant configurations of archaeological practice.[3] The challenge facing archaeologists is not just learning more about how the material culture of memory operates but also about coming to recognize the selective nature of the memories that are preserved in this way. It is likely, also, that no single set of criteria will be universally appropriate. Instead, historically and contextually specific models will be called for. As a first step in this direction, understanding the epistemological basis of other, non-Western 'archaeologies' seems all the more urgent.

Notes

1. As the term implies, soil micromorphology entails the study of microscopic traces of debris and the variable form of soil particles in different archaeological contexts so as to determine the nature of human activities performed in different areas across a site. Being microscopic in nature, such traces are believed to be less susceptible to the distorting effects of post-depositional processes than the macroscopic elements of the archaeological record, such as artefacts and structural remains, that form the focus of most archaeological analyses.
2. For other 'readings' of how the Haya interpret and recreate their past, see Césard 1927 and Schmidt 1996.
3. Of course, the reality is far more complex than this, since there are depositional contexts within Dogon settlements that are distinctly associated with women

and their routine practices. These include a special midden where all household cooking pots are deliberately broken as part of a process of ritual cleansing performed when particular taboos governing a woman's movements during menstruation have been broken, and the accumulation of body-oil pots that are left close to the village cemetery each time a woman is buried. However, as I have argued elsewhere, these are highly structured deposits which record only certain aspects of women's history and frequently do so in a male idiom (Lane 1986b).

References

Appadurai, A. (ed.) (1986), *The Social Life of Things: Commodities in Cultural Perspective*, Cambridge: Cambridge University Press.

Atwood, Margaret (2000), *The Blind Assassin*, Toronto: McClelland and Stewart.

Bedaux, R.M.A. (1986), 'Pottery variation in present-day Dogon compounds (Mali): preliminary results', in R. Singer and J.K. Lundy (eds), *Variation, Culture and Evolution in African Populations*, Johannesburg: Witwatersrand University Press.

Binford, L.R. (1962), 'Archaeology as Anthropology', *American Antiquity* 28: 217–25.

Bourdieu, P. (1977), *Outline of a Theory of Practice,* Cambridge: Cambridge University Press.

Bradley, R. (2002), *The Past in Prehistoric Societies*, London: Routledge.

Brasseur, G. (1968), *Les Établissements humains au Mali*, Dakar: Institut Fondementale d'Afrique Noire, Mémoire 83.

Brown, J.L. (1980), 'Miji-Kenda grave and memorial sculptures', *African Arts* 13: 36–9, 88.

Césard, P. (1927), 'Comment les *Bahaya* interprètent leurs origines', *Anthropos* 22: 447–53.

Chevalier, S. (1996), 'Transmettre son mobilier?' *Ethnologie Française* 26: 115–28.

Connerton, P. (1989), *How Societies Remember*, Cambridge: Cambridge University Press.

Costello, S.K. (2000), 'Memory tools in early Mesopotamia', *Antiquity* 74: 475–6.

Daniel, G.E. (1950), *A Hundred Years of Archaeology*, London: Duckworth.

Denyer, S. (1978), *African Traditional Architecture*, London: Heinemann.

Fforde, C., Hubert, J. and Turnbull, P. (eds) (2002), *The Dead and Their Possessions: Repatriation in Principle, Policy and Practice*, London: Routledge.

Foucault, M. (1979), 'Governmentality', *Ideology and Consciousness*, 6: 5–21.

Friedman, J. (1992), 'The past in the future: history and the politics of identity', *American Anthropologist* 94: 837–59.

Geary, P. (1986), 'Sacred commodities: the circulation of medieval relics', in A. Appadurai (ed.), *The Social Life of Things: Commodities in Cultural Perspective*, Cambridge: Cambridge University Press.

Hendon, J.A. (2000), 'Having and holding: storage, memory, knowledge and social relations', *American Anthropologist* 102: 42–53.

Hoskins, J. (1998), *Biographical Objects*, London: Routledge.

Küchler, S. (1987), 'Malangan: art and memory in a Melanesian society', *Man*, 22: 238–55.

Lane, P.J. (1986a), 'Past practices in the ritual present: examples from the Welsh Bronze Age', *Archaeological Review from Cambridge* 5(2): 181–91.

—— (1986b), 'Settlement as History: A Study of Space and Time among the Dogon of Mali', University of Cambridge, PhD Thesis.

—— (1987), 'Reordering residues of the past', in I. Hodder, (ed.), *Archaeology as Long-Term History*, Cambridge: Cambridge University Press.

—— (1994), 'The temporal structuring of settlement among the Dogon: an ethnoarchaeological study', in M. Parker Pearson and C. Richards, (eds), *Architecture and Order: Approaches to Social Space*, London: Routledge.

—— (1996), 'Rethinking ethnoarchaeology', in G. Pwiti and R. Soper (eds), *Aspects of African Archaeology*, Harare: University of Zimbabwe Publications, 727–32.

Layton, R. (ed.) (1989a), *Who Needs the Past? Indigenous Values and Archaeology*, London: Unwin Hyman.

—— (ed.) (1989b), *Conflict in the Archaeology of Living Traditions*, London: Unwin Hyman.

Lemonnier, P. (1986), 'The study of material culture today: towards an anthropology of technical systems', *Journal of Anthropological Archaeology* 5: 147–86.

Lillios, K.T. (1999), 'Objects of memory: the ethnography and archaeology of heirlooms', *Journal of Archaeological Method and Theory* 6: 235–62.

Lyons, D. (1998), 'Witchcraft, gender, power and intimate relations in Mura compounds in Déla, northern Cameroon', *World Archaeology* 29: 344–62.

Malinowski, B. (1922), *Argonauts of the Western Pacific*, London: Routledge.

Marcoux, J-S. (2001), 'The *'casser maison'* ritual: constructing the self by emptying the house', *Journal of Material Culture* 6: 213–35.

Mines, D.P. (1997), 'Making the past past: objects and the spatialization of time in Tamilnadu', *Anthropological Quarterly* 70: 173–86.

Parsons, K. (2001), 'Crossing boundaries', *Kenya Past and Present* 32: 57–62.

Roberts, M.N. and Roberts, A.F. (eds) (1996), *Memory: Luba Art and the Making of History*, New York: The Museum of Modern Art and Munich: Prestel.

Paul Lane

Robertshaw, P. and Kamuhangire, E. (1996), 'The present in the past: archaeological sites, oral traditions, shrines and politics in Uganda', in G. Pwiti and R. Soper (eds), *Aspects of African Archaeology*, Harare: University of Zimbabwe Publications, 739–43.

Rowlands, M. (1993), 'The role of memory in the transmission of culture', *World Archaeology* 25: 141–51.

Schmidt, P.R. (1996), 'Rhythmed time and its archaeological implications', in G. Pwiti and R. Soper (eds), *Aspects of African Archaeology*, Harare: University of Zimbabwe Publications, 655–62.

Semple, S. (1998), 'A fear of the past: the place of the prehistoric burial mound in the ideology of middle and later Anglo-Saxon England', *World Archaeology* 30: 109–26.

Sillitoe, A. (1998), 'The development of indigenous knowledge: a new applied anthropology', *Current Anthropology* 39: 223–52.

Smith, A.B. (1999), 'Encapsulation or not: The Ju/'hoan example', paper presented at the 4th World Archaeological Congress, Cape Town, 10–14 January 1999.

Stahl, A.B. (2001), *Making History in Banda: Anthropological Visions of Africa's Past*, Cambridge: Cambridge University Press.

Stevenson, M.G. (1991), 'Beyond the formation of hearth-associated artefact assemblages', in E.M. Kroll and T.D. Price (eds), *The Interpretation of Archaeological Spatial Patterning*, London: Plenum Press.

Trouillot, (1995), *Silencing the Past: Power and the Production of History*, Boston: Beacon Press.

Vickery, A. (1993), 'Women and the world of goods: a Lancashire consumer and her possessions, 1751–81', in J. Brewer and R. Porter (eds), *Consumption and the World of Goods*, London: Routledge.

Weiner, A.B. (1992), *Inalienable Possessions: The Paradox of Keeping-While-Giving*, Berkeley: University of California Press.

Weiss, B. (1996), *The Making and Unmaking of the Haya Lived World: Consumption in Everyday Practice*, Durham NC: Duke University Press.

—— (1997), 'Forgetting your dead: alienable and inalienable objects in Northwest Tanzania', *Anthropological Quarterly* 70: 164–72.

Williams, H. (1998), 'Monuments and the past in early Anglo-Saxon England', *World Archaeology* 30: 90–108.

–2–

'Varimu Valale': Rock Art as World Heritage in a Ritual Landscape of Central Tanzania
Jasper Chalcraft

The past is not dead nor its meaning singular and decided. It is always precariously perched on the present.

Arjun Singh (cited in Bernbeck and Pollock 1996)

Varimu valale, 'spirits sleep well',[1] is a key phrase uttered during the rituals that some locals practise in Kondoa-Irangi, Tanzania mostly under fig trees or next to sacred springs, but also in the painted rock shelter of Mungumi wa Kolo, a site that is being nominated for UNESCO's World Heritage List.

This highlights a discordance between the way the global 'World Heritage' initiative conceives of the past and the way a place is lived in and used by local ritual specialists. There are several official pointers, as article 3.1.3 of Tanzania's new Cultural Policy, Sera ya Utamaduni (inaugurated 23 August 1997), states in article 3.1.6 that cultural heritage sites are to be 'identified, delineated and developed', as well as used for education and tourism. Moreover, 'All man-made objects shall become national monuments on attaining the age of one hundred years' (article 3.1.11). In line with Appadurai's (1981) view of 'the past as a scarce resource' we find this antiquity defined variously: by those who live around and use it, local elites, archaeologists and researchers, and national and international institutions. For archaeologists, the rock art of Central Tanzania spans a period from at least 3,500 BP[2] to paintings known as the 'Late Whites' created up to 200 years ago. These are unique in East Africa in being produced, probably, by iron-working agriculturists, rather than pastoralists (Nooter 1986: 104). The early paintings are seen by some to relate to the Khoisan-speaking Sandawe hunter-gatherers (now settled) who live to the south-west. The fragility of these paintings and their uniqueness and the high level of research interest in the corpus of southern African rock art are of predominant concern to the archaeologists involved with the nomination: their conservation is not only being threatened by environmental factors, but also by human interaction (graffiti, fires and dancing in shelters, the ritual spitting of beer onto the paintings, and so on.) For the Rangi and

Alagwa who live in the area these paintings were created by Wareno (a Kiswahili term probably denoting the Portuguese, possibly seen as spirit beings), or by 'Germans'. Nonetheless, for the Rangi they belong to the deep past, for 'Most Rangi distinguish only two periods of time: *siku iji* (these days, the present time); and *hara kali* (long ago). *Hara kali* includes, not only the very beginnings of the Rangi as a distinct people, but also events as recent as 1916, the year when German administration effectively came to an end' (Kesby 1981: 22).

Thus, an emic reckoning of time by the local people themselves consigns the paintings to antiquity. The view of the Tanzanian state is not dissimilar, for in the narrative of the nation the paintings represent where Tanzanians have come from, an antiquity second only to the country's palaeoanthropological finds.

World Heritage too, manipulates the temporal sphere. Indeed, drawing a particular past from history and keeping it remote (such as placing it into an evolutionary schema, and romanticizing it) combined with the act of imagining a global unity, confines some heritages to 'glacial time';[3] for 'Under glacial time remnants of the past are treasured as symbols of culture and nature that had value and have been lost' (MacNaughton and Urry 1998: 160). An attitude to the past based on objects and places seems to be on the ascendancy. This preference for the tangible in thinking about and claiming possession of the past noted by Gillis (1994: 15), is evidenced across a wide range of societies in the fierce debates surrounding the repatriation of antiquities and human remains (e.g. NAGPRA – Native American Graves Protection and Repatriation Act), and the international legal struggle to create effective (and 'indigenous') intellectual property regimes (e.g. TRIPS – Agreement on Trade-Related Aspects of Intellectual Property Rights). These issues go hand in hand with a growing precision, described in the reconsideration of Hubert in this volume's introduction, of the representation of things in time.

Universalist 'heritage' as a conceptual category is on the rise, while contextually and individually particular embodied social memory is challenged by a new regime; a kind of heritage arms-race in which various identities (nationalisms, ethnicities, sexualities, etc.) claim places and objects as their 'property', and international institutions reify those claims through creating new legal instruments.

The objective of this research conducted in 2001 was to see how the rock art sites (or, 'rock imagery places') of Kondoa-Irangi were engaged with at the local level. Apart from graffiti, and some subsistence activities, the other significant use of sites was of a ritual nature. In local accounts this latter use was limited to only two clusters of sites actually containing rock art, although the whole area formed a ritual landscape. Here we focus on the most widely used and known site, Mungumi wa Kolo. The sensitivity of this site was emphasized in the SARAP (Southern African Rock Art Project) report of 2000 which recommended 'ongoing traditional use of the sites by the local community' (ibid.: 28). Here I present

Figure 3 The painted rock shelter at the ritual site of Mungumi wa Kolo, the flagship site of the proposed World Heritage nomination, with remains of a protective wall built by the Antiquities Department. Photo: Jasper Chalcraft

some of the data and challenges relevant to this objective. Mungumi wa Kolo can also be considered as the 'flagship' site for the rock art of Kondoa-Irangi, a role in which it will probably be presented in the nomination to UNESCO's World Heritage List.

I consider World Heritage here as a system of values and practices, over and above the clear ideological mission phrased in the documents that gave it birth[4] – principally the United Nations' 1948 Universal Declaration of Human Rights and the World Heritage Convention of 1972. My investigation, as far as it touches on UNESCO, considers how far the key values and practices of the organization *frame* activities (in Giddens' sense of constraining or enabling action) at the local level. The ethnographic material that follows is presented in outline only, because my primary objective here is to relate this local use of sites to the assumptions of the World Heritage project.

The importance of continuing ritual practice by some Rangi and Alagwa (Wasi) in an area earmarked for standard World Heritage status is rather different from the basis on which that status is assumed to rest. It seems unlikely that current ritual practice has relevance to Kondoa's early paintings as such, although there may possibly be some connections with the Late Whites. (One informant stated that 'witchdoctors' would paint a 'scorpion' onto a shelter wall – he mentioned Pahi-Lusangi – in order to create illness for a victim who could buy his health back from the painter.) The ongoing use of sites for 'ritual practices' does not in fact match the logic of 'cultural heritage' according to World Heritage (see criteria (iii) and (iv) identified in the SARAP report; 2000: 23). Under these criteria the sites are reduced to paintings and shelters alone, valorized only as archaeological testimony to past cultural activity rather than in the context of their current local significance. It is argued here that nomination under World Heritage's 'cultural landscape' category rather than 'cultural heritage' would better suit the lived reality of the sites. However, UNESCO's means of identifying cultural landscapes reflects Western preoccupation with centralized political systems, with landscapes that can be bounded and defined; for instance, 'functionality and intelligibility' are preconditions necessary for inclusion of cultural landscapes on the World Heritage List (Layton and Titchen 1995: 178).

Kondoa-Irangi, The Rangi, and The Alagwa

Kondoa District is a semi-arid area in the Dodoma Region of central Tanzania. The Kondoa-Irangi Hills (known locally as 'Upper Irangi'), rise to an altitude of 1,200 to 2,200 metres above sea level, and used to be covered with *miombo* forest, but intensive agro-pastoralism, combined with other factors, has changed the environment, leading to severe erosion in the highlands (Christiansson et al. 1993: 4; Madulu 1999). To the east of the Hills is the Maasai Steppe ('Lower Irangi'), where a large number of Rangi have recently settled. The area north from Kolo has seen Rangi expansion into areas originally settled by Alagwa and Gorowa.

Here I give a brief sketch of Rangi society, and an even more partial view of that of the Alagwa. Rangi society was segmentary (Fosbrooke 1958a: 21; Kesby 1981: i), and before the imposition of a chiefdom in 1919, it was their language that had long been the focal point of their mutual identification as Rangi. They are isolated as Bantu-speakers in the Eastern Rift Highlands, being surrounded by the three other African language groups. Chasi, the language of the Alagwa, is classified as 'Cushitic'. At first Rangi expansion pushed Alagwa further away from the area in which they lived, though now one is struck by the degree of assimilation between the groups; for instance many Alagwa children speak

Kirangi as a first language. Rangi settlement has tended to be scattered, though this has been affected markedly by colonial period resettlement schemes, and the 'villagization' of Nyerere's Ujamaa.[5]

I focus on two categories of individuals in Irangi. *Veneese* (pl., sg. *mweneese*: 'men of the land') are ritual practitioners who control the state of affairs between humans and ancestors.[6] It is a title given only to the descendants of those who have established new settlements as part of a Rangi land-rights ideology known as *mawunda-ya-sakame* ('fields of blood').[7] The second category are the *vaanga* (Kesby 1982: 195), 'diviner-healers', though most Rangi I spoke to referred to them by the Kiswahili *ngoma ya shetani* ('djinn music').[8] Their role is to divine and heal for their extended family. These categories are found also among the Alagwa, who are key players in the history of Irangi, having had a privileged role in rainmaking ritual (Fosbrooke 1958a), as have famed rainmakers of other ethnicities (e.g. Gorowa).[9] A number of Rangi informants commented pointedly that the Alagwa are still 'pagan', and that only they continue to blow horns, *irimo*, during rainmaking. The potency attributed to them is perhaps due to the extension of the Rangi land rights ideology to the Alagwa who had clearly been the first to settle certain areas. Indeed, some elderly Rangi maintain that *varimu*, the ancestral spirits to whom all rituals are addressed, are in fact Alagwa (see Kesby 1981: 32), thus pointing to a perceived shared past for both ethnicities.

Ritual practice in Irangi is varied. Diviner-healers perform either at home or in rock shelters. We can group current ritual practice into four general types: rainmaking, which usually takes place under a fig tree near the homestead; 'land-magic'; boundary marking (connected to the previous two, and perhaps not really a separate category); and the 'djinn' music of the diviner-healers who perform either at home or in rock shelters. Many rainmakers stated that they were also *veneese* (or *hapaloe* in Chasi).[10] Those I spoke to who mark boundaries were all *veneese*, and in the past this practice may have been inseparable from 'land-magic' and rainmaking. Rapid population growth, newly settled areas and subsequent changes such as a shift from matrilineal to patrilineal inheritance, and a colonially-imposed chieftancy based in Kolo, have interwoven clan and ethnic histories. The clarity of the ritual division of the area has been reduced.

UNESCO and 'World Heritage'

The conceptual origins of UNESCO and the World Heritage Programme in the Enlightenment and in Romanticism characterize it as universalist, with 'heritage' seen as a 'public good'. However, actual management of sites often contrasts with local values. Put crudely, the impending paradigm of World Heritage may necessitate a renegotiation of the relationship that a number of Rangi and Alagwa maintain with their ancestors via the painted shelter of Mungumi wa Kolo. This is despite recent initiatives, such as UNESCO's 'Intangible Heritage' programme, which acknowledge distinctive cultural perspectives. Richard Fardon (this volume) notes the amenability of the 'histories of material treasures' for temporal resignification, and World Heritage can be seen to be resignifying sites temporally, spatially and symbolically.

Despite the sensitivity of the management of the Kondoa-Irangi nomination, the representation and interpretation of the site will probably rest in the minds and hands of outsiders. Their interest may be more nationalistic than local, for it is likely that Village Councils will share responsibility for any such sites with the Antiquities Department. Furthermore, the 'stakeholders' who were consulted throughout the nomination process were the local elite (Village Councils, District Council, officials from government and NGO programmes in the area): this may be seen to have excluded ritual specialists. In the consultative process their prevailing concern was with the perceived benefits (tourism, roads, bridges, clinics and electricity) that a World Heritage nomination could bring to their villages. Increased international tourism may impose a market value on the sites, and to what degree this is incompatible with local use of the sites is not yet clear. Local opinions on the history of the sites themselves, or on the paintings, were not, as far as I am aware, either gathered or sought.

Local Use of Sites

How do locals use the rock art sites of central Tanzania? Paintings at Mungumi wa Kolo, Pahi and Kandaga are visited on educational outings by local schools, and also by Bustani Teachers' College from Kondoa town. Other local visits involve interaction with the paintings through graffiti (Pahi, Kandaga), and interaction with the site through ritual (Mungumi wa Kolo, Pahi), as well as possible socio-economic use (the overhanging top of the Pahi shelter Kwa-Nyange IV (B8) appears to have been used as a threshing floor for millet). To simplify the case, these are examples of heritage as Bourdieu's habitus, not, as is implicit in the World Heritage model, heritage as *choice* (Appadurai 2001).

In local accounts only Mungumi wa Kolo (including the two nearby small shelters known as Majilili: sites B1, B2 and B3) sees significant ritual use. We can identify two main reasons for its importance: it forms part of a well-known ritual border, and is home to powerful spirits and djinns (spirits here being clan ancestors, and djinns being capricious 'genies'). The site is seen as particularly potent by a number of local diviner-healers – 'djinn musicians' – who come here to cure their patients, to divine the future, and in some cases to gain power themselves (this may also be a reason for some *veneese* to visit the site). Both the first and second reasons contribute to why Mungumi is also used by a few rainmakers as well. Just below the large shelter known as Mungumi wa Kolo there is a boulder with a 'hole' underneath it. This shows clear signs of recent use, described by some ritual specialists as something similar to a 'vision-quest' hole, and as a repository for the portion of the sacrifice designated for the ancestors. Of the forty-eight ritual specialists whom I spoke to, some lived over forty kilometres from Mungumi, but over half either used the shelter themselves for ritual purposes, or knew of other groups that did.

Power of Place

Not a single informant attributed any ritual importance to the paintings in Mungumi wa Kolo or elsewhere. The importance of such places in traditional terms may therefore reside in the spatiality of a site (after Blake 1998: 60), more than in the painted figures so central to the World Heritage nomination.

According to Prins and Woodhouse it was Janette Deacon who brought the landscape back into focus in Southern African rock art studies (Deacon 1988; Prins and Woodhouse 1996: 78). She pointed out the importance of hills and springs as key nodes in the landscape of the creators of southern African sites. Deacon's ideas were taken up strongly by Lim in her thesis on the rock art sites of Usandawe (southwest of Kondoa-Irangi), 'There is power in the place and this is

Figure 4 Detail of the rock paintings at Kandaga, showing 'Late Whites' painted over earlier 'red' paintings; numrous tuyères around this site attest to its use for iron-smelting, to which people/period the 'Late Whites' are probably attributable. Photo: Jasper Chalcraft

what attracted and localised the rock art ... the importance of the place is primary and ... painting is secondary' (1992: 268). Certainly the sites of Kondoa-Irangi appear to have been selected: they are mostly shelters that constitute vantage points over the surrounding countryside. This general orientation of shelters, considered with the red paintings, seems to point to their use by hunters.[11] 'Late White' paintings, mostly geometrics, occur at some sites superposed on early reds (Kandaga A9 for example), suggesting some kind of significance attributed to the original painters (and/or paintings) by those who followed them. Such a continuity, albeit without such temporal disjuncture, was noted by Culwick in the 1930s to the south of Irangi. Wagogo ('Bantu' pastoralists) adopted sites at Bahi said to have been painted by the area's previous inhabitants, the Wamia. They maintained Wamia funerary ceremonies, repainting with fat from a sacrificial animal and using the sites for their own rainmaking rituals (Culwick 1931: 443), suggesting an attribution of ritual potency to the indigenous 'Other' by the 'Bantu' incomers. If the landscape was important to the painters, we may note that today Rangi and Alagwa do not generally 'venerate' hills, as is claimed of the Sandawe and Rimi. In ritual terms other elements are of importance, predominantly fig trees, and sacred springs that provide water vital for rainmaking. There could be something in the supposition that the importance of Mungumi wa Kolo to Rangi and Alagwa (and possibly others) may in part derive from the shelter's evident importance to Irangi's previous inhabitants, who would probably have been regarded as particularly potent ritually, as has been noted elsewhere with 'Bantu'-Khoisan relations (e.g. Prins and Hall, 1994).

Making Rain: Ritual Apparatus and Practice

The following attempts an overview of Rangi and Alagwa rainmaking and land-magic, in terms of tools and practice. Site location for a ritual was in most cases a large fig tree near to the homestead / village. A black sheep was the sacrificial animal of choice for rainmaking, chosen 'because rain clouds are black'. This was normally killed on site, roasted, and a portion left for the spirit. Sometimes this portion was a half of the animal, in a significant number of cases it was the head alone, buried next to the fig tree. The skin was usually retained for practical uses; a strip of it being tied to the fig tree by a few specialists.

A calabash (*mumbu* in Kirangi) was normally prepared, filled with local beer (*pombe*) to spit or splatter over the site. The calabash was invariably decorated with 'white-soil water', often with vertical lines placed to mark the four cardinal directions. A string of white beads might encircle the neck of the calabash; these are the same white beads known as *kichingo* (sg., pl. *vichingo*) that are worn around the waist by young girls, and around the neck by women. These decorative additions to the calabash were seen 'to make the spirit come', and to make the calabash 'natural' and 'beautiful'.

There was almost always also a half-calabash holding water and 'white-soil'. In most cases this 'white-soil' was ground python-droppings. This was mixed either with water taken from a special spring, frequently called *Ntarii* ('nose', here designating a spring that never runs dry), or from any ordinary water source. This mixture was then flicked with either the leaves of the castor plant (*mnonyo*)[12] or the *kongo* tree. Alagwa informants often used leaves from the *gindai* plant (*mlami* in Kirangi). It is this mixture that was used to mark the calabash of *pombe*, and often to mark the head of the sheep as well. According to an informant from Changamisa the sheep was only marked during rainmaking rituals.

The most common reasons for a *mweneese* or rainmaker to perform a ritual were when there was too much or too little rain (winds from the west are seen to bring destructive rain), or to abate the sun, or disease. Other reasons included the death of elders, the drying up of springs, the violent deaths of village men, or when *varimu* are disturbed when a fig tree or other trees around a mountain spring or circumcision grove are cut down.

It should be noted that change in ritual practice has been subtle. Bound-beating and initiation ceremonies appear to have declined, and the toolkit too seems to have been modified. I refer to a possible shift from the use of chyme in *muuda* (medicine), to that of python droppings,[13] which may have served to integrate and/or appropriate symbolic ideas emanating from the Lake Victoria region. One group who may have mediated these ideas in Irangi were the Nyamwezi whose involvement in the ivory and slave trades had repercussions in the area perhaps from as early as the late 1700s.

Ritual Uses of Mungumi wa Kolo

In the following section I set out who is using Mungumi wa Kolo and the reasons they give for doing so. Differences in ritual format are briefly described; this emphasizes the distinctness of each clan/ritual group while establishing the conceptual commonalities and attachment to the site that they share.

Mungumi wa Kolo as a Border

An Alagwa *hapaloe* from Tlawi Juu claimed he used Mungumi wa Kolo occasionally. An elder with two uncircumcised and 'very black' boys would go and spit *pombe* around the shelter and talk to the spirits. They should then walk day and night around their whole border from Mungumi wa Kolo, a circumambulation of about thirty-four hours. He described it as a ritual performed once every three years, undertaken because 'All the *hapaloe* want to know the area – and they can greet the spirit(s) (*Gieri*)'. They perform another ritual like the one at Mungumi when they reach Tlawi Chini. His account was slightly contradictory in the discussion – before telling us about the use of Mungumi wa Kolo as part of their border-marking, he said that *hapaloe* from Tlawi Juu and Kwadinu used the 'hole' at Mungumi (though one of the *mweneese* from Kwadinu claimed that Mungumi was used by people from Haubi), which he denied later on.

A non-specialist from Kolo said that people of all clans sacrifice at Mungumi wa Kolo for rain, and use it for healing. Wahaire (poss. Vahagire) also have a border running through it, from the Chief's house at Kolo to the east. Two *veneese* from Mnenia of the Vasiru clan designated Mungumi as important because it was a border, a boundary marker. When asked whether the paintings themselves have any 'power', they ascribed the ritual potency of Mungumi wa Kolo to the fact that previous inhabitants had been there, and a 'boundary marker is important because people are always meeting there'.

Mungumi wa Kolo for Djinn Musicians

A *mweneese* and rainmaker from Bumbuta who also heals at her home, claimed that djinn musicians and 'medicine men' from both Pahi and Kinyasi use Mungumi wa Kolo. She believed they use it because the paintings were done by *varimu* and this made the place powerful. She also described how people 'dance and sing, go into the hole [just below the main shelter at Mungumi] and the spirit marks their cheeks to show all is good, and gives them a calabash of medicine'. This account of what happens inside the hole at Mungumi correlates strongly with that of a *mweneese* from Nchulunchuli (see below).

A *mweneese* and rainmaker from Chungai stated that djinn musicians used Mungumi wa Kolo, though he would not be more specific. A non-specialist from the same village was more forthcoming; he talked of djinn musicians and medicine men still using the 'hole' at Mungumi 'to see the spirit', his reason for their doing so was that 'Mungumi is the place of here.' They would enter the hole while others dance and sing 'special songs' outside, and sacrifice a black sheep. When they come out of the hole the (nameless) spirit has marked their face. It leaves a line on the forehead, made from a paste of ground python-droppings.

A *mweneese* of Chora stated that the Vasalu of Mnenia use Mungumi wa Kolo, because Mungumi is part of their area: 'Many medicine men go to Mungumi as it is special for medicine. They start at – go first to – Mariwi (mountain spring), but for more power they go to Mungumi. First they take python-droppings from Mariwi, for Mungumi they take a calabash of medicine. People dance and sing special songs around Mungumi, and at a special time he [the spirit] comes with medicine.'

In the village of Mnenia a djinn musician initially denied using the shelter but later admitted that she and her group go and 'dance to special songs in Mungumi. The spirit puts medicine (*muuda*) into each person's hand...' and it marks their right temples with python-droppings. (This 'medicine' is a stick that can either be ground into a powder or boiled and drunk: either way its effect is to make the djinn leave the patient.) Prior to this the leader of their group spits *pombe*, and using their hands they splatter water from Ntarii spring mixed with python-droppings around the site 'to tell the spirit we are here'. The names she gave for the djinns in the shelter were: Mrangi, Mwarabu, Sharifu, Maasai, Simba, Njoka. She claims that her group do not, however, use the 'hole' at Mungumi, only the shelter; another (unnamed) group use it. Yet the *veneese* of Kinyasi insisted that it is the 'hole' at Mungumi that is the focus for djinn musicians.

A group of djinn musicians from Lusangi said they use Mungumi wa Kolo for healing. On arrival they (ideally) find that half the *pombe* in the calabash they took there the previous day has disappeared. They appeal to the djinn(s) of Mungumi to leave their patients. 'White-soil' water in a half-calabash is flicked around the site with castor leaves. A white chicken is sacrificed. They say special words, they 'beg the spirit' and dance. They stated that Mungumi is their last resort for healing, and they come here having tried unsuccessfully with a session of djinn music at the homestead with the patient. They also said that the Vawombe of Mnenia sacrifice in Mungumi wa Kolo for rain with either a goat or sheep, while for their own rainmakers they prefer to use a mountain spring near Lusangi.

Mungumi wa Kolo for Rainmakers / Veneese

An informant from Nchulunchuli initially did not mention that he used Mungumi wa Kolo. In fact, he uses it for rainmaking, and considers the site to fall under his ritual jurisdiction (as *mweneese*). He claims that djinn musicians cannot use the shelter or hole until they have his permission to do so; however an informant from Potea described the procedure for accessing the 'hole' as follows, 'If you are ill with a djinn you go to a medicine man, then you go to the *mweneese* [the one of your area] for permission to go to the hole [to be cured].' The *mweneese* of Nchulunchuli described the shelter as being used by people of this area, both djinn musicians and rainmakers: the Vasi Nduu clan, and the group of a well-known female *mweneese* of the Vawombe Ntinuu clan (she herself explicitly denied using Mungumi, though other informants confirmed that she does). He maintained that all Warangi clan spirits are present in the shelter. Furthermore, he described the 'power of the place' as pre-existing the paintings, which he believes the Germans painted. 'Majilili is for the djinn musicians... We use python-droppings ['white-soil' water] and flick the mixture with *kongo* leaves. Djinn musicians use *mnonyo* leaves. We spit *pombe*.' On being asked what happened at the 'hole' he replied: 'If you are inside the hole one of the spirits will give you something: a calabash full of medicine, a knife, an arrow, or a chicken. If the spirit gives you a chicken it is bad luck, it means famine... Getting the knife or arrow is good luck, so is the calabash of medicine.' Mungumi wa Kolo's 'hole' is not, apparently, unique. An Mjeja clan *mweneese* from Kinyasi detailed how he and *veneese* of Vakanya clan use a hole there. A sheep is killed, roasted, and half put next to the hole with a quantity of *pombe*. The disappearance of the sheep and *pombe* the next day means the spirit has heard them. The hole is also used to divine the year.

Other 'holes' known in the area include one near Sambua, which is apparently a special place for calming strong winds, and a hole at Pahi called Kwagaiu used to perform 'land-magic'.

A *mweneese* from Pahi said he uses Mungumi wa Kolo, though he also uses another hole called Sokoreda to divine the future:

> There is a special place here for 'looking at the future'... There are many spirits. The place is where two rocks come very close together and a Vanaja goes into that place between the rocks. Meanwhile they go to the meeting place with a black sheep which they then take to the cave [not Mungumi] and they throw python-dropping water. They do not kill the sheep. They also spit *pombe* and say *varimu valale*. Afterwards the person comes out of the hole and tells them what the future is.

A renowned rainmaker of the Vafuchu clan from Cheke had this to say about Mungumi wa Kolo:

> Some time ago [*hara kali*] a group of Visave rainmakers were lost in the Mungumi area and they found shelter and sacrificed there so that the [resident] spirit showed them the way home. They had been lost for one week. This group of rainmakers – these Visave – they lived in Isabe. The rainmakers of Mungumi, they are still from Isabe. The Vanaja clan of Pahi also use Mungumi.

He also identified two ancestral Gorowa spirits in Mungumi: Mungu and Singana.[14] However, he himself used another 'hole' in the past, near to a mountain spring at Masange, which he stayed in without food or water for five days so that the spirits could 'teach' him. He also said that Visave and Hagire *veneese* use the 'hole' at Mungumi to get 'visions'.

Conclusion

We have seen that a number of ritual specialists use Mungumi wa Kolo. It is not clear what the effect of site management in regulating use of this shelter inhabited by clan ancestors, connected to spirit possession, the revelation of ancestral dreams, rainmaking and border-marking might be. How central or marginal this is should depend on how 'cultural heritage' is defined, though in this case it is not open to discussion, as the nature of its management is to be brokered between local government (at the village level) and the Antiquities Department, under the guidance of national policy and international institutions.

Where the paintings are known locally, they are seen not to belong in any meaningful way to the area's present inhabitants; they were created by *Wareno*, or by Germans, (only one informant believed that *varimu* painted them). There is, of course, the possibility that the explicit denial of connection to authorship of the paintings 'may simply be expressions of the dangerous powers of such places' (Kenny 1976: 148). Some Late White paintings of 'scorpions' may be connected to recent witchcraft, while others, given their isolation as single figures in holes or restricted spaces and a certain amount of conjecture, may have been painted by initiates during, or following a trance-state (e.g. there are possible 'entoptic' grids in a tiny enclosed space on the top of the rock-shelter Pahi-Lusangi kwa Nyange IV). By and large, however, the paintings are said to be from a temporal elsewhere, not significant in themselves, despite the potency attributed to these sites on account of their prior use by peoples seen as ritually potent.

'Heritage' values confine the paintings and local traditions to 'glacial time', and there is some resonance between this and the Rangi temporal category of *hara kali* (long ago). However, this masks the ongoing ritual utility of the deep past, and a privileging of the heritage values of the paintings over the ritual values of the sites. This might represent the loss of a cultural resource for those to whom the shelter was important. If the values of ritual practice are recognized, it seems likely that they become a 'value' relating specifically to the foreign tourist market, and we might well feel pessimistic about the commoditizing effect this might have. Given that the draft management plan focuses on the infrastructural and interpretative development of Mungumi wa Kolo as the 'flagship' site, it is unlikely that local use of the site will go unregulated. For instance, the nomination itself is part of a reinscription of national territory, resting on the new objectives of Tanzania's Cultural Policy of 1997 mentioned at the opening of this chapter. The State too, it seems, has its own version of *hara kali*, and this in turns holds its own ritual utility.

More problematic than the notion of glacial time inherent in nominating the rock art sites under cultural criteria alone, is that this reification of the paintings may overshadow the landscape in which locals negotiate their history, and thus be detrimental to the area's 'intangible heritage'. The 'cultural landscape' category within World Heritage was conceived to address this kind of problem, and does to a certain degree represent the re-entry of space and place into time, therefore foregrounding a more holistic view of the 'site'. However, even if the nomination were to be proposed as a 'cultural landscape', temporal and spatial dimensions may be conceived of differently by Rangi ritual specialists, village and district level government functionaries, Tanzanian archaeologists, UNESCO policy makers, and heritage tourists.

Notwithstanding the importance of Mungumi wa Kolo as a ritual site, it is clear that the whole area projected to become a World Heritage site is populated with Rangi, Alagwa (and to a lesser extent Burunge and Gorowa) ancestral clan-spirits. However, the ritual landscape is more complex than the sacrificial sites, 'holes', circumcision groves, previous initiation zones in the ravines, and sacred springs where they are said to be located: it is delineated and rationalized by ritual boundaries that appear to have been tied to hereditary ownership of areas of land. A relationship exists between ritual practice and an indigenous politics of land ownership and management. A World Heritage nomination should take account of this, though even as a cultural landscape its 'functionality and intelligibility' would be problematic, not least because of a traditionally decentralized Rangi social structure, and the contestation of these areas between different ritual (and political) groups, probably due to an apparent decline in border-marking/bound-beating, and the degree to which they share these values and beliefs with local government.[15] Furthermore, and fundamentally, it may be the ongoing ritual practice within this landscape that helps order the past for Rangi and Alagwa, and justify land-ownership in the present.[16]

That ancestral-spirits of various clans and ethnicities are said to inhabit Mungumi wa Kolo may well reflect both the historical and actual social relationships between these groups. It has been suggested that taking spirit possession as a form of embodied memory is a necessary part of African historiography (Larsen 2000: 280). Thus, the different djinns which possess the patients of the djinn musician from Mnenia have much to tell us about the culture history of the area. Echoing once more Gregory Bateson's perception of one of the key roles of ritual being the preservation and utilization of knowledge (Janzen 1992: 176), Mungumi wa Kolo is more than a central node in the ritual landscape; it is key to the social and political history of the area, while also offering testament to a deep-history via its rock-paintings. However, a World Heritage nomination that privileges the latter, risks the former – thus the rock art itself becomes no more than conceptual 'graffiti' partially or totally obliterating the other pasts and other values connected to the rock shelter.

Such an obfuscation or obliteration of the past is unlikely to occur without local agency. The tools and institutions through which the West organizes and appropriates the past (amongst others, books and museums; see Adams 1995: 143, 146–50) may in turn be reappropriated as part of a reorientation of heritage (the concern with consolidating the tangible as mentioned earlier), and put to local – political – needs.[17] There are signs that the Rangi too have recognized the

potential in being an object of study (Kesby 1982: 397), and that there is a desire
to have their history, *written*, and presented in a *book*: this modern form of cultural
reproduction being seen as both desirable and necessary. The impending paradigm
of World Heritage may therefore necessitate a reorientation of the *loci* of cultural
reproduction, as a landscape of different values and practices reframes the history
that locals at present negotiate for themselves.

Notes

1. Fosbrooke translates this as: 'let the spirits sleep' (1958a: 24).
2. Masao has a c14 date for an ochre pencil of 3,665 +/– 140 B.P. (1979:
   271), though it is probable that some paintings date to an earlier period, and
   archaeological assemblages of the Later Stone Age date back to 19,000 BP;
   however Anati gives a surprising earliest date for the paintings of 40,000 BP
   (1986: 61).
3. As MacNaughton and Urry have pointed out, contemporary ways of thinking
   globally, of imagining ourselves part of a global community (in their example
   particularly evident in the growth of environmental thinking, the ideal of
   saving the environment depending on a shared – imagined – notion of global
   citizenship) rely on a 'glacial sense of time' in order to imagine themselves
   part of 'not just their locality, but humanity or nature and the planet as a whole'
   (1998: 152).
4. Important modifications and clarifications of the 1948 Declaration occurred
   with the two 1966 International Human Rights Covenants that covered civil and
   political rights, and economic, social and cultural rights. The World Heritage
   Convention's official title is 'The Convention Concerning the Protection of the
   World Cultural and Natural Heritage'.
5. On change in Rangi settlement and social structure see, for example,
   Mung'ong'o (1999).
6. *Veneese* were also called upon in the past for dispute settlement along with
   another category of leader: these were the *nkabaku* (literally 'bulls'), 'big-men'
   who acquired reputations and a certain amount of power either through their
   knowledge, or through their status as 'war leaders' by successfully leading
   cattle-raids (Kesby 1981: 62).
7. 'These were inheritable rights to clan lands which a pioneer locally known as
   the *mweneisi* had occupied, cleared of bush, and generally made habitable for
   himself and his descendants ... any Mrangi who possessed a piece of land in

the core areas in the Hills could and was qualified to legally "inherit from the ancestors" any unutilised piece of land in the surrounding areas. This cultural ideology has since been widely used to rationalise and justify the geographical expansion of the Rangi people and their territoriality from their homeland in the Hills to the surrounding areas in Lower Irangi' (Mung'ong'o 1999: 47). Kesby renders the term as *maunda ya sákame*, literally meaning 'fields of blood'. For further details see Kesby (1981: 110).

8. I give this as 'djinn music' in line with local translations of the term in full knowledge of Victor Turner's 'drums of affliction' / 'cults of affliction', and recognize local practice in Kondoa-Irangi as part of what Janzen identifies as a widespread 'institution' present throughout much of Central and Southern Africa (Janzen 1992: 4).

9. It is of interest that the Sandawe also associate the Alagwa with rainmaking (Lim 1992: 208).

10. Fosbrooke gives this as both *hapaloimo*, and *hapoloimo* (1958: 21). It is of interest that an Alagwa informant from Fenga Hill gave a different Chasi title, *Isabe*, though nobody else confirmed the use of this term. Isabe is actually a village, that, according to a well-known Rangi *mweneese* from Cheke, is where the original Visave clan rainmakers of Mungumi wa Kolo came from.

11. On non-visual aspects of rock art (e.g. acoustic, tactile, flaking and geophagic) see Ouzman 2001, and Fagg 1997.

12. Fosbrooke (1958b: 31) also mentions that the 'Master of Ceremonies' must 'carry a twig of castor oil plant' during the circumcision ceremony. The boys being circumcised also sit in the shade of a castor oil tree during their operation (ibid.: 35). Jannie Loubser (pers. comm. November 2001) believes that castor oil leaves may have hallucinogenic properties similar to jimsonweed [used in the *chinigchinich* cult of the Coso Range, and perhaps connected to the rock art there (Layton 2000: 172)], which could lead to a new understanding of the paintings known as the Late Whites in Kondoa. A *mweneese* gave me a creeper root that gives you 'special dreams'. He called it *'musekia'* (lit. 'cheerful' in Kirangi) which, according to Tanzanian ethnobotanist Norbert Ngowi, is *Tarena Suaveolens*.

13. With regard to possible significances of serpents, Tanzania's 'snake-men' guilds come to mind, and their significance is notable with regard to rainmakers further south (see Jolly 1996).

14. Although the rainmaker describes himself as Rangi of the Vafuchu clan, the fact that Wafuchu (the Kiswahili term for the Gorowa ethnicity) have been described as very powerful rainmakers, opens up the possibility that his ancestors were in fact Gorowa, as his Rangi clan name attests.

15. It should be noted that the Rangi have a long history of antipathy to governance generally (see Kesby 1982: 241, 231, 27). Government was government,

and had been, and continued to be seen primarily as responsible for loss of money through taxation (ibid.: 208, 53). Furthermore, the only explicit use of ritual in the mediation of modernity I came across was from a centenarian of Tumbelo, a *mweneese*, who took ritual measures to counteract the threat he felt *Ujamaa* posed to his people: 'During *Ujamaa* people were moved from here. I was afraid and made a medicine [*muuda*] that made everyone come [return] here'.

16. On the importance of landscape to the ordering of prehistoric pasts (in Britain), see Gosden and Lock 1998: 6.

17. I make this point also to emphasize that the 'tourist gaze' is not a monolithic culturally-bounded optique upon the world (see also Guneratne 2001): frequently it is mediated by local intermediaries who may pursue their own individual, class, or other interests in their presentation of a site to others.

References

Adams, K.M. (1995), 'Making up the Toraja? The appropriation of tourism, anthropology, and museums for politics in upland Sulawesi, Indonesia', *Ethnology* 34(2): 143–53.

Anati, E. (1986), 'The state of research in rock art: rock art of Tanzania and the East African Sequence', *Bolletino del Centro Camuno di Studi Preistorici* 23: 15–68.

Appadurai, A. (1981), ' The past as a scarce resource', *Man* 16(2): 201–19.

—— (2001), 'The globalisation of archaeology and heritage: a discussion with Arjun Appadurai', *Journal of Social Archaeology* 1: 35–49.

Barclay, P. (1999), *Anthropology and Colonialism in Asia and Oceania,* Review of Jan van Bremen and Akitoshi Shimizu, (eds), *Anthropology and Colonialism in Asia and Oceania*, Richmond, Surrey: Curzon Press. Referred to May 2000. Location: www.h-asia.msu.edu

Bateson, G. ((1958[1936]), *Naven: The Culture of the Iatmul People of New Guinea as Revealed through a Study of the Naven Ceremonial*, London: Wildwood House.

Bernbeck, R. and Pollock, S. (1996), 'Ayodhya, archaeology, and identity', *Current Anthropology* 37(1), Supp.: S138–42.

Bessières, M. (2001), 'Indiana Jones has no future', *The UNESCO Courier,* April. Referred to February 2002. Location: www.unesco.org/courier/2001_04/uk/doss22.htm

Blake, E. (1998), 'Sardinia's nuraghi: four millenia of becoming', *World Archaeology* 30(1): 59–71.

Bourdieu, P. (1972), *Esquisse d'une théorie de la pratique*, Paris: Droz.

——(1986), 'Habitus code et codification', *Actes de la Recherche en Sciences Sociales*, 64: 40–4.

Christiansson, C., Mbegu, A.C., and Yrgård, A. (1993), *The Hand of Man: Soil Conservation in Kondoa Eroded Area, Tanzania,* Nairobi: Regional Soil Conservation Unit, Swedish International Development Authority.

Culwick, A.T. (1931), 'Some rock-paintings in central Tanganyika', *Journal of the Royal Anthropological Institute of Great Britain and Ireland* 61: 443–53.

Deacon, J. (1988), 'The power of place in understanding southern San rock engravings', *World Archaeology* (Edition titled 'Archaeology in Africa') 20(1): 129–40.

Fagg, M.C. (1997), *Rock Music*, Pitt Rivers Museum, University of Oxford, Occasional Paper on Technology No.14. Totton: Hobbs the Printers.

Fosbrooke, H.A. (1958a), 'Blessing the year: a Wasi / Rangi Ceremony', *Tanganyika Notes and Records* 50: 21–7.

——(1958b), 'A Rangi circumcision ceremony: blessing a new grove', *Tanganyika Notes and Records* 50: 30–8.

Giddens, A. (1984), *The Constitution of Society*, Berkeley CA., University of California Press.

Gillis, J.R. (1994), 'Memory and identity: the history of a relationship', in J. R. Gillis (ed.) *Commemorations: The Politics of National Identity*, Princeton N.J., Princeton University Press.

Gosden, C. and Lock, G. (1998), 'Prehistoric histories', *World Archaeology* 30(1): 2–12.

Guneratne, A. (2001), 'Shaping the tourist's gaze: representing ethnic difference in a Nepali village', *Journal of the Royal Anthropological Institute* 7(3): 527–43.

Janzen, J.M. (1992), *Ngoma: Discourses of Healing in Central and Southern Africa*, Berkeley: University of California Press.

Jolly, P. (1996), 'Symbiotic interaction between black farmers and south-eastern San', *Current Anthropology* 37(2): 277–305.

Kesby, J.D. (1981), *The Rangi of Tanzania: An Introduction to their Culture*, New Haven, Connecticut: Human Relations Area Files, HRAFlex Series, FN16–001.

——(1982), *Process and the Past among the Rangi of Tanzania*, New Haven, Connecticut: Human Relations Area Files, HRAFlex Series, FN16–002.

Kenny, M. G. (1976), 'The symbolism of East African rock art', *Zeitschrift für Ethnologie* 101(1): 147–60.

Larson, P.M. (2000), *History and Memory in the Age of Enslavement. Becoming Merina in Highland Madagascar, 1770–1822*, Portsmouth, NH: Heinemann.

Layton, R. (2000), 'Shamanism, totemism and rock art: Les Chamanes de la Préhistoire in the context of rock art research', *Cambridge Archaeological Journal* 10(1): 169–86.

Layton, R. and Titchen, S. (1995), 'Uluru: an outstanding Australian Aboriginal cultural landscape', in B. von Droste, H. Plachter, and M. Rossler (eds), *Cultural Landscapes of Universal Value*, New York: Gustav Fischer Verlag.

Lim, I. (1992), *A Site-Oriented Approach to Rock Art: A Study from Usandawe, Central Tanzania*, PhD Thesis, Boston: Brown University.

MacNaughton, P. and Urry, J. (1998), *Contested Natures*, London: Sage.

Madulu, N. (1999), 'Sustainable agriculture under population stress in semi-arid Tanzania', in J. Boeseu, I.S. Kikula and F.P. Maganga (eds) *Sustainable Agriculture in Semi-Arid Tanzania*, Dar es Salaam: Dar es Salaam University Press.

Masao, F.T. (1979), *The Later Stone Age and the Rock Paintings of Central Tanzania*, Wiesbaden: Franz Steiner Verlag.

——(1990), 'Possible meaning of the rock art of central Tanzania' *Paideuma* 36: 189–99.

Mung'ong'o, C.G. (1999), 'Sustainable agriculture in semi-arid Tanzania. Some sociological insights from Kondoa-Irangi, Ukara Island, Matengo Plateau and Mbulu Highlands', in J. Boesen, I.S. Kikula and F.P. Maganga (eds) *Sustainable Agriculture in Semi-Arid Tanzania*, Dar es Salaam: Dar es Salaam University Press.

Nooter, N.I. (1986), 'The Late Whites of Kondoa: an interpretation of Tanzanian rock art', *Res* 12: 97–108.

Ouzman, S. (2001), 'Seeing is deceiving: rock art and the non-visual', *World Archaeology* 33: 237–56.

Prins, F.E. and S. Hall (1994), 'Expressions of fertility in the rock art of Bantu-speaking agriculturalists', *African Archaeological Review* 12: 171–203.

Prins, F.E. and Woodhouse, H.C. (1996), 'Subsaharan Africa: the state of the art: rock art in southern and tropical Africa – the last five years', in P.G. Bahn and A. Fossati (eds), *Rock Art Studies: News of the World,* Oxford: Information Press.

SARAP / ICCROM [International Council for the Conservation and Restoration of Monuments] (2000), *Kondoa-Irangi Workshop: Final Report.*

SARAP (2000), Workshop on the nomination of the Kondoa Irangi Rock Paintings of Tanzania to the World Heritage List. SARAP / AFRICA-2009 (ICCROM).

Thornton, R.J. (1980), *Space, Time, and Culture among the Iraqw of Tanzania*, New York: Academic Press.

Tilley, C. (1994), *A Phenomenology of Landscape: Places, Paths and Monuments*, Oxford: Berg.

–3–

The Time of Place in West Mexico
Trevor Stack

This chapter is about talk on the history of towns in west Mexico, which I treat as part of a 'moral geography' as recently defined by Thomas: a 'complex of associations among ideas of person, people, place, and history' (Thomas, 2002: 372). I describe how talk about history helped to link persons to place and particularly to mark some people as townspeople as opposed to villagers. My focus is on the temporal dimensions of such links – hence the title of this chapter.[1] 'Place can be defined in a variety of ways. Among them is this: place can be whatever stable object catches our eye' (Yuan, 1977: 161).[2] Following Yuan, 'place' is defined here as a singularity that is conceived primarily in spatial terms. 'Place' in this sense can be distinguished from 'position' but also from 'event' as a singularity conceived primarily in temporal terms. It should be emphasized that the distinction is one of degree: any construal of place has temporal dimensions just as any construal of event has spatial dimensions.

One focus of the literature on the subject has been on the ways in which people are linked to place. Such links are often related to other attributes of the person. People can be linked to the same place in different ways: this is one way in which distinctions are made between individuals. Thomas writes, for example, of the importance of various metaphors of 'rooting' that are used to link Malagasy to places and to people in other places. He points out that such imagery 'also signifies division and hierarchy within the [Malagasy] polity' even though ritual ranking was abandoned in the nineteenth century. However, distinctions are also made by linking people to different places – and particularly to different kinds of place. One important example among Malagasy is the distinction made between townspeople and villagers (Thomas, 2002: 371–2, 373–8, see also Malkki 1992).

Thomas notes that this particular distinction bears comparison to that described by Raymond Williams in *The Country and the City* (Thomas, 2002: 377, Williams, 1973). Similar distinctions are also made in Mexico and Latin America, although often crosscut and complicated by other distinctions. Redfield, for example, described the struggle of the residents of Chan Kom, Yucatán to turn their village into a proper town: 'To "become a pueblo" meant to adopt many of the ways and political forms and ambitions of townspeople. It meant to accept the tools, leadership, and conceptions of progress which were then [in the 1910's] being offered to the villagers of Yucatan by the leaders of Mexico's social revolution' (Redfield, 1950: 1). Becoming a town, in other words, involved not just an increase in population or in urban services, but a transformation in the personhood of Chan Kom's residents. It marked, indeed, an important shift in the moral geography of the region.

My fieldwork in west Mexico was conducted during the 1990s in the Sierra de Tapalpa region, south of Guadalajara in the state of Jalisco, and particularly in Tapalpa itself, a town of about 6,000 inhabitants and seat of its municipal district. I found that people were indeed linked to Tapalpa in different ways. Wealthier families, many of whom owned nearby lands, were often associated with the centre of Tapalpa, where many also lived or owned businesses. The outlying barrios were associated with poorer families, many of whom worked in some capacity for the wealthier families (see also Serrano, 2002). But I also found that people were linked to different kinds of place. Places were sometimes distinguished on ethnic grounds: for example, the people of Tapalpa often described residents of the neighbouring town Atacco as *indios* (Indians). Places were also distinguished in terms of civic status, as among Malagasy and in Yucatán. I focus here on the distinction made in the Sierra de Tapalpa between the people of *pueblos* (small towns) and of *ranchos* (villages or hamlets).

I have said that 'place' is conceived primarily in spatial terms, but also has temporal dimensions. This is resonant with the argument of Boyarin and others that the dimensions of time and space – he uses the term 'timespace' – cannot easily be separated (Boyarin, 1994). Indeed, we have already defined place implicitly in terms of time: the temporal stability of place is clearly part of what 'catches our eye'. But stability is not the only temporal ingredient of place, as we will see; nor is it the only singular quality of place.[3]

There were, in fact, various ways in which Tapalpa was temporalized, one of which was critical to Tapalpa's tourist image. Tapalpa was visited by large numbers of weekenders, mainly from Guadalajara. Many of the businesses in the centre of the town, particularly the hotels and restaurants, catered to these weekenders. Part of the town's attraction was the image of Tapalpa as a *pueblo típico*: a rustic kind of place in which time stood still. This was a kind of ultra-place, a place of extreme stability. However, some Tapalpans rejected that temporalization. Two middle-aged women, for example, lamented that 'Tapalpa is not Tapalpa any more', blaming this on tourism together with migration and television. They were denying the stability of Tapalpa on which the tourist image rested; ironically, tourism itself had helped to undermine this stability.

There is a further temporalization of place in west Mexico: that of talk about the history of Tapalpa. In particular talk about history is linked to the distinction between townspeople and villagers.

The Public Past of History

I went to west Mexico originally as a historian after completing an undergraduate degree in History at Oxford University. In 1992, I began a project of local history in Tapalpa, but I ended up by focusing on how others talked – and wrote – about Tapalpa's history. These others included long- and short-term residents of the town, those of the neighbouring town Atacco and of some other surrounding communities, migrants in California, other visitors including weekenders and bureaucrats, and academics who had written about Tapalpa's history. In this chapter I focus on 'Tapalpans' in the loose sense of long-term residents of the town, particularly those who identified closely with it.[4] I lived in Tapalpa for most of 1992–1994, then returned for most of 1997–1999. Although I had since begun postgraduate studies in anthropology, most Tapalpans still knew me as an historian. As a result, much of my data was what people saw fit to tell someone writing the history of their town.

When I asked Tapalpans 'what is history?' they often answered something like *lo que de hecho pasó* (what in fact happened). They would agree that anything that in fact happened was history; their category of history was, in this respect, broader than that of Oxford historians. Very little was actually told as history, however. Tapalpans usually volunteered something about how Tapalpa was founded, something about a period of prosperity in the past, and about the revolutions that took place in the youth of the elderly people. This is not to say that Tapalpans talked little about the past. They talked at length about their own personal experience and that of their family, about the misfortunes of others, about town politics and the corruption of politicians, and so on. When pushed, most conceded that all this could be considered 'history' as long as it had 'in fact happened'. In practice, however, they only rarely volunteered any of this as history. Why was so little told as history? I have said that 'what in fact happened' was the only explicit criterion for history, but there is also an implicit criterion: it should be something that could be said publicly. For example, I was once accused by my landlady of writing a book of *chisme* (gossip). There were two things she could have meant by that. The first was that my information was mere hearsay; the second was that I was being intrusive. Tapalpans often drew a line of privacy around the affairs of the extended family and my landlady seemed to suspect that I was going to write about members of her own. This was not only inappropriate behaviour for a lodger, it also made for bad history: history should be fit for public consumption.

There was a temporal dimension to this. The 'past' of history was not just any old past. It was a past that was comfortably past, comfortably removed from the present. Indeed, we might better translate the *pasó* of *lo que hecho pasó* as 'passed' rather than simply 'happened'.[5] This removal was precisely what made it a public kind of past. There was much talk of violent revolutions, for example, and indeed the blood seemed to spice up what was told as history. But people did not tell as 'history' details of a bloody dispute that took place some thirty years ago, partly at least because some of the protagonists – and issues – were still alive. This kind of talk – as much as gossip – was too relevant to make for good history.[6] This attitude cut out of history most of what Tapalpans liked to talk about. They found what was told as history rather insipid and talked only rarely – and even then briefly – about history as such. They often asked me about it, but I found that most were distracted by more immediate concerns – children, *telenovelas*, politics, and so on – and quickly lost interest in my answers. Yet the idea that Tapalpa had its history continued to be reproduced together with a few tokens of that history. Tapalpans continued to ask about the town's history, confident that such a question was sensible. Most could reply that Atacco was older than Tapalpa, as is discussed further below. Then they would suggest that I talk to someone else who knew more, sure that someone must know Tapalpa's history, even if they did not.

Why did people talk at all about history given that other topics such as gossip were more interesting? History provided an emblem that was of use in various practices. It offered an unproblematic way of alluding to Tapalpa when more than just a place-name was required. History was not just a useful ingredient of Tapalpa's tourist image; it was also employed in bureaucratic documents, often together with population statistics and an etymology of its place-name as a prelude to municipal surveys (e.g. Camarena y Gutiérrez de Lariz, 1987, Nava López and Nava Aguilar, 1985). I will suggest in the next section, however, that there was a more specific motive for people to talk about history. History was not just any old emblem – nor was it attached to any old place. It was one of several marks that distinguished a *pueblo* from a *rancho*.

The Quality of *Cultura*

The distinction between *pueblos* and *ranchos* was complex: it could be made in terms of population, urban services, civic architecture, urban layout, and so on. It could also be made in terms of what was called *cultura* and it is a quality that merits closer attention.

Zárate has written of the distinction between *ranchos* and *pueblos* in the neighbouring Llano Grande region. He observes, for example, that 'the interest shown [by the people of *ranchos*] in reconstructing houses and buying electronic apparatus contrasts with their disinterest in common space' (Zárate Hernández, 1997: 180). This was largely consistent with my experience in the Sierra de Tapalpa. What people called *ranchos* were, roughly speaking, settlements that consisted of clusters of houses surrounded by plots of land, inhabited by a few extended families, who were expected to compete with each other, each one in pursuit of its own interests. There was little sense of a common interest – still less one that people could debate publicly. What people called *pueblos*, on the other hand, were settlements consisting of neat lines of houses, laid out in ordered fashion along streets, which centred on a public square or *plaza* surrounded by public architecture, such as a church and civic administration. *Pueblos* were also inhabited by families and other groups competing with each other, but the difference was that townspeople – or some of them – were felt able and willing to discuss their common interests in a public arena.

The quality of *cultura* was linked to this distinction. The term was used most often in the negative, taking the form of 'so-and-so lacks *cultura*', in the sense that such an individual lacked the ability to apprehend whatever lay beyond the immediate. It was not just any immediate need or issue that was involved, but usually what were considered to be short-sighted private interests. Those found lacking in *cultura* included peasants who sold their land for short-term gain, individuals who threw trash out of car windows, migrants who forsook their civic duty for wage labour, citizens who traded their vote for promised favours, and politicians who were corrupted by personal, familiar, or partisan interests. Those who did have *cultura*, on the other hand, were considered able to apprehend the public good that lay beyond the pettiness of such interests. They had authority over those who lacked that ability. *Ranchos* were considered lacking in *cultura* and thus in people with the ability to apprehend the public good: the good of *ranchos* would be determined elsewhere.

Several aspects of this distinction are, I suggest, widely resonant. The notion of *cultura* was resonant with the sense of 'culture' as cultivation that Williams has described (Williams, 1976: 76–82). It was also similar to notions held elsewhere in Mexico. What Zárate glosses as the 'supposed refinement' of townspeople in the Llano Grande, for example, was clearly similar to *cultura* (Zárate Hernández, 1997: 181). Redfield discusses in similar terms the success of Don Eustaquio Ceme in Chan Kom: he was 'one of the few people who think about the condition of their community, those who look beyond their private problems to those of the entire village' (Redfield, 1950: 1971).

Not everyone was linked to place in the same way. Being 'from here' was one important category of town politics: for example, the mayor of Tapalpa in 1998–2000 was quick to reject the complaint of anyone that he considered 'not from here'. Conversely but more subtly, those considered most obviously 'from here' often seemed to play a prominent part in town politics. Not surprisingly, these included the families that owned lands in the surrounding area and properties in Tapalpa's centre. This distinction was made, as far as I could tell, both in *ranchos* and in *pueblos*.

Within *pueblos* there was a further distinction, for in *pueblos* only a handful of individuals were expected to have a full measure of *cultura*. This gave such people certain authority over those others – not just in *ranchos* but in the town itself – who did not have *cultura*. For example, Don Lupe, an elderly resident of Tapalpa, was often said to have *cultura*; he was also remembered as the most public-spirited mayor that Tapalpa had ever had. The town mayor mentioned above, on the other hand, was not always so highly regarded, precisely because he was held by many to lack *cultura*.

Cultura and the Public Past

History, then, represented a past that was comfortably 'passed' and part of the motivation to talk about history came from its identification with towns. The distinction made between *pueblos* and *ranchos* with particular reference to the quality of *cultura* has also been explored, but the third step is to establish the link between the knowing of history and the possessing of *cultura*.

Several British towns were awarded the status of cities on the occasion of the Millennium. One criterion that was often invoked was the history of the town in question.[7] The same association between civic status and history was evident in Mexico. Both Redfield and Zárate, for example, appear to sense a link between towns, *cultura* and history. Redfield begins his second ethnography of Chan Kom with an account of its history, while Zárate describes towns in the Llano Grande as having a 'certain historical profundity', but neither articulates the nature of this link (Redfield, 1950: 1–21, Zárate Hernández, 1997: 183).

I asked the question 'what is the history of this place?' in various settlements of the Sierra. The answer differed, of course, from one place to another, but it also differed from one kind of place to another. When I asked the question in Tapalpa, most people had a ready-made answer: they gave a kind of potted history of the town. The same was true of other *pueblos* in the Sierra. When I asked in *ranchos*, people also attempted to answer the question, since in principle any place could have its history. However, they did not find much to say: there was no ready-made answer, nor were they sure that anyone else would know more.

It may be that history is linked to *pueblos* on two levels. First, it is linked on the level of substantive content. When people talked about history, they usually include the founding of their towns. 'Founding' is not just the first person to settle in that place, but involved the laying out of streets, the building of a public square, and so on.[8] Thus when people talk about history, they are talking about the kind of things that made their town a town. It was a kind of social 'charter' in Malinowski's sense: a narrative that contained the birthright of a social entity (Malinowski 1992: 91).

But history was also linked to towns on a second level: talk about history was exemplary of how townspeople should behave. I have said that history must be fit for public consumption: it should be something that could be said publicly. Talk about history is talk about a past removed from the present – about a specifically public kind of past. It shows the ability to apprehend whatever lies beyond an immediate present. As such, it is a mark of a particular kind of place – and of a particular kind of person. It shows in people talking publicly about issues of common interest instead of, for example, monetary gain. Thus it is not just that history is a charter for towns, but that talk about history is exemplary of town-like behaviour.

In the field-work, people were linked to the same places in different ways. Talk about history tended to give authority to certain people in each town. Again, this occurred both through what was talked about and through the talking itself. There was not much naming of names – a mark of gossip rather than history – but people did sometimes mention the name of families, such as those who participated in the revolutions. The main effect was simply to link those families more closely to the town or, more precisely, to help make them indisputably 'from here'. This, as we have seen, was an important category in town politics. But people in *pueblos* were also distinguished in terms of *cultura*. Townspeople usually gave a potted history of their town, before suggesting that I talk to someone else who knew more history. That someone else was often from a family considered 'from here', but equally often a person held to have a greater degree of *cultura*. The best example of the latter was the former mayor Don Lupe: I was sent to talk to him soon after I arrived in Tapalpa in 1992 and he was also one of the few Tapalpans who had written about Tapalpa's history (Nava López, 2002, Nava López and Nava Aguilar, 1985).[9]

Places That Were Prior

I found that when most people spoke of Tapalpa's founding they referred at some point to the neighbouring town of Atacco. This was so throughout the period of my research in the 1990s. There were disparities in the accounts that people would give, but one distinction was made consistently: Atacco was older than Tapalpa. More specifically, it was often said that Atacco was the *pueblo* when Tapalpa was an *hacienda*. By *hacienda*, Tapalpans meant something slightly different from a *rancho*. *Haciendas* were the large rural estates – the pride of a landed oligarchy – that were broken up by the Agrarian Reform from the 1920s. The point of the contrast, however, was to emphasize that Atacco was then the only *pueblo*; Tapalpa was, at that time, not yet a *pueblo*. Several Tapalpans suggested in 1992 that I visit Atacco in my quest for Tapalpa's history. Atacco was situated about two miles away, within the municipal district of which Tapalpa was the seat. It had about 2,500 inhabitants, the second-largest population in the district. I thought Atacco had a fair claim to being a *pueblo*, as it was usually so described by its residents. It did, moreover, seem to have its own history: Tapalpans referred to Atacco's history and the people of Atacco also found something to say. What they said, in fact, was very similar to what was said in Tapalpa: Atacco was the *pueblo* when Tapalpa was just an *hacienda*. The two places seemed to share a history to the extent that it was difficult to tell the history of one without the other.

Embedded in this history, however, was a clear distinction between the two places. We have encountered several kinds of pastness in the Sierra de Tapalpa: the past of history, of legal discourse, of gossip, and so on. This was a further kind of pastness: Atacco was before Tapalpa. 'Being before' was, as it is so often, an ambiguous kind of pastness. One group in Atacco, for example, had sought since the 1980s to 'reclaim' lands belonging to Tapalpa's land-owning families in the name of the 'indigenous community of Atacco'. For this group, Tapalpa – and particularly its wealthy land-owning families – had usurped Atacco and its communal lands. Another group, in contrast, preferred to see the history of Atacco as evidence of its potential. Indeed, they argued that an awareness of Atacco's history could bring about a renaissance in the town.[10] But this same history was told more often in ironic tones: Atacco was then as dependent on Tapalpa as Tapalpa had – ironically – once been on Atacco. In fact, sometimes people would gloss this by saying that Atacco was Tapalpa. I have explained elsewhere that Atacco was usually described not as old and venerable but as the most backward place on earth (Stack, 2002: 65–79).

This did not necessarily make Atacco a *rancho*. Tapalpans did sometimes lump Atacco together with the *ranchos*, but Atacco was generally regarded as being something other. *Ranchos* might become *pueblos* – just as Tapalpa's *hacienda* had become a *pueblo* – but it was considered unlikely that Atacco would become again a *pueblo*. Tapalpans were quick to temporalize Atacco by relegating it to a past that had been left behind. Indeed, they seemed to place Atacco less in the history than in the pre-history of Tapalpa. This resonated with the labelling of Atacco's people as *indios*. This term *indio* was used ethnically for those considered to descend from the pre-Hispanic inhabitants of Mexico; it was also used metaphorically for all those who were held to lack *cultura*. Atacco was a place that had lost whatever *cultura* it might once have had.

This kind of place – with its people – was easy to dismiss. While Atacco was the second-largest settlement in the district, it was consistently sidelined by the municipal government in Tapalpa. It was given a measure of autonomy in 1999 by raising its civic status, but there were several voices of protest. The municipal Secretary, for example, complained that there were too few persons in Atacco with the capacity to exercise self-government. Even the Human Rights Group (of which I was a member from 1997–1999) paid little attention to the people of Atacco and seemed to dismiss them as a lost cause.[11]

Consequentiality

So far this chapter has traced the contours of a particular moral geography, focusing on the linking of persons to places and particularly on the temporal dimensions of this linking. However, I should emphasize that moral geographies are both consequential for events and are the consequence of events. In order to trace this web of consequences, moral geographies must themselves be carefully situated in an analytical time and space of events.[12] Every linking of person to place has its consequences, however slight. Minimally, each telling of history helped to keep history in circulation (see Urban, 1996). Despite the slight interest in Tapalpa's history, the idea that the town had its history – together with tokens of that history – was still being reproduced. Each telling of history could also have an effect on the distinctions made between persons. For example, each assertion that Don Lupe was the person who knew most history could only bolster his claim to *cultura* and thus his authority over other townspeople. At the same time, it could only strengthen the conviction that Tapalpa was a place that had its history – and thus a likely setting for such eminent citizens. Similarly, each mention of Atacco as a place that was stubbornly 'before' had the effect of putting down the people of Atacco. It helped to reinforce the numbing inadequacy felt by many residents of Atacco.

Such linkings of person to place could also be challenged, as has been discussed in the case of the two groups in Atacco: one arguing that Atacco had been usurped by Tapalpa, the other insisting that Atacco was indeed a home to *cultura*. I found, however, that much of this moral geography, including the history of towns, had been quite resilient. Certain elements had been particularly longstanding, despite the considerable population movement in the region during the twentieth century.[13] In 1879, for example, two Tapalpan residents wrote a municipal survey that included an account of the town's founding. I have argued elsewhere that this account probably does represent what Tapalpans were saying of their town's history in 1879. If so, there has been a shift in ethnic distinctions: the 1879 authors described Tapalpa's founders as a 'tribe of indigenous people' and not as a family of Spanish *hacendados*. They still made, however, a distinction between Tapalpa and Atacco: when this 'tribe of indigenous people' settled in Tapalpa, Atacco 'already existed and was the principal town, made up of pure indigenous people'. There may be an ethnic distinction implicit in the 'purity' of the 'indigenous people' of Atacco. What is clear is that the same temporal distinction was being made: Atacco was as prior to Tapalpa in 1879 as it was in the 1990s (Camarena y Gutiérrez de Lariz, 1987: 24–5).

This moral geography was not just resilient over time; certain elements were also widely disseminated through space. It was remarkable that Tapalpa's founding was told in such similar ways not only through the 1990s but also across the social space of Tapalpa and Atacco. More broadly, I found that many of my observations – about the idea of history itself and its association with towns – also held for other places in which I conducted research in Mexico.[14] They may also hold beyond Mexico. I have suggested, for example, that there has been an association between history and towns in the UK.[15] What shaped and maintained this linking of person to place? Of what events and processes was it a consequence? One set of formative events were those of Spanish colonization. The indigenous population was uprooted in the sixteenth century and forced to resettle in *pueblos* that were designated by missionaries and constructed according to their designs (see Farriss 1984, Hanks 1987, Markman 1977). These places were defined bureaucratically in surveys such as in the 1579 *Relaciones Geográficas*, which included questions about the 'founding' of these *pueblos* (Acuna, 1988, see also Little-Siebold, 1998). It should not, then, be surprising that 'founding' has become a central feature of the history of *pueblos*.

The genre of history was also shaped by the actions of the Mexican state, particularly by the extension of mass schooling (e.g. Pérez Siller and Radkau García, 1998). This involved the linking of persons to a different kind of place, that of nations. However, the teaching of national history may still have shaped and encouraged talk about the history of towns. This may have been particularly the case in recent years, since teachers have taught local history together with regional and national history (Stack 2003). Indeed, when I asked why Tapalpa's history was important, several parents responded that their children might be asked to write homework on the topic.

History, however, was not as monolithic as I have implied up to now, even in the Sierra de Tapalpa. I have explored elsewhere the differences and disjunctures between, for example, history in bureaucratic documents, in school homework and in civic parades (Stack 2002). Each strain of history had its own peculiar genealogy through space and time. Another strain, for example, was encouraged by the expansion of tourism since the building of a road to Tapalpa in 1957, where for weekenders, it was a place in which time stood still. History had its part in this tourist image, but it was a quaint history of idiosyncrasies rather than a cultivated history of civic actions. The archetypal knower of this history was not Don Lupe but Don Beto, who served up in his *cantina* a colourful repertoire of singular narratives.

The Insidious Time of Place

The various dimensions of place are intertwined, moving in and out of focus, sometimes explicit and sometimes not. I suggest that the temporal dimensions of place are particularly insidious. Hence the survival of the temporal distinction between Atacco and Tapalpa, despite apparent changes in the ethnic distinction being made. Ethnic distinctions come and go, we might conclude, but temporal distinctions go on and on.

I have three possible explanations for this. The first follows from our definition of place as a singularity conceived primarily in spatial terms. This focus distracts our attention from other dimensions, such as that of time. By the same token, it may be that space is an insidious dimension in the imagining of event. We might not discard, secondly, the possibility that temporal distinctions are generally less transparent to consciousness than certain other kinds of distinctions. This may be particularly the case when such distinctions are made by the use of a verb tense. Whorf, at least, suggested that verb tense (together with noun classifiers and so on) may create 'a much more far-reaching compulsion' than 'single words, phrases, and patterns of limited range' (Whorf 1956: 137). Thirdly, we anthropologists, together with Tapalpans, are heirs to a peculiarly modern obsession with the marking of difference in terms of time. Fabian has written of the importance of time in this respect. He argued that anthropology has itself tended to mark difference temporally, partly through the use of the present tense in ethnographic description (Fabian 1983).[16] History has been yet another resource for the temporal marking of modern difference. This modern abundance of time has, I suggest, helped to make time as insidious for Tapalpans as for anthropologists.

Notes

1. This research was conducted in 1997–99 with a Horniman Scholarship from the Royal Anthropological Institute and a Penfield Fellowship from the School of Arts and Sciences at the University of Pennsylvania. I am grateful to Alex King, Katrin Lund and Allice Legat for their comments.
2. I am grateful to Katrin Lund for her paper, 'The Highest Mountain in Spain: Locating Places and Non-Places' (forthcoming) which added to my thoughts on this subject.

3. It is not just places themselves that have temporal dimensions but also the links of persons to places. For example, people would often narrate their migration from one place to another since their own birth, as well as that of their parents and sometimes grandparents.

4. My analytical categories of ethnographic subjects are culled from categories that are used in the Sierra, but these are of course contentious. The same is true of my own use of terms such as *pueblo* or town to refer to places such as Tapalpa. We will see below that Atacco in particular is not always considered to be a *pueblo*.

5. The events of history took place in a time that was felt to be distant but in a space that was felt to be immediate. Indeed, many events of history took place in the proximity of Tapalpa's plaza: for example, the old church and the first houses were built around the same plaza that was later the scene of shootouts during the revolutions.

6. This was not inconsistent with my experience of history at Oxford. Academic historians were often reluctant to write about events that were felt to be too recent. This was usually justified in the name of objectivity: one must 'allow the dust to settle' before hazarding an account of events.

7. Officially there were no such criteria, since it was felt this could lead to towns claiming city status as a right, rather than as an honour conferred on unique occasions by personal Command of the Queen (personal communication, Lord Chancellor's Department). However, several criteria were invoked in the discussions, including many on the Internet, that were raised by the awards (e.g. Dexer, accessed 25.02.03).

8. This is also reflected in histories written in the region and beyond. The most famous example is *Pueblo en vilo*, a microhistory of San José de Gracia in the neighbouring state of Michoacán, written by the distinguished Mexican historian Luis González, who was also a native of the town. An important part of the book focuses on the 'founding' of San José – the transition from *rancho* to *pueblo* – and on the civic qualities of its 'founders'. These included some of the author's own ancestors (González y González, 1968).

9. However, what was written of Tapalpa's history was quite different from what was spoken of Tapalpa's history: I discuss the implications elsewhere (Stack, 2002: 35–46).

10. The first group made much of a colonial land title that was in their possession. I have argued elsewhere that the second group denied the 'legal' validity of the document while continuing to value it as a relic of 'history' (Stack, 2002: 20–22).

11. Atacco seemed to have history – it was old, after all. I have argued elsewhere, however, that Atacco was only felt to have history in the limited sense that history was known of Atacco and not in the sense that history could be known

in Atacco itself. Briefly, the old people of Atacco might find something to say about past times, but were not expected to produce an authoritative history of the kind produced by Don Lupe in Tapalpa. Atacco's history would be told by those from elsewhere – perhaps even by Don Lupe himself (Stack, 2002: 65-79).

12. There is a difficulty here with the term 'event' since I defined the term above as the temporal equivalent of 'place': a singularity conceived primarily in spatial terms. I should perhaps distinguish between 'event' and 'happening' just as I distinguished 'place' from mere 'position'.

13. One wave of population movements was a result of the series of rebellions between 1912–1937: inhabitants of many *ranchos* were resettled in *pueblos*, while several wealthy families left the highland area for more secure surroundings. Since then, there has also been a high level of labour migration to the state capital Guadalajara and to California: many Tapalpans had lived and worked for extended periods in the US (see also Serrano, 2002).

14. I also spent some time in the city of Zamora in the neighbouring state of Michoacán, in the small town San Sebastián del Oeste and the tourist resort Puerto Vallarta, both further west in the state of Jalisco, as well as in the city of Concord, California, where many Tapalpans live and work.

15. I have suggested elsewhere that some elements of this moral geography are also common to nationalist history (Stack, 2002: 5, Stack, 2003).

16. Of course, this happens in various ways. Even within the Sierra de Tapalpa, I have mentioned several kinds of 'pastness' of which history is but one example.

References

Acuna, René (1988), *Relaciones geográficas del siglo XVI (10: Nueva Galicia)*. México, D.F.: Universidad Nacional Autónoma de México.

Boyarin, Jonathan (1994), 'Space, time, and the politics of memory', in Jonathan Boyarin (ed.) *Remapping Memory: The Politics of TimeSpace* Minneapolis: University of Minnesota Press.

Camarena y Gutiérrez de Lariz, Gabriel de Jesús (1987), 'Villa de Tapalpa', *Revista Jalisco* 1987: 20–52.

Dexer, Ian N (accessed 25.02.03), *Inverness*. http://website.lineone.net/~indexer/.

Fabian, Johannes (1983), *Time and the Other: How Anthropology Makes Its Object*, New York: Columbia University Press.

Farriss, Nancy (1984), *Maya Society Under Colonial Rule: The Collective Enterprise of Survival*, Princeton, NJ: Princeton University Press.

González y González, Luis (1968), *Pueblo en vilo: una microhistoria de San José de Gracia*. México, D. F.: El Colegio de México.

Hanks, William (1987), 'Discourse genres in a theory of practice', *American Ethnologist* 14: 668–92.

Little-Siebold, Todd (1998), 'Monografías, memoria y la producción local de historia', *Mesoamérica* 36: 343–369.

Malinowski, Bronislaw (1992), *Malinowski and the Work of Myth,* Ivan Strenski (ed.), Princeton: Princeton University Press.

Malkki, Lisa (1992), 'National Geographic: the rooting of peoples and the territorialization of national identity among scholars and refugees', *Cultural Anthropology* 7: 24–44.

Markman, Sidney D. (1977), 'The gridiron plan and the caste system in colonial Central America', in Elías Sevilla-Casas (ed.), *Western Expansion and Indigenous Peoples: The Heritage of Las Casas,* The Hague: Mouton.

Nava López, J. Guadalupe (2002), 'Relatos de un pueblo mágico: su pasado, sus creencias, sus tradiciones', *Un rincón en la Sierra Tapalpa* 2: 5–6.

—— and Ma. Patricia Nava Aguilar (1985), *Monografía de Tapalpa, Jal.* Tapalpa, Jal., Mexico: Biblioteca Pública Municipal de Tapalpa, Jalisco.

Pérez Siller, Javier and Verena Radkau García, (eds) (1998), *Identidad en el imaginario nacional: reescritura y enseñanza de la historia,* Puebla: Universidad Autónoma de Puebla, El Colegio de San Luis, Georg-Eckert-Institut.

Redfield, Robert (1950), *A Village That Chose Progress: Chan Kom Revisited,* Chicago: University of Chicago Press.

Serrano, Javier (2002), *La dimensión cultural de las remesas: los tapalpenses y su comunidad transnacional,* Guadalajara: Tesis de Maestría en Antropología Social del CIESAS-Occidente.

Stack, Trevor (2002), *Places That Have History: The Public Knowledge of Mexican Towns*, Philadelphia, PA: University of Pennsylvania.

—— (2003), 'Citizens of towns, citizens of nations: the knowing of history in Mexico', *Critique of Anthropology* 23(2): 193–208.

Thomas, Philip (2002), 'The river, the road, and the rural-urban divide: a postcolonial moral geography from Southeast Madagascar', *American Ethnologist* 29: 366–391.

Urban, Greg (1996), *Metaphysical Community: The Interplay of the Senses and the Intellect*, Austin, TX: University of Texas Press.

Whorf, Benjamin Lee (1956), *Language, Thought, and Reality*, Cambridge, MA: MIT Press.

Williams, Raymond (1973), *The Country and the City*, London: Chatto & Windus.

—— (1976), *Keywords: A Vocabulary of Culture and Society*, London: Fontana and Croom Helm.

Yuan, Y.F. (1977), *Space and Place: The Perspective of Experience*, Minneapolis: University of Minneapolis Press.

Zárate Hernández, José Eduardo (1997), *Procesos de Identidad y Globalización Económica: El Llano Grande en el Sur de Jalisco*, Zamora, Michoacán (Mexico): El Colegio de Michoacán.

Part II
Mythical Times, Presentism, and the Critique from History

Tiger in an African Palace[1]

Richard Fardon

What looked like modernist social anthropology's theory of history was – so this essay will argue – nothing of the sort but instead a theory of identity in need of a historical dimension. With some help from a tiger in a Cameroonian palace, I shall argue that even in the hands of sophisticated mid-twentieth-century anthropological theorists – such as Franz Baermann Steiner – a 'charter' theory of history was incapable of explaining why certain mementoes of the past became treasures. Because the transvaluation of material traces of the past into present-day treasures offers a close analogy, or so I shall claim, to the translation of past events into charters for contemporary affairs, examining the historic labour invested in creating a treasure can highlight some of the problems we face when trying to track changes in identities and their charters. These problems congregate densely around the fundamental issue of historic continuity: what remains the same when ground and figure may both change? I shall argue that no convincing sociological answer to this question can ignore the historic engagement of human labour in the project of creating historic continuity and, furthermore, that the most powerful of these connections are usually not established propositionally.

Present Problems

As a modernist movement the social anthropology of Bronislaw Malinowski and the (more or less) two intellectual generations of anthropologists who succeeded him, set both itself and its theories firmly in the present. *Itself*, partly because modern simply means 'of the now', and *partly*, because functional anthropology made much of its displacement of evolutionist, diffusionist and outmoded intellectualist theories by its own vivid explanations of practices and institutions in terms of their very contemporaneity, their very 'here-and-nowness'. Merging the temporal nearness of the present with the spatial nearness of presence, functional explanations proposed that cause and effect merged in an actuality of social existence. Hence the investigation of functional processes had to occur proximately in both spatial and temporal senses: in the 'here-and-now' of the investigator's research. When experience-based description and functional explanation were written up in the ethnographic present, a third 'now' – writerly and generic – was made the medium of a presentism that was simultaneously methodological and theoretical. The consistency of this high valuation of the 'here and now' elevates it, to my mind, beyond mere preference towards an aesthetic disposition characteristic of its time.

A preference for the 'here and now' was nowhere more obvious than in functional approaches to history itself. Malinowski's famous theory of mythical charters (1944: 111, 162–4) suggested that accounts of the origins and purposes of institutions had to be studied as justifications of a present order; charters were used in the present and should be studied and explained as such. For instance, in societies that conserved them to any depth, genealogies needed to be investigated in those contexts when people felt moved to bring them forward to support arguments, and their being so moved should be explained in terms of the interests, both personal and collective, that genealogical charters served. Evans-Pritchard for the Nuer (1940: 229–34) and such of his students as Laura and Paul Bohannan (1952, 1955) for Tiv and Emrys Peters (1960) for Bedouin demonstrated the power of this line of argument in explaining the invariant depth of genealogies despite the passage of time and generations. More generally, the argument was taken up to emphasize how far rhetorical uses of the past needed to be construed as the expression of identity interests in the present (whether of individuals or collectivities).

All this is well-worked ground, and my traversal of it hasn't involved new paths. My purpose is to spotlight just how recursively and insistently the intellectual strategies of modern social anthropology urge the present upon us. Self-consciously a modern intellectual movement, social anthropology researched into the present, explained in terms of the present, and wrote in its own specialized expansion and condensation of the present tense. A quality of 'now-ness' recommended whatever it touched; and 'pastness' seemed correspondingly unattractive. Those of us trained by the mid-century modernists probably absorbed presentism as we acquired a sense for the aesthetics of a properly proportioned anthropological argument.

Our editors' observation that there has been little dialogue between anthropological theories of time and history, applies especially to functional or charter theories of history. If history is to be understood only as a construction subservient to current interests, a more or less serviceable past designed for the present, then no theory about the passage of time is required. Value is attributed to a (rather one dimensional) 'pastness' existing entirely in the present.

All this emphasis on the present was not, as we know, unproblematic. Slightly amending Johannes Fabian's argument of the 1980s (1983, 1991) to my interests, I would argue that the tendency to use the present as an answer to all of anthropology's problems (whether of theory, method or genre) had the perverse effect, like a goodwill gesture over-used, of rendering all – and thereby no

– ethnographic scenarios coeval. Writing in the ethnographic present, as has been amply demonstrated, compounded the problem of undiscriminating coevalness by conflating the 'now' of writing, with the various 'nows' of local research, reported events, recurrent processes, reconstructions of the eve of colonization and so forth. Functional anthropology deserves to lose credibility less on account of its arguments from effects, the usual villain of the piece, than on account of the unsustainable weight it places upon the idea of the present. Arguments from effect come in more and less justifiable forms, but a theory of history entirely invested in the present, and wholly devoid of reference to the passage of time, becomes unsustainable even in its own terms. If the present is baldly counterpoised to the past, and attempts to narrate that past are only efforts to underwrite present interests, then it is difficult to understand how present interests could have any temporal trajectory that is not simply their own justification? In short, radical presentism makes the present itself incomprehensible (and something we cannot understand can scarcely be asked to explain its own history). This said, it may seem surprising now to argue that this modernist theory has a future in social anthropology; however, I believe it raises interesting questions so long as it is treated not as a theory of either history or of time, but only as a theory of how some 'pastness' is transfigured for the 'now'. Fundamentally, this is a theory of identity transformation in need of temporal specification rather than a theory of history.

The most succinct, mid-century, expression of the operator imagined to animate such identity work – at least that I have come across – occurs in one of Franz Baermann Steiner's *Statements and essays*, the semi-private prequels to extended and considered statements he did not, for the most part, live to make.

> The chief sociological principle is probably this: that no individual can have a position [*eine Stelle*] without identifying themself with something, and there is no identification without transformation. The necessity for identification is primary. This is the chief difference between human and animal social forms. The 'I' of human society is at the apex of a triangle of which the other corners are called communication and identification. The sides [*Schenkel*, also thighs] adjacent to the I-point are called language and transformation [*Verwandlung*]. The circumscribing circle is 'society' – in its metaphysical sense (based on Schüttpelz 2003: 44).

As Erhard Schüttpelz points out, Steiner's formulation maps a tension: in order to occupy a status there must be identification, but identification implies transformation. The image evoked by Steiner's prose recalls the most famous of Leonardo's 'measurement' drawings[2] of the proportions of the human figure (an illustration to the first chapter of the third book of Marcus Vitruvius Pollio's first century BC treatise *De architectura* that was rediscovered as an inspiration to the Italian Renaissance). The outstretched limbs of Leonardo's human figure touch the inner edge of the circle circumscribing him. This circle, Steiner tells us, is 'society', but not in its actuality (as described perhaps by Radcliffe-Brown [1952]) but in terms of its presence to the individual.

Schüttpelz notes that a second aphoristic statement, following directly upon it in Steiner's notebooks, seems to extend the same train of thought:

> No transformation is conceivable without previous identification. The goal of transformation is thus communicable, lies within language. The process of transformation is only indirectly language-related – through the goal towards which it points but which does not interpret it. The mythical occurrence is a transformation that is wholly expressible through identifications; thus it is comprehensible through language. As such it is not irrational, rather the series of mythic transformations are the quasi-rational organizing principles of all non-communicable series, that is the whole chaotic transformative potentiality of the human universe. (Schüttpelz 2003: 45)

So far as can be ascertained in the present state of research, Steiner's only explicit development of the concept of transformation[3] occurs in his lectures on taboo during a discussion of Arnold van Gennep's *rites de passage*. This suggests that Steiner imported into his native German philosophical references a cluster of French-language sociological ideas that make up – as our editors' Introduction notes – one of the informing images of mid-century British social anthropology. Identification is treated as a status (thus communicable), whereas movement between status positions, or more precisely the state of being in movement between them, cannot be expressed propositionally (and may be apprehended only through evocation of the experience of liminal excursus, or by analogy with the effects of mythological operators – functions that Steiner himself seems forced to conjure up visually). Steiner adds two unusual elements to this sophisticated but also typical, quintessentially mid-century, British social anthropological analysis: these concern positionality and movement (the second envisaged as distinct operations of detachment and attachment). From others of his writings it is clear that Steiner habitually considered individuals (whether persons or societies) as composite, thus potentially conflictual entities. This is entirely consistent with the sense of restless instability between identification and transformation in Steiner's aphorism. Transformation necessitates identification, but identification in its turn entails transformation. In short, identities are in constant movement within the human universe's 'chaotic transformative potentiality', which we may take as a summation of all the finally inexpressible processes of being in movement between momentarily determinable positions. If the image of triangle within circle is indeed meant to suggest such hermetic devices as Leonardo's implausibly proportioned encircled human figure – as well as the cabbalist literature of the renaissance, and the generative and combinatorial operators of the aphoristic tradition[4] – then we should envisage it not as static but as spinning in that chaos of transformative energy to which Steiner refers. Perhaps Steiner intended another parallel here to Leonardo's derivation (via Vitruvius) of man-made architectural symmetries from the given potentialities of the human form (see Fig. 5).

If the reader is able to accept my proposition that Steiner's idiosyncratic imagery nonetheless encapsulates much of the essential mood of mid-century social anthropological thought, then it is worth posing once more the problem of the notorious absence of a historical dimension. And, in terms of Steiner's imagery, it would seem that the problem arises because individuals in movement between positions are envisaged to be outside structural determination and therefore in a state that may only be evoked – diagrammatically or perhaps by analogy with myth. While finding Steiner's identity operator a fertile thought object, I see no reason why some effort cannot be made to specify its operations temporally – even in terms of a strong benchmark conception of historical time, such as that proposed by Georg Simmel.

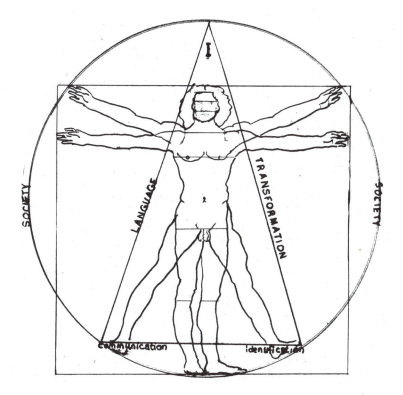

Figure 5 Steiner's operator superimposed on Leonardo's measurement drawing

Richard Fardon

In the 1916 essay translated as on 'The problem of historical time', Georg Simmel (1980: 127–44) provides an ambitious standard. For an 'item' to qualify as historical for Simmel: it ought both to be fully understandable to us, and to be uniquely located in a temporal frame. The two criteria should intermesh such that it is on the basis of our understanding that we realize the item could not be located temporally other than in the position – relative to other items – it in fact occupies. His own summary at this point in his argument reads:

> ...from the fact that an item has a *temporal status*, it does not follow that it is historical. And from the fact that this item is *understood*, it does not follow that it is historical. Suppose, however, that both of these conditions are satisfied. An item is historical when it is temporalized on the basis of an atemporal interpretation. In principle, this criterion for historicity can be satisfied only if interpretation embraces the totality of contents. This is because the single item can really be understood only in its relationship to the absolute totality. It follows that in this context temporalization can only mean location within a specific temporal frame. (ibid.: 1980: 131, added emphases)

Continuing, Simmel explains why 'temporalization' is so important to the understanding of events.

> This logical consequence is based on the following two considerations. First if temporalization is based on the total process, then every event can have only one unique location that cannot be exchanged with any other. Second, interpretation is possible only given the relatively precise determination of time. It is not possible to understand an item simply by ascribing a general temporal location to it. To ascribe a general temporal location to an item is simply a way of saying that the event in question really happened. And that is precisely what cannot be achieved by interpretation (ibid).

Simmel's requirements to cross the threshold of historicity may be unfeasibly high in many cases but, as such, they usefully highlight just how far short of a theory of history modern social anthropology's account of the uses of the past fell. Modern social anthropology revealed ways that 'past-ness' was mobilized in present processes of identification and transformation. Explanatory weight fell (as it did iteratively) upon the present: deployment of the past made sense in terms of its impact now. The social anthropologists' account ignored both of Simmel's threshold criteria of historicity: the past was not (in some cases, anthropologists believed, could not be) temporally specified, and there was no attempt to understand the past 'item' other than in terms of its present use. It hardly needs to be added that achieving the two-pronged criterion of uniquely placing the past event temporally in terms of our understanding of it, could not be addressed at all. Instead, to return to my opening, explanatory weight was thrust onto the present as the context in which to explain how recollections of the past were transacted.

However, to repeat what now should seem only mildly paradoxical, this hectic and reiterative presentism ended by having no account of why the present was as it was, or – and this is fundamentally damaging – any way of delimiting what 'present' designated. This became abundantly clear when commentators attempted to define any consistent temporality to the written 'ethnographic present'.[5] Mid-century anthropology, in short, was not predisposed to see the present as the product of the past, hence – despite the intentions of many of its practitioners – its apolitical character as a theoretical project. I expressly say 'as a theoretical project' since social anthropology in practice had a redeeming characteristic: the experience of ethnographic actualities usually prompted writers to go beyond what we are able to read retrospectively into the theoretical pronouncements of their times. Ethnographic experience as corrective to anthropological precept would, however, be another paper on the same subject.[6] Here, I have been concerned instead with what, following Fredric Jameson (1981), might be called the generative political unconscious of anthropological precept.

To recap: what looked like mid-twentieth-century social anthropology's contribution to the study of history was nothing of the sort. Rather, it was a demonstration that all contemporary individual and collective identifications had recourse to the past. Effective in a crude kind of way in dealing with contemporary uses of the past, and important as a methodological caution against naïve derivation of history from present sources, social anthropology's 'identity operator' drew from notions current in turn of the century French-language sociology – including van Gennep's – the precept that resting points in identification had a propositionality that processes of transformation between identities did not (a harbinger of V.W. Turner's more thoroughgoing sense of the necessity of liminality to change). Steiner's originality within his circle – even if he didn't follow it through – was to produce a formulation that implicitly challenged the possibility of a distinction between identity and identity transformation by showing the two to be mutually entailed. I think these remain fertile ideas, and I want now to explore them in a direction Wendy James anticipates in her discussion of Marcel Mauss's rather hesitant relation to time and history in Africa. His difficulty, as James sees it in introducing her subject, is that the ideas of the *Année sociologique* school rested heavily on a distinction between archaic and modern time that could at least *seem* to be made to work better in the Arctic or Australia than it could in Africa. 'The distinction between "traditional" and "modern" time ... collapses into the history which has produced it: in particular, the history of the concepts of modernity and progress themselves, and in the special case of anthropology, the colonial encounter' (James 1998: 226).

The counterpoising of the traditional with the modern is a feature of widespread contemporary African sensibility that itself, as James suggests more generally, is a product of a particular historical process rather than the shape that history has taken. Evaluations like traditional versus modern assume some life of their own in so far as they come to inflect human agency by becoming part of its context. Ethnicity in Africa has been a striking example of the simultaneous changes in item and context that makes identity transformation so difficult to express in terms that are clear without being oversimplifications. Our problem is that changes over time occur both in the 'figure' (say, a particular ethnicity) and in the 'ground' (current anticipations of ethnicity as a type of difference) (Fardon 1996, 1999a, 1999b). To take up James's comment on the significance of colonialism: colonial administration, based on colonial presuppositions about difference, acted upon both ethnicity as ground and ethnicities as figures. Often it could affect the latter indirectly: where local administrative practices were mediated through already dominant ethnicities, less powerful ethnicities were obliged to resort to a kind of catching up exercise by carrying out identity work in a changing context that, while generally unfavourable to them, nonetheless offered the possibility of an emergent rights discourse related to affirmations of distinct identity. Analytic arguments as to whether ethnicities were, or were not, invented or constructed or however made up – or whether they either did, or did not, have histories – do considerable injustice to both the modulations between mutually implicated fields and figures in these historical processes of change and to the increasingly undecidable status of quite what should be construed local and what imported in such processes. Following Simmel, we need to temporalize these processes, such that the terms in which we understand them simultaneously fix them as having to have occurred at one time rather than another. Here I find it helpful to explore these issues in the light of some rather literal fields and figures: in this case images of tigers, how they were framed, and quite what they are doing in a trope-filled, African palace.

Tiger in an African Palace

The existence of tigers in Africa has engaged some notable minds. Nelson Mandela and his prison companions' celebrated debate raised some germane points.

> One subject we harkened back to again and again was whether there were tigers in Africa. Some argued that although it was popularly assumed that tigers lived in Africa, this was a myth and that they were native to Asia and the Indian subcontinent. Africa had leopards in abundance, but no tigers. The other side argued that tigers were native to Africa and some still lived there. Some claimed to have seen with their own eyes this most powerful and beautiful of cats in the jungles of Africa.
>
> I maintained that while there were no tigers to be found in contemporary Africa, there was a Xhosa word for tiger, a word different from the one for leopard, and that if the word existed in our language, the creature must once have existed in Africa. (Mandela 1994: 511)[7]

There is some truth in most of the views expressed here. There are archaeological traces of tigers north of the Sahara (Wilson 1995: 537); tigers have entered African English via translation of local terms, so that tiger masquerades are reported from southern Nigeria (Oha 2001); nowadays there are football teams called 'The Tigers' – notably the national team of the Central African Republic (Royer 2002: 462); and numerous products are tiger branded.[8] As some listeners asked at the conference in Arusha, why are tigers in Africa more problematic than, say, the tigers that a particular brand of petrol promised to put in European petrol tanks, or the lions of European heraldry, or indeed the British annexation of Tippoo's mechanical tiger from India that now occupies a prominent spot in the Victoria and Albert Museum in London (Karp and Kratz 2000)? No reason at all, of course, except that in the African case – or at least the particular one to which I turn – it is possible to chart the stages of the tiger's introduction as a cultural item and, on this basis, to develop some more general points about the relation of imagery to identity.

This case study concerns what, in general terms, might be called a 'durbar' ceremony – if by that term we understand not just its Indian 'original' but a variety of local martial displays that were able to be incorporated into colonial 'ornamentalism'.[9] In the course of their north to south raiding before establishing the Bali chiefdoms in the Grassfields of present-day Cameroon, Chamba leaders had incorporated various peoples, and their Lela festival developed from earlier martial ritual to become an occasion for – among other things – this motley crew to pledge loyalty to their king. The ceremony crystallized into something recognizable as that performed today during the earliest years of German colonization of Kamerun, of which the chiefdom of Bali Nyonga was an important intermediary. In May 2001, when the opportunity arose to take part in a block seminar in Basel[10] where many of the most important early photographs of this event are housed in the mission archive, I was fascinated to see a video of the 1999 Lela taken by a Swiss cooperant, Andres Wanner. I have not myself seen Lela since 1984, so this is vicarious 'fieldwork' in the digital age. Much remained the same fifteen years on, but among the things that had changed was a mural depicting a tiger painted on a bright red background behind the King's throne in the palace forecourt, an area that accommodated much of the activity of the Lela celebration. Why a tiger in an African tropical kingdom? The lions and elephant to either side of the tiger were at first sight less incongruous, but this was misleading since they transpired to share much of their inspiration with the tiger. Finding a still image and some information about all this involved me in more digital-age research. Days before the conference, scouring the internet more in desperation than expectation, I found myself indebted to a site belonging to Peter Sengbusch, a biologist based at the University of Hamburg, who had posted photographs taken in 1997 on his website, Afrika-online (see Fig. 6).[11] Further enquiry to Ted Johnson, proprietor

Figure 6 The Palace of Bali Nyonga (1997) © Peter v. Sengbusch

of a Bali Nyonga website and an American volunteer who worked with coffee co-operatives in the early 1990s, provided the information that the murals had been undertaken in 1993–4 by David Louis Musi. Musi, who had died some time in 2000, had been a schoolteacher and the town's leading electric guitarist as well as an artist and carver.[12] His services had been engaged during palace improvements undertaken at the behest of the reigning monarch, HRH Fon Dr Ganyonga III, who succeeded to his father's throne in 1985.[13] So we know when the tiger – and the elephant and lions – were painted as a palace mural, but we are none the wiser why a tiger.

A clue to the *proximate* origin of these images – and of their blue and white patterned borders – comes in an early twentieth-century record of the treasure displayed during Lela. In those days, fences encircling the palace were renewed, and to the right of the entrance from the orientation of the exiting monarch – that is, in the position that the murals now occupy – were hung cloths. In a photograph of the 1908 ceremony we see a display of royal wealth including ivory horns, a throne placed upon leopard and cow skins, a stool, statues, an umbrella, a fog horn and cloths hung upon the palace fencing (Fig. 7). Three layers of cloth can be discerned: at bottom are patterned blue and white cloths imported as part of the regional trade from either the Jukun to the west or, more likely, the Ndop plains closer by. (The missionary Jakob Keller refers to them as *ndi ndob*, 1919: 65.) These types of prestige cloths predate European colonization.[14] That a figurative

Figure 7 Treasure displayed at the 1908 Lela. Basel E-30.27.003

cloth overlays these becomes clearer in a photograph taken in either 1909 or 1910 to which I turn shortly. The topmost layer of cloth in the 1908 display consists of two simulacra of leopard skins. To the best of my knowledge, these fabrics are not recorded as reappearing at later Lela (but the record is uneven, so this absence of evidence is not evidence that they were never used again); and it is readily apparent that they are not displayed for want of real leopard skins (since some skins lie upon the ground). It looks more as if we are dealing with a decorative aesthetic that finds cloth appropriate for hangings and skins for footings.

The middle layer of cloth is visible in a (somewhat blurred and crudely retouched) photograph that comes from the Lela of either 1909 or 1910 (Fig. 8).[15] Three animals may be discerned with difficulty: clearest is an elephant in the centre of the photograph, to the viewer's right is a standing lion, and to the left a tiger. The animals are abundantly clear in a colour photograph taken over a half century later, in 1963, showing that one of the cloths (the elephant), all of which had a red background, was by that time patched (Fig. 9).[16] Another dozen years on, the cloths were again photographed by the curator and ethnographer Hans-Joachim Koloss. One of Koloss's photographs reveals for the first time that there were actually three lion panels, although apparently only one each of tiger and elephant (and the elephant panel has the patch apparent in 1963; Fig. 10). Despite lion and elephant being African mammals, it seems likely that all three creatures

Figure 8 Treasure displayed at the 1909 or 1910 Lela. Basel E-30.27.008

were originally of exotic inspiration: the elephant is a small-eared Indian example and, given that it clearly belongs to a set including the tiger and elephant, the lion is likely to have been Asian-derived as well. The earliest definite textual reference to these animal cloths occurs in the description that the missionary Jakob Keller published in 1919, although it is based on information he collected before the First World War: he mentions 'European carpets/tapestries with woven animal figures' (*'europaïsche Teppische mit eingewebten Tierfiguren'*, 1919: 65). Max Esser who visited Bali Nyonga in 1896 had referred to the King having a costly carpet spread before his ivory throne (Chilver and Röschenthaler 2001: 82), but this might or might not have been the hangings in the photographs of which we know.

Where might the hangings have come from? Since Jakob Keller does not state that they were a missionary gift, they are likely to have come via Bali's other contacts with the coast; perhaps they were the gift of a trader, or of one of the labour recruiters on behalf of the coastal plantations who visited in Bali in the decade around the turn of the nineteenth century between the closure of the first German military station and the establishment of a missionary presence. Most likely European-manufactured but of Indian inspiration, extensive enquiries of British, Dutch and German museums have not – as yet – pinned down their provenance.[17]

Figure 9 HRH Fon Galega II during Lela in 1963. © Hans-Peter Straumann

Figure 10 Treasure displayed at the 1975 Lela. © Hans-Joachim Koloss

The animal tapestries are not particularly exotic in the context of the Bali palace treasures: the inventory of 1908 encompasses items like the matting fences that are locally argued to be of northern origin (like the Chamba leadership), prestige items local to the Grassfields (wooden stools and a throne copying Grassfield style), as well as a variety of European imports (including glassware, pottery and a ship's foghorn – the last already present by the time of Esser's visit, as perhaps were our draperies). However, the animal panels have left an enduring trace. Presumably – since I have not had the opportunity to enquire into this on the spot – when David Louis Musi undertook the palace murals at the behest of his relatively recently installed Fon, he was under instructions to take inspiration from the animal panels. Interestingly enough, he positioned the tiger panel behind the throne, retaining its red background and adding an oliphant and a calabash (presumably for transporting palm wine). He added a couple of other panels too: one depicting a double gong like that the Fon strikes at Lela, and another with a pair of fighting warriors, presumably a reminder that the Bali had fought their way to their present kingdom However, most of the decoration derives from the early twentieth-century cloth images. The lion panels were doubled and placed at either end of the display wall (which may reflect an actual disposition of cloths at some Lela, given that photographic evidence suggests the lion panels to be the only cloths of which the Bali Fon had more than one example). A single elephant panel has been retained, and the elephant depicted remains the small-eared Indian variety (although its head is partly obscured in Figure 6 by the pronged posts which are a part of the *lela* apparatus, this feature is clearly visible from other photographs not reproduced here). Is it accidental that the 'indigenous' animals – elephant and lion – have been given a relatively naturalistic background of sky and grass, while the tiger alone has retained the scarlet backdrop of its cloth version? The prestige cloths that hung behind the imported animal cloths in the photographs from 1908–10 have morphed into decorative borders painted around the panels of the mural.

My final piece of photographic evidence – at least for now – dates from 2002, and I owe it to Ernst Elsenhans who visited Bali in August that year. Elsenhans's photographs show that the external murals were still intact, although peeling, and that the fabric panels were pinned up in the hall of the palace, looking rather threadbare given that they must be around a hundred years old. New to the photographic record is a tiger panel behind the Fon's throne within the palace (Fig. 11). Framed by a border inspired by indigo cloth patterns, a powerful and markedly naturalistic tiger – which certainly looks as if it had been taken from an original source other than the cloth – bares its teeth behind the throne dais. A winged crown is painted directly above the Fon's throne, itself a compelling exercise in the accumulation of symbols of power. The whole assemblage – but particularly the tiger – seems to speak to the renewal of power of chiefship,

Figure 11 The throne dais of HRH Fon Dr Ganyonga III (2002). © Ernst Elsenhans

including the power to exercise violence, at the close of the twentieth century not just in Cameroon, but in many African countries where 'modern' state institutions are locally weak.

So much for proximate origins of the animal images but, following Nelson Mandela's lead, presumably other ideas paved the path to their acceptance: a noisy, oliphant-using ceremonial culture readily accommodated a ship's foghorn, and the kingly attributes of the leopard must have provided a welcoming niche for the import of what – with apologies to Wole Soyinka – we could call symbolic tigritude. Perhaps there always is some sense in which a new idea is already there in the environment that receives it, that is to say in the abilities people have to forge continuities.

Treasures and Translations

My brief example has traced how some past treasures have been re-evoked in the service of contemporary identifications. The vagaries of my own 'research' through old photographs and texts, internet and e-mail, conversations and letters of enquiry seems to mirror with respect to its accidental progress, something in the processes of transfer occurring more than a century ago. Materials were imported into Bali and redeployed, figures have literally (in the case of the local patterned cloths) become frames. The reworking of treasures bears a close resemblance to the reworking of identities: change occurs subtly and simultaneously in figure and ground. Similarity is produced over time in terms of a project that is driven (but not entirely guided) by local perceptions of means and ends. When Paul Bohannan – who had skilfully edited Steiner's papers on economics after his death – came to use some of Steiner's ideas to explore his own ethnography, he decided to change a term that was quite telling in Steiner's original usage. Bohannan (1955) wrote of conversion when goods from one sphere of exchange (say subsistence goods) were traded for goods of another sphere (say prestige goods). Bohannan wanted to draw attention to the transaction itself. Steiner seems more explicitly to have been concerned with questions of value, and he referred not to conversion but 'translation'. Something was translated into a treasure when it brought to mind for people the memorably intensive effort that had gone into creating or acquiring it. Like identities, treasures were conceivable only in terms of their having a past. Modernist social anthropology did all its explaining – as I emphasized at the outset – in terms of the present. But throwing so much weight upon the present is problematic, not least because for most people, most of the time, it is the present that is full of uncertainties and problems, and the past that seems a source of stability. The audacity of modernist social anthropology's approach was to eschew the popular view and seek resolution where there is typically instability – in the present. I do not think this modernist insight is entirely exhausted, but neither do I feel that it is wholly sustainable. A modest proposal to extend its working life would involve historicizing those mutually entailed processes of identification and transformation of which Steiner spoke in his aphorism. Contrary to his words, this would entail a close investigation of identifications as processes in time in order to ask about the conditions under which mementoes of memorably intensive time are objectified, reified and even fetishized. Identity work, I would suggest, has much in common with the creation (and indeed loss) of value by treasured objects. Both involve an investment of labour that must be studied historically; both treasures and identities are subject to temporal resignification; both may lose as well as gain value; both are materialized in ways that may resist or subvert people's attempts to annex or use them in particular ways. A labour theory of value necessarily begs questions of history in ways that an exchange theory (rooting value entirely in the present) need not. Presentism, in this respect, relies heavily on an exchange theory of value, whereas a labour theory of value recognizes that present value is not autonomous of past labour.

Notes

1. Specific acknowledgements may be found in notes, but I want to thank the British Academy and Research Committee of the School of Oriental and African Studies for making possible my attendance at the ASA Conference in Arusha, and the audience to this paper, given as a plenary lecture, for their astute questions and amused generosity towards the near invisibility of tigers in the illustrative material I managed to find by the time of the event. Johannes Fabian and Sjaak van der Geest suggested specific references which I have been glad to follow up.

2. Pen on paper, 34.3 × 24.5 cm, Venice, Accademia, No. 228, c. 1492. Apparently the text Leonardo copied to accompany his original drawing did not include the sentences he illustrated: 'The navel is naturally placed in the centre of the human body, and if a circle be described of a man lying with his face upward and his hands and feet extended, it will touch his fingers and his toes. It is not alone by a circle that the human body is thus circumscribed, as may be seen by placing it within a square. For if we measure from the feet to the crown of the head, and then across the arms fully extended, we should find the latter measure equal to the former; so that the lines at right angles to each other enclosing the figure would form a square' (Vitruvius quoted by Ludwig Goldscheider 1945: Note 48, p. 29).

3. To judge both from Schüttpelz's perusal of the unpublished aphorisms and from the index to Adler and Fardon's (1999) edition of Steiner's selected writings.

4. Jeremy Adler and I discuss the notion of what H.G. Adler called a 'universal mathesis' in Steiner's work in our Introduction the first volume of Steiner's selected works (1999 I: 36, 48–9). The translation presented here of 'The chief sociological principle...' benefits from Erhard Schüttpelz's research on Steiner's original manuscripts. Obscurities that Adler and I were unable to resolve in our earlier translation (Steiner 1999 II: 240) had their source in (reasoned but probably erroneous) transcription decisions made in H.G. Adler's typescript from which we worked.

5. Within an extensive debate, see Davis 1992 and Sinclair 1993.

6. Lyn Shumaker's recent account of research at the Rhodes-Livingstone Institute in Northern Rhodesia (2001) shows just how far precept and practice might diverge.

7. Gemetchu Megerssa was kind enough to point out that many of the questions I raised were prefigured in this excerpt. I have only subsequently come across Carmel Schrire's engaging lecture which uses the same device and quotation (Schrire 2002).

8. Thanks to Christine Stelzig's retentive memory for the historic reference and to David Pratten's advice on the interpretation of references to tiger masquerades in Nigeria.

9. I am indebted to Umar Buratai, who visited the University of London as an A.G. Leventis Fellow in autumn 2001, for conversations on this shared interest. The durbar itself might have served as well as the tiger for my example. Ornamentalism is, of course, the title of David Cannadine's account of British imperial ritual and display (2001).

10. I am grateful to Paul Jenkins for adding this invitation to his other kindnesses (including permission to reproduce photographs from the collection of the Basel Mission Archive), and to the seminar participants for stimulating responses that I shall acknowledge more fully in a detailed account of Lela that is in preparation. Here, I want to acknowledge two participants particularly: Ernst Elsenhans and Hans-Peter Straumann who sent me photographs after the seminar two of which appear here.

11. At the time of writing, there are three colour photographs of the Bali Nyonga palace at http://www.biologie.uni-hamburg.de/b-online/afrika/kamerun/bali.htm

12. At the time of writing, his photograph appears at http://www.bamenda.org/ted/drmoses/crydie/musi.jpg

13. At the time of writing, photographs of the cry die of Galega II and the installation of Ganyonga III were to be found on the website of the Bali Cultural Association of the USA: http://www.bca-usa.org/bea/galega.html

14. E-30.27.003 is one of a series of photographs of the 1908 ceremony in the Basel Mission Archive. The circumstances under which they were taken can be reconstructed with a high degree of likelihood and seems to rest on the simultaneous presence in Bali of the German museum ethnologist, Bernhard Ankermann, the missionary and counsellor to the Bali chief, Ferdinand Ernst, and the trainee missionary, Jonathan Striebel, who was responsible for most of the photographs finding their to way to Switzerland along with his written account. A fuller account of these circumstances will appear in a *Festschrift* for Paul Jenkins (Fardon 2004).

15. Basel E-30.27.008 is attributed to Clara Schultze-Reinhardt who was in Bali during the month of Lela only in 1909 and 1910. An interesting feature of this photograph is that the lion to the viewer's right appears to be facing left. Since the lion panels otherwise always appear facing right, this suggests the panels to have been reversible (Keller, as mentioned earlier, suggests the figures were woven). Close inspection of later photographs suggest that the panels may subsequently have been backed with a blue material, so they were no longer reversible.

16. A series of photographs was taken by Hans-Peter Straumann when he was a teacher in Bali Nyonga. These have been copied for the Basel archive and

are used here with permission. A roughly contemporaneous history of Bali compiled by the Headmaster of the Cameroon Protestant College, Bamenda, refers to 'large red cloth draperies with elephants and tigers pictured on them' used during Lela (1971, originally 1965: 18). The survival of cloth for long periods is apparently not unusual: a photograph of his 1940 installation shows the mid-century Fon of Bali Nyonga wearing – apparently in pristine condition – a robe that his father used decades earlier (Basel E30.85.215).

17. For their attempts to clarify this question, sincere thanks are due in the UK to Rosemary Crill and Deborah Swallow of the Victoria and Albert Museum, June Hill of the Bankfield Museum, and John Picton at SOAS; in Germany to Brigitte Tietzel of the Deutsches Textil Museum in Krefeld, Heide Nixdorf (Professorin Kulturgeschichte der Textilien) of the University of Dortmund, and to Hans-Joachim Koloss and Christine Stelzig of the Ethnologisches Museum, Berlin; in the Netherlands to Annemieke Hogervorst of the Gemeentemuseum, Helmond, and Pieter ter Keurs of the Rijksmuseum voor Volkenkunde, Leiden; in the USA to Lisa Aronson of Skidmore College, Saratoga Springs. Vibha Arora, Oxford, suggests a possible origin in Western India for these cloths.

References

Adler, Jeremy and Richard Fardon (eds), (1999), 'Orientpolitik, value, and civilisation: the anthropological thought of Franz Baermann Steiner', Introduction to *Franz Baermann Steiner Selected Writings Volume II*, Oxford: Berghahn.

Bohannan, Laura (1952), 'A genealogical charter', *Africa* 22: 301–15.

Bohannan, Paul (1955), 'Some principles of exchange and investment among the Tiv', *American Anthropologist* 58: 60–9.

Cameroon Protestant College (C.E.G.) (1971 [1965]), *Bali History*, mimeographed, CPC: Bamenda, Cameroon (copy in Basel Mission Archive)

Cannadine, David (2001), *Ornamentalism: How the British saw their Empire*, London: Allen Lane.

Chilver, E.M. and Ute Röschenthaler (eds), (2001), *Cameroon's Tycoon: Max Esser's Expedition and its Consequences*, Oxford: Berghahn Cameroon Studies, Vol. 3.

Davis, John (1992), 'Tense in ethnography: some practical considerations', in Judith Okely and Helen Callaway (eds) *Anthropology and Autobiography*, ASA Monograph 29, London and New York: Routledge.

Evans-Pritchard, E.E. (1940), *The Nuer. A Description of Modes of Livelihood and Political Institutions of a Nilotic People*, Oxford: Clarendon Press.

Fabian, Johannes (1983), *Time and the Other: How Anthropology Makes its Object*, New York: Columbia University Press.

——(1991) *Time and the Work of Anthropology: Critical Essays*, Reading: Harwood.

Fardon, Richard (1996), '"Crossed destinies": the entangled histories of West African ethnic and national identities', in Louise de la Gorgendière, Kenneth King and Sarah Vaughan (eds), *Ethnicity in Africa: Roots, Meanings and Implications*, Edinburgh: Centre of African Studies, 117–46.

——(1999a), 'Ethnic pervasion', in Tim Allen and Jean Seaton (eds), *The Media in Conflict: War Reporting and Representations of Ethnic Violence*, London: Zed, 64–80.

——(1999b), *Contrast and Comparison: Notes from a Middle-Belt, West African Practice*, (Inaugural Lecture, May 1998), London: SOAS (University of London).

—— (2004), 'The ethnologist and the missionaries: recording the 1908 Lela in Bali Nyonga', in Michael Albrecht, Veit Arlt, Barbara Müller and Jürg Schneider (eds), *Getting Pictures Right*, Köln: Rüdiger Köppe Verlag.

Goldscheider, Ludwig (1945), *Leonardo da Vinci*, Oxford and London: Phaidon Press.

James, Wendy (1998), 'Mauss in Africa: on time, history and politics', in Wendy James and N.J. Allen (eds), *Marcel Mauss. A Centenary Tribute*, Oxford and New York: Berghahn.

Jameson, Fredric (1981), *The Political Unconscious. Narrative as Socially Symbolic Act*, London: Methuen.

Karp, Ivan and Corinne Kratz (2000), 'Reflections on the fate of Tippoo's Tiger: defining cultures through public display', in Elizabeth Hallam and Brian V.Street (eds), *Cultural Encounters: Representing Otherness*, London and New York: Routledge.

Keller, Jakob (1919), 'Das Lelafest in Bali', *Der Evangelischer Heidenbote*, Juni: 63–66, Juli: 78–81, Oktober: 116–18.

Malinowksi, Bronislaw (1944), *A Scientific Theory of Culture and Other Essays*, Chapel Hill: University of North Carolina Press.

Mandela, Nelson (1994), *Long Walk to Freedom*, London: Little, Brown & Co.

Oha, Obododimma (2001), 'Mmanwu Awusa: masquerading the Hausa Muslim in Igbo tiger performance', in *Africa at the Crossroads: Complex Political Emergencies in the 21st Century*, UNESCO/ENA: Most Ethno-Net Africa Publications (www.unesco.org/most/crossroadsoha.htm).

Peter, Emrys (1960), 'The proliferation of segments in the lineage of the Bedouins of Cyrenaica', *JRAI* 90: 29–53.

Radcliffe Brown, Alfred R. (1952), *Structure and Function in Primitive Society*, London: Cohen & West.

Royer, Patrick (2002), 'The spirit of competition: *wak* and sport in Burkina Faso', *Africa* 72(3): 464–83.

Schrire, Carmel (2002), *Tigers in Africa: Stalking the Past at the Cape of Good Hope*, Landsdowne, and Windhoek: LLAREC Series in Visual History, University of Cape Town Press.

Schumaker, Lyn (2001), *Africanizing Anthropology: Fieldwork, Networks, and the Making of Cultural Knowledge in Central Africa*, Durham and London: Duke University Press.

Schüttpelz, Erhard (2003), 'Transformation and identification: Franz Baermann Steiner's "chief sociological principle"', in Jeremy Adler, Richard Fardon and Carol Tully (eds), *From Prague Poet to Oxford Anthropologist: Franz Baermann Steiner Celebrated,* Munich: Iudicium; London: Publications of the Institute of Germanic Studies (University of London School of Advanced Studies), 80.

Simmel, Georg (1980), *Essays on Interpretation in Social Science*, edited and translated by Guy Oakes, Manchester: Manchester University Press.

Sinclair, Simon (1993), 'The present tense again', *Journal of the Anthropological Society of Oxford* 24 (1): 33–48.

Steiner, Franz Baermann (1999), *Selected Writings, Volumes I and II*, Jeremy Adler and Richard Fardon (eds), Oxford: Berghahn.

Van Gennep, A. (1960 [1909]), *The Rites of Passage*, London: Routledge & Kegan Paul.

Wilson, R.J.A. (1995), 'Carthaginian, Numidian, Roman', in Tom Phillips (ed.) *Africa: the Art of a Continent*, London: Royal Academy.

–5–

'Time, Too, Grows on the Moon': Some Evidence for Knight's Theory of a Human Universal[1]

Ian Watts

Our species evolved in Africa between 150 to 200 thousand years ago, dispersing across the world within the last 100 thousand years (White et al. 2003; Oppenheimer 2003). There is growing archaeological evidence that by the time this dispersal began, the essential elements of symbolic culture were already established.[2] Some of the earliest direct evidence concerns engravings on pieces of red ochre and sets of shell beads from Blombos Cave in South Africa, dated over 70 thousand years ago (Henshilwood *et al.* 2002, 2004). Red ochre is an earth pigment widely used by recent hunter-gatherers for body-painting and decorating artefacts. Its *regular* use – from early in the Late Pleistocene[3] of southern and northern Africa[4] – may be used to infer habitual collective ritual (Watts 2002) of the kind long viewed as central to the generation and transmission of symbolic constructs (Durkheim [1912] 1965; Deacon 1997).

Taken together, these developments oblige cultural anthropologists to consider the possibility of significant universals underpinning symbolic culture. Ambitious endeavours to identify and explain supposed symbolic universals were standard during the infancy of anthropology but have fared poorly since the 1920s, the last notable example being Lévi-Strauss's *Mythologiques* (1970–1981). The validity of some cross-cultural symbolic findings – for example, the incompatibility between cooking and noise (Lévi-Strauss 1978), or between menstruation and sunshine (Frazer 1900) – has never been refuted, but with no plausible theoretical model to account for these correlations, research agendas have moved on.[5]

As the 'out of Africa' model of modern human origins gained acceptance, Chris Knight (1991) proposed his 'sex-strike' theory of a unitary origin to symbolic culture, subsequently elaborated with the more rigorously Darwinian 'sham-menstruation' hypothesis (Knight et al. 1995; Power and Aiello 1997). According to this model, selection pressures for larger-brained offspring placed heavy energetic burdens on evolving hominin mothers during the last half million years. In low latitudes, these burdens would have been most acute in the dry season. In meeting these challenges, females could seek support from (a) local kin-related females, (b) male kin and/or (c) out-group males. The optimal strategy would have been to combine all three, co-operating with male and female kin in the task of extracting regular provisioning from sexual partners. According to Knight et al. (1995), ancestral 'modern' females achieved this by making sexual access dependent upon male co-operative hunting success.

Menstruation would have been uniquely salient to males as a reliable indicator of imminent fertility. By painting up in shared blood, or using blood-coloured substitutes such as red ochre, coalitions of nursing, pregnant and cycling females could 'scramble' the relevant information, preventing 'philanderer' males from discriminating between them. By declaring themselves imminently fertile yet currently unavailable, females established the beginnings of group-level sexual 'morality'. With 'blood' used to signal 'ritual inviolability', the same logic could be extended to the blood of game animals, marking raw meat as taboo to hunters. Hunters were obliged to return to camp and surrender their kills to affines, whereupon 'raw' flesh was rendered available through being 'cooked'.

Synchronized female 'sex strike' presupposes an appropriate external clock. With late Middle Pleistocene technology, hunting expeditions would often require overnight travel, presupposing nocturnal light. The only time sunset is not followed by darkness is the second quarter of the waxing moon. With ritual power (in Knight's model) either 'on' or 'off', the 'sex strike' should climax with the hunters' successful return at full moon, whereupon the community switches to a phase of feasting and marital sex. This binary alternation between opposed ritual states, mapped onto lunar periodicity, implies that women's ritual action began at dark moon.

The improbability of Knight's scenario renders it eminently falsifiable. The predicted ritual syntax can be summarized as follows. Ritual potency is switched 'on' by a 'blood'-signal at dark moon. There should be no cooking-fire. In triggering menstrual withdrawal, the 'on' signal connotes 'temporary death', 'fasting', 'hunger', 'raw food', 'darkness' and 'wetness'. Since females must emphatically *reverse* signs of sexual availability, we expect displays indicating not only 'wrong time' but also 'wrong sex' and 'wrong species' (Power and Watts 1997, 1999). Here I test those predictions concerning the cultural construction of time in the light of Khoisan ethno-historical data. The Khoisan – the First Peoples of southern Africa – historically comprise a cluster of hunter-gatherer and herder cultures; genetically they include one of Africa's oldest human lineages. Although I will primarily be addressing hunter-gatherer data, Khoekhoe pastoralist sources will also be drawn upon, on the grounds that despite differences in economy and language, Khoisan cultures have shared structural features across several domains, including ritual and cosmology (Barnard 1992). In what follows, detailed references to sources are placed in the endnotes, to make for clarity in the main argument.

The Moon in Khoisan Ritual and Belief

Recent analyses of Khoisan religion (Barnard 1992: 251–64; Guenther 1999) broadly agree on a set of distinctive shared elements, central to which are 'a dual notion of divinity' and 'a trickster figure who is both protagonist and god' (Guenther 1999: 88). Barnard speaks of a 'high' god and a 'lesser' deity.[6] Barnard and Guenther differ with respect to the Moon; both reject earlier notions of 'moon worship', but Barnard includes the moon as a pan-Khoisan supernatural being, while Guenther regards it as a 'relatively minor element in Bushman myth and lore' (ibid.: 231). Barnard criticizes past and recent ethnographers for failing 'either to see the structural position of the Moon in relation to other entities, or to explore the cosmo-semantic or syntactic context of indigenous statements about the Moon' (1992: 254). Guenther sees the moon's waxing and waning merely as an inevitable metaphor for life, death and regeneration (1999: 65).

The status of the moon bears upon a more theoretical disagreement between the two authors – the relative significance of structural elements in Khoisan religion. Minimizing structure in religion, belief and myth, Guenther treats ambiguity as the 'ontological and conceptual substance' of Khoisan beings and states (1999: 236). Barnard by contrast emphasizes shared structural features of Khoisan cosmology. The case for a coherence of structure and metaphor operating across ritual arenas was developed by Lewis-Williams (1981; Lewis-Williams and Biesele 1978).

The Moon in Khoekhoe Ritual and Belief

As European commentators first regularly encountered Cape Khoekhoe pastoralists in the later seventeenth century, they almost invariably reported dances at the appearance of the new moon and/or at full moon. Over the first fifty years of colonization, of twenty-four authors referring to such dancing, the largest proportion only mention new moon dances.[7] While some accounts were based on hearsay and others were plagiarized, it seems that relative to full moon, the new moon was of equal or greater ritual significance. The majority opinion was that the Khoekhoe 'worshipped' or 'venerated' the moon. A proponent of the opposite view was Langhansz (1694), who held that the timing of dances was attributable to the light afforded, enabling participants to play with their shadows (Raven-Hart [RH] 1971: 406) – this despite an immediately preceding assertion that dances occurred 'especially at the New Moon'. I cite Langhansz as the first in a long line of commentators (some supported by indigenous statements) who regarded the need for light as sufficient explanation for lunar phase-locked dancing.[8]

As for practices accompanying these dances, several accounts mention red cosmetics. Schouten (1655) reported that when people dance, 'they sometimes turn their eyes to heaven, and then with a red stone write stripes and crosses on each others' foreheads' (RH 1971: 84).[9] Meister (1688) independently records the use of 'red earth and fat' for face-painting in preparation for a full-moon dance (RH 1971: 349). Kolbe states that women in particular painted up with red ochre for such assemblies, while Valentyn reported that at new moon, men threw balls of clay into the river,[10] possibly indicating a symbolic association between the new moon and water. Heeck, in 1655, reported that new moon dances involved sexual licence; on these occasions: 'those who are yet unmarried (after their fashion) that night take women, one, two or more as they meet them, whether old or young, pretty or ugly' (RH 1971: 35). This account of 'orgiastic' (as opposed to marital) union is consistent in its timing with Knight's model. It should not be dismissed as literary licence, since later accounts describe similar Korana (Khoe pastoralist) rituals, although failing to specify anything about timing.[11] By contrast, Bolling (RH 1971: 147) describes Khoekhoe marriage as a full-moon ceremony, held at the beginning of the winter rains (May). Similarly, Grevenbroek (1933: 211) included betrothal ceremonies among various full-moon rites.

Recorded beliefs about the moon are rare. Cowley says that it was believed to control the weather, expressing its pleasure or displeasure with people by showing itself or not (RH 1971 [1686]: 310). According to Grevenbroek, the Khoekhoe 'imputed to the moon all diseases of men and beasts, the inclemency of the sky, and the prevalence of disasters of every kind. When the moon is full, women who are in their monthly courses blame it for their illness' (1933 [1695]: 207). This last remark, flatly contradicting Knight's model, will be evaluated shortly. Both accounts need to be seen alongside those ascribing similar attributes to an otiose heavenly Supreme Being.[12]

The view that the Khoekhoe 'worshipped' the moon was eloquently defended by Kolbe.[13] Drawing on Hahn's free translation of Kolbe's original, Barnard (1992: 294) says that 'the Moon is not the Khoekhoe God himself', but 'the visible manifestation of God'. Kolbe's example of a 'prayer' to the new moon provides a different picture to that given by Grevenbroek (see above): 'Be welcome, give us plenty of honey, give grass to our cattle, that we may get plenty of milk' (Hahn 1881: 41). The paradox would be resolved if benefits were attributed to the waxing phase, and illness to the waning, consistent with a Nama (Khoe pastoralist) healer's report that medicines were never prepared during the waning moon (Laidler 1928: 434).

According to Hahn, both the Nama trickster – Heitsi-eibib, and God – Tsûillgoab or !Khub, shared attributes with the Moon – llKhāb (1881: 130–7). All three beings come from the east, the sacred direction. All promise immortality, alter their shape and disappear only to reappear. Tsûillgoab and Heitsi-eibib are engaged in recurrent conflicts with 'bad Beings' in which their powers wax and wane. Hahn interpreted Heitsi-eibib's maternal incest as a metaphor of lunar periodicity

(1881: 136), while P.W. Schmidt (1933, cited in S. Schmidt 1986: 210) elaborated on Hahn's notion of the lunar character of Heitsi-eibib's repeated conflicts with ≠Gama≠gorib. Sigrid Schmidt (1986) and Barnard (1992: 259) come to broadly similar conclusions.

Clearly, the moon was central to Khoekhoe conceptions of the 'high god', the trickster, material abundance and scarcity, the overall pattern appearing consistent with Knight's model.

Sources on the /Xam Bushman

The first detailed insights into Bushman belief come with Wilhelm Bleek's and Lucy Lloyd's transcriptions of oral narratives provided by /Xam speakers from what is now Northern Cape Province.[14] Influenced by Max Müller's theories (cf. Bleek 1874: 98), Wilhelm Bleek was predisposed to look for sidereal elements, resulting in some interpretative exaggeration (Bleek 1874, 1875: 9); but this hardly detracts from narrative content. A less well-known nineteenth-century source is von Wielligh's (1921) Afrikaans collection of narratives, largely based on accounts collected in a former /Xam speaking area in the 1880s.

/Kaggen and !Khwa

The two principal supernatural beings in /Xam mythology are /Kaggen, the trickster, and !Khwa, the Rain-Beast. /Kaggen created the moon and game animals, most notably the eland; he was also protector of the game. !Khwa means 'water' or 'rain'; the term could also be applied to menstrual blood.[15] In personified form !Khwa is primarily the enforcer of menstrual observances; he appears as a male being, generally described as a bull-ox, dwelling in water-sources (Hewitt 1986: 78). Prior to the arrival of Khoe pastoralism, !Khwa probably took the form of an eland bull (Schmidt 1979). In enforcing menstrual taboos, !Khwa was identified with the violent, 'male' rain. His principal means of punishment was to send lightning or whisk up transgressors in a whirlwind, transforming them into the Rain's creatures – typically frogs. He threatened not only excessive wetness but cultural reversal. Outside menstrual contexts, !Khwa could be a beneficent Rain-Cow. Von Wielligh's informants also spoke of the Watersnake, a supernatural being sharing several attributes with !Khwa and identically related to menstruating women. Descendants of the /Xam have recently corroborated and elaborated these beliefs (Hoff 1997). Barnard identifies !Khwa with the 'high god' of other Khoisan religions and points out that an association of the Moon 'either' with !Khwa 'or' /Kaggen has long been argued (1992: 255 with refs.). I suggest both associations are valid.

Prefacing Remarks on the Moon in Bushman Belief

Guenther states:

> It appears that to some Bushmen the moon represents, in its crescent form as the new moon, life and well-being, as among the /Xam, whose menarcheal rites were timed by the new moon. *Alternatively*, we find that the Nharo associate the waning moon with death: its crescent is seen as a boat carrying dead souls to god ... because of its waxing and waning, the moon appears as a symbol of life (and death) and regeneration throughout Khoisan belief and myth.
>
> In sum, we once again find a considerable *diversity and divergence* of views on this enigmatic stellar body...' (1999: 65, emphases added)

Unfortunately, this otherwise accurate summary is hedged about with misleading qualifications. The new moon is consistently associated with 'life and well being', identification of the waning moon with death and illness seems almost as widespread.[16] This is not a negative 'alternative' view, inconsistent with positive beliefs about the new moon. Instead, it offers a complementary image of the opposite side of the lunar cycle, culminating in Moon's 'temporary death'. Rather than 'diversity and divergence', these two views represent a coherent structure of belief.

Among Khoisan languages with grammatical gender (Khoe family), the moon is masculine; but as an object engendering beliefs it is frequently gender-ambivalent – sometimes male, sometimes female (Power and Watts 1997, 1999; Solomon 1992). From Guenther's discussion of the moon's gender (1999: 130, but see Guenther 1989: 51), one might think this was another example of 'diversity and divergence'. But the moon's gender is tightly structured by phase: new/waxing moon is regarded as male (or sometimes as a child); the full moon is female.[17] The /Xam full Moon was sometimes regarded as wife to the waxing Moon, consistent with the prediction that men hunt during the waxing moon for 'full moon wives'.

The Moon and Menstruation

Moon-menstruation linkages inspire Khoisan metaphors.[18] These do not specify lunar phase, but ritual traditions and associated myths connect menstruation with the dark moon; blood-flow should have ceased by new moon. Following menarche, a /Xam 'new maiden' was released from seclusion at the appearance of the new moon (L. VI, 2: 4000–4002). Guenther (1999: 65) mentions this timing to argue for 'diversity and divergence' of perspectives on the moon, but identical timings are reported for the Angolan !Xŭ (a !Kung dialect group) (Bleek 1928a: 122) and for the G/wi or closely related G//ana of the central Kalahari (Valiente-Noailles

1993: 94–7), a Khoe-speaking Bushman group. Spanning more than a century and encompassing all three traditionally recognized Khoisan language families (Bleek 1929b, but see Barnard 1992: 22–3), these accounts indicate a deep structure of Khoisan ritual practice. The only contrary account known to me is Bjerre's (1960: 146) report that the Zu/'hoãsi only performed the Eland Bull Dance on the evening of the girl's emergence 'if the moon is shining', going on to state: 'If it is full moon, and there is enough food, the dancing goes on all night...' (ibid). The timing of the new maiden's emergence casts doubt on Grevenbroek's earlier-cited remark that Khoekhoe women 'blamed' the full moon for menstruation; they were probably 'blaming' the moon in general.

Menstruation is implicitly associated with the dark moon in several versions of a /Xam myth about the Leopard Tortoise.[19] Qing's account to Orpen (1874: 9), in which the trickster Cagn (/Kaggen) has his hand trapped by a river-dwelling creature, may be a Maluti San variant. The Leopard Tortoise is one of !Khwa's creatures, set aside as his meat and tabooed to girls and unmarried men. The tortoise is menorrhagic: 'she is always ill with bleeding'.[20] She continues to bleed 'after the moon died, and another moon came, while she still lay ill'. In all versions she is encountered by a male passer-by, generally either out hunting or seeking honey. The tortoise is either a 'grandmother' or 'elder sister' of her victim. She tricks him into assuaging her menstrual cramps by massaging her neck, she then retracts her neck, trapping the hand of her victim and causing the flesh to rot. In //Kabbo's version, where /Kaggen is the victim, rain poured down and 'cold seized him' as his flesh decayed. In Qing's account, the threatened permanence of the union is played out (in a river) according to seasonal rather than lunar periodicity. Flesh falling away suggests extreme hunger. In von Wielligh's version, the two victims return home while the moon is still young. Using dew – 'water from the moon' – they restore their flesh by washing their hands each morning until the moon is full.

There are indications that the severe food and drink restrictions on a /Xam 'new maiden' extended to her immediate kin.[21] Viegas Guerreiro was told that among the !Xũ in Ondova district (Angola), at the first sign of menarche, 'all the fires in the camp are extinguished'. The taboo against cooking during menstruation is epitomized in the versions of the story of the menarcheal girl who attempted to cook flesh. She goes to the waterhole and captures and kills one of !Khwa's children (resembling a young bovid, not to be confused with !Khwa's creatures). She places it on the fire to roast, but water bubbles up out of the ground, extinguishing the fire with hissing and spluttering. The girl and her kin are whisked up by whirlwinds and dropped into the waterhole as frogs.

If !Khwa's relationship to secluded menstruants associates him with the dark moon, then logically he should stand in opposition to cooking in other narrative contexts. A hunter who shot !Khwa as an eland (L.VIII, 16: 7461–2, 17: 7463–72) found the meat instantly transformed to ashes when placed on the fire; he and his companions suffer a similar fate to the disobedient menstruant. /Xam women expected their husbands' hunting to be unsuccessful during dark moon (Lewis-Williams 2000: 249). An association of meat-hunger with the dark moon is implied by the //Xegwi phrase for scarcity: 'Au! The moon is small (dark)' (Potgieter1955: 30, parentheses in original). Hunger is also associated with the new moon (B. V: 588).

Like the moon's gender, the gender of the Khoisan menarcheal girl is emphatically mutable (Power and Watts 1997, 1999). She adopts male roles and attributes. She may be identified with the gender-anomalous eland bull or with the hunter who has shot an eland (Lewis-Williams 1981) or gemsbok (Heinz 1994). While in seclusion, the /Xam menstruant possesses !Khwa's destructive supernatural potency. Her emergence at new moon magically assists forthcoming hunts and attracts the desired 'female' rain. She is reintroduced to water and appeases !Khwa by sprinkling haematite over it (recall Valentyn's account indicating Khoekhoe ritual attitudes to bodies of water at new moon). The female rain, like the female initiate, is visualized as red (Power and Watts 1997: 545–6).

The /Xam moon was also conceptually red,[22] variously ascribed to the red dust on /Kaggen's shoe when he used the shoe to create the moon, to the blood of game about to be killed, or simply because 'cold' things are red. Other Bushman groups hold similar conceptions. Redness and brilliance are consistently associated with Khoisan constructs of supernatural potency, connoting both beauty and danger, attracting and setting apart (Watts 1999: 133–7). Menarcheal observances are the only Khoisan ritual context where red pigments were almost invariably used (Knight et al. 1995: 93–5 with refs.). Among the /Xam and Zu/'hoãsi, the girl's reincorporation into the band appears to have been the occasion for the most socially inclusive use of red ochre. Unlike Khoisan male initiation, menarcheal ritual is ubiquitous, relatively invariant in structure and unequivocally of the classic three-stage structure proposed by van Gennep ([1909] 1960). Guenther (1999: 176) has argued that together with trance dancing, this was the occasion where 'ontological transformation' is most pronounced.

Waxing Moon, Hunting and Rain

Guenther asserts: 'In neither the /Xam nor the Nharo case is there any evidence that the moon was regarded as the bringer of rain, game and food' (1989: 82), yet in the same paragraph he acknowledges that the /Xam addressed the new moon 'in prayer' for assistance in the hunt. Bleek and Lloyd recorded three such /Xam appeals[23] along with a ritualized greeting of the new moon. /Xam women would consult the waxing moon or an eponymous moon-like insect to determine whether their husbands would succeed in the hunt. The 'Moon' insect (and by extension the moon itself) was spoken of as 'possessing' the game. While the dark moon was blamed for hunting failure, the new or waxing moon – particularly if it appeared red – was a good hunting omen (Lewis-Williams 2000: 250). The new moon's association with game may have informed its description both as the 'moon horn' and as a hunter's bow. Moon's ownership of the game was explicitly asserted by Dorothea Bleek's Nharo informants. It permitted hunting during its waxing, but not at full moon. Bleek also reported a Nharo appeal for rain, addressed to the new moon. Appeals to the new moon for success in hunting antelope are reported for the Kxoe and others. The accounts are remarkably consistent in context and verbal form; most appeals included stereotyped hand-gestures before the face; in several reports, the hunter blew on an antelope horn.

The !Xũ also asked the new moon for rain (Bleek 1928a: 122; Lebzelter 1934: 6). Their term for the new moon was interchangeable with that of the 'high god' Huwe (Bleek 1928a: 123; see also Estermann 1979 [1956]: 12). In the 1960s, they still associated the new moon with success in the hunt (Viegas Guerreiro 1968: 97, 298). Appeals to the new moon are absent in recent Zu/'hoã ethnographies, but the same idiom ('struck') is used when an arrow finds its mark and when the new moon first appears (Shostak 2000: 127). Orpen (1874: 5) reported seeing southern San throw sand in the air and shouting out on first seeing the new moon, while the //Xegwi (also southern San) believed that the new moon brought rain (Potgieter 1955: 29). An identification of both the dark and new moon with rain is made in Greef's (1996: 12) Namibian Khoisan story from which this chapter takes its title.

Observations of this kind led some authors, most notably Dorothea Bleek (1928a: 122; 1928b: 27) and Schapera (1930: 177), to characterize Bushman religions in terms of 'moon worship'. Guenther (1999: 64–5) rightly criticizes this view, but misrepresents its basis. It had nothing to do with the timing of healing dances. Prosaic indigenous explanations for dancing at full moon cannot explain ritual attitudes to the waxing moon. Far from the !Xũ and Zu/'hoã (!Kung ethno-linguistic groups) showing a 'discrepancy' of views regarding the moon (ibid.: 65), the summarized evidence indicates considerable consistency.

It was widely considered the height of disrespect for a hunter to look at the moon when game had been shot and the poison had yet to take effect (Bleek 1928b: 16; Vedder 1937: 433–4). For the /Xam, such disrespect would prompt the Moon to swallow the game's fat or dilute the hunter's poison with 'Moon's water' (Bleek and Lloyd 1911: 67; Lewis-Williams 2000: 250). Guenther points out that in his role as protector of the game, the /Xam Moon shares an identity with /Kaggen (1989: 81). While there is much to be said for this, to infer that the moon must therefore have been 'the adversary ... of hunters' (ibid.) is to disregard the contrary evidence. The paradox dissolves if we grant that the Moon stands in a similar relationship to the availability of game (and their fatness) as does the New Maiden. If the menarcheal girl ate game procured by anyone other than her father, or gazed upon springbok, she would invite identical consequences to those befalling the disrespectful hunter (Bleek and Lloyd 1911: 77). By adhering to protocol, she mirrors the moon's role in helping ensure hunters' success.

/Xam Myths of the Moon's Creation

/Kaggen created the Moon (implicitly the new moon) by throwing a curling veld-shoe or feather into the sky. Hewitt (1986: 213–25) analysed four versions of this myth, three from Bleek and Lloyd and one from von Wielligh's collection. In the Bleek and Lloyd versions, the action is precipitated by /Kaggen's intervention in the butchery of an eland, where – by piercing the eland's gall bladder – he angrily eclipses the sun, producing total darkness (cf. Lewis-Williams 1997). Where a shoe is used to remedy the darkness, its dirtiness and redness – being covered in red dust – is emphasized, accounting for the redness of the moon. Arguably, the 'soiled shoe' is a menstruating vagina (cf. Dundes 1980: 47; Vinnicombe 1975: 386), adding to /Kaggen's repertoire of gender ambiguous traits (Hewitt 1986: 153–4). In /Han≠kass'o's version (L.VIII, 6: 6505–85) the feather – licked and used to wipe gall-fluid from /Kaggen's eyes – is also soiled. Having thrown up the feather, /Kaggen instructs it on waxing and waning. The narrator concludes by describing nocturnal porcupine hunting, made possible by /Kaggen's creation.

According to Hewitt,[24] both of //Kabbo's versions end in similar fashion, with the narrator extolling the social benefits of /Kaggen's act, permitting – *inter alia* – nocturnal hunting. I was unable to corroborate this. Hewitt may have had in mind /Kabbo' narrative about the Sun's conflict with the Moon, featuring a lengthy digression on the benefits of moonlight in allowing springbok hunters to return at night (B. XVI: 1526–52).

In von Wielligh's version,[25] /Kaggen made for himself a pair of shoes. But the right shoe chafed or pinched his foot, so he instructed his daughter the Hammerkop (a bird) to soften it by throwing it into the waterhole. The shoe may have been bloodied as a result of the chafing – which would accord with the redness of the shoe in other versions. We learn elsewhere (von Wielligh 1921 [1]: 110) that the Hammerkop was responsible for informing the Watersnake whenever 'young maids' polluted the waterhole with ash. Dwelling at the bottom of the waterhole, the Watersnake is enraged by the polluting shoe and causes the water to freeze overnight. When the Hammerkop retrieves the shoe, it comes out with a piece of ice attached. Now /Kaggen is angered, and throws the ice-bound shoe into the air. The Hammerkop calls on the Windbird to take the shoe up high: 'so that we will have light at night!'.[26] Hewitt's translation ends with the summary sentence: 'The shoe with the piece of ice on it then became the moon', but von Wielligh's text continues: 'When the ancestors saw the moon for the first time, they covered their faces with their hands and praised the moon. Ever since, they had light at night and could hunt porcupines and wait for game at waterholes to shoot them' (1921 [1]: 98). The Sun, jealous of the moon, fires arrows that melt the ice until only /Kaggen's shoe remains. People cried because the moon had died; in response to their crying, the Watersnake created a fountain on the moon to fill up the shoe, renewing the cycle. So, the Watersnake, standing in the same relation to menstruants as !Khwa, is responsible for the moon's waxing.

Moon and Hunting in Practice

In recent Bushman ethnographies, references to nocturnal hunting are rare (Marshall 1960: 342; Cashdan 1986: 164; Valiente-Noailles 1993: 64). Nevertheless, 1970s research (Crowell and Hitchcock 1978) indicated that the most productive strategy traditionally practised by the Zu/'hoãsi of Dobe (western Botswana) and Eastern Khoe Bushmen along the Nata River (eastern Botswana) was *night-stand ambush hunting by water sources*. This was restricted to dry-season moonlit nights (normally during the gibbous moon). At this season, water-dependent game aggregate around remaining water-sources. Many species do a considerable proportion of their drinking after sunset, approaching by game-trails (Weir and Davidson 1965; du Preez and Grobler 1977). By exploiting these regularities and optimizing available light, moon-conscious hunters reduce their search-time, greatly increase encounter rates and make it possible to get close to prey. The strategy is similarly productive for the Tanzanian Hadza (Hawkes et al. 1991: table 2; Bunn et al. 1988: 424).

Presumably because of the abundance of big game before the later nineteenth century, descriptions of Khoisan nocturnal hunting – explicitly or implicitly lunar phase-locked and mostly comprising waterhole ambushes – are more common in earlier accounts.[27] Of the /Xam, in addition to the moonlit hunting that completes two of the moon-creation narratives, and the account of hunters returning laden with springbok meat at full moon (B.XVI: 1542–3), there are numerous passages in the Bleek and Lloyd collection referring to nocturnal hunting of springbok, the /Xam's principal prey antelope. Holub (1881: 34) reported that springbok were particularly susceptible to dry-season ambush hunting by waterholes (see also Chapman 1971 [1868] II: 141).

It can be inferred that similar strategies would have played a much greater role in the economies of the early Later Stone Age, 12 to 25 thousand years ago, and Middle Stone Age, between 25 and 250 thousand years ago, when spears were the primary weapon and proximity to prey was therefore at an even greater premium

(Knight et al. 1995). It should be recalled that the 'sex strike' model accords dry-season nutritional stress a critical role in the evolution of symbolic culture. The threat posed by lions during night-stand hunting is mitigated by the fact that lions do most of their nocturnal hunting when there is no moonlight (Joubert and Joubert 1997: 86–8). This carving up of lunar time between humans and lions is echoed in a Zu/'hoãsi belief about lunar eclipses: 'on very bright nights a lion may cover the moon's face with a great paw, giving himself darkness for better hunting' (Thomas 1960: 43; cf. Marshall 1986: 183; Biesele 1993: 24, 111, 114).

Trance Dancing and 'Honeymoon'

Full moon was a common occasion for a trance dance (e.g. Marshall 1969; Barnard 1979: 73, 1992: 253), sometimes indigenously explained in terms of the light afforded.[28] Trance dances were also often held on the return of a successful big-game hunt. Hunting of large game (e.g. eland or giraffe) frequently lasted several days (Marshall 1959: 354, fn.1, 1961: 239); it is likely, therefore, that – like ambush-hunting – logistic hunts occurred during the gibbous moon. Indirect support for such a coincidence includes Estermann's account of a !Xũ hunting ceremony after killing 'a big antelope', which took place 'at the full moon or a little later' (1979 [1956]: 12), and Mapote's account of how Maluti Bushmen prepared pigment for rock painting (How 1962: 35). Haematite had to be ground and roasted, outside, under a *full moon*, by a post-menopausal woman. It was mixed with the blood of a *freshly* killed eland. The indigenous ideal appears to be one in which the successful conclusion of a big game hunt, trance dance and full moon would all coincide.

Consistent with the Cape Khoekhoe accounts, the //Xegwi considered full moon to be the ideal time for surrendering game as an initial bride-service gift (Potgieter 1955: 11–12). A //Xegwi expression when given something nice to eat was: 'Au! the moon is full' (1955: 30). For the Zu/'hoãsi: 'The round full moon is a sign of satisfaction' (Marshall 1986: 181), while for the /Xam, the full moon was fatness personified, it had 'put on a big stomach' (L.II, 6: 657). In short, full moon is the proper time for feasting.

Myth as Deep History

G/wi and G//ana mythology addresses the origin of the sex-based division of labour in the idiom of lunar periodicity. Domestic pressure from a woman and her children – or from the first woman – motivates the first man to go hunting (Silberbauer 1965: 101; Valiente-Noailles 1993: 192–3). In his 1790 travelogue,

Le Vaillant reported a behavioural counterpart to this logic. Asking the Khoekhoe leader of a Bushman band why they raided livestock, he was told that when there was no longer any meat, the women took off their pubic aprons and slapped the men's faces with them. The raiders' successful return inaugurated a phase of feasting and intimacy for as long as the meat lasted (Glenn 1996: 43). That Khoisan women might insult husbands in precisely this manner is corroborated by Hoernlé (1918: 69).

The following is a condensed rendition of a story told by a Namibian Khoisan storyteller:

> The Moon is nearly dead. Tonight it is a bowl throwing water to the earth:... Tomorrow night the Moon will start to grow again. Time, too, grows on the Moon... We are the Moon People. After we die, the good people ... they walk to the Moon. Everyone is very happy and content in the Moon Kalahari... You say I have told you a charming story? You wish you could tell me that you believe it to be true. But you have to tell me that Americans travelled to the Moon in some kind of super aeroplane... The Moon is a desert, you say... You say you're sorry to have to tell me this. Why are you sorry? I know you're not a liar and a thief – and I, I am also not a liar and a thief... But tell me this: when the Americans travelled to the Moon, was the Moon full?... When the Moon has grown until it's full it is a wonderful place ... not, of course, when it is dying. (Greef 1996: 12–14)

I suggest that such narratives know what they are talking about. Treated with appropriate respect, they are as important to understanding our species' recent African origin as archaeology or genetics.

Conclusion

Among the Khoisan we have traces of a lunar encoded, binary temporal structure. Dark moon is associated with menstruation, seclusion and hunger; it is a period of awesome supernatural potency, threatening cultural reversal and excessive wetness. The mobilization of this potency to secure future abundance begins at new moon. Any sexual connotations of this period are of a parodic, anti-marital character (incestuous or 'animal'). Hunting is a preoccupation of the waxing phase. At full moon, men normatively surrender meat to in-laws, inaugurating a period of cooking, feasting, and marital sex. In terms of supernatural potency, the full moon is marked by a community-wide healing dance. The waning moon is unmarked in terms of ritual power. These structural oppositions testify to the continuing conceptual force of a unifying lunar periodicity to economic, sexual and ritual life. Some of these patterns might be explained in terms of the moon as metaphor for life, death and regeneration. Such an approach could readily equate menstruation ('temporary death') with dark moon. But would it also predict marriage at full moon? Where would rituals of sexual licence fit in? Would wetness be predicted at dark moon or full? Inexplicable on any other basis, the beliefs and practices outlined here confirm the predictions of 'sex-strike' theory. It would appear, therefore, that there is more structure to Khoisan cosmology than Guenther would grant. Far from negating binary structures, ambiguity and paradox may be essential to their construction (cf. Power and Watts 1999).

Notes

1. I am grateful for an Honorary Research Associateship in the Department of Archaeology, University of Cape Town. I also thank the Manuscripts and Archives Library, University of Cape Town, for permission to cite from the Bleek and Lloyd collection. Thanks also to Janine van Niekerk for translations of von Wielligh, and Alan Barnard, Chris Knight, Camilla Power, and Elena Mouriki for critical comments; and to the editors of this volume.
2. McBrearty and Brooks 2000 for review; Watts 1999; D'Errico et al. 2001; Henshilwood et al. 2001; Hovers et al. 2003.
3. Onset of the Late Pleistocene, 128ka, the beginning of the Last Interglacial.
4. Watts 1999; Wendorf et al. 1993; earlier within the African tropics, McBrearty 2001; Barham 2002.
5. See D'Andrade (1995) re 'agenda hopping'.
6. This distinction is more evocatively rendered by Wilmsen's terms of 'Creator' and 'Administrator' deities (Wilmsen 1989, 1999)
7. Nine of 24 authors refer exclusively to dances at the appearance of the new moon: (Raven-Hart [RH] 1971: 35, 218, 239, 388, 406, 423, 463, 487; Schapera 1933: 37); five refer to both new and full moon dances (RH 1971: 56, 321, 384, 394, 433); six refer only to full moon (RH 1971: 148, 163, 205, 297, 349; Schapera 1933: 211); two probably refer to full moon dances (RH 1971: 127; Schapera 1933: 139); and two are indeterminate (RH 1971: 20, 310).
8. For further references see Boeving quoted in Kolbe 1731 [1]: 97; Leguat [1698] in RH 1971: 433; Sparrman 1975 [1785-86]: 205; Gusinde 1966: 39; Guenther 1999: 64–5.
9. Schouten's account appears to have been copied (unaccredited) by Vogel in 1679 (Raven-Hart 1971: 218), and it is Vogel whom Kolbe (1731: 97) credits when repeating the account. While Schouten made no mention of lunar periodicity, this can reasonably be inferred on the basis of the wider literature. Vogel's

account explicitly links face-painting with a red stone with new moon dances. The reference to painting with red ochre is from Kolbe (1731 (2): 201).

10. See Valentyn ([1726] 1971: 261). His editor, E.Raidt suggests (260 fn.15) this detail was taken from Schreyer (1681: 40, unseen), he also reports two similar accounts (Meister 1677: 254, unseen) and Ten Rhyne (1933 [1686]: 141). Ten Ryhne asserts that this was done in honour of the sun, but seen against the wider body of Khoisan beliefs and practices, a lunar association seems likely. That he also states that the hurling of the balls into the water was accompanied 'with a great noise' would be consistent with a new moon ritual according to the derived predictions of the 'sex strike' model.

11. Wuras 1929 [1858]: 294; Stow 1905: 114–15; Kirby 1933; Engelbrecht 1936: 148.

12. Dapper 1933 [1668]: 75; Ten Rhyne 1933 [1686]: 140–141; Valentyn 1971 [1726], vol. 2: 95, 261.

13. Peter Kolbe (1791, trs. Medley 1731) was probably the most perceptive and certainly the most scientific of early observers (Raum 1998; Barnard 1992: 253). For Hahn see (1881: 41). As discussed by Raum, it is unfortunate that hardly any Khoisan specialists have used Kolbe's original text.

14. Bleek 1873, 1875; Lloyd 1889; Bleek and Lloyd 1911; Bleek 1923, 1929a, 1931–1936, 1936; Hewitt 1986; Guenther 1989; Lewis-Williams 2000; James 2001; and unpublished notebooks. For 'sidereal elements', see Hewitt 1986: 59; Guenther 1999: 64, 231. Where notebooks in the Bleek and Lloyd archive (University of Cape Town Manuscripts and Archives Library) are referred to, Wilhelm Bleek's notebooks are indicated by the letter B followed by the notebook number in Roman numerals and pages in Arabic numerals. Lucy Lloyd's notebooks are indicated by the letter L followed by the informant number in Roman numerals (II = //Kabbo, V = Dia!kwain, VI = !Kweiten ta //ken, VIII = /Han≠kass'o), followed by notebook number and page numbers in Arabic numerals. Where Dorothea Bleek's notebooks are referred to (relating to fieldwork with Nharo and !Xũ), citation is by archive number (e.g. A.3.16), followed by page number.

15. 'Water' or 'rain', see Bleek and Lloyd 1911: 149. Hewitt (1986: 284) mistakenly cites L. V, 6: 4393 as the source where !Khwa is used to refer to 'menstrual fluid'. Neither 4393 nor its reverse mentions !Khwa. Hewitt probably had in mind one or all of the following passages, firstly on pp. 4389 rev. and 4390 rev., where, in the context of describing the identity of young men with menarcheal girls, Dia!kwain said: 'he should be afraid of the girls, for the girl's rain would come out upon him'. A similar injunction is given on p. 4399 rev., with a variant on pp. 4405 rev. and 4406 rev., where he talks of the precautions the girl must take in preparing food for her parents, otherwise: 'her rain/water would come out of her parents' teeth'. In all three passages,

the term !Khwa seems to be used as a circumlocution for menstrual blood itself, rather than designating the intervention of the eponymous supernatural being who punishes breaches of menstrual observances. No mediating being is required in these cases of contagion by direct contact.

16. Guenther's example of Nharo belief concerning the waning moon carrying dead souls has a /Xam counterpart (Bleek and Lloyd 1911: 399). Hewitt's (1986: 93) statement that the /Xam did not relate any celestial body to illness, while strictly correct, needs qualification in so far as death was associated with the waning moon.

17. L.II, 1: 285–287, continued L.II, 2: 292; Bleek 1928a: 122; Marshall 1986: 181. Lloyd comments (L.II, 2: 291 rev.) that 'the moon should not be she in this tale as it is not a woman'. However, I suspect that the gender assignation may have been correct, as this narrative concerns the 'great moon' with a stomach. For 'wife to the waxing moon', see Lewis-Williams 2000: 247; L. VIII 28: 8843–46; see also Silberbauer 1965: 101 re. the G/wi.

18. Moon-menstruation metaphors, see Power and Watts 1997: 544 with refs; Schultze 1907: 296; Wilmsen 1999: 86, 89, 127.

19. Bleek and Lloyd 1911: 36–41; L.II, 5: 565–624; L.II, 8: 811–882; L.V, 5: 4265–4288; von Wielligh 1921 [1]: 145-148. Re 'tabooed to girls...' see Bleek 1991–36, Part V: 303; Hewitt 1986: 281.

20. The attribution of menorrhagia to the Leopard Tortoise or 'Great Tortoise' (*Geochelone pardalis*) is probably due to its habit of urinating copiously both when laying eggs (Branch 1988: 26) and if picked up. This is the largest of southern African chelonians. Copious urination when picked up (a stress response) is a common trait across species. /Xam girls were instructed that if they found a tortoise (apparently *Psammobates geometricus*, cf. L.VIII, 21: 7843), they were not to pick it up with their hands but to use a stick to put it into their collecting bag 'lest the tortoise should soil her' (L.V, 6: 4383). It may also be significant that Angulate tortoises in the western Cape (*Chersina angulata*) have bright red abdominal plates on the plastron, giving rise to their Afrikaans name of 'rooipens' (red belly) (Branch 1988: 27). In Dia!kwain's version, the protagonist is 'a great water schilpad' (L.V, 5: 4265), probably the freshwater terrapin (*Pelamadusa sp.*); this might also be the unidentified, river-dwelling creature in Qing's version of the myth. For 'always ill with bleeding', see (L.II, 5: 568); 'after the moon died' (Bleek and Lloyd 1911: 38), 'male passer-by' (ibid.; L.II, 5: 569), 'seeking honey', (L.V, 5: 4265; Orpen 1874: 9), 'grandmother' (L.II, 5: 569), or 'elder sister' (Bleek and Lloyd 1911: 39). 'Flesh decayed' (L.II, 5: 566) and 'water from the moon' (von Wieilligh 1921 [1]: 147). Cf. the recent study by Waldman (2003).

21. For 'new maidens' see (Hewitt 1986: 280; Lewis-Williams 2000: 279); for 'fires extinguished', Viegas Guerreiro (1968: 221); for 'cooking flesh'

(Guenther 1989: 106–9; Hewitt 1986: 80–81; Bleek and Lloyd 1911: 199–205).

22. For 'conceptually red' see (B. II: 378, 382; B. III: 440, 458; B. IV: 551-560; L. II, 6: 656), 'create the moon' (B. II: 384, 424; L. II, 4: 484–5), 'game to be killed' (Lewis-Williams 2000: 250), 'cold' things are red (B. II: 378–9) 'similar conceptions among other groups' (Viegas Guerreiro 1968: 298; Köhler 1978/9: 20; Marshall 1986: 180).

23. Bleek 1929a: 306; Lewis-Williams 2000: 248. Also for 'ritualised greeting of the new moon' (Bleek and Lloyd 1911: 57). For 'success in the hunt', (Lewis-Williams 2000: 249–51; James 2001: 75–6, 194). 'Moon horn' (B. III: 455; L. II, 6: 654); 'hunter's bow' (B. V: 588). For Nharo informants, (Power and Watts 1999: 113); this is the second of two quotations appearing at the top of p.113, incorrectly cited as from Lucy Lloyd's /Xam notebooks. The correct citation is A3.16: 328 rev., recorded 28.2.21, informant's name //axas (a woman). The punctuation is added. See also (Bleek m.s. A.3. 18: 369). For 'not at full moon' (ibid; A.3.16: 302 rev.); Nharo appeal (1928b: 26) Kxoe appeals, (Köhler 1978/79: 17), and others: the !Xũ (Bleek and Lloyd 1911: 415, cf. Dickens 1996 re linguistic identity), Zu/'hoãsi (Wilhelm 1954; Köhler 1978/79: 17) and G/wi (Silberbauer 1981: 108).

24. Hewitt, 1986: 219, 222. For //Kabbo's versions: (B.II, 379–433 [The more precise citation for this version is B.II: 379-390, continued on 421–428 and B.III: 429–433], and L.II, 4: 482-6). //Kabbo's version to Lucy Lloyd makes no mention of benefits arising from the moon's creation and in the version given to Wilhelm Bleek, the only explicit social benefit occurs in the line: '/Kaggen said: "people shall see bushes in the dark..."' (B.II: 386). Hewitt may have misread the passage at the end of the narrative (B.III: 432–3), concerning hunting by sunlight.

25. 1921 [1]: 97–100; see also Hewitt 1986: 217. For /Kaggen's shoes, compare 'sandals' (Lewis-Williams 2000: 15).

26. The Windbird manifests as a whirlwind (a detail omitted by Hewitt), which would, on the basis of the Bleek and Lloyd material, link the magic action to !Khwa's typical *modus operandi*. Given that the Watersnake is fulfilling equivalent functions to !Khwa, it could be argued that the Watersnake was ultimately responsible for the whirlwind.

27. For 'abundance of big game', Passarge [1904] in Wilmsen 1997: 80; ibid [1907]: 175–6. For 'earlier accounts' see Wikar 1935 [1779]: 103; Tindall 1856: 22; Livingstone 1857: 161–2, 165–6; Chapman 1971 [1868] II: 50; Hahn 1870: 103; Passarge [1905] in Wilmsen 1997: 257–8; Wilhelm 1954: 124. For references to '/Xam's principal prey' see Bleek and Lloyd 1911: 283; Bleek 1931-36, Pt. V: 311; L. II, 6: 629–630; L. II, 14: 1374–1376; L. VIII, 14: 7224 rev. – 7227.

28. Gusinde 1966: 39; Guenther 1989: 82. Guenther reports that it was because he was told by a Nharo man that they danced at full moon so as not to 'bump into each other' that he ceased all enquiry into the 'stock notion of "moon worship"' (ibid.: 82, see also 1999: 64). In a manner alarmingly reminiscent of Langhansz, Guenther seems not to have noticed that all the recorded 'appeals' to the moon concerned the new rather than the full moon. For references to 'trance dances' following a successful big-game hunt, see Metzger 1950: 74–8; Marshall 1969: 355–6; Barnard 1979: 73; Katz 1982: 39.

References

Barham, L. (2002), 'Systematic pigment use in the Middle Pleistocene of south-central Africa' *Current Anthropology* 43: 181–90.

Barnard, A. (1979), 'Nharo Bushman medicine and medicine men', *Africa* 49: 68–80.

—— (1992), *Hunters and Herders of Southern Africa*, Cambridge: Cambridge University Press.

Biesele, M. (1993), *Women Like Meat*, Johannesburg: Witwatersrand University Press.

Bleek, D. (1923), *The Mantis and his Friends*, Cape Town: Maskew Miller.

—— (1928a), 'Bushmen of Central Angola', *Bantu Studies* 3: 105–25.

—— (1928b), *The Naron: a Bushman tribe of the Central Kalahari*, Cambridge: Cambridge University Press.

—— (1929a), 'Bushman folklore', *Africa* 2: 302–13.

—— (1929b), *Comparative Vocabularies of Bushman Languages*, London: Cambridge University Press.

Bleek, D. (ed.), (1931–6), 'Customs and beliefs of the /Xam Bushmen: From material collected by Dr. W.H.I. Bleek and Miss L.C. Lloyd between 1870 and 1880', *Bantu Studies* 5: 167–79 (Part I); 6: 47–63 (Part II); 6: 233–49 (Part III); 6: 323–42 (Part IV); 7: 297–312 (Part V); 7: 375–92 (Part VI); 9: 1–47 (Part VII); 10: 131–62 (Part VIII).

—— (ed.), (1936), 'Special speech of animals and Moon used by the /Xam Bushmen: From material collected by Dr. W.H.I. Bleek and Miss. L.C. Lloyd between 1870 and 1880', *Bantu Studies* 10: 163–99.

Bleek, W. (1873), 'Report of Dr. Bleek concerning his researches into the Bushman language and customs presented to the Honourable the House of Assembly', Cape Town: Cape Parliamentary Papers A17–'73.

—— (1874), 'On resemblances in Bushman and Australian mythology', *Cape Monthly Magazine* February 1874: 98–102.

—— (1875), *A Brief Account of Bushman Folklore and Other Texts*, Cape Town: J.C. Juta.

Bleek, W.H.I. and L.C. Lloyd (1911), *Specimens of Bushman Folklore*, London: Allen.

Bjerre, J. (1960), *Kalahari*, London: Michael Joseph.

Branch, B. (1988), *Field Guide to the Snakes and Other Reptiles of Southern Africa*, Cape Town: Struik.

Bunn, H.T., L.E. Bartram and E.M. Kroll (1988), 'Variability in bone assemblage formation from Hadza hunting, scavenging, and carcass processing', *Journal of Anthropological Archaeology* 7: 412–57.

Cashdan, E.A. (1986), 'Hunter-gatherers of the northern Kalahari', in R. Vossen and K. Keuthmann (eds), *Contemporary Studies on Khoisan I*, Hamburg: Helmut Buske Verlag (Quellen zur Khoisan-Forschung 5.1).

Chapman, J. ([1868] 1971), *Travels in the Interior of South Africa, 1849–1863*, E. Tabler (ed.), Cape Town: A.A. Balkema, 2 vols.

Crowell, A.L. and R.K. Hitchcock (1978), 'Basarwa ambush hunting in Botswana', *Botswana Notes and Records* 10: 37–51.

D'Andrade, R. (1995), *The Development of Cognitive Anthropology*, Cambridge: Cambridge University Press.

Dapper, O. ([1668] 1933), 'Kaffraria, or land of the Hottentots', trs. I. Schapera, in I. Schapera (ed.), *The Early Cape Hottentots*, Cape Town: The Van Riebeeck Society, 14: 6–77.

Deacon, T. (1997), *The Symbolic Species*, London: Penguin Books.

D'Errico, F., C. Henshilwood and P. Nilssen (2001), 'An engraved bone fragment from ca. 70 ka-year-old Middle Stone Age levels at Blombos Cave, South Africa', *Antiquity* 73: 309–18.

Dickens, P. (1996), 'The place of Lloyd's !Kun texts in the Ju dialects', in J. Deacon and T. Dowson (eds), *Voices from the Past: /Xam Bushmen and the Bleek and Lloyd Collection*, Johannesburg: Witwatersrand University Press, 161–211.

Dundes, A. (1980), *Interpreting Folklore*, Bloomington: Indiana University Press.

du Preez, J.S. and I.D. Grobler (1977), 'Drinking times and behaviour at waterholes of some game species in the Etosha National Park', *Madoqua* 10: 61–9.

Durkheim, E. ([1912] 1965), *The Elementary Forms of Religious Life*, New York: Free Press.

Engelbrecht, J. A. (1936), *The Koranna*, Cape Town: Maskew Miller.

Estermann, C. ([1956] 1979), 'The Non-Bantu Peoples; the Ambo Ethnic Group', in G. D. Gibson (ed.), *The Ethnography of Southwestern Angola*, New York: African Publishing Company, Vol 1.

Frazer, J.G. 1900. (2nd edn.), *The Golden Bough*, London: Macmillan, 3 vols.

Gennep, van A. ([1909] 1960), *The Rites of Passage*, London: Routledge and Kegan Paul.

Glenn, I. (1996), 'The Bushmen in early South African literature' in P. Skotnes (ed.), *Miscast: Negotiating the Presence of the Bushmen*, Cape Town: University of Cape Town Press, 41–9.

Greef, D.M. (1996), 'The Moon People', in K. Fischer-Buder (ed.), *The Moon People and other Namibian Stories*, Windhoek: New Namibia Books, 12–14.

Grevenbroek, J. ([1695] 1933), 'An account of the Hottentots', trs. B. Farrington, in I. Schapera (ed.), *The Early Cape Hottentots*, Cape Town: The Van Riebeeck Society 14: 161–299.

Guenther, M. G. (1989), *Bushmen Folktales: Oral Traditions of the Nharo of Botswana and the /Xam of the Cape*, Stuttgart: Franz Steiner Verlag Wiesbaden, Studien zur Kulturkunde 93.

——(1999), *Tricksters and Trancers: Bushman Religion and Society*, Bloomington and Indianapolis: Indiana University Press.

Gusinde, M. (1966) *Von Gelben und Schwarzen Buschmännern*, Gratz: Akademische Drukund Verlagsanstalt.

Hahn, T. (1870), 'Die Buschmänner', *Globus* 18: 65–8, 81–5, 102–5, 120–3, 140–3, 153–5.

——(1881), *Tsuni!-Goam: The Supreme Being of the Khoi-Khoi,* London: Trübner.

Hawkes, K., J.F. O'Connell and N.G. Blurton-Jones (1991), 'Hunting income patterns among the Hadza', *Philosophical Transactions of the Royal Society of London,* Series B, 334: 243–51.

Heinz, H. J. (1994), *Social Organization of the !Kõ Bushmen*, Köln: Rüdiger Köppe Verlag, Quellen zur Khoisan-Forschung 10.

Henshilwood, C., J. Sealy, R. Yates, C. Cruz-Uribe, P. Goldberg, F. Grine, R. Klein, C. Poggenpoel, K. Van Niekerk, and I. Watts (2001), 'Blombos Cave, southern Cape, South Africa: preliminary report on the 1992–1999 excavations of the Middle Stone Age levels', *Journal of Archaeological Science* 28: 421–48.

——, F. d'Errico, R. Yates, Z. Jacobs, C. Tribolo, G. Duller, N. Mercier, J. Sealy, H. Valladas, I. Watts, and A. Wintle (2002), 'Emergence of modern human behaviour: Middle Stone Age engravings from South Africa', *Science* 295: 1278–80.

——, F. d'Errico, M. Vanhaeren, K. van Niekerk, Z. Jacobs (2004), 'Middle Stone Age shell beads from South Africa', *Science* 304: 404.

Hewitt, R. L. (1986), *Structure, Meaning and Ritual in the Narratives of the Southern San*, Hamburg: Helmut Buske Verlag, (Quellen zur Khoisanforschung 2).

Hoff, A. (1997), 'The Water Snake of the Khoekhoen and /Xam', *South African Archaeological Bulletin* 52: 21–37.

Holub, E. (1881), *Seven Years in South Africa*, London: Sampson Low, Marston, Searle, and Rivington, Vol 1.

Hovers, E., S. Ilani, O. Bar-Yosef, and B. Vandermeersch. (2003), 'An early case of color symbolism', *Current Anthropology* 44: 491–522.

How, M.W. (1962), *The Mountain Bushmen of Basutoland*, Pretoria: J.L. van Schaik.

James, A. (2001), *The First Bushman's Path: Stories, Songs and Testimonies of the /Xam of the Northern Cape*, Pietermaritzburg: University of Natal Press.

Joubert, D. and B. Joubert (1997), *The Lions of Savuti: Hunting with the Moon*, National Geographic Society.

Katz, R. (1982), *Boiling Energy*, Cambridge: Harvard University Press.

Kirby, P. (1933), 'The reed-flute ensembles of South Africa', *Journal of the Royal Anthropological Institute* 63: 313–389.

Knight, C.D. (1991), *Blood Relations*, New Haven and London: Yale University Press.

Knight, C., C. Power, I. Watts (1995), 'The human symbolic revolution: A Darwinian account', *Cambridge Archaeological Journal* 5: 75–114.

Köhler, O. (1978–9), 'Mythus, Glaube und Magie bei den Kxoe-Buschmännern', *Journal of the South West African Scientific Society* 33: 9–49.

Kolbe, P. (1719), *Caput Bonae Spei Hodiernum*, Nürnberg: Monath.

—— (1731), *The Present State of the Cape of Good Hope,* trs. G. Medley, London: W. Innys, 2 Vols.

Laidler, P.W. (1928), 'The magic medicine of the Hottentots', *South African Journal of Science* 25: 433–47.

Lebzelter, V. (1934), *Eingeborenenkulturen von Südwestafrika*, Leipzig: Verlag Karl W. Hiersemann.

Lévi-Strauss, C. (1970–1981), *Mythologiques: An Introduction to a Science of Mythology,* London: Jonathan Cape, 4 Vols.

—— (1978), *The Origin of Table Manners*, London: Jonathan Cape, Introduction to a Science of Mythology Vol. 3.

Lewis-Williams, J.D. (1981), *Believing and Seeing*, London: Academic Press.

—— (1997), 'The Mantis, the Eland and the Meercats', in: P. McAllister (ed.), *Culture and the Commonplace: Anthropological Essays in Honour of David Hammond-Tooke*, Johannesburg: Witwatersrand University Press 195–216.

Lewis-Williams, J.D. (ed.), (2000), *Stories that Float from Afar*, Cape Town: David Phillip.

Lewis-Williams, J. D. and M. Besiele (1978), 'Eland hunting rituals among the northern and southern San groups', *Africa* 48: 117–34.

Livingstone, D. (1857), *Missionary Travels and Researches in South Africa*, London: John Murray.

Lloyd, L. (1889), *A Short Account of further Bushman Material Collected,* London: David Nutt.

Marshall, L. (1959), 'Marriage among !Kung Bushmen', *Africa* 29: 335–65.

—— (1960), '/Kung Bushman bands', *Africa* 30: 325–55.

—— (1961), 'Sharing, talking and giving: relief of tension among the !Kung Bushmen', *Africa* 31: 231–49.

—— (1969), 'The medicine dance of the !Kung Bushmen', *Africa* 39: 347–81.

—— (1986), 'Some Bushmen star lore', in R. Vossen and K. Keuthmann (eds), *Contemporary Studies on Khoisan, 2*, Hamburg: Buske Verlag (Quellen zur Khoisan-Forschung 4).

McBrearty, S. (2001), 'The Middle Pleistocene of East Africa', in Barham, L. and Robson-Brown, K. (eds), *Human Roots: Africa and Asia in the Middle Pleistocene*, Bristol: Western Academic and Specialist Press, 81–98.

McBrearty, S. and A. Brooks (2000), 'The revolution that wasn't: a new interpretation of the origin of modern human behavior', *Journal of Human Evolution* 39: 453–563.

Metzger, F. (1950), *Narro and his Clan*, Windhoek: John Meinert.

Oppenheimer, S. (2003), *Out of Eden: The Peopling of the World*, London: Constable.

Orpen, J.M. (1874), 'A glimpse into the mythology of the Maluti Bushmen', *Cape Monthly Magazine* 9 (49): 1–13.

Potgieter, E. F. (1955), *The Disappearing Bushmen of Lake Chrissie*, Pretoria: J. L. Van Schaik.

Power, C. and L. Aiello. (1997), 'Female proto-symbolic strategies', in Lori D. Hager (ed.), *Women In Human Evolution*, Routledge: London and New York, 153–71.

Power, C. and I. Watts (1997), 'The woman with the zebra's penis: gender, mutability and performance', *Journal of the Royal Anthropological Institute* 3: 1–24.

Power, C. and I. Watts (1999), 'First gender, wrong sex', in H. Moore, T. Sanders and B. Kaare (eds), *Those who Play with Fire*, London: Athlone Press 101–132.

Raven-Hart, R. (1971), *Cape of Good Hope 1652–1702. The First Fifty Years of Dutch Colonisation as seen by Callers*, Cape Town: Balkema, 2 Vols.

Raum, J. (1998), 'Reflections on rereading Peter Kolb with regard to the cultural heritage of the Khoisan', in A. Bank (ed.), *The Proceedings of the Khoisan Identities and Cultural Heritage Conference, July 1997*, Cape Town: The Institute for Historical Research, University of the Western Cape and Infosource CC, 172–79.

Schapera, I. (1930), *The Khoisan Peoples of South Africa*, London: Routledge.

Schapera, I. (ed.), (1933), *The Early Cape Hottentots*, Cape Town: The Van Riebeeck Society Vol. 14.

Schmidt, P.W. (1933), *Der Ursprung der Gottesidee*, Die Religionen der Urvolker Afrikas, Band 4, Münster: Ascherdorff.

Schmidt, S. (1979), 'The rain bull of the South African Bushmen', *African Studies* 38: 201–24.

Schmidt, S. (1986), 'Heiseb — Trickster und Gott der Nama und Damara in Südwestafrika/Namibia', in R. Vossen and K. Keuthmann (eds), *Contemporary*

Studies on Khoisan 2, Hamburg: Helmut Buske Verlag, Quellen zur Khoisan-Forschung 5 (2): 205–56.

Schultze, L. (1907), *Aus Namaland und Kalahari*, Jena: Gustav Fischer.

Silberbauer, G. (1965), *Report to the Government of Bechuanaland on the Bushman Survey*, Gaberones: Bechuanaland Government.

——(1981), *Hunter and Habitat in the Central Kalahari Desert*, Cambridge: Cambridge University Press.

Shostak, M. (2000), *Return to Nisa*, Cambridge Massachusetts and London: Harvard University Press.

Solomon, A. (1992), 'Gender, representation and power in San ethnography and rock art', *Journal of Anthropological Archaeology* 11: 291–329.

Sparrman, A. (1975 [1785–86]), *A Voyage to the Cape of Good Hope*, V. Forbes (ed.), Cape Town: Van Riebeeck Society.

Stow, G.W. (1905), *The Native Races of South Africa*, London: Swan Sonnenschein.

Ten Rhyne, W. (1933 [1686]), 'An account of the Cape of Good Hope', trs. B. Farrington, in I. Schapera (ed.), *The early Cape Hottentots*, Cape Town: The Van Riebeeck Society, 14: 84–157.

Tindall, H. (1856), *Two Lectures on Great Namaqualand and its Inhabitants*, Cape Town: G.J. Pike.

Thomas, E.M. (1960), *The Harmless People*, London: Readers Union.

Valentyn, F. ([1726] 1971), *Description of the Cape of Good Hope*, trs. R. Raven-Hart, E. Raidt (ed.), Cape Town: Van Riebeeck Society.

Valiente-Noailles, C. (1993), *The Kua*, Rotterdam and Brookfield: Balkema.

Vedder, H. (1937), 'Die Bushmänner Südwestafrikas und ihre Weltanschauung', *South African Journal of Science* 334: 416–36.

Viegas Guerreiro, M. (1968), *Bochimanes !khu de Angola*, Lisbon: Instituto de Investigação Científica de Angola, Junta de Investigações do Ultramar.

Vinnicombe, P. (1975), 'The ritual significance of eland (Taurotragus oryx) in the rock art of Southern Africa', in *Valcamonica Symposium 1972 – Actes du Symposium International sur les Religions de la Préhistoire*, Capo di Pointe: Ediziones Del Centro, 379–400.

von Wielligh, G.R. (1921), *Boesman Stories. Deel 1: Mitologie en Legendes*, Cape Town: De Nationale Pers, Beperkt.

Waldman, L. (2003), 'Houses and the ritual construction of gendered homes in South Africa', *JRAI* 9: 65–79.

Watts, I. (1999), 'The origin of symbolic culture', in Dunbar, R., Knight, C. and Power, C. (eds), *The Evolution of Culture*, Edinburgh: Edinburgh University Press, 113–46.

Watts, I. (2002), 'Ochre in the Middle Stone Age of southern Africa: Ritualised display or hide preservative?' *South African Archaeological Bulletin* 57: 2–16.

Wendorf, F., R. Schild, A. Close *et al.* (1993), *Egypt during the Last Interglacial*, New York and London: Plenum Press.

Weir, J. and E. Davidson (1965) 'Daily occurrence of African game animals at water holes during dry weather', *Zoologica Africana* 1: 353–68.

White, T., B. Asfaw, D. DeGusta, H. Gilbert, G. Richards, G. Suwa and F.C. Howell (2003), 'Pleistocene *Homo sapiens* from Middle Awash, Ethiopia', *Nature* 423: 742–52.

Wikar, H.J. ([1779] 1935), 'The journal of Hendrik Jacab Wikar', in E.E. Mossop (ed.), *The Journals of Wikar, Coetsé and van Reenen*, Cape Town: The Van Riebeeck Society, 15: 20–219.

Wilhelm, J.H. (1954), 'Die !Kung-Bushleute', *Jahrbuch des Museums für Völkerkunde zu Leipzig* 12: 111–89.

Wilmsen, E. (1989), *Land Filled with Flies*, Chicago: The University of Chicago Press.

—— (1999), *Journeys with Flies*, Chicago: University of Chicago Press.

Wilmsen, E. (ed.), (1997), *The Kalahari Ethnographies (1896–1898) of Siegfried Passarge*, Koln: Rüdiger Köpper Verlag, Quellen zur Khoisan: Forschung 13.

Wuras, C.F. ([1858] 1929), 'An account of the !Korana', *Bantu Studies* 3: 287–96.

–6–

Historical Time versus the Imagination of Antiquity: Critical Perspectives from the Kalahari

Chris Wingfield

Anthropologists have long distinguished between the narrative forms of myth and history in human retellings of the past. Evans-Pritchard in his lecture 'Anthropology and history' noted the different character of myth and history, stating that myth 'is not concerned so much with a succession of events as with the moral significance of situations, and is hence often allegorical or symbolical in form'. He went on to suggest that it is not incapsulated[1] as history is, but is a re-enactment fusing present and past. It tends to be timeless, 'placed in thought beyond, or above, historical time; and where it is firmly placed in historical time, it is also, nevertheless timeless in that it could have happened at any time, the archetypal not being bound by time or space' (1961: 8). History, on the other hand, according to Collingwood (1946: 10–11), on whom Evans-Pritchard draws, is '(a) a science, or an answering of questions; (b) concerned with human actions in the past; (c) pursued by the interpretation of evidence; and (d) for the sake of human self-knowledge,' and as such is related to problems of specific places and times. Science, according to Collingwood, 'consists in fastening upon something we do not know, and trying to discover it ... Science is finding things out: and in that sense history is science' (ibid.: 9).

These definitions are perhaps ideal types that represent two poles between which many works may fall, but they are nonetheless useful in highlighting some qualitative differences found in renderings of the past. In attempting a critique of Watts's chapter (this volume), which relies heavily on Knight's evolutionary theory of cultural origins as an explanatory framework, I shall suggest that this theory may be characterized by the above description of myth. Beyond this specific example such mythic form may be said to characterize a certain genre of speculation, popular of late, about human origins especially in the field of evolutionary psychology. This work often claims to be scientific in its reliance on Darwinian frameworks, but is not scientific in Collingwood's sense, since it offers an explanation for something that it seems we already know – what it means to be human – rather than 'fastening upon something we do not know,' i.e. how to deal best with the extremely limited archaeological evidence for the biological origins of *homo sapiens*. After this critique I shall then attempt to present a different framework, derived from Marcel Mauss, through which I have attempted to deal with similar questions and material from southern Africa to that of Watts but from the starting point that all evidence about the past must be read as incapsulated in the complexities of the present. This is especially true of recent and contemporary practice, which I shall argue cannot be used in any straightforward way as evidence for the ancient past, whether people are hunter-gatherers and therefore 'know' what they are talking about (see Watts above, p. 107) or not. It seems likely that people do know what they are talking about, but whether they are talking about the same things as Knight and Watts is questionable.

The critique of Knight's theory as myth is not unanticipated, since Knight himself (1991: 5) states 'because I am motivated politically – I am constructing a myth'. He suggests following Landau (1991) that mythmaking is what all palaeoanthropological storytellers have been doing since the birth of their science. While there is considerable justification in this assertion, does this necessarily legitimize such ongoing self-conscious creation of myths? An awareness of the ease with which speculation about the remote human past falls into legitimizing mythology should surely motivate us to be extremely wary of this temptation.

Knight (ibid.: 4) suggests that the value of the study of human origins 'is that it demonstrates, firstly, that early life was communist. Secondly, it teaches us that revolution lies at the very heart of what we are.' He goes on to state that 'everything distinctively human about our nature – above all, our capacities for language, self-consciousness, symbolically regulated co-operation and creative work – are precisely the products of that immense social, sexual and political revolution out of whose travails we were born.' I shall offer a brief précis of Knight's theory, but it may be found more extensively stated in his book *Blood Relations* (1991) and is described in Watts's chapter (this volume). The revolution at the core of his theory involves women/females initiating a coordinated 'sex-strike' (as in Aristophanes' *Lysistrata*). This involves cooperation through the masking of signs of fertility with ochre, and a consequence is that men/males must cooperate to provide them with meat, in order to be allowed periodic access to sex. This myth, proposed as a Darwinian evolutionary model, ties together an edifice by which Knight ingeniously relates archaeological evidence of ochre use, biological ideas about human menstrual cycles, and aspects of contemporary hunter-gatherer ethnography relating to hunting and initiation; and of course this relates to the moon and its cyclicity as we see from Watts's paper.

According to Collingwood (1939, 1946) any historian is inevitably constrained by their own historical position and perspective. Their craft is an attempt to work their way imaginatively through the preoccupations of the present to understand the preoccupations of the past, much as any ethnographer attempts to work their way into the preoccupations of people in different places. An awareness of the often radical alterity of the past, as well as of its complexity, is often the most concrete result of historical work. Knight (1991) however, seems keen to affect the contemporary world through establishing a charter myth for a different order of things and such a philosophical conception of history does not straightforwardly fulfil this ambition. However Collingwood (who wrote that when he read Marx a part of him used to stand up and cheer (1939: 152)), is clear that there is a point to history that extends beyond reflection and self-knowledge. His answer is to suggest that 'The historian's business is to reveal the less obvious features hidden from a careless eye in the present situation. What history can bring to moral and political life is a trained eye for the situation in which one has to act' (ibid.: 100).

In interpreting archaeological evidence about the past, there lies a crossroads between the possibility of becoming historical in Collingwood's sense, and the self-conscious propagation of myths. This is a choice between the investigation of the past as incapsulated in the present and a timeless 're-enactment fusing present and past'. The fusing of present and past in myth is perhaps what Lévi-Strauss (1966) might refer to as *bricolage*, drawing on a number of elements of the present to create a mythic narrative. However the transformative consequences for the elements of such *bricolage* are clear: they are drawn together and shaped by the process of making them fit a desired end, of which they become a part. The ethnographic and historical accounts in Watts's chapter which are important for Knight's theory become altered as certain aspects are focussed on, to the exclusion of other features of the narrative. It is quite clear that only the features which relate to attitudes to the moon are important and only these are recounted. These original texts are transformed into particular elements of Knight's mythic structure, rather than remaining features of a different context, which includes certain contradictory elements.

What is more, while a myth may be constructed as a charter (Malinowski 1926) for particular interests in the present (in Knight's case he makes it clear that this is revolutionary Marxism), the myth once created may be put to any number of purposes by parties with alternative ends. Myths are multi-vocal creatures which may easily evade the control of their creators. In this case the highly politically charged circumstances of indigenous rights in the Kalahari and in other African countries make the centrality of African hunter-gatherers in Knight's myth and in Watts's paper somewhat problematic. A myth that in a northern metropolitan context appears to challenge the grounds of western capitalism, may be taken in the south as one which legitimizes the conception and treatment of hunter-gatherer minorities as primitive and subhuman.

It is clearly not the first time that the people remote from the centres of metropolitan power have found themselves central figures in western metropolitan myths. Wengrow's chapter (this volume) documents some of the uses made of the notion of ancient society in post-revolutionary France, again in attempts to construct a new alternative society. This practice has a very long history involving hunter-gatherers (Barnard 1999), whereby 'primitives' are made to play the role of 'other'. Their position in these narratives however appears to have oscillated frequently between that of Rousseau-esque noble savages and Hobbesian brutes whose undeveloped lives are nasty, brutish and short. It is this later conception that one might be tempted to suggest underlies the thinking and policy-making of certain contemporary institutions on the African continent. In anthropological contexts, the Kalahari debate (Barnard 1992) exemplifies the ease with which African hunter-gatherers may be modelled by alternative versions of Marxism, first as 'primitive communists' (Lee 1988) and as then as an encapsulated rural proletariat (Wilmsen 1989). The major problem with making people stand in either one of these archetypal positions is that it has the effect of lifting them out of the present, their day-to-day struggle for existence, and of placing them into a mythical realm. As Johannes Fabian (1983) has made clear, the denial of coevalness in the contemporary world by anthropologists to the people they study is one of the chief violences in which anthropology has played a part. It is a key feature of the construction of alterity, by which people come to stand as mythical exemplars or archetypes. A part of the recognition of coevalness and shared humanity is the recognition of a full range of characteristics. People may cooperate for social ends but may in equal measure pursue their self-interest in a thoroughly capitalist manner. People may engage in rites of initiation involving ochre and animal products, but they may equally drive 4x4s, drink beer, smoke cigarettes and talk on mobile telephones. The construction of myths inevitably concentrates on particular aspects of contemporary practice, which in the case of evolutionary explanations tend to suggest continuity with ancient practices.

Ancient African Hunter-gatherers

The reasons why African hunter-gatherers are focussed on in the construction of myths about human antiquity are obvious. In terms of our systems of anthropological categorization they are following the subsistence strategy of our remote ancestors in the same environment. We were all once African hunter-gatherers and now they are the remnant population – our 'contemporary ancestors'. However we must question whether our academic categories are necessarily useful. What it means to be an African hunter-gatherer in a time where you belong to an encapsulated minority population in a capitalist nation-state which has appropriated most of the commercially viable land, and what it means to be an African hunter-gatherer 100,000 years ago when there was no alternative are surely very different. In addition their existence on a common landmass by no means necessarily implies a common environment. Much of the evidence about the remote period of the human past comes from coastal or lacustrine settings, and there are suggestions that even the fauna populating the land may have been quite different at the time (Klein 1989; Klein and Cruz-Uribe 1996). The lush mountainous southern Cape coast, where Henshilwood and Sealy's (1997) discoveries of geometric engravings on red ochre come from, and the harsh sandy scrub desert of the Kalahari are clearly very different environments even if one ignores a plethora of features of the contemporary landscape such as roads and towns which did not exist all that time ago.

In addition there is a frequently made argument for a direct line of descent and continuity. Linguists state that Khoisan languages are amongst the most diverse in the world, while geneticists state that contemporary Khoisan DNA is also exceptionally diverse. But the conclusion that is jumped to on these results more often than not is that this suggests the ancientness of Khoisan peoples. Indeed Watts states that genetically Khoisan peoples include one of Africa's oldest lineages (p. 96). There is however considerable sleight-of-hand in this interpretation. Is it possible to directly infer evidence of temporal depth on the basis of variability? Is there not after all a direct line of descent and continuity of equal 'temporal depth' between remote human ancestors and all living humans? Rather than seeking an explanation for this diversity by the comparison of Khoisan subsequent history with that of other human groups, an attribution of 'ancientness' is offered as an explanation. But is not all DNA equally ancient? Do all languages not probably have antecedents that reach back to language origins? Do the cultural traditions of contemporary and historical Khoisan people living in different parts of the African continent necessarily tell us any more about the cultural practices of our remote ancestors than any other contemporary practices? Are Khoisan people and their religious practices living anachronisms, 'stone age tribes' and survivals in the contemporary world, or do they rather represent populations and practices that are attempting to live in the world in which they find themselves?

Furthermore we must be aware of the dangers of mistaking analytic categories for things with an ontological existence. While discussion of Khoisan or even Bushman belief and ritual may make sense to those who use, and have invented these categories, the latter may serve to unify and mask a great deal of variability in both language and cultural practice. There is no necessary reason why accounts of 'Khoisan' attitudes to the moon should necessarily be the same across large geographical distances, let alone the spans of historical time that Watts is dealing with. The atemporal category of Khoisan is one which exists only in the anthropological and linguistic imagination. Paul Lane (1994–95: 58) has argued that 'By using anthropological data as a source of ethnographic analogues without an equally critical assessment of their historical context, archaeologists only serve to perpetuate a similarly timeless view of African societies.' This echoes Evans-

Pritchard's warning that one of the consequences of social anthropology's breach with history is the uncritical use anthropologists tend to make of documentary sources (1961: 5). If, in the case of Watts's considerations, in spite of considerable historical and geographical differences, these accounts turn out to suggest considerable similarity, then it seems that this poses a question about why this is the case, rather than straightforwardly providing evidence for a myth.

The commonalities in the accounts of various Khoisan groups at different times and their attitude to the moon, which Watts highlights, is of considerable interest, and his analysis points to a number of significant associations made by a different Khoisan peoples between various aspects of their lived worlds, such as the moon, menstruation and the blood of hunted animals. But to substitute these mythic structures for an historical argument about human antiquity is a dangerous proposition. Pocock suggested that 'It is by recognising that he is engaged in a dialogue of three – himself, the society studied and his fellow sociologists – that the objectivity peculiar to [the ethnographer] is preserved... It is clear that if he eliminates any one of the partners ... the dialogue is broken and he falls back into the collective representations of his own or the other society' (1961: 105). One might substitute fellow-historians in place of fellow-sociologists for a very Collingwoodian notion of history, but the retention of this dialogue of three is essential as a tool to prevent a lapsing into collective representations. Myths on the other hand, are almost by definition reflective or rather refractive of particular collective representations.

The Search for Origins

If a myth is, as in Malinowski's (1926) conception, a charter or an explanation of the past, what in this case is Knight's theory of cultural origins an explanation or charter for? Knight explicitly claims that it is quite clearly a charter for revolution at the heart of human affairs (Knight 1991: 11). This revolution is seen to bring about the transition from an exclusively Darwinian level of determination to cultural history as the product of symbolically constituted agents (cf. Watts above). However the interesting thing about the myth as charter is that it seems unavoidably to smuggle in a whole set of other collective representations which are not necessarily the mythmaker's intention and which indeed might subvert it. This myth continues a grand Western tradition of emphasizing the gulf between humanity and animality, and one might argue is a contemporary retelling of the narrative of 'the fall of man', a narrative central to the Judaeo-Christian tradition (Genesis Ch. 3). It is a myth which in nineteenth-century terms brings humanity closer to the angels than the apes (Genesis 3: 22 'man is become as one of us, to know good and evil'). Central to what brings about this fall is the fruit of the tree of knowledge, 'symbolic culture', which comes about as a result of the temptation of women's carnality. This myth demonstrates how 'culture' gains ascendancy over 'nature', playing on two of the most powerful and ideologically laden notions of contemporary Western thought (Williams 1958 and 1976; Ingold 1986). The image of primal humanity and the aspects which set this humanity aside from preceding animality in Knight and Watts's version of the myth are clearly those of symbolic culture. Yet the birth of 'culture' lies in certain contradictions present in the world of 'nature', its roots lie in biology and the biological mechanisms of evolution and reproduction.

However, Knight's theory is not a simple retelling of the narrative of the fall, since it attempts to subvert particular aspects in order to make them speak to a contemporary setting. This should not be surprising to an anthropological audience since Claude Lévi-Strauss (1981) pointed out in the last volume of *Mythologiques* that '*conter* (to tell a story) is always, *conte redire* (to retell a story) which can also be written *contredire* (to contradict)...' Interestingly, Knight's (1991) theory of a unitary origin to symbolic culture is also a retelling of a more recent archaeological version of the myth of the fall. This has tended to place the origins of 'symbolism' in the Eurasian Upper Palaeolithic, referred to as 'The Human Revolution' (Mellars and Stringer 1989). This interestingly Eurocentric myth has suggested that 'behaviourally modern humans' come onto the scene with the arrival in Eurasia of 'anatomically modern humans' which are happily supplied by Africa. The origins of true humanity and modern behaviour are made clear in archaeological terms (Klein 1995: 168) by the presence of:

- Substantial growth in the diversity and standardization of artefact types.
- Rapid increase in the rate of artefactual change through time and diversity through space.
- First shaping of bone, ivory, shell and related materials into formal artefacts.
- Earliest appearance of incontrovertible art.

Interestingly the first three criteria might almost be meta-descriptions of industrialization. The focus on technology and its advancement and improvement clearly resonates strongly with contemporary Western preoccupations. The last criterion, that of incontrovertible art, is suggested by the presence of painting, sculpture and personal adornment, all key features of modern conceptions of the edifice that characterizes particularly European notions of high culture. One gains a sense of early Europeans who would be as at home in art galleries as their bourgeois descendants (Bourdieu 1989), and may prompt one to ask whether modern behaviour in people forty thousand years ago might not be classed as an anachronism. The largely European focus of the myth has tended to reflect the massive concentration of archaeological work on Europe. Roger Lewin (1993) has suggested that there has been about two hundred times as much archaeological investigation in Europe as in Africa relating to this period.

As Watts points out, certain finds in Africa have increasingly tended to subvert these myths, suggesting evidence for features of 'behavioural modernity', as defined above, or what he calls 'symbolic culture' in Africa before those in Europe. However to transfer the locus of the first European enlightenment to Africa in a politically correct gesture of inclusivity hardly seems to come to terms with the fundamental problems of categorization inherent in the mythic narrative. As anthropological studies of art (Price 1989; Morphy et al. 1994; Gell 1998) have increasingly suggested that the western category of art is inapplicable cross-culturally and analytically in unaltered form, so it seems important to recognize that it may not be applicable over such long periods of time. Unfortunately the term 'symbolic culture' appears to conjure up images of metaphorically laden Renaissance paintings, and does not take sufficient note of anthropological challenges to the use of both terms, symbolism and culture (Sperber 1974; Kuper 1999). Can the discourse survive if we abandon or challenge so many of the key terms? The history of anthropology suggests that if anything the discourse on humanity may be fertilized by the refinement of terms and categories as those previously used are found to be too culturally and historically restricted. However the ideological, headline grabbing, punch which comes when we speak of 'the first art' and the 'the origins of culture' is considerably weakened if we challenge the applicability of these terms. As Collingwood seems to suggest (1939 : 100), an awareness of the true complexity and the radical alterity of other forms of life may be the ultimate result of an historical, and we might add anthropological, approach. Is it not in many ways more truly subversive and challenging to refuse to recognize categories of popular political discourse in anthropological analysis?

Techniques of the Body

In my work on ostrich eggshell beads from the Kalahari I have found Marcel Mauss's idea of body techniques (Mauss 1979 [1935]) extremely useful, and this in its time was just such an ideological challenge to contemporary political categories (Schlanger 1998). In the context of a nationalistic Europe, techniques appeared to fly against the notion of bounded cultures and particular histories since they flow so easily from group to group. Indeed the study of body techniques continues to be subversive since it denies any obvious and straightforward distinctions between culture and nature, body and society. Body techniques are certainly socially transmitted but they are equally integral to the operation of bodies in such seemingly 'biological' functions as eating and walking. Contrary to Watts's suggestion (1999: 138) that 'body-painting' might be 'the most rudimentary of Mauss's (1979) *"techniques du corps"*' it seems quite clear that an action far more rudimentary such as walking or even chimpanzee nut-cracking (Wrangham 1994) must occupy this position. The social aspect of bodily action is not something which suddenly appears; body-painting is not 'the first means through which people were ritualized' (Watts 1999: 138), but rather a ceremonial aspect of human behaviour of a kind that seems to pervade all social action and integrates seamlessly with the flow of life (Wittgenstein 1979; James 2003). Equally, human groups and coalitions do not seem to exist in an either/or state, since it would seem that coalition or relationship formation (Evans-Pritchard 1940; Mauss 1990) permeates human behaviour and does not come about in a revolutionary moment of human existential decision. Such social action extends into the remote human past, and it would not be difficult to argue that primates also have body techniques that are socially transmitted, and are, perhaps to a very slight degree when compared to humans, ceremonial (such as leaf stripping as a display of male aggression). It is the sociality of primate lives which makes this the case, rather than anything distinctive about their genetic structure.

Bourdieu (1977) adopted Mauss' term *habitus,* which he coined in his paper on techniques of the body, since it begins to get away from more rigid conceptions of cultural tradition and rules, and allows for a more bodily and fluid 'theory of practice'. When we are dealing with evidence such as ochre in the archaeological record, it is clear at some level that we are dealing with evidence of techniques of the body. The extent to which we can or should try to abstract from this evidence 'structures of thought' and the existence of 'symbolic culture', since both terms are highly contested in contemporary anthropological discourse, is much more questionable. However the continuity of a technique of the body does not necessarily tell us all that much about other long-term continuities, since the techniques involved are often fairly flexible and fluid. Ostrich eggshell bead making in the Kalahari is an example of a body technique which at first sight appears to demonstrate a great deal about long term cultural continuity, since there is archaeological evidence for the continuous practice of the technique in the region over thirty thousand years (Robbins et al. 2000: 1111); but a more detailed analysis of contemporary practice suggests a myriad of ways in which the technique is implicated in contemporary geopolitical realities. It is in no simple way 'an ancient tradition'. For the archaeologists of the future, the apparent continuity of this practice, suggested by a material which survives well in the archaeological record, might serve to mask a whole range of discontinuities in people's relationships with their environments in the present.

I shall briefly introduce some comparative ethnography to suggest the variations possible for a technique of the body. I have adopted from Lemonnier a *chaîne opératoire* approach, since this emphasizes the technology of bead production as a part of a wider system of relations between people and the world. Lemonnier renders *chaîne opératoire* in English as 'operational sequence' and suggests that this may be considered as 'the series of operations involved in any transformation of matter by human beings' (1992: 26). This method leaves plenty of scope for considering the importance of materials, and their presence and absence, in this system of action. As Lemonnier points out, 'By its own specificities and, of course, by being present and or absent in a given environment the material may partially determine the technological behaviour of a people' (1992: 6). Thus it is suggested that materials and objects may play a subtly active role in the human body techniques by which they are transformed. The availability and relative plenty of particular materials may be very important in furnishing a resource landscape from which people, in practising their technique, may draw.

The basic outline of this technique is that you must turn ostrich eggshell into small rounded pieces that are strung together. The main steps in the process are outlined in the diagram below. Inevitability there is a certain arbitrariness in the different ways in which this is achieved. This allows for local and regional variation when performing these actions, and the variations may be anything but arbitrary, revealing significant local differences in situation (Lemonnier 1992). Through considering bead making in two different locations, D'Kar and Kgalagadi district, I hope the significance of these variations and the possibility of considerable variation over temporal distances may become apparent (Fig 12).

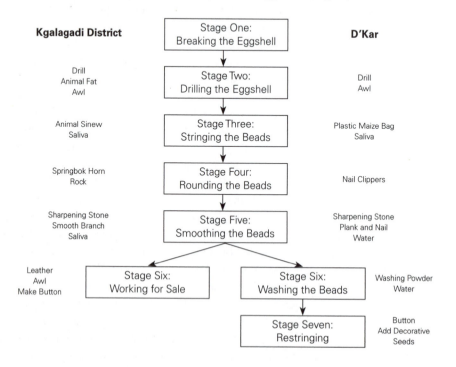

Figure 12 Producing egg-shell beads: 'chaînes opératoires' compared

Making Beads at Dqãe Qare

D'Kar, is in Kalahari terms, relatively urbanized. It was once part of a farm block but has now developed into a settlement around a mission. The bead making I learned here was largely on a farm, Dqãe Qare, that was bought for the community in 1993 by the Dutch Government, and had been stocked with game in a community-based tourism project (van den Berg 2000: 35). Bead making was carried out by the women in slack times when other jobs such as cooking, and cleaning the guest rooms, had been done.

There are five main stages in the manufacture of ostrich eggshell beads; breaking the eggshell into bead sized pieces, drilling the pieces, stringing the beads, rounding them, and finally smoothing them. These are essential to the process and the materials involved and would be found anywhere that a similar technique were practised. However there are some specific features to these practices and materials at Dqãe Qare. For instance, the eggshell was supplied by the craft shop in D'Kar, since access to wild ostriches is difficult because of the surrounding cattle farms. The eggshell comes from commercial ostrich farms in Namibia and South Africa.

At D'Kar the drill used is a long piece of wood with a flattened nail attached at one end (Fig 13). A piece of carpet is used as a surface on which the beads can be drilled. To make a twine, people unpicked the threads of plastic used to make strong sacks of maize, and then rubbed them with their hands on their thighs. One

Figure 13 Making beads at Dqae Qare 2001. Photo: Chris Wingfield

end of the plastic is singed with the flame of a lighter to create a hard point. The preliminary rounding of beads was done with a large nail clipper bought from one of the local shops. Starting at one end of the string, one clips off the edges, getting the beads to an approximately rounded shape. The final rounding of the beads is done when a loop is made at one end of the string of beads, which is hooked onto a nail in a piece of wood: the beads are held tight and pushed against a knot at one end of the string with the left hand, while the right hand rubs the beads with a sharpening stone (made in China), wetting the beads with water from a cup. When this procedure is finished the beads are well rounded, but are covered in a white goo of ground eggshell. The beads are then cleaned in a cup with some washing powder and rinsed until sparkling white.

Making Beads at Ngwatle

Ngwatle from where my comparison is drawn is in the considerably more remote Kgalagadi District. Buying trips there are made by Gantsi Craft approximately once every three months. The district has a mixed population of Bakgalagadi and !Xõ Bushmen and there have long been relations between these two groups often of clientship (Silberbauer and Kuper 1966; Kuper 1970). The land is communally held, and hunting quotas have been agreed on by the settlements. Access to wild resources is therefore far easier than at D'Kar and, as we shall see, at some stages of the *chaîne opératoire* these replace shop-bought items used at D'Kar.

The stages of bead making in the Kgalagadi District largely follows that outlined above but there are some significant differences. Instead of using nail cutters to shape the beads, people chip them using the horn of a springbok. While some people also make twine from maize meal sacks as at D'Kar, most have animal sinew from hunting which they use for the same technique. Another animal product missing from D'Kar was animal fat, applied to the drills, so they move more smoothly in the hands. Interestingly, a disputed feature of quality with the buyer is the roughness of beads which was due to the smoothing technique. Though similar to D'Kar, people did not use water, but saliva, to lubricate the beads during grinding. People said that they did not know that water could be used and the shortage of water in the area, contrasting with the relative plenty of water around D'Kar, seems significant. Interestingly, the beads were rubbed on a piece of straight wood from the bush, rather than a square plank as at D'Kar, and more wild ostrich eggshell seemed to be used here.

The diagrammatic representation comparing the *chaînes opératoires* makes clear the differences between the two places. The first five stages are very similar and allow only relatively minor variations. The main difference between D'Kar and the Kgalagadi district involves the tools used and the differential access to hunted animal products and shop-bought materials. It seems that bead workers at

Ngwatle are operating in different resource landscapes to those of D'Kar. This is a landscape where water is scarce, stone and springbok horn more easily accessible than nail clippers, and animal sinew and fat relatively easy to obtain. At D'Kar sinew and springbok horns are more difficult to come by, but maize sacks and shop bought commodities such as nail clippers and washing powder are similarly easier to come by. It is easier to find a flat plank lying around, than to hew and smooth a tree branch. This should give a sense of how sensitive technical procedures may be to environmental change. In this case while retaining the same end goal – the manufacture of an ostrich eggshell bead – these different communities achieve it in ways which profoundly reflect the environment in which they operate.

Technological opportunism appears to be a *modus operandi* for people making beads in the Kalahari, and the use of a variety of materials does not seem to be constrained by conservative notions of tradition. Rather, people opportunistically forage, practising a literal form of *bricolage* (Lévi-Strauss 1966) in relation to their technical procedures. Without some very detailed studies involving microscopy and possibly chemical analysis, the details of different technical procedures, finely attuned as they are to their resource landscapes would be lost in an archaeological context, where the presence of ostrich eggshell beads might be all that was noted. This degree of technical variation demonstrated largely reflects the different political and geographical influences in two locations separated by just a few hundred kilometres in the contemporary Kalahari. How much more significant are the variations we must imagine for the historical past? What transformations have taken place in this relatively specific geological location over the last thirty thousand years since the beginning of ostrich eggshell bead production? The introduction of metal as a material for drills is clearly one significant transformation.

It hardly seems sensible to ignore the whole complex of behaviour and activities which surround the manufacture of ostrich eggshell beads, to focus on the beads themselves and proclaim the continuity of an unbroken tradition. The fact that nearly all ostrich eggshell is now supplied by ostrich farms and that it is now nearly all ultimately sold to international tourists is also significant. The continuity of particular aspects of technique and their material products may serve to mask a great deal of history and change which are integral to contemporary forms and practices. These continuities are incapsulated, to use Collingwood's term (1939: 114), by a whole range of other practices, which must be taken seriously for a historical consideration to be possible.

Conclusion

In conclusion, I shall return my focus to the subject of Watts's chapter. It seems that to consider Khoisan practices as evidence for human origins without taking seriously the incapsulated nature of this evidence does considerable violence to the coevalness and contemporaneity of these people. It would seem justified to argue that aspects of the environment, such as the moon and sun, have considerably more influence on the temporal patterning of human activity prior to the use of electric lighting and an indoor lifestyle in contemporary metropolitan centres, but this does not justify an exclusive focus on African hunter-gatherers, since there are many populations worldwide for whom this is true. Watts's argument raises all sorts of interesting questions about peoples' relations with their environments and the associations they make between different features of these and themselves, but the mythic framework in which he sets these out is problematic and disturbing, not least because it tends to lead to the reification of certain questionable categories.

The presentism of structural-functionalist and much twentieth-century anthropology has been remarked upon (see Fardon this volume) and it certainly seems reasonable to attempt to adopt less presentist theoretical positions. I would argue that this must be by becoming historical rather than by becoming mythical. To prevent anthropology from falling into collective representations, the dialogue of three is essential to maintain where possible, not only in ethnography but also in historical approaches. The past may be another country, but it is not a blank canvas, and it is important to allow the evidence to speak with and against its narrator.

In short, I am not opposed to speculation on long-term history, to arguments for the importance of the periodicity of the moon in affecting human notions of periodicity, or against arguments about the significance of pigments and colours in human ceremonial life. Indeed, these are important elements in some of my own work. However I regard the framework in which Watts, as well as Knight and Power seek to place their work as untenable since it reifies so many categories which anthropology has sought to challenge, and because it is framed in mythic terms. If Watts, Knight and Power were to demythologize their theory, a strategy that the theologian Rudolph Bultmann suggested was useful in the understanding of much Biblical myth (Gogarten 1955), they might find that it would be possible to have a much more fruitful dialogue in anthropological contexts.

Note

1. I shall retain Collingwood and Evans-Pritchard's spelling of incapsulation when referring to the past's incapsulation in the present, but shall use encapsulation when referring to the physical encapsulation of hunter-gatherer by food-producing communities in contemporary Africa.

References

Barnard, A. (1992), *The Kalahari Debate: A Bibliographical Essay,* Edinburgh: Centre of African Studies, Edinburgh University.

Barnard, A. (1999), 'Images of hunters and gatherers in European social thought', in R.H. Daly, (ed.), *The Cambridge Encyclopedia of Hunters and Gatherers,* Cambridge: Cambridge University Press.

Bourdieu, P. (1977), *Outline of a Theory of Practice,* Cambridge: Cambridge University Press.

——(1989), *Distinction: A Social Critique of the Judgement of Taste,* London: Routledge.

Collingwood, R.G. (1939), *An Autobiography,* Oxford: Clarendon Press.

Collingwood, R.G. (1946), *The Idea of History,* Oxford: Clarendon Press.

Evans-Pritchard, E.E. (1940), *The Nuer: A Description of the Modes of Livelihood and Political Institutions of a Nilotic People,* Oxford: Clarendon Press.

——(1961), *Anthropology and History, a lecture delivered in the University of Manchester with the support of the Simon Fund for the Social Sciences,* Manchester: Manchester University Press.

Fabian, J. (1983), *Time and the Other: How Anthropology Makes its Object,* New York: Columbia University Press.

Gell, A. (1998), *Art and Agency: An Anthropological Theory,* Oxford: Clarendon Press.

Gogarten, F. (1955), *Demythologizing and History,* London: SCM Press Ltd.

Henshilwood, C. and J.C. Sealy (1997), 'Bone artifacts from the Middle Stone Age site at Blombos Cave, southern Cape, South Africa', *Current Anthropology* 38: 890–5.

Ingold, T. (1986), *Evolution and Social Life,* Cambridge: Cambridge University Press.

James, W. (2003), *The Ceremonial Animal: A New Portrait of Anthropology,* Oxford: Oxford University Press.

Klein, R.G. (1989), 'Biological and behavioural perspectives on modern human origins in southern Africa', *Journal of World Prehistory* 9: 167–98.

Klein, R.G. (1995), 'Anatomy, behaviour and modern human origins', *Journal of World Prehistory* 9: 167–98.

Klein, R.G. and L. Cruz-Uribe (1996), 'Exploitation of large bovids and seals at Middle and Later Stone Age sites in South Africa', *Journal of Human Evolution* 31: 315–34.

Knight, C. (1991), *Blood Relations: Menstruation and the Origins of Culture,* New Haven and London: Yale University Press.

Kuper, A. (1970), *Kalahari Village Politics: an African Democracy,* London: Cambridge University Press.

——(1999), *Culture: The Anthropologists' Account*, Cambridge, Mass. and London: Harvard University Press.

Landau, M. (1991), *Narratives of Human Evolution*, New Haven and London: Yale University Press.

Lane, P. (1994–95). 'The use and abuse of ethnography in the study of the South African Iron Age', *Azania* 29/30: 51–64.

Lee, R.B. (1988), 'Reflections of primitive communism' in T. Ingold, D. Riches and J. Woodburn, *Hunters and Gatherers: Volume 1, History, Evolution and Social Change*, Oxford, Berg.

Lemonnier, P. (1992), *Elements for an Anthropology of Technology*, Ann Arbor: Museum of Anthropology, University of Michigan.

Lévi-Strauss, C. (1966), *The Savage Mind (La pensée sauvage)*, London: Weidenfeld & Nicolson.

——(1981), *The Naked Man*, London: Jonathan Cape.

Lewin, R. (1993), *The Origin of Modern Humans*, New York: Scientific American Library.

Malinowski, B. (1926), *Myth in Primitive Psychology*, London: K. Paul Trench Trubner & Co. Ltd.

Mauss, M. (1979 [1935]), 'Les techniques du corps', *Journal de Psychologie* 32 (3–4): 271–93.

——(1990 [1925]), *The Gift: The Form and Reason for Exchange in Archaic Societies*, London: Routledge.

Mellars, P. and C. Stringer (1989), *The Human Revolution: Behavioural and Biological Perspectives on the Origins of Modern Humans*, Edinburgh: Edinburgh University Press.

Morphy, *et al.* (1994). *Aesthetics is a cross-cultural category: a debate held in the Muriel Stott Centre, John Rylands University Library of Manchester, on 30th October 1993*, Manchester: Group for Debates in Anthropological Theory.

Pocock, D. (1961), *Social Anthropology*, London: Sheed & Ward.

Price, S. (1989), *Primitive Art in Civilised Places*, Chicago: Chicago University Press.

Robbins, L.H., M.L. Murphy, *et al.* (2000), 'Archaeology, palaeoenvironment, and chronology of the Tsodilo Hills White Paintings rock shelter, Northwest Kalahari Desert, Botswana', *Journal of Archaeological Science* 27(11): 1086–113.

Schlanger, N. (1998), 'The study of techniques as an ideological challenge: technology, nation, and humanity in the work of Marcel Mauss' in W. James and N.J. Allen (eds), *Marcel Mauss: a centenary tribute*. Oxford: Berghahn Books.

Silberbauer, G.B. and A.J. Kuper (1966), 'Kgalagari masters and Bushman serfs: some observations', *African Studies* 25(4): 171–9.

Sperber, D. (1974), *Rethinking Symbolism,* Cambridge: Cambridge University Press.

van den Berg, E. (2000), 'At the Dqãe Qare game farm in Ghanzi', in N. Rozemeijer (ed), *Community-based Tourism in Botswana*, Gaborone: SNV Botswana, 35–45.

Watts, I. (1999), 'The origins of symbolic culture', in R.I.M. Dunbar et al. (eds), *The Evolution of Culture: An Interdisciplinary View*, Edinburgh: Edinburgh University Press.

Williams, R. (1958), *Culture and Society, 1780–1950*, London: Chatto & Windus.

——(1976), *Keywords: A Vocabulary of Culture and Society*, London: Fontana.

Wilmsen, E.N. (1989), *Land Filled with Flies: A Political Economy of the Kalahari*, Chicago: University of Chicago Press.

Wittgenstein, L. (1979), *Remarks on Frazer's Golden Bough* trs. A.C. Miles, revised by Rush Rhees, Atlantic Highlands NJ: Humanities Press.

Wrangham, R.W. (1994), *Chimpanzee Cultures*, Cambridge, Mass: London: Harvard University Press in cooperation with The Chicago Academy of Sciences.

–7–

Kingship, Revolution, and Time:
Perspectives on Materiality and Modernity
David Wengrow

As William Arens (1984) observed some years ago, studies of kingship provide a sensitive indicator of the schism between historical and anthropological approaches to power, and by implication between Western representations of European and non-European time. While European history has tended to associate significant political transformations with the personal agency or fortunes of particular rulers, anthropology has tended to embed non-European kingship within abstract notions of cosmology, social structure, or personhood. There are of course important exceptions on both fronts, which have been steadily increasing in number and draw their inspiration primarily from the *Annales* school in history (for example, Boureau and Ingerflom 1992), and in anthropology from various strands of Marxist thought (see Rowlands 1998). The study of divine kingship therefore presents a fertile ground within which the rapprochement of anthropology and history appears to be taking root, and upon which traditional disciplinary constructions of European and non-European experience are now openly challenged.

This chapter aims to contribute to this process by situating the anthropological practice of observing and studying exotic forms of divine kingship within a longer European tradition of critical thought and practice, extending back into pre-colonial times, that is, into the period of absolute monarchy itself. It seeks to outline how a cultural strategy of alienation that originated in Europe as a form of internal resistance to royal power was transformed, in the context of colonial rule, into one of external domination. In documenting this process a particular emphasis is placed upon the role of material culture in forming cultural memories of, and temporal perspectives on, sacred kingship. Specifically it is argued that the experience of kingship as an exotic phenomenon, engendered by the practice of archaeology and anthropology, has been recursively linked both to the formation of the modern political subject in Europe, and to the interaction of colonial governments with elites under their control.

David Wengrow

Forgetting Divine Kingship in Revolutionary France

At their various moments of birth, the modern nations of Europe, whether they followed a republican path or that of constitutional monarchy, found themselves confronted by the cultural remnants of an old regime. Their urban centres in particular were still saturated with the tangible memories of a more hierarchical past, in which political life gravitated around some form of sacred monarchy. In her study of the role of festivals in the French revolution, Mona Ozouf has highlighted the cultural strategies through which this memory was either suppressed or incorporated during the passage to political modernism in France. In laying to rest what Michelet called the vampires of the *ancien régime*, Ozouf argues that the revolutionary festivals were 'an indispensable complement to the legislative system, for although the legislator makes the laws for the people, festivals make the people for the laws' (1988: 9). Participants were expected to enact a utopian vision of the modern political subject, emerging from the ashes of the old regime fully formed and imbued with the responsibilities of democratic and national life. They were therefore festivals of forgetting and purification; a collective attempt to efface both the deep monarchical past and the violent means of its termination. In Louis Dumont's (1980) terms, they sought to dramatize the death of *Homo hierarchicus*, and his rebirth as *Homo aequalis*.

'Time', writes Ozouf, 'was not merely the formal framework within which the Revolution took place; it was also the raw material on which it obstinately worked… The first thing to be done was to manifest the discontinuity brought about by the Revolution in the flow of time, to signify, quite unequivocally, that the era of the Republic was no longer the era of kings, and to mark this absolute beginning' (1988: 158–9). Paul Connerton notes the particular significance of the beheading of Louis XVI in marking this rupture. For centuries the phases of dynastic rule had been the 'benchmarks of time', each coronation signified by the anointing of the ruler's head. The mode of his execution ensured that 'not simply the natural body of the king but also and above all his political body was killed' (1989: 8–9).

The desire to inscribe the memory of revolution into popular experience of time is most clearly reflected in the invention of the revolutionary calendar, which aimed to align the enactment of commemorative festivals with the passing of the seasons. It also found concrete expression in the organization of human activity within them, notably the system of age groups through which participation was regulated. At the Festival of Youth, sixteen-year-old boys, each grasping a flower, stepped across a human circle formed around the altar of the nation, to emerge subsequently with a weapon in hand. The ceremonial of ages also involved a circulation of gifts; usually a reciprocal exchange of bread and fruit between the age groups (Ozouf 1988: 161–6, 193).

Regicide, the gift, age groups, male initiation: between the bonfires of Monarchy and Church, an image of primitive society was enacted on the festival grounds of Paris long before the scholars of the *Année sociologique* would seek to historicize it, or ethnographers travel to the ends of empire in search of it. Perhaps in these fleeting, orchestrated dramatizations of the social contract, it achieved a greater coherence than in any community more remote in time or space.

In seeking to make the present and future comprehensible as a natural progression from the past, the intelligentsia of the revolution also had recourse to an idealized and exemplary image of classical antiquity. To this end it became necessary to forget the divine emperors and dictators of Rome, even as Napoleon Bonaparte prepared to fashion himself into a new Caesar, just as the institution of slavery within the ancient *polis* had somehow to be excused. Like the enactment of noble savagery the evocation of republican antiquity served a dual function. It made possible the forgetting of recent history by infusing present action with meaning drawn from a deep imaginary past. This process of remembering in order to forget had a truly archaeological character (*pace* Foucault). After all, in digging down to create new material environments for social memory to inhabit, excavation always incurs the destruction of the upper layers, and hence of the potential for future memories of a more recent, and perhaps more disturbing, past. Archaeology is as much about forgetting as remembering.

For some modern political philosophers and historians, forgetting the formative role of sacred monarchy in European political experience appears to be a *fait accompli*. Werner Maihofer, for instance, asserts that: 'Love of freedom, respect for the law, equality before the law, rule through agreement of the ruled, and government through the consent of the governed, are the decisive characteristics of Attic democracy at the very birth of Europe's political culture, as opposed to the Asiatic despotism that faced it on the other side of the Aegean' (1990: 23). Here the cultural distance between Athens and Persia, as represented by the Athenians, is substituted for the political distance between ruler and ruled which has characterized most European societies since the fall of the Roman Empire. This amounts to a reiteration of Montesquieu's famous assertion that despotism is a natural part of the Oriental scenery, while Occidental despotism is like a weed taken root in foreign soil (Montesquieu 1949 [1748]: 266).

Notions of cultural distance and disciplinary constructions of 'the other' have received considerable attention in recent decades. Their study has been directed primarily towards understanding the cultural processes underpinning European colonial domination of non-Europeans, a subject that will be reviewed in concluding this chapter. Initially, however, I wish to discuss in more detail the role of the exotic in Europe's own passage to political modernism.

David Wengrow

The Royal Body and the Savage Gaze

The notion of the ruler's body as a legal and religious entity, irreducible to the physical body of a particular king or queen, was central to the political thought of Medieval and Renaissance Europe. In England and France these distinct entities, united in the living monarch, were separated upon his physical demise. As a temporary conduit of sacred and temporal authority the image of the king, or rather of his 'body politic', was fashioned as an effigy to be displayed and rendered services until the kingship passed into a new living form. While the natural body was subject to decay the body politic remained a 'likeness of the "holy sprites and angels"', because it represents, like the angels, the Immutable within Time' (Kantorowicz 1957: 8).

Paul Monod (1999) has linked this ritual practice to contemporary notions of the Christian self as comprising an individual soul lodged within a particular bodily form, an integration which was believed to continue after death. Accordingly the institution of sacred kingship promoted the harmony of the body politic as a magnification of the personal harmony sought between body and soul. Medieval notions of utopia envisioned an earthly paradise brought about through the government of an ideal ruler. The quest for the fabled kingdom of Prester John, which motivated early European travellers to Africa and the Orient, was therefore a journey towards inner salvation, as well as a precursor to outward conquest (Melville 1992). Likewise negative images of the 'evil ruler' evoked by opponents of royal power drew consistently upon notions of physical ugliness, religious abomination, and the violations of subjects' bodies by torture, experimentation, rape, and even anthropophagy. The corpse of the tyrannical ruler was imagined too foul for proper burial, foreshadowing his return from the dead or reincarnation in another form (Klaniczay 1992).

Monod characterizes the development of an open theatre of monarchy during the seventeenth century as a strategic response to assaults upon the notion of bodily sacredness launched during the Reformation. The ruler's body began to command authority less through its status as a hidden, sacred object than through its involvement in open dramatizations of royal power or virtue, the audience for which extended from nobles to artisans (1999: 83–84). In central Europe this gave rise to the confessionalized monarch, seeking to embody Catholic values of self-sacrifice and purity; in northern Europe to the Protestant hero-king, distinguished by discipline and martial prowess. By contrast, the baroque kings of western Europe sought to maintain the inherent sacredness of royal power by bringing the rewards of heaven down into the realm of the court, and by continuing to invest in a mystical notion of the ruler's body. During the period of absolutism, on most major religious festivals, the Great Gallery of the Louvre would be opened to subjects afflicted with scrofula, who arrived in their thousands to receive the miraculous healing power of the royal touch (Bloch 1973 [1924]).

A common aim of these strategies was to maintain a relationship between ruler and subject based upon fundamental personal values, and articulated at a level that was emotional and sensual rather than reflexive or discursive. In this context it is interesting to consider a recurring figure in the popularizing tradition of courtly literature, recently discussed by Carlo Ginzburg: the lowly but enlightened outsider who enters the court and challenges the moral authority of the ruler. The character of Milenus, the Peasant of the Danube, is among the earliest examples cited, appearing in Guevara's *Golden Book of Marcus Aurelius*, published in 1529 and widely reproduced throughout Europe. He is an ambivalent figure, described as having a monstrous physical form mid-way between human and animal, as though heightened awareness has come at the price of a loss of humanity. Ginzburg places Guevara's text at the head of a genre in which 'the savage, the peasant, and the animal, together or singly, have offered a viewpoint from which it is possible to turn upon society [and specifically upon hierarchy] a distance, estranged, and critical gaze' (2001: 12). In Montaigne's sixteenth-century essay *Des cannibales* three natives of the New World leave their idyllic homeland (where they speak an agreeable language reminiscent of Greek) to visit the court of Charles IX, and are shocked to see armed, adult men in the service of a 'beardless child' (reproduced in Thibaudet and Rat, 1962: 200–212). And in his (1721) *Lettres Persanes*, under the guise of Persian Rica, Montesquieu would later write of Louis XIV in terms prefiguring the cruder nineteenth-century caricatures of primitive kingship among non-European peoples: 'This king is a great magician: he rules even over the mind of his subjects... He even goes so far as to make them believe he can heal them of all sorts of evils by touching them, so great is the strength and power he has over their spirits' (see Bloch 1973: 29).

Simon Schama describes how, in the prelude to revolution, the bodily habits and practices of Bourbon rulers became the focus of a vitriolic attack on monarchy, disseminated through pornographic images and satirical literature. The court of Versailles was vividly characterized as a site of orgy, with Marie-Antoinette vilified as the chief agent of sexual depravity and the king mocked as a cuckold. A fake confession was distributed and updated in the decade preceding her execution: 'Catherine de Medici, Cleopatra, Agrippina, Messalina, my deeds have surpassed yours, and if the memory of your infamies still provokes a shudder, if its frightful detail makes the hair stand on end and tears pour from the eyes, what sentiments will issue from knowledge of the cruel and lascivious life of Marie-Antoinette' (1989: 203–47). Such slander derived its force from the cultural logic of royal power itself: 'Few states were as body centred as seventeenth- and eighteenth-century France. The rhetoric, rites, and rhythm of political life derived from bodies' (Melzer and Norberg 1998: 1). In portraying the king as subject both to an unruly libido and a wayward wife, republican rhetoric ate away at the ideology of masculine control and comportment which 'connected order in the royal body with order in the body politic' (Merrick 1998: 30).

The transformation of individual rulers into timeless anti-heroes continued in the celebratory festivals that followed the revolution (Ozouf 1988: 30–31, 93, 174–7, 211). Among the effigies carted through the streets the figure of the dead king was represented, not primarily as Louis XVI, but through a series of archetypes symbolizing 'Tyranny', 'The Perjurer', and so on. Simulacra of royal and religious relics – statues, images, sceptres – were burned and broken, and at Morteau the 'Burial of Monarchy' was enacted, as if to speed it forcibly into an antiquarian domain of ruin and loss. Revolutionary orators spoke in allegories (which Walter Benjamin said are to thought as ruins are to architecture), substituting abstract concepts such as liberty and despotism for the specificity of remembered events and personalities.

Ancient Egypt and the Objectification of Political Memory

Against the background of these developments there emerged in Europe a parallel discourse on divine kingship, which took ancient Egypt as its *topos* (in Yates's (1966) sense of a real or imaginary space in which memory can be anchored). Until recently, studies of ancient Egypt's place in European culture and imagination have tended either to seek Renaissance precursors for the modern discipline of Egyptology, or to chart the development of Egyptianizing fashions in elite circles as 'Egyptomania'. The latter term has been particularly detrimental to understanding, and is reminiscent of the social pathologies ('Masai-itis') invented by colonial officers to excuse their propensity for 'going native' in the field. I will not be concerned here with the exemplary Egypt of Graeco-Roman and Hermetic texts, which enchanted the scholars and courtiers of the Renaissance and Enlightenment, but with the oppressive and desolate Egypt of the Old Testament and of romantic literature.

In a penetrating essay, Peter Hughes (1995) recalls Volney's meditation on the ruins of the Orient as an allegory for the fall of French monarchy. *The Ruins*, published during the early stages of revolution in France and swiftly translated into English in 1800, relates the reflections of a traveller passing through the lands of the Near East: 'Hail solitary ruins, holy sepulchres and silent walls!... When the whole earth, in chains and silence, bowed the neck before its tyrants, you had already proclaimed the truths which they abhor; and, confounding the dust of the king with that of the meanest slave, had announced to man the sacred dogma of Equality' (Volney, cited in Hughes 1995: 284).

In Volney's premonition that the banks of the Seine and the Thames might one day become a landscape of monumental ruins, like those of the Nile or the Euphrates, Hughes detects a clear sense of nostalgia for what had barely begun to pass. Drawing upon Kubler (1962), he observes that ruins serve to commemorate past desires, offering 'a way of overcoming the absence of the past when it is limited to paper and ink or condemned to fading memory' (1995: 284). Their materiality brings the past into the sensory domain of the present, even as their weathered and fragmented forms summon the sensations aroused back into a ruptured past.

Much of this is echoed in Jan Assmann's recent discussion of Egypt's mnemonic role in maintaining the conceptual distinction between true and false religion in western ontology. The biblical opposition between Israel and Egypt provides a 'map of memory' upon which the spaces of western monotheism and its opposites, polytheism, paganism, and idolatry, have been constructed. The narrative of the exodus translates this distinction into spatial terms so that Egypt stands not only for idolatry but also for a past that is rejected. Remembering Egypt constitutes an 'overcoming and a liberation from one's own past which is no longer one's own … Egypt must be remembered in order to know what lies in the past, and what must not be allowed to come back' (1997: 7–8).

There can be few more direct materializations of this dual process of remembering and distancing than the Egyptian galleries of the Louvre. Andrew McClellan (1994: 7, 91–123) describes how, in its transformation from palace into modern museum (an 'imposing school' of the nation), the Louvre of the revolution had become a shrine to 'popular sovereignty and the triumph over despotism', shaping republican identity in a comparable manner to the Revolutionary festivals. The Egyptian galleries opened in 1826 under the restored monarchy of Charles X (Humbert 1997). Displays of ancient, exotic objects were installed in the former apartments of the queens of France, and organized didactically according to general themes: two galleries were devoted to royal funerary practices, one to precious items and materials, and a fourth to religious beliefs. The ceiling of the latter chamber was adorned with an allegorical painting portraying a transition from the decadence of tyranny to the rewards of enlightened government as *L'Étude et le Génie des arts dévoilant l'Égypte à la Gréce*. Contemporary oil paintings depict Napoleon Bonaparte during his conquest of Egypt in 1798, directing the excavation of royal mummies from their subterranean tombs (see Larsen 1994, fig.1; Humbert et al. 1994: 226–7).

At the heart of the lavish *salle funéraire* stood a large platform, on which were arranged the upper casings of elaborate sarcophagi, their lower casings and contents exposed on the floor beneath. In the space of the Louvre, where crowds had gathered to receive the miracle of the royal touch, citizens could now come to measure their own being against the exposed husk of a divine king, at the same

–143–

time measuring the latter against his boastful monuments. On display here was not merely the fantastic 'otherness' of oriental civilization (cf. Said 1978; Mitchell 1991), but also the very embodiment of dynastic rule, grafted onto the inscrutable remains of a derelict culture and located safely behind the threshold of modernity. In unveiling and laying to rest the ghost of monarchy, the guillotine had given way to the intrusive public gaze. In this sense the museum anticipated in concrete form the aspirations of Michelet's *Histoire de la Révolution française*: 'That dead man is Old France, and that bier, the coffin of the Old Monarchy. Therein let us bury, and for ever, the dreams in which we once fondly trusted, – paternal royalty, the government of grace, the clemency of monarchy, and the charity of the priest; filial confidence, implicit belief in the gods here below' (Michelet 1967 [1879–80]: 55).

While in some respects entirely new in their impact, these displays also marked the secular culmination of an earlier theological dialogue between 'death the master' and 'kingship the subject'. During the fourteenth century mummies were depicted in the *danse macabre* where death, the great leveller, guides both beggar and king towards the same inevitable fate. Throughout the fifteenth and sixteenth centuries the skeletal figure of death was often shown with trappings of monarchy, marking out his space as one in which earthly hierarchy becomes subject to the power of mortality (Ariès 1983: 110–16).

Egyptian mummies, or parts of them, had first entered Europe centuries before the French Revolution. As early as the thirteenth century they were highly valued, not primarily as visual spectacles, but for the medicinal properties of a resin they contained (*mumia*). This substance was often extracted at source for shipment to Europe in powdered form, where it was used to treat coughs, colds, and other ailments (see Dannenfeldt 1985). As pre-preserved curiosities, intact mummies were also natural commodities, which joined the flow of pickled, salted, tanned, and dried organic goods from the Orient into the dockyards of early modern Europe (Cook 2002). By the early seventeenth century, the unwrapping and dissection of Egyptian 'royal' mummies had become a popular urban spectacle, attracting large crowds lured by sensational advertisements.[1]

As a body that alters the ordinary processes of time and decay, the status of the mummy as an object of curiosity *par excellence* resided on the cusps of the clinical and the bizarre, an observation which gains additional interest in relation to the healing powers attributed to the bodies of contemporary living rulers. As an object of scrutiny the mummy may be seen as the nexus of a popular discourse in which the awed gaze inspired by the sacred body of monarchy was displaced by the lurid gaze of the horrified spectator, and by that nemesis of the irrational: the surgeon's knife.

It seems paradoxical, then, that architectural forms of ancient Egyptian derivation came to occupy a central place as monuments to republicanism in the festivals of the French Revolution (Humbert 1997: 65ff.). In 1792 the Conseil Géneral de la Commune ordered that a prominent statue of Louis XVI in the Place des Victoires be demolished and replaced by an obelisk, wrongly described in their directive as a 'pyramid', inscribed with the names of fallen revolutionary leaders. The same year witnessed a major festival in the Tuileries for the martyrs of the revolution, at which the focal monument was an enormous wooden pyramid. A leaflet was distributed appealing to each citizen to place a garland at its base in honour of those heroes 'qui nos ont aidé à vaincre les tyrans!' One year later, a monumental statue of the goddess of Nature in Egyptian costume was erected on the ruins of the Bastille for the Festival of Regeneration. Water spouted from its breasts into a basin below where speeches were made celebrating the return of the people to an original state of innocence and freedom.

It is unlikely that stark geometrical forms such as obelisks and pyramids would have carried connotations of ancient Egypt, let alone sacred monarchy, to contemporary observers, as they do to the eye of the modern art historian. Prior to the revolution, the designer Étienne-Louis Boullée had already envisaged the use of Egyptian architectural forms in the construction of cenotaphs for the civilian and military dead (Humbert et al. 1994: 103–5). In the eyes of the revolutionary intelligentsia they answered a need to fill the aesthetic and emotional void left by the rejection of Christianity, with its powerful symbolic rhetoric of sacrifice and resurrection (Laurens 1999: 2; Ozouf 1988: 203–12). Their austere forms also provided an empty canvas for the didactic construction of memory through oratory or surface inscription. As Michael Rowlands has observed, remembering the dead by inscribing their names on an eternal monument 'requires that its form should be timeless; that it should resonate identity with a remote past, escaping the conflicts of the present' (1993: 145).

Conclusion: Sacred Kingship, Time, and the Colonial Encounter

In 1943 P.P. Howell, district commissioner in the Upper Nile Province of the Anglo-Egyptian Sudan (who later combined Oxford anthropology with his career), set out to observe and record 'as accurately as possible' the funeral of a Shilluk king, Reth Papiti Yor, and the installation of his successor, Reth Aney Kur. It was to be the first of a number of such ceremonies that he recorded during his service in the Condominium. The British government had made itself known to the Shilluk in 1903 by deposing Reth Kur, the predecessor of Papiti Yor, whom they considered a potential ally of Mahdism. It had subsequently suppressed an armed rebellion against Papiti Yor by Nawelo, the son of Reth Kur and brother of Aney, and presented him with 'a brightly-coloured sash and turban, a dark beret, blue sheepskin, deck chair and a saddle' (Arens 1979: 172).

Howell describes the *reth* as a 'classic example of Frazer's conception of the divine king', referring both to the power over nature attributed to him by his subjects, and also to the periodic practice of ritual regicide among the Shilluk (Howell and Thompson 1946: 10). The veracity of this latter practice was famously cast into doubt by Evans-Pritchard in his 1948 Frazer Lecture. It has since been affirmed from a number of other sources (Arens 1979; Simonse 1992), conforming to a wider pattern of what Friedman (1991) terms the 'involution of sacred kingship' in pre-colonial and colonial Africa (compare Meillassoux 1991; Simonse 1992). Subsequent studies have, however, supported Evans-Pritchard's (Frazerian) view that the main purpose of customary regicide was to preserve the values of fertility embodied in kingship which were being weakened by the individual in office: 'not revolutions but rebellions against the king in the name of kingship' (1962 [1948]: 83).

In writing up his reports for *Sudan Notes and Records*, Howell cited as a pretext for his study an observation made by C.G. Seligman in his 1933 Frazer Lecture, *Egypt and Negro Africa: A study in divine kingship*. Seligman, it should be added, subscribed to (and to some extent pioneered) a widely held view that contemporary African kingship was a surviving, but contaminated, remnant of ancient Egyptian kingship (see O'Connor and Reid 2003). Close observation of the 'complicated installation ritual of the Divine King' would, Seligman suggested, expose the cultural formulas binding the people emotionally to the ruler. The power of the Nilotic king over his people was materially inscribed within the actions and orations of the installation ceremony. By implication it could have had little to do with any personal qualities, beliefs, deeds, or affiliations that might have endeared Reth Aney Kur to, or estranged him from, his people during the course of his life.

This basic understanding of African royal ritual may be supported by a great deal of ethnographic evidence. Luc de Heusch, for instance, has recently argued that royal installation ceremonies throughout a wide range of African societies, including the Shilluk, have typically involved the dissolution of the individual person of the king into a 'fetish-body'. The ritual, rather than the political, function is, he suggests 'at the core of the institution', endowing the king with his essential function in articulating the natural and social orders, 'just as Frazer envisaged it' (1997: 231). It would then become crucial to understand the impact of an observer such as Howell upon the performance of these rituals, not because ethnographic writing was a poetic idiom of domination (cf. Parkin 1990), but because his very presence inserted the British government into the heart of the proceedings.

On this subject, Howell in fact gives us a considerable amount of information, perhaps slightly more than he intended. The joint funerary and installation rites of the king involved both private and public rituals. The latter included a long enactment of ritualized warfare, collective processions, and animal sacrifice.

These ceremonies, which centred upon controlled displays of violence, lasted for a number of days, and occasioned a mass congregation of Shilluk from all social ranks and parts of their country. There is a striking sense of powerlessness in Howell's confessed inability to interrupt their rhythmic fervour in order to 'interrogate the performers'; in his frustration at being physically prevented from entering the secluded hut-shrine of Nyikang, the ancestral hero embodied by the *reth*; in his consciousness that informants are lying to him about key aspects of the ritual process (Howell and Thompson 1946: 12, 56, 66). There is also a sense of self-alienation in his acquiescence to the atmosphere of secrecy surrounding the ritual duties of the *reth*, and in his muted admiration for the disciplined displays of the Shilluk warrior 'regiments' (ibid., 26, 64). The performers, moreover, took steps to incorporate Howell into the framework of the ceremony at a critical moment, much to his chagrin. During the orations given by Shilluk leaders to confirm the installation of the new *reth*:

> Some forty or fifty chiefs and elders each had their say in turn, and after each speech the spokesman thrust his spear into the ground... Most of the speeches... were rather trite... An untraditional but common topic was: 'The Government needs no introduction, you and it must co-operate; it is not like the Dervishes or Turkia; you must help to collect its taxes.' (Howell and Thompson 1946: 71–2)

In his 1996 Frazer Lecture, Alfred Gell (1997) proposed a reinterpretation of royal rituals in the Bastar kingdom of central India under British rule, which may have a bearing on our understanding of these events. He demonstrated that periodic rebellion and royal ritual in fact derived from a shared cultural logic, the strategic aim of which was to insulate the kingdom from outside interference by the state, and in particular to keep tax revenues low. Secular rebellions were prompted, not by oppressive acts of the king, but by the government's desire to weaken his authority or remove him from his people, and took the form of his capture and confinement by an assembled crowd. Gell perceived a link here with royal ritual (Dasara), which involved a temporary dethronement (symbolically equated to death) and subsequent abduction of the king by his people, followed by his final revival and restoration to power. Like the calendrical rituals which 'assure a "happy normality" against the possibility of adverse alterations' in nature, this ritualized political disruption formed a kind of 'pre-emptive unrest'. Its aim was 'the assertion of tribal control over the Raja's person and, through him, the capacity to resist the extension of the power of the state' (Gell 1997: 437). The ultimate audience for these *en masse* dramatizations of popular force, though largely effaced from the rituals themselves, was the British authorities (ibid.: 445).

Gell's account highlights how existing temporal frameworks of royal ritual provided colonial subjects with a sanctioned vehicle for popular demonstrations of strength and intransigence, which would otherwise have been suppressed as open resistance to the government. The irony, surely, is that resistance embedded within royal ritual was translated back into the language of timeless tradition by colonial observers, for whom the true meaning of sacred kingship was, as Howell puts it, 'lost in antiquity' (Howell and Thompson 1946: 12). His account stands as testimony to a familiar, but self-defeating desire: to peel back the wrappings of the mummy and glimpse 'the Immutable within Time'.

Notes

1. For example: 'Two Mommies or Mummies are being exhibited in their entirety: such rare and fine examples have never hitherto been seen. They have been brought out of the Royal Sepulchres. If we have never seen their like before, the reason is the difficulty of obtaining them. For, since time immemorial no-one dared lay a finger on a single one of the Tombs of the Nobility, for fear of retribution. Yes, here are two, taken from the very Tombs of the Kings themselves, and you would scarcely credit the sums that we have been obliged to expend so as to bring them here.' Public advertisement, c. 1648, (cited in Aufrère 1990: 166). (With thanks to Prof. Christopher Robinson for translation.)

References

Arens, W. (1979), 'The divine kingship of the Shilluk: a contemporary re-evaluation', *Ethnos* 3–4: 167–81.

—— (1984), 'The demise of kings and the meaning of kingship: royal funerary ceremony in the contemporary southern Sudan and Renaissance France', *Anthropos* 79: 355–67.

Ariès, P. (1983), *The Hour of Death*, Harmondsworth: Penguin.

Assmann, J. (1997), *Moses the Egyptian: The Memory of Egypt in Western Monotheism*, Cambridge, Mass. and London: Harvard University Press.

Aufrère, S. (1990), *La momie et la tempête. Nicolas-Claude Fabri de Peiresc et la "curiosité egyptienne" en Provence au début du VIIe siècle*, Avignon: Éditions A. Barthélemy.

Bloch, M. (1973 [1924]), *The Royal Touch: Sacred Monarchy and Scrofula in England and France*, trs. J.E. Anderson, London: Routledge & Kegan Paul.

Boureau, A. and C.S. Ingerflom, C.S. (1992), *La royauté sacrée dans le monde chrétien*, Paris: École des Hautes Études en Sciences Sociales.

Connerton, P. (1989), *How Societies Remember,* Cambridge: Cambridge University Press.

Cook, H.J. (2002), 'Time's bodies. Crafting the preparation and preservation of Naturalia', in P.H. Smith and P. Findlen (eds), *Merchants and Marvels: Commerce, Science, and Art in Early Modern Europe*, Routledge: New York and London, 223–47.

Copans, J. and J. Jamin (1994), *Aux origines de l'anthropologie française,* Paris: Jean-Michel Place.

Dannenfeldt, K.H. (1985), 'Egyptian Mumia: the sixteenth-century experience and debate', *Sixteenth-Century Journal* 16: 163–80.

De Heusch, L. (1997), 'The symbolic mechanism of sacred kingship: rediscovering Frazer', *Journal of the Royal Anthropological Institute* (N.S.) 3 (2): 213–32.

Dumont, L. (1980), *Homo Hierarchicus. The Caste System and its Implications,* Chicago and London: University of Chicago Press.

Evans-Pritchard, E.E. (1962 [1948]), 'The divine kingship of the Shilluk of the Nilotic Sudan' in *Essays in Social Anthropology*, London: Faber.

Frazer, J.G. (1890), *The Golden Bough: A Study in Comparative Religion,* London: Macmillan.

Friedman, K.E. (1991), *Catastrophe and Creation: The Transformation of an African Culture*, Chur, Reading: Harwood Academic Publishers.

Foucault M. (1989), *The Archaeology of Knowledge,* trs. A.M. Sheridan Smith, London: Routledge.

Gell, A. (1997), 'Exalting the king and obstructing the state: a political interpretation of royal ritual in Bastar District, Central India', *Journal of the Royal Anthropological Institute* 3 (3), 433–50.

Ginzburg, C. (2001), *Wooden Eyes. Nine Reflections on Distance*, New York: Columbia University Press.

Guillemette, A., M-H. Rutschowscaya and C. Ziegler (1997), *L'Égypte ancienne au Louvre,* Paris: Hachette.

Howell, P.P. and W.P.G. Thompson (1946), 'The death of a *reth* of the Shilluk and the installation of his successor', *Sudan Notes and Records* 27: 5–85.

Hughes, P. (1995), 'Ruins of time: estranging history and ethnology in the Enlightenment and after', in D.O. Hughes and T.R. Trautmann (eds), *Time: Histories and Ethnologies*, Michigan: University of Michigan Press, pp. 269–90.

Humbert, J-M. (1997), *L'Egypte à Paris*, Paris: Action Artistique de la Ville de Paris.

Humbert, J-M., M. Pantazzi, W. Seipel, and C. Ziegler (1994), *Ägyptomanie. Ägypten in der Europäischen Kunst, 1730–1930*, Vienna: Kunsthistorisches Museum.

Kantorowicz, E.H. (1957), *The King's Two Bodies: A Study in Mediaeval Political Theology*, Princeton: Princeton University Press.

Klaniczay, G. (1992), 'Representations of the evil ruler in the Middle Ages', in H. Duchhardt, R.A. Jackson, and D. Sturdy (eds), *European Monarchy: its Evolution and Practice from Roman Antiquity to Modern Times,* Stuttgart: Franz Steiner Verlag.

Kubler, G. (1962), *The Shape of Time: Remarks on the History of Things,* New Haven and London: Yale University Press.

Larsen, M.T. (1994), 'The appropriation of the Near Eastern past: contrasts and contradictions', in *The East and the Meaning of History: international conference, 23–27 November 1992.* Rome: Università degli studi di Roma 'La Sapienza', 29–51.

Laurens, H. (1999), 'Les lumières et l'Égypte', in P. Bret (ed.), *L'éxpedition d'Égypte: une entreprise des lumières,* 1798–1801, Paris: Technique et Documentation, 1–6.

McClellan, A. (1994), *Inventing the Louvre. Art, Politics, and the Origins of the Modern Museum in Eighteenth-century Paris,* Cambridge: Cambridge University Press.

Maihofer, W. (1990), 'The ethos of the republic and the reality of politics', in G. Bock, Q. Skinner, and M. Viroli (eds), *Machiavelli and Republicanism,* Cambridge: Cambridge University Press.

Meillassoux, C. (1991), *The Anthropology of Slavery: The Womb of Iron and Gold,* London: Athlone.

Melville, G. (1992), 'Le prêtre Jean, figure imaginaire du roi sacré', in A. Boureau and C. S. Ingerflom (eds), (above).

Melzer, S.E. and K. Norberg (eds), (1998), *From the Royal to the Republican Body: Incorporating the Political in Seventeenth- and Eighteenth-century France,* Berkeley, Los Angeles, London: University of California Press.

Merrick, J. (1998), 'The body politics of French absolutism', in S.E. Melzer and K. Norberg (eds), (above).

Michelet, J. (1967 [1879–80]), *History of the French Revolution,* trs. C. Cocks, Chicago and London: University of Chicago Press.

Mitchell, T. (1991), *Colonising Egypt,* Cambridge: Cambridge University Press.

Monod, P.K. (1999), *The Power of Kings: Monarchy and Religion in Europe, 1589–1715,* New Haven and London: Yale University Press.

Montesquieu, Baron de (1949 [1748]), *The Spirit of Laws,* trs. T. Nugent, New York and London: Hafner Press.

O'Connor, D. and A. Reid (2003), *Ancient Egypt in Africa,* London: UCL Press, Institute of Archaeology.

Ozouf, M. (1988), *Festivals and the French Revolution,* Cambridge, Mass. and London: Harvard University Press.

Parkin, D. (1990), 'Eastern Africa: the view from the office and the voice from the field', in R. Fardon (ed.), *Localizing Strategies: Regional Traditions of Ethnographic Writing,* Scottish Academic Press and Smithsonian Institution.

Rowlands, M. (1993), 'The role of memory in the transmission of culture', *World Archaeology* 25 (2), 141–51.

——(1998), 'Ritual killing and historical transformation in a West African kingdom', in K. Kristiansen and M. Rowlands (eds), *Social Transformations in Archaeology: Global and Local Perspectives*, London: Routledge.

Said, E. (1978), *Orientalism*, New York: Vintage.

Schama, S. (1989), *Citizens: A Chronicle of the French Revolution,* New York: Knopf.

Seligman, C.G. (1934), *Egypt and Negro Africa: A Study of Divine Kingship*, London: Routledge.

Simonse, S. (1992), *Kings of Disaster. Dualism, Centralism and the Scapegoat King in Southeastern Sudan*, E.J. Brill: Leiden.

Thibaudet, A. and M. Rat, (eds) (1962), *Montaigne: oeuvres complètes*, Paris: Gallimard.

Yates, F. (1966), *The Art of Memory*, London: Routledge & Kegan Paul.

Part III
Modern Times?

Time Inscribed in Space, and the Process of Diagnosis in African and Chinese Medical Practices

Elisabeth Hsu

This chapter relates to Alfred Gell's (1992) work on the anthropology of time in that it critically examines a generally held belief about the temporal sequencing of allegedly distinctive processes in a medical encounter: diagnosis and treatment. The belief is that good medical practice consists of making a diagnosis first, and then delivering medical treatment accordingly. The aim of the diagnosis is to identify the cause of the illness; and treatment is considered effective if it eliminates not only the symptoms, but also the underlying cause. We all are familiar with this reasoning, yet as this chapter will show not all medical practice is grounded on this principle, and perhaps, the view that diagnosis and treatment take place in two consecutive phases reflects more of a claim within Western biomedicine of an ideal than a lived practice.

My argument thus provides further material for the claim that diagnosis itself constitutes an integral part of the treatment. It demonstrates that there is no such thing in medicine as a context-free 'objective' diagnosis, because every diagnosis is implicitly already an aspect of the treatment itself (e.g. Laderman and Roseman 1996, McGuire 1988). Since the processes of making a diagnosis and delivering treatment cannot easily be separated, one needs to question whether 'good medical practice' – not only 'traditional' but also 'advanced-traditional', 'modern-traditional' and 'modern' medical practice – necessarily has to be grounded in a distinction between them. This analysis, which differentiates between these kinds of medical practice in ways the actors did, will point to various forms of synchronicity between diagnosis and treatment.

Alfred Gell's *The Anthropology of Time* is central to the method applied in this study insofar as Gell, who criticizes anthropologists for being unduly preoccupied with culturally constructed notions of time-cosmologies, advocates a more pragmatic approach to the study of time. If one investigates what people do, he claims, there is always a 'before versus an after'; but this need not mean, he immediately adds, that the awareness of 'pastness, presentness and futurity' are 'real characteristics

Elisabeth Hsu

of events'. Rather, he says, 'they arise from our relation to them as conscious subjects' (1992: 157). Gell builds on the work of philosophers in nineteenth and twentieth century Europe in order to provide a 'coherent philosophical account of time' and to elaborate a 'general model of time cognition'. This, he thinks, should save anthropologists from 'unwarranted metaphysical speculation' and remove them from the 'generalized sense of puzzlement that the ghostly notion of time evokes' (ibid.: 149).

The Anthropology of Time is a *tour de force* that introduces the reader into European philosophy, psychology, linguistics, economy, and eventually also Bourdieu's theory of practice. Of particular relevance is his discussion of chrono-geography and time-economics (ibid.: 190–216), for he considers researchers within this field to have laid important foundations for an anthropology of time '"objectively" understood' (ibid.: 321). 'The problem at the moment', he says, 'is that no real effort has been made to bridge the gap between time-budget studies (a pretty dull subject in the estimation of most anthropologists I know) and "exciting" topics having to do with collective representations and the mediation of social processes' (ibid.: 322). While Durkheimian anthropology has focused on concepts of time which become evident in the context of ritual, he points out that studies of time 'must proceed along a broad front', including everyday life practices. Ritual representations of time have been misunderstood to provide a 'world-view' when, in fact, they represent not more than 'a series of special-purpose commentaries on a world...' (ibid.: 326). Anthropologists are thus admonished to pursue a strategy that on the one hand investigates 'the inherent choreographical possibilities of social actions in their space-time frame' and on the other, the symbolic aspects of these actions, i.e., the 'schemes of temporal interpretation' that the ethnographic subjects themselves have (ibid.: 325). While chrono-geographers have done the former, anthropologists should combine both approaches by engaging in an analysis of the language and cognition of the subjects studied to achieve the latter (ibid.: 327).

When Gell says that the study of 'opportunity costs provides the bridging concept between subjectivity and objectivity in the sociological interpretation of action in the world' (ibid.: 323), one is bound to think that he applies a highly culture-specific framework for assessing the 'objectivity' in the sociological interpretation of action. Indeed, as Wendy James and David Mills in the introduction to this volume state, these 'clean' and 'clear' categories, which appear 'culture-free', convey a sense of temporality that is in fact 'culture-bound' and based on a protestant work ethic. Yet Gell does advocate a 'dual strategy' that involves both the choreography of action from an outsider's viewpoint (an outsider who may well have a protestant work ethic) with analysis of the actors' schemes that involves knowledge of their language and cognition. Gell speaks of an analysis that combines the subjective and seemingly objective interpretation of action.

Nevertheless, if one assumes, as do Gell and the editors of this book, that people have multiple notions of time, extending from time concepts surfacing in ritual, to those intrinsic to daily life routines, different approaches to the analysis of time appear justified. Gell himself says that the approach he advocates is useful for analysing 'the action frame of reference and the shallow time of everyday life' (ibid.: 314).

By following people's movements through space in a specific activity of daily life (that can also be framed as a form of ritual interaction), as is demonstrated in this chapter, we get a sense of their sequencing of their actions, admittedly only from an outsider's viewpoint. If we investigate the objects, and their positions in space, and ask for the meanings attributed to these objects and to their orientation in space, we may indirectly learn how people conceive of their actions from an insider's viewpoint. All human beings move through space, and this movement happens within an 'action-frame' governed by a sequencing 'before versus after'. Comparative research into very different cultural settings – for example, of the medical encounter between doctor and patient – is thus possible, because we have a common denominator.[1]

Time and the Process of Diagnosis in Medical Anthropological Literature

The diagnostic process is a complex one, as is already demonstrated in the flow diagram of an early study (Lewis 1975: 250). Conditions of patients differ, some may be treated instantly, others may not be treated at all. For some one may have determined a cause before treatment, others are treated without searching for a cause. In some cases the sequencing 'identification of cause – treatment of cause' is straightforward, in others the process is several times repeated. Also, the cause may be diagnosed at different stages of the course of the illness, and occasionally, Gilbert Lewis says, an explanation is given retrospectively.

In her article 'Time and the process of diagnosis in Sinhalese ritual treatment', Lorna Rhodes (1984) discusses a case of such retrospective diagnosis. The cause of a woman's barrenness is in retrospect attributed to the demon Kandavara and linked to events that took place many years earlier, at menarche, and that previously had not been considered significant. The explanation of this woman's barrenness consists of a process whereby previously insignificant events gain significance over time. Since the performance of the ritual for Kandavara takes place three months after the birth of the child, the performance itself cannot be considered to have effected the birth.[2] Rhodes writes about this particular case, not because she considers such retrospective diagnosis 'occasional', but because she considers it relevant to a more general critique of the claim that, in the patient's view or within her 'action-frame', diagnosis always precedes treatment.

In a first instance, Mark Nichter (1996) seems to provide a framework for understanding this: biomedical diagnoses, he suggests, search for the cause of the illness in the past and produce disease 'taxonomies', while in other medicines, the process of illness labelling (such as retrospectively blaming the demon Kandavara) results in 'taskonomies': tasks for the patient's social entourage to strategically deal with the illness in a manner that is primarily concerned with the well-being of the patient in the future (e.g. by performing the ritual for Kandavara). In cases of establishing taxonomies, diagnosis precedes treatment, but in cases of taskonomies, treatment prospects determine the label of the illness. Nichter's distinction has however the flaw that it idealizes both Western biomedicine and folk medical reasoning, and artificially increases the difference between them. After all, treatment prospects can determine diagnosis, also in biomedical practice. The availability of certain treatments can lead to preference for certain diagnoses. For instance, availability of treatment with lithium led to an increase in diagnoses of manic-depression (Kleinman 1988). In other words, even in biomedical practice diagnosis may be determined by treatment prospects.

Diagnosis is furthermore closely linked to prognosis, as Mary-Jo Good points out in an article on the 'discourse of hope' among cancer patients: 'Consideration about how to maintain hope while still being truthful, about what and how much to tell, thus occurs in the context of discussions not simply of diagnosis but of prognosis and treatment' (1990: 64–5). Also Allen Young (1998: 268–9) stresses the importance of generating hope through a diagnosis when speaking about 'meaningful time' in his study of PTSD (post-traumatic stress disorder). He points out that some patients may receive a certain diagnosis and treatment, temporarily considered the best, while an atmosphere of hope is generated that a more concise diagnosis and treatment will be found in the future. Such generation of hope thus draws out a slightly altered sequencing: diagnosis precedes treatment precedes diagnosis. The tenor of hope that Young alludes to, namely, that for any diagnosis a better diagnosis may be found in the future, is not only important for the individual patient's understanding and treatment of his or her condition, but for the entire apparatus of biotechnology that surrounds biomedical practice: as Young (1998) and Good (1990: 60) emphasize, the funding of biomedical research depends critically on this 'political economy of hope'. Neither Young nor Good directly call into question that 'modern' biomedical practice provides diagnosis and treatment in consecutive phases, yet by pointing to the importance of hope and its political economy, they highlight how treatment, diagnosis and prognosis are bound into a complex web of interdependencies and fleeting temporalities.

There are many more studies in medical anthropology that tangentially discuss time and the process of diagnosis in medical treatment. The few given here illustrate vividly that diagnosis may retrospectively be attributed to a certain condition, that prognosis (which is closely linked to treatment availability) is an important aspect of any diagnosis; and that therefore the interrelation between diagnosis and treatment is much more intricate than implied by the claim that diagnosis and treatment take place in distinct consecutive phases.

Time Inscribed in Space, and in Objects

Among the studies mentioned, there are two diagrams, by Lewis (1975: 250) and Rhodes (1984: 51), both of which depict time as a unidirectional vector. The time vector orders various events along a gradient from past to future events. However, as useful as a time vector may be, it ultimately represents an ordering device of the ethnographer. This present study, which builds on my own fieldwork data, attempts to derive from the spatial ordering of a ritual setting (i.e. a medical practice) the temporal order of seemingly insignificant everyday activity or form of ritual interaction (i.e. the medical encounter).[3] By way of methodology, however, it is difficult to derive any temporal sequencing from a spatial arrangement with no knowledge of the language (a point that I will expand on below in more detail), and it is impossible to derive anything from the spatial order itself, without observation of how people move through the spaces.

Therefore, I will seek to follow the movement of patients through the spatial layout of Chinese and African medical practices, and explore what we can derive from this about diagnosis and treatment, and their temporal interrelatedness, in the respective medical encounters.[4] Between March 2001 and August 2002 (four months in four visits), I worked with Chinese doctors in Africa (Tanzania and Kenya).[5] In what follows, I will first discuss the spatial layout of 'advanced traditional' Chinese medical practices, second, that of 'traditional' African ones on the Swahili coast, and, third, before emphasizing too strongly the cultural distinction between the African and Chinese, point to 'modern traditional clinics' (MTC).[6] These recent fieldwork observations will then be evaluated in the light of an earlier language-oriented investigation of the medical encounter in modernized traditional acupuncture wards of the People's Republic of China.

'Advanced Traditional' Chinese Medical Practices of Dar es Salaam and Arusha, Nairobi and Mombasa

Traditional Chinese Medicine (TCM) is a recently revived form of Chinese elite medical teachings and practices, which since the 1950s has been standardized in government-run Chinese medical universities and colleges, hospitals and clinics (e.g. Farquhar 1994, Hsu 1999, Scheid 2002). In Tanzania, it classifies as an 'advanced traditional' medicine (Hsu 2002), and indeed the spatial layout of the consultation rooms has much in common with 'modern' biomedicine.

By looking at photo portraits of the Chinese doctors , one central object of the ritual space in a Chinese medical practice becomes obvious: the table. The table can certainly be taken as a sign of the doctor's literacy: s/he writes the patient's case record and prescriptions at the table and s/he uses the table for storing books (not only medical ones but also books for learning English or Swahili, novels, and newspapers, or also pamphlets about investment in Kenya). The table is used not only as storage place for books but also for other openly displayed instruments like that for taking blood-pressure measurements, the stethoscope, calendars (Western-type), and also Chinese medical paraphernalia like plastic models of men with colourful acupuncture-channels, medicines, and the like.

The table is often situated at the centre of the room. It is the place where most discussion and the 'diagnosis' takes place. The patient may face the doctor, with the table separating them; or doctor and interpreter may sit on opposite sides of the table, but fairly close to each other, and the patient will be between the two, at the far end and at a greater distance. The table demarcates difference and distance between practitioner and patient.

Inspection of the spatial layout of Chinese medical practices shows, however, that this table is central only to one among several rooms. As the layout of the medical practices in Dar es Salaam, Kariakoo (Fig. 14) shows, and also those at Pangani shopping centre and in the newly established Hurlingham private medical centre in Nairobi, most Chinese medical practices have various rooms each with a specific function. Thus, the patient, often in the company of another person, enters the medical practice via the waiting room. He or she is greeted by a receptionist, who typically is an African woman, often in a white coat. Then, after waiting for a short while – one to two or ten minutes, or twenty at most – the patient enters the consultation room where the table is the central feature. Many patients leave this room within a few moments, with a prescription in hand and a bag full of medicines, without venturing further into the spaces of a Chinese medical practice. Yet, without exception, all the Chinese medical practices I visited (about twenty-five) had a separate room for a bed, or, at least, a separate space within the same room, usually behind white or light blue curtains. The bed signifies the place where treatment takes place, which is generally being administered to patients lying in an outstretched and passive posture.[7] The spatial layout of an 'advanced traditional' Chinese medical practice, which appears similar to a 'modern' Western medical practice, would thus suggest that indeed, the ideology of 'Phase 1: diagnosis, Phase 2: treatment' is carried out in these spaces.

This movement, which entails staying in a waiting room, often among a group of people, moving into a space where the doctor is faced alone or with the interpreter, and perhaps moving from there onto a bed, has several variations. Many Chinese medical practices contain a laboratory for conducting simple Western medical tests, carried out by an African laboratory-technician, usually

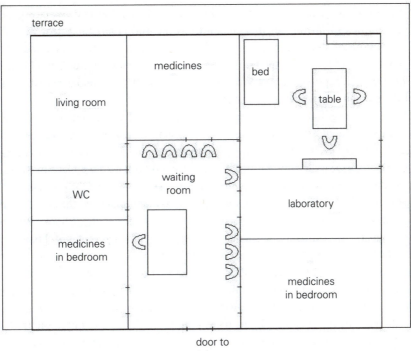

Figure 14 Layout of an 'advanced' Chinese medical practice in Dar es Salaam, Tanzania

male, for identifying malaria, urinary infections, stomach ulcers, and, rarely, HIV infection. The importance of this biomedical laboratory in a Chinese medical practice cannot be overemphasized, as it produces rapid results, i.e. in less than half an hour; results which are considered reliable (by Euro-American medical professionals whom I consulted, by Chinese doctors and by the African clientele). This 'ritual space' of biomedical laboratories in Chinese medical practices is one the patient generally does not enter, just as a patient is not allowed to enter the inner sanctum in a religious setting, and yet it is precisely the activities undertaken in that space, and their results, which give these medical and religious places their utmost significance.

Clearly, it is not primarily the Chinese medical rationale and the Chinese philosophy of life that attracts the African clientele, but the entrepreneurial structure of their practices. The Chinese meet the needs of the patients which are, as I gathered from various remarks, to work through the nuisance of a medical procedure as quickly and as efficiently as possible. Western medical services are known for 'red tapism', and are referred to as 'a waste of time', because they provide each of the above services in separate spaces, often in different buildings, and require the patient to stand in line for each, 'And at last, we are given prescriptions for medicines that cannot be purchased in any pharmacy because they run out of stock', a patient in a Chinese clinic in Nairobi exclaimed. One of the main reasons why such African patients seek out Chinese doctors is that Chinese doctors provide the services of consultation, lab-test, and the handing out of the relevant medicines in one space.

It is the case that every Chinese medical practice I visited featured not only a table (for diagnostics) but also a bed (for treatment). However, whereas beds were regularly used in the Chinese acupuncture clinics of the People's Republic of China, the treatment-on-the-bed phase frequently did not take place in African contexts, despite the spatial arrangements provided. During the three weeks that I spent at a clinic in Dar es Salaam, I never saw a patient treated on the bed; the bed was instead used as a storage place, for the telephone, the telephone books, and for newspapers. So, although the spatial arrangement seemed to hint at it, Phase two 'treatment-on-the-bed', did not really feature in many Chinese medical encounters in Africa. Instead, the purchase of drugs featured prominently as Phase two.

This is perfectly obvious from the spatial layout of one of the busiest medical practices I saw where the room with the bed was used for storing cleaning utensils while most of the space of the medical practice was occupied by a pharmacy. In this medical practice, many patients missed out phase one, i.e. the diagnosis with the doctor, and they entered the medical practice solely for the purchase of medicines. Thus, the Chinese medical practice had the function of a pharmacy. In one afternoon, I saw mainly men going to the counter. They were served by two smart-looking African women, and as far as I judged, the majority of them bought Chinese drugs that boost potency.[8]

In other Chinese medical practices, there was a separate storage room for medicines, which like the biomedical laboratory, was closed to the public. It was in fact often locked, and thus veiled in secrecy, even more so than was the biomedical laboratory. Typically, it would store not only Chinese medical drugs, but also Western medicines. In Tanzania this secrecy has been reinforced by the regulations on pharmaceuticals which prohibit the sale of biomedical drugs by Chinese doctors. However, in Kenya, where according to the Chinese doctors I spoke with legislation is less discriminatory, I discovered that doctors were similarly secretive about their drugs and their storage places. Might this suggest that the drugs are the essential 'treasure' that attracts the African clientele, even more so than the biomedical laboratory?

'Traditional' African Practices on the Swahili Coast

The bed is generally absent in African healers' practices. That could be understood to mean that treatment on a physical body which passively lies prostrate in front of the healer does not feature prominently in African healing. The table is not a prominent feature either.[9] Can we take this as an indication that the above temporality of 'diagnosis first, delivery of treatment to the physical body second' is not central to African healing?

More striking than the absence or presence of any particular item, like table and bed, is the great variation between the spatial layouts of different African practices. African practitioners work in spaces that are far less similar in structure to each other than are those of Chinese doctors, which I take to indicate that TCM has been subject to more rigorous standardization than 'traditional African' medical practices, even when considering only those few visited on the Swahili coast between Dar es Salaam and Tanga.

In Swahili coast practices, sometimes one entered first into a space for people to wait – the courtyard or chairs on a terrace – separate from the consultation room; at others the patients waiting for treatment formed an audience for the healing performances that took place within the same ritual space. Sometimes the diagnostic conversation and healing procedures occurred in a sprawling complex of buildings, at others in a single tiny room. Indeed, the ritual space for most of the 'traditional' African healing did not reflect a division of the medical encounter into the two different temporal phases 'diagnosis first, treatment second'.

On the Swahili coast, practices did feature one recurrent motif: it was neither bed nor table but a fireplace; most healers had a fairly clearly defined fireplace even though it was often portable and small (Fig. 15). The healer usually was

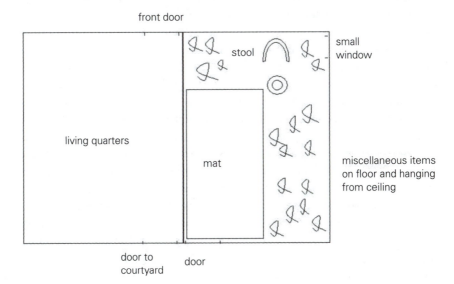

Figure 15 Layout of a 'traditional' African healer's practice in Bagamoyo, Tanzania

seated close to the fire place but I never observed him (woman healers seem to be rare) seated directly in front of it, as though the fireplace were the central place of the practice, more central to it than the healer himself. The healer could handle the fire while remaining seated, he could light it, add incense to it and feed it with various kinds of wood, thereby generating smoke or scents of various kinds. From observation alone, it is difficult to understand the significance of the fire and the incense burning. The scent was always pleasant, sometimes almost intoxicating, the smoke could suddenly become quite thick and white, but just like spirit beings, it remained intangible as it ascended, and accumulated underneath the iron sheet roof or dissipated into the foliage of a tree or through a window in the wall. One can easily comprehend that the fire, the scent and the smoke make present spiritual forces.

Susan Whyte (1997), in her study of Nyole divination by spirit possession and by the examination of Arabic books, emphasizes that this practice is governed by several 'principles of uncertainty'. Firstly, the patient is supposed not to know the cause of his or her illness or misfortune; second, the healer also is expected not to know any details of the case beforehand. Uncertainty, Whyte emphasizes, is the point of departure for a Nyole séance, and Whyte points out that 'this uncertainty is not simply "there". It is constructed and emphasized' (ibid.: 68). The foremost principle of this constructed uncertainty is, in Whyte's analysis, the 'relative privacy' of a séance. The spatial layout of the ritual setting is likely to contribute to the construction of such uncertainty.

Indeed, several healers I visited worked in ritual spaces that were marked by a certain cosiness or intimacy. More than once my colleague and I were cramped into a small space, with 'stuff' 'lying about' or hanging from the roof, the room being filled with ritual paraphernalia to the extent that one barely found space to put one's legs, or that it was so small and stuffy and hot that ventilation was a problem. In one practice, the healer turned on an electric fan to alleviate the suffocating atmosphere during most the medical encounter, except for the phase of fumigation that featured in almost all the treatments he performed.

Having said this, it is important to bear in mind that there was great variation in spatial layout among African healers, and not every healer cramped his patients into tiny rooms. Nevertheless, the spatial arrangement in many practices emphasized synchronicity of events and solidarity, the healer sitting often beside the patient, rather than facing him or her, a feature that created a certain closeness between them. Table and bed, on the other hand, rather than emphasizing synchronicity, divides the medical encounter into two phases, diagnosis and treatment; and, rather than enhancing solidarity, this institutes distance between doctor and patient, and thereby enhances the doctor's authority.

'Modern Traditional' Clinics in Dar es Salaam

Before committing the fallacy of working out a clear-cut contrast between 'traditional' African and 'advanced' Chinese practices, let us once again be reminded of the great variety of African practices. So far, I have not mentioned a spatial arrangement that one occasionally finds in Dar es Salaam; this is a room with a large table, a large chair for the practitioner and one or two smaller chairs for the clients, and also a separate room in which medicines are stored and dispensed. Considering that practitioners themselves have given such practices the name 'modern traditional clinic', with (MTC), we now can be quite certain that it is not a cultural difference between Chinese and African healing that is reflected in the spatial arrangements, but a difference between so-called 'traditional' and 'modern traditional' practices (or perhaps, if we insist on the cultural aspect, of Westernized Chinese medicine, TCM, and Westernized African medicine, MTC).

As shown above, the consultation room of African practitioners on the Swahili coast of Tanzania typically has a fireplace, but no bed or table. The question that then arises is whether non-Westernized or non-modernized Chinese medical encounters also took place in spaces without tables and beds, a question that I cannot answer immediately. In ancient China pulse diagnostics certainly did not take place at a table but on a mat, much the same, we may surmise, illustrated in a work on pulse diagnostics in more recent Japan (Kuriyama 1999: 58–9). The chair was introduced into China through Buddhism, by the sixth century AD (Kieschnick 2003: 241), centuries after the foundations of what we now recognize as Chinese medical practice had been laid. Tables with long legs must represent an adaptation that the introduction of the chair required.

However, we need not go into the history of furniture in China in order to show that the temporal sequence of 'diagnosis first, treatment second' need not necessarily always apply to Chinese medical practice. As will be shown here, it may well reflect a claim about 'modern scientific' or 'advanced traditional' Chinese medical practice, rather than a lived reality. For showing this, however, inspection of spatial arrangements in medical practice and observation of how patients move through these spaces is insufficient; it now becomes indispensable to resort to language skills.

The Synchronicity of Diagnosis and Treatment in 'Advanced Traditional' Acupuncture

In acupuncture clinics of the People's Republic of China, it is common practice for a patient to sit in Phase one at a table, opposite the doctor, have tongue, pulse, complexion, smell, voice and words examined. The patient will see the doctor jot a 'diagnosis' into the case history booklet (that typically is in the client's care), and then move onto a bed where a doctor will work with acupuncture needles on the body. When I read such case histories, however, I found that most 'diagnoses' were fairly similar, they often read ' "blood" of the "liver" and "kidneys" is depleted' (*ganshen xuexu*).[10] The sameness of 'diagnosis' contradicted my observation by the bedside, however, where a doctor would rarely select the same acupuncture points for inserting needles. This would suggest that it was by the bedside, in the process of deciding which acupuncture point was to be needled in which way, that the doctor made a diagnosis of the particular condition from which the patient suffered. This observation among Chinese acupuncturists suggests that the spatial layout reflects only a claim about an ideology that diagnosis and treatment should happen separately in separate spaces.

No TCM doctor would agree with me that 'diagnoses' are made by the bedside and not at the table, because no TCM doctor would consider the silent procedures of the acupuncturist by the bedside as 'diagnosis'. The diagnosis was the verbally expressed statement, made at the table, and written into the case history booklet. However, it is evident that what was written down at the table was far too general to have a great bearing on the doctor's choice of acupuncture points, varying from one patient to the other. From an observer's point of view, individual diagnosis and treatment thus took place, at least in acupuncture, in one and the same space, synchronously, by the bedside.

TCM medical colleagues have ridiculed acupuncturists for treating basically only one condition, the 'liver kidney blood depletion', and few others; they feel superior to them on the grounds that they believe that acupuncture involves 'just treatment'. Since they are so literacy-dominated, they cannot see that the acupuncturist engages in diagnosis by the bedside, and that good acupuncturists give very different treatments for each patient, even if the 'diagnosis' in the notes is much the same. TCM doctors consider the choice of acupuncture points a 'therapeutic skill' rather than a 'diagnostic procedure', and thereby delegate it to the domain of what sociologists of science call the 'tacit knowledge' of a skill. They adhere to what an anthropologist considers the 'actors' claim', which reflects a standpoint diametrically opposed to that of outside observers, who call the procedure by the bedside a 'diagnosis', or more precisely a 'diagnosis-cum-treatment'.

For these reasons, one is entitled to ask: what is the significance of the procedure by the table? Why do TCM doctors insist that the medical encounter consists of two phases: a diagnostic phase by the table (which produces a 'diagnosis' that is so general that it is basically irrelevant for the following therapeutic intervention) and a therapeutic phase by the bedside (which, as seen above, from an observer's viewpoint, consists of 'diagnosis-cum-treatment')? Is it that doctors who claim this, wish to state their alignment with 'modern' science? After all, 'modern' doctors stand by the claim that 'diagnosis first, treatment second' is good medical practice. But we have just observed that both African healers, and Chinese acupuncturists, make the diagnosis and provide the treatment in one and the same space.

Earlier research into pulse 'diagnosis', and my question as to why this particular diagnostic method has been so popular in so many places, and for over two thousand years, has led me eventually to the idea that it was perhaps the 'therapeutic touch' that the doctor gave the patient in the process of diagnosis and not merely the tactile perception of the patient's pulse that made this 'diagnostic' method so successful. This is further evidence, from yet another angle, that questions the validity of the notion that diagnostic procedures can clearly be separated from therapeutic ones.

Discussion

Time as inscribed in space, and the movement of patients in those spaces, has provided a common denominator for comparing and contrasting ' traditional' African, 'modern traditional' African (MTC), 'advanced traditional' Chinese medicine (TCM), and 'modern' biomedical consultation rooms. It has provided an 'action-frame' of various forms of medical encounter. Gell's conviction that all human beings relate to time in ways that 'are not markedly unlike the way in which we do ourselves', made the comparison between culturally disparate phenomena possible. Gell discourages the differentiating between 'physical', 'biological', 'social' or 'psychological' time, when he remarks : 'The whole point of an abstract category such as 'time' is precisely that it provides a means for the relative unification of otherwise diverse categories of processes' (1992: 315). The movement of the patients through the spaces of the consultation rooms, can be understood to have as common denominator the before-versus-after 'action-frame'.

The spatial arrangements of many 'traditional' African healers on the Tanzanian Swahili coast suggest that diagnosis and therapy happen simultaneously, in the same space, at the same time. One could argue that this simply underlines how unscientific 'traditional' African healers are; but I have shown that also among 'advanced traditional' Chinese acupuncturists the 'diagnosis' by the table is diagnostically insignificant. A sceptic could insist that the diagnostic process by the table is 'fake' only in those cases where 'traditional' medicines, African or Chinese, are being 'modernized'. The sceptic would point to a huge gap between principles of 'traditional' and 'modern' knowledge production, and emphasize that each system is grounded in a fundamentally different rationale.

One could point to the importance of the fireplace in Swahili coast practices, and be reminded of the presence of spirits instantiated through smoke and rising vapours, and see in this a typical feature of pre-modern, 'traditional' medical practice which is absent in the more secular 'advanced traditional' and 'modern' medicines. However, one would thereby disregard moments of synchronicity and diagnosis-cum-treatment which persist in those 'modern' practices. Given the diversity of conditions that people present to healers and doctors, it is unlikely that there is one single principle that rules 'good medical practice'. Interestingly, it was Western biomedical practitioners themselves who called into question the belief that diagnosis and treatment take place in consecutive phases by stating that 'diagnosis is treatment' (Brody and Waters 1980). Perhaps 'modern' medical practitioners need to look at 'traditional' forms of healing to recognize that in their practice, particularly for persistent problems, the moments of synchronicity might be precisely those that are conducive to healing, even though they are now hidden by biotechnology and an ideology that likens medicine to a science. My study of 'traditional', 'modern traditional', 'advanced traditional', and 'modern' practice has emphasized, rather, the continuities, after comparison within a common framework of 'time'.

Notes

1. This study draws on research in East Africa, a new geographical region for me which could not have been carried out without the help of many colleagues, too many to mention here. First and foremost, I thank Dr Edmund Kayombo and Ms Nargis Simmons in Dar es Salaam, and Dr Mwenda Ntarangwi in Nairobi. Without their knowledge of whom to locate where and without their interpretive skills I would not have been able to accumulate the data presented in such a short time. I would also like to thank Julia Powles, Sonia Scott-Fleming, Kent Maynard and the editors for valuable comments, and David Parkin and Gilbert Lewis for supporting this project from its inception. It was funded by a small grant of the British Academy.

2. Perhaps, its significance consists of consolidating among a wider circle of people a private explanation given for the ten years of suffering? The performance ensures that the individual suffering becomes, very tangibly, one of a collectivity and makes it, as Parkin (1992) would say: 'culturally loud'. It terminates suffering by scapegoating an insignificant past event, by seeing in it the 'cause' of the illness.

3. The time scale I looked at rarely exceeded an hour and often concerned a few minutes only; it did not concern days, months, years, and even decades, so

arguably, given the difference in time scale, this study does not link directly to the above ones.

4. Following the advice of a senior Tanzanian colleague I studied 'traditional Chinese' in conjunction with 'traditional African' medical practice, particularly in urban settings (for the latter see, for instance, Swantz 1990).

5. My Swahili is rudimentary but so is that of most Chinese practitioners with whom I conversed in Chinese; they themselves used English or depended on Tanzanian interpreters (from Chinese into Swahili) to speak with their mostly African clientele.

6. A profile of the Chinese practitioners and their clientele is given elsewhere (Hsu 2002).

7. Note that 'time' as inscribed into space, and the objects table and bed, does not always apply to a sequencing of diagnosis and treatment in 'modern' biomedicine: the bed is also used for examining the patient.

8. This is a short-term observation but it may not be entirely unrepresentative, given that 'impotence' stood out on the advert as the only hand written item. I interpret this to mean that the item of 'impotence' was sufficiently important to be added to the other ones at a more recent stage.

9. I visited about twenty practitioners on the Swahili coast between Tanga and Dar es Salaam.

10. Blood, kidneys, and liver all have specific Chinese medical meanings, and should not be mistaken for what these words designate in biomedicine. Depletion is a typical sign of old age, and the liver is the organ that typically stores the blood that dries out during menopause and old age. Acupuncture wards in the PRC took on functions of a day-care centre for the elderly, mostly women but also men (from fieldwork, 1988–9.)

References

Brody, H. and Waters, D.B. (1980), 'Diagnosis is treatment', *Journal of Family Practice* 10 (3): 445–9.

Farquhar, J. (1994), *Knowing Practice: The Clinical Encounter of Chinese Medicine*, Boulder: Westview.

Gell, A. (1992), *The Anthropology of Time: Cultural Constructions of Temporal Maps and Images*, Oxford: Berg.

Good, M.-J. Del Vecchio (1990), 'American oncology and the discourse on hope', *Culture, Medicine, and Psychiatry* 14: 59–79.

Hsu, E. (1999), *The Transmission of Chinese Medicine*, Cambridge: Cambridge University Press.

—— (2002), '"The medicine from China has rapid effects": Chinese Medicine Patients in Tanzania' in E. Hsu and E. Hoeg (eds), *Anthropology and Medicine,*

Special Issue: Countervailing Creativity: Patient Agency in the Globalisation of Asian Medicines, *Anthropology and Medicine* 9 (3): 291–313.

Kieschnick, J. (2003), *The Impact of Buddhism on Chinese Material Culture*, Princeton: Princeton University Press.

Kleinman, A. (1988), *Rethinking Psychiatry: From Cultural Category to Personal Experience*, New York: Free Press.

Kuriyama, S. (1999), *The Expressiveness of the Body and the Divergence of Greek and Chinese Medicine*, New York: Zone Books.

Laderman, C. and Roseman, M. (1996), *The Performance of Healing*, London: Routledge.

Lewis, G. (1975), *Knowledge of Illness in a Sepik Society*, London: Athlone Press.

McGuire (1988), *Ritual Healing in Suburban America,* New Brunswick: Rutgers University Press.

Nichter, M. (1996), *Anthropology and International Health*, Amsterdam: Gordon and Breach.

Parkin, D. (1992), 'Ritual as spatial direction and bodily division' in D. de Coppet (ed.), *Understanding Rituals*, London: Routledge.

Rhodes, L. Amarasingham (1984), 'Time and the process of diagnosis in Sinhalese ritual treatment', *Contributions to Asian Studies* 18: 46–59.

Scheid, V. (2002), *Chinese Medicine in Contemporary China: Plurality and Synthesis*, Durham: Duke University Press.

Swantz, L. (1990), *The Medicine Man of the Zaramo of Dar es Salaam*, Bohuslaningen: Uddevalla, Sweden.

Whyte, S. Reynolds (1997), *Questioning Misfortune: The Pragmatics of Uncertainty in Eastern Uganda,* Cambridge: Cambridge University Press.

Young, A. (1998), *The Harmony of Illusions: Inventing Post-traumatic Stress Disorder*, Princeton: Princeton University Press.

–9–

Time and the Work Ethic in Post-Socialist Romania
Monica Heintz

The operative must be in the mill at half past five in the morning; if he comes a couple of minutes late, he is fined; if he comes ten minutes late, he is not let in until breakfast is over, and a quarter of the day's wages is withheld, though he loses only two and one half hours' work out of twelve.

> Engels, *The Condition of the Working Class in England*, 1887

Sometimes when women go to work they say they have come for a rest.

> Ashwin and Bowers 1997, on Russia

Work is not to be measured in how many hours you spent with your buttock on a chair.

> Manager of organization Alpha

Let the clients wait, it tells them who is the boss, who decides.

> Manager of organization Beta

The capitalist understanding of time as money generates the dependence of work practices and values on the management of time at the workplace. However, what happens when capitalist structures are suddenly introduced in a society, whose perceptions of time management derive from a non-capitalist organization of labour? Do they create a parallel understanding of time proper to workplaces or do they allow 'time' as defined outside the workplace to enter freely into such enterprises? What effect does the confrontation of different understandings of time use have on work values and work practices? Who manages the individual's time on a daily basis and at the lifetime level? In this essay I will focus on the relation between time and work values, using ethnographic material gathered from service enterprises in Bucharest, Romania (1999–2000). Most data come from two private organizations, each of which belongs to a different segment of the labour market: the private enterprise Beta (the marketing department of a foreign language school), representative of the new local business initiatives, and the NGO Alpha, typical of the top-end labour market under Western guidance. In order to explain work practices, the trends in the management of time at the workplace are put into their cultural and historical context. The main actors in time management and the aim (or meaning) of time use at both the daily and lifetime level are considered. Finally, I draw a parallel between individual and national time, with respect to their measurement, management and orientation.

Time Discipline

E. P. Thompson's study, 'Time, Work-Discipline and the Making of Capitalism' (1967) opened the way for analyses on the link between the organization of work and the perception of time. The study shows how the demands of the capitalist organization of work gradually imposed a new understanding of time during the process of industrialization in England and how impressively individuals resisted the change in their perception of time – the complete 'conversion' to the new notion of time taking some centuries. This imposition was reinforced by a moral endorsement from the Protestant ethic, while other notions of time were condemned. 'Waste of time is thus the first and in principle the deadliest of sins', declared Richard Baxter's *Christian Directory* (Weber, 1984[1904]: 157).

The introduction of clocks and time-pieces in factories became an early tool for imposing the new work discipline. In Engels' account of work conditions in nineteenth-century England quoted above, punctuality and precision in time keeping are essential means for the exploitation of workers. Attali asserts that the invention of instruments for measuring time is a reflection of the desire for power: for mastering metaphysical uncertainty, for mastering the time of others and one's own, in the present and the future. In *Histoires du temps* (1983) he studies the history of these instruments and through it the history of the perceptions of time and of human inscriptions in time. 'The use and then the abandonment of an instrument for time measurement reveal the contemporary social order, while participating in it' (Attali, 1983: 9, my translation). At any time in history, several instruments of time measurement, and thus several notions of time, coexist.

In the two business enterprises that I will refer to in this essay, the organization of time was a proof that the spirit of strict discipline of capitalism (Benjamin Franklin's 'time is money') and the dictatorship of time decried by Engels had no translation into daily practice, though emphasized in managerial discourses.

Beta is the marketing department of a language school, which claims to be 'Western' and 'modern' in its marketing techniques, teaching environments and methods. Forty employees aged twenty to thirty (mostly good-looking women) try to sell ten-month English language courses to potential clients recruited from the street (in order to obtain their telephone numbers), subsequently re-contacted by phone (to persuade them to come to a presentation of the school) and given a full survey of courses on site, during which sales were negotiated. Employees have no fixed minimal wage and are paid only a small percentage of the price obtained for each course sold. While the appointments with the clients were strictly monitored (the clients were reminded twice of the appointment-time by phone, which made them arrive on time), the manager often summoned his own employees only to let them wait for ten or fifteen minutes as a test of their commitment. He also called them in every day one to two hours earlier than needed, for so-called training that seldom took place, and kept them after work for motivational talks, even though employees were paid per sale and not per hour. Despite the manager's rhetoric which emphasized the importance of getting a profit out of every activity, his behaviour indicated a loose perception of time: he thought it normal himself to spend the whole day at work, even if he had nothing to do. He also demonstrated his power through a manifest lack of consideration for the time of the others. Clients – at least, those whose appointment hour was respected – perceived arriving on time and respecting the appointment hour as a positive sign of a Western-style work culture, and liked to stress how pleased they were to have been treated this way. Clients who were made to wait tended to get angry because this contradicted their expectations of a Western style business – and often vented their feelings when they saw the high price of the courses. Employees, caught between the manager's incoherent discourses and wayward practice of 'Western' time management and the even less convincing financial rewards of the enterprise, offered no open resistance but simply left the job. Staff turnover took place every six weeks. This indicates that most service employees take into account, at least symbolically, the equation that time equals money: to them is stands for capitalistic practice and personal affluence.

The NGO Alpha is a humanitarian organization, funded from European sources, in which managers trust that work practices will arise naturally out of the humanitarian commitment of its employees. The headquarters comprise employees, mostly twenty-five- to thirty-five-year-old social sciences graduates, who are well remunerated. Here, where the flexibility of the hour of arrival at work is balanced only by the flexibility of the hour of departure from work, it is the organization of tasks over longer periods of time that is problematic. Report deadlines always force employees to work extra hours, while less pressurized periods give way to coffee breaks (though the preparation of reports could have taken place in advance). This slackness is especially unproductive when several persons depend on each other's work, as this is often the case. People have to waste days waiting for an essential response from somebody else, who is caught up trying to meet a deadline. Attempts are made to plan at least one to two weeks in advance, but timetables are not respected when another 'priority' arises. Changes in legislation or changes of appointments with other institutions are then offered as reasons for the disruption of work-schedules. The employees' main complaint is the organization's 'lack of management', which prevents them from having reasonable work systems, or 'restraints' (e.g. successive deadlines, quality norms) to act as markers of their time. This does not stop the organization surviving, but prevents it from expanding its activities. The scarcity and preciousness of time implied in 'time is money' is not embedded in this organization, because there has been no coherent attempt to make it real.

The importance of the discipline of time required by capitalist organization is such that the use of time in the enterprise might provide us with a key factor for understanding disorder and failure to improve work and business practices. However, given that the managers are unable to inject or implement a sense of time proper to the organization, the perception of time use coming from the larger urban context is what penetrates through external constraints. In general it still rules in organizations. I will focus on the perception of time in the urban environment in the following part of this chapter.

Changing Trends in the Allocation/Management of Daily Personal Time

I will survey the main historical changes in the management of time in the last half of the twentieth century in Romania, because of their continuous relevance to the lived experience of service employees through different eras.

Comparative studies between the way people express and measure time reveal that ecology (Thompson, 1967) and occupations (Whipp, 1987) are the decisive factors in shaping their perceptions. Thompson asserts that task-oriented time is characteristic for non-industrial societies. For example, Nuer time is structured by the daily needs of the cattle and by their seasonal needs (change of pasture, etc) (Evans-Pritchard, 1940). Similarly in English rural life in the past, the timetable for work used to be a function of the seasonal needs. The way people measured the time was loose: dawn, morning, dusk. In Romania, where industrialization was forced upon peasants only about thirty to forty years ago, Thompson's analysis of the industrialization process in England still holds true. The perception of time takes more than a few years to change. In rural Romania, during busy times (which are seasonal or linked to the imminence of feasts) people will work until they finish their duties, but will rest most of the day during the winter when there is less to do and the days are shorter.

In urban Romania, where the enterprises I have studied were situated, life contrasts radically with rural areas, because of the difference in the organization of daily work: in the countryside tasks are still dictated by the seasons and the consequent amount of work they bring, whereas in the city the hours of work are strictly regulated and the watch or clock gives the measure. There should therefore be two different notions of time. But this can hardly be the case, since there is no clear distinction between rural and urban people: migration to and from the countryside at different ages is common and everybody's extended family contains both rural and urban members. Having been educated to use daily time in a certain manner, later external constraints are likely to be resisted (which does not mean that people cannot succeed in imposing these themselves). What becomes then of Bloch's assertion (1977) in response to Geertz's suggestion that people could freely oscillate between several perceptions of time, each linked to a particular context? It is certainly true that if the context had the power to impose a certain notion of time, people would be constrained to learn it and comply with it. Yet, as the preceding part of this paper has shown, the reverse is often the case.

The socialist period was characterized by the gradual imposition of the state as manager of people's daily time. Logically, this should have been restricted to the workplace, to the eight hours work per day plus additional time for work meetings, party meetings, organized party demonstrations or compulsory 'voluntary' extra hours. However, the economy of shortage imposed additional hours for queueing, from which no family could escape (Schwartz, 1975; Câmpeanu, 1994). Queueing would normally take two or three hours every day (much more for retired people and children), in order to buy different types of food from different shops, which generally sold only one product at the time. Queueing was not only time-consuming, but domestically disruptive as it was impossible to foresee it. While queueing especially appears to disturb family life, waiting for buses for hours while heading for an appointment affects punctuality in relation to others (including people at the workplace). Planning and control over one's own time is thus difficult. Phenomena like this '*étatisation*' of time as Katherine Verdery has called it (1996) undermined people's own responsibility for their use of time, especially in the public sphere, reduced the importance of time-keeping and the potential for its fruitful use. Time was an efficient political tool and the 'colonization' of individual time was an important way of counteracting possible acts of resistance.

If queueing has disappeared from shops in post-socialist Romania, it has not disappeared from administrative offices (witness the huge queues for paying taxes). There are several other forms of time-wasting that these offices impose through their bureaucracy, lack of information and lack of appropriate internal services. Each time one finds out that s/he needs a fiscal stamp or a copy or a blank paper while dealing with officialdom, one has to go to the nearest post office or library (supposing s/he knows how to find the way), then back for another queue at the office requiring the stamp or paper. Most administrative branches have not internalized these services and have not displayed information on the procedures. To obtain the smallest bit of information, one is forced to queue. But this might also prove useless, if the employee is unable to provide information or is unwilling to investigate further. For solving each administrative problem, an employee loses one or more half-days of work.

What has changed, however, since socialist times is that the imposition of the state and of enterprises on one's time is increasingly understood and contested. Quite naturally, those who did not realize the value of their time under the socialist period understand it now, since the capitalist concept of Time as Money has become familiar. As a result, people tend to be meaner with their time and complain more if it is stolen from them. But when allocating personal time between activities, we can still see some surprising behaviour. Yes, time *is* money, but how much money?

One of the most striking behaviours to a Western eye is to see how people are prepared to save just a little money by spending so much of their time. While many could not afford to give up any opportunity for saving (for instance: retired people who do not have any other means of obtaining money), others simply do not equate time and money. One of my informants who was a high school teacher would spend twenty or thirty minutes to go to his school in order to make urban phone calls for free from there, while this would save him only a fifth of what he would earn by giving a private lesson in the same half hour – or so his wife complained. (One might note also that he was making private calls on public money.) However, she herself would shop in five different supermarkets in order to get the best prices.

Who attempts to play God the Father in Romania after 1989? On a short-term basis: enterprises. Urban dwellers are dependent on them for financial reasons and most private enterprises exercise their power through time abuse. This is common both in enterprises that pay by commission and in those where wages are paid for an eight-hour working day. In the marketing department that I observed, the working day was called 'flexible': i.e. rather unexpected and chaotic. It was typical to send employees home for two hours to change their clothes and eat and to come back afterwards. Thus, while there were only six hours per day of effective employment, the employee was at the company's disposal for ten hours or more. 'Staying around' was a constant requirement and justified by the fact that one should 'catch the job'. If one considers that these requirements also took place in the 'training' period, and that they were accompanied by a complete lack of security about a possible contract and possible payment (the training period simply grew longer and longer), the feeling that one's time was not respected also grew more justified. Indeed, new employees would not know if the month they had already spent in this rhythm would bring financial rewards or assure them of a job. Some employees were called to work but deliberately not given any clients, thus being deprived of the possibility of making any money. (If the contract was not concluded, work with the clients was not paid for at all. Also the risk of going to work but not having any client was a constant pressure, but the manager who could foresee it again preferred to keep employees around 'just in case'.) Consequently the working day of the employees at Beta was neither task-oriented, nor strictly measured; it was just as loose as their income opportunities. As for the better paid and often more secure jobs in the top labour market: there is a frequent requirement to do unpaid extra hours. As one of the top labour market employees told me, 'As soon as they pay you more than usual, they think they can ask you to do anything.' So time, after all, is still of less value than money.

Though the 'time is money' equation rhetorically rules in many enterprises, neither the managers, nor the employees have changed their behaviour in consequence, both lacking the practice of responsibility towards their own time. This means that when work or business commitments are not respected, the individual believes that this has happened because of external causes beyond their control, not that s/he transgressed any ethical principles. The manager of Beta expressed his regret that the employee called upon to work had no client (i.e. no possibility at least to try to earn some money), but he believed he had no responsibility for this and blamed the poor situation of the Romanian economy. This lack of accountability becomes more obvious when trying to discover what *does* manage the individual's life in the long run.

Managers of Time, Managers of Lives

In the socialist period, the state was overwhelmingly present on a daily basis, impinging on the personal management of daily time. Individuals remained free to organize their lives within the limits pre-set by the system. Lifetime jobs and fixed wages generated a feeling of long-term stability. Professional and/or financial events that would dramatically change one's life hardly existed. Typically, people would get married, acquire a house, have children, then retire on a state pension and raise their grandchildren. This could easily appear to be the result of one's own life choices – a consequence of the hegemony of representation exercised by the state (Yurchak, 1997). The state's authority over one's lifetime was not more contested than God's will – except by intellectuals.

While private enterprises have replaced the state in many cases as the managers of individual time on a daily basis, they appear to have no great impact for the long term. This is due to the fragility of both the enterprises and the individual's position within them. While commercial pressures could prevent young women from having children, for example, women would always have the option of giving up the job, if they wanted to.

Therefore on a long-term basis, one could master one's life, but can one see that far ahead in a survival economy? Living from one day to the next because of economic constraints and social instability renders long-term life planning obsolete. The bank in which you saved your money for a private flat could collapse tomorrow and you might recuperate your money (partially) in two to five years' time; the company for which you work may get restructured tomorrow or you may get fired without notice; the political regime might change or you may have the chance to win in one of the TV game shows, which you play every day. Fate is finally responsible for events that you have assumed you initiated for yourself.

Though there are more risks than in long established capitalist societies, usually there is some freedom of choice about how to employ one's time and how to trade it against money and pleasure. This also depends on how 'choice' is defined and by whom. The notion of freedom of choice in general is a new concept in Romania; during the socialist period, state control made most people think that they had no freedom of choice. There was choice, but not in the consumerist sense where both choice X and choice Y would bring you a certain satisfaction. Applying rational thinking when choosing between being obediently conformist and taking the dangerous path of dissent was tantamount to no choice in the end. As in the case of daily time, which appears determined by external factors (the climate for the rural population, the state during the socialist period, or commercial enterprises today in urban areas), one's lifetime tends to be perceived as predetermined or at least to have its main limits set by external factors or 'opportunities'. That does not mean that life itself would be thought or lived as predetermined. But we cannot refer to choices in terms of time unless we consider the orientation of time: the meaning or the reason for this choice.

Meaning/Purpose of Everyday Time

Time is measured in the Time of Codes (Attali, 1983) by sophisticated and precise watches. People are reminded by them of the existence of every second, of every tenth of a second. The value of the second is remembered, however, only during activities that are viewed negatively. One is aware of every minute one unwillingly spends in a waiting room, but we do not notice time passing when engaged in pleasant activities. This may appear to be a common trend in industrial societies, but there are some fine details. The readiness with which we forget what time it is when happily engaged in an activity belongs, in a way, to an 'age of innocence'. Responsible, mature women will arrive late because they met with neighbours on their way, engaged in a conversation and simply forgot to consult their watches. As the awareness of the flow of time surfaces only now and then, so does the awareness of its value. The 'why' that should accompany the allocation of a time-limit is often absent, even when it is entirely one's own responsibility to manage one's time. The way people express how time is used contains an implicit judgement on the meaning of its duration. In Romania 'time wasted' is referred to as 'time lost' (*timp pierdut*). The difference from the English expression is that while 'waste' extends over a period of time (necessary for the activity of 'wasting' to take place), the 'loss' is a sudden, immediate event, almost an accident. This also implies that the agent has less power to stop the process and that s/he becomes aware that it took place only after the event. Time that is positively 'spent' is referred to as *timp petrecut,* literally 'time passed'. (In English we refer to time 'spent', as for any other consumable.) Linguistic uses provide some comfort in the situations observed above.

For many of my informants who were in full-time employment (sometimes also on second jobs), the aim of a busy day was to make it to the end and go to bed. This could unfortunately also be said of many Westerners. The French call this kind of life *'metro-boulot-dodo'*, (tube-work-sleep). Romanian urban dwellers however, have much more diversity in their spatial destinations: they need to visit five shops rather than one to buy food, they have dozens of offices to go to for paying their bills and other matters, they have second jobs and greater family commitments. They must have some way of restoring their energy! The explanation may be quite simply: they go to work in order to rest, as Ashwin and Bowers were told by their Russian informants (1997: 28). Between the multitudes of commitments they have every day, most service employees count on their work hours as the most stable and reliable amount of time for collecting thoughts and recovering energy. People describe the time they spend at their workplace as 'I stayed at work' and a very widely circulated joke about the state employees is a pun on the similarity between state (*stat*) and stay (*sta*). When the only purpose of an activity is its end, its 'destination', it is easy to understand why in the absence of coherent time management at the workplace, work time and work obligations are respected as little as possible, and why extra activities of a more pleasant or of a greater personal value are performed in order to 'fill' the time (knitting, chatting, phoning home, solving personal problems).

The slack attitude at the work place is not to the liking of all service employees and in the NGO Alpha, the sense of duty and interest in its progress does not allow for any rest during the working day. But employees complain that their daily time has no planned shape or 'destination' either. The succession of events in the workplace is too rapid and does not allow them to plan, look back on their planning or realize that they have accomplished anything during the day. Thus, in the first half hour when employees arrive at work, they wonder how, when and what they should do, whereas before the monthly deadlines everybody has to work non-stop to finish. These times are so pressurized that they are treated as a constraint, not as an opportunity to give real meaning to employees' jobs. Deadlines are not creating positive rhythms; they remain disruptive events (for example, by forcing employees beyond the eight hours of their normal working day).

Monica Heintz

Daily time appears to have no proper purpose. The capitalist measure of work in terms of hours, not tasks, is imposed on employees who used to understand time as task-oriented. It encourages the meaninglessness of daily time and incites the employees to wait for work time to pass (when they can). Daily time contains only an alternation between a time of constraint and a time of pleasure, time 'spent' and time 'lost', time of sleep and time awake. This echoes on a small scale Leach's structuralist view of time as a sequence of oscillations between polar opposites, a pendulum-like movement (1961). Repetitive daily activities receive meaning only in the long term, when a succession of accomplishments can be reviewed.

Individual Time and National Time

In his lecture, 'Times and Identities' (1991), John Davis asserts that while all people experience duration, they have different notions of time that are relevant for their social life and the construction of their identities. Two different symbolic representations of time can coexist in one culture, depending on whether they refer to time in its daily acceptance or to time as 'history'. The way people perceive 'daily' time is relevant for their social behaviour and the way they perceive 'history' for their identities. The concordance or contradiction between these two scales also generates distinct structures of perception.

What a close look at Romanian history reveals is the fact that the present transition from socialism to capitalism could be situated within a long series of historical transitions: from an agrarian to a modern capitalist state, from capitalism to Soviet socialism, from the Stalinist form of socialism to Romanian national socialism (to mention only the most recent), most of them against the background of external wars and treaties constantly reshaping the borders. 'Being Romanian has meant centuries of being survivors, principally by mechanisms other than overt conflicts' (Verdery, 1983: 370). One could establish linearity in the flow of history, where key events are remembered to be written in history, while 'transition' periods are erased. The positive history of the nation was generally written, especially during the last fifty years of Marxism, through this process of selected memory. However, if the periods of transition are not to be erased, we should follow rather the interpretation of the Romanian philosopher Lucian Blaga (1969) who sees Romanian history as alternating, but what defines it is the alternation between periods of peace and periods of war, i.e. between periods of the assertion of the national soul and periods of survival. This, together with the geographical alternation of hill/valley that characterizes the Romanian territory, says Blaga, has shaped the Romanian soul. This interpretation re-evaluates and reconciles current 'transitional' abnormalities. It also echoes on the historical scale the understanding of time we have noted on the daily scale, which resembles Leach's pendulum model. Unfortunately this interpretation of history is not popular.

Other similarities between the time of the individual and the time of the nation (or history) can be found. Understanding agency in the management of national time helps in understanding agency (or the lack of it) in the management of individual time. History remains an important frame within which Romanians define their identity. Making sense of recent events and of their relevance for the history of the nation is thus of utmost importance for the understanding of individuals' histories, which gain meaning as part of a national project. The answer to questions of the management and orientation of historical time is called 'the Romanian destiny'.

Most philosophical and even sociological works on this issue concentrate on Romania's 'fate' in the world and have strong historicist views. The existence of a national destiny is taken for granted in Romanian social sciences. A recent call for papers for the Annual Conference of the Centre for Romanian Studies (a prestigious research centre that has published many history books since 1989) states that 'The Romanian lands have traditionally been a crossroads of Europe, a land and people influenced by contacts with various peoples and cultures, a land traditionally on the border of vast and mighty empires which have influenced its destiny.' This underlines both that national destiny exists as such and that it has largely been determined by external factors. The national anthem urges on Romanians: 'Now or never/ Build yourselves another destiny/ That would astonish/Your cruel enemies' (my translation).

Indeed, the history of Romania cannot be understood apart from European history: first, the extension of various empires, then in the twentieth century of zones of influence; and currently, the economic needs of the European market (Chirot, 1976: 121). The Roman *principates* of which modern Romania is composed have always turned toward Western Europe, though some historians claim that this model, borrowed or imposed from the West has proved inadequate to solve Romania's problems and has become a major handicap (Roberts, 1951). The revelation of power-games such as the Yalta Conference or the Kosovo crisis in Spring 1999 has often led to disillusionment with the West and to the reinforcement of nationalistic movements. However, neither the pressure of Western agencies, nor the revolt of national pride in the face of the Romanian government's present servitude towards Western countries, seems to change the Romanians' will to join the European Union and NATO, which are viewed as guarantors of future stability and economic prosperity.

Conclusion

The recurrent theme in my ethnography is that time and timing in Rumania are not rigorous and their control is minimal. Both the individual and the nation tend to let events occur. They are not left to chance, but to destiny, the external benevolent co-ordinator of human/national life. This concept enters into conflict with the necessities of capitalist organization. The absence of work discipline and the lack of education in the management of time allows 'time' as defined outside the workplace to run freely into enterprises. This 'laissez-faire' in time discipline is due to a tradition of non-agency in time management, which has been shaped by historical circumstances throughout the twentieth century. Time is a rare thing and it is appreciated as such. While a capitalist logic would conclude that time is 'expensive' and scarce and should be managed accordingly, most Romanians do not consider time as a commodity at all: it is neither for sale, nor for purchase. They do not manage their time – they simply use it. Some of the paradoxical behaviour signalled above (the willingness to give all of one's time to a Western style manager, but the impatience over a waste of time with state administration) comes from the fact that Romanian urbanites try to comprehend the capitalist notion of time as a commodified value through their own notion of time.

The dialogue with history allows for a parallel between individual and national time regarding their orientation and meaning. While history does not yield a strong sense of direction or 'destination' and continues to appear meaningless, the individual's understanding of her/his personal life will follow the same trajectory. A lack of meaning is an inevitable consequence, both in work practices and values, and in the individual's sense of self.

References

Ashwin, S. and Bowers, E. (1997), 'Do Russian women want to work', in Buckley, M (ed.), *Post-Soviet Women: from the Baltic to Central Asia*, Cambridge: Cambridge University Press.

Attali, J. (1983), *Histoires du temps*, Paris: Fayard.

Blaga, L (1969 [1944]) *Trilogia Culturii*, Bucuresti: Editura pentru Literatura Universala.

Bloch, M. (1977), 'The past and the present in the present', *Man* 12: 278–292.

Câmpeanu, P. (1994), *România: Coada la hrană, un mod de viapă*, Bucuresti: Editura Litera.

Chirot, D. (1976), *Social Change in a Peripheral Society: The Creation of a Balkan Colony*, London: Academic Press

Davis, J. (1991), *Times and Identities: An Inaugural Lecture delivered before the University of Oxford on 1 May 1991*, Oxford: Clarendon Press.

Evans-Pritchard, E.E. (1940), *The Nuer,* Oxford: Clarendon Press.

Leach, E. (1961), *Rethinking Anthropology*, London: Athlone Press.

Roberts, H.L. (1951), *Rumania: Political Problems of an Agrarian State*, New Haven: Yale University Press.

Schwartz, B. (1975), *Queuing and Waiting: Studies in the Social Organization of Access and Delay*, Chicago: Chicago University Press.

Thomas, K. (1999), *The Oxford Book of Work*, Oxford: Oxford University Press.

Thompson, E.P. (1967), 'Time, work discipline and industrial capitalism', *Past and Present* 38: 56–97.

Verdery, K. (1983), *Transylvanian Villagers: Three Centuries of Political, Economic and Ethnic Change*, Berkeley: University of California Press.

Verdery, K. (1996), *What Was Socialism, and What Comes Next?*, Chichester: Princeton University Press.

Weber, M. (1984 [1904]), *The Protestant Ethic and the Spirit of Capitalism*, London: Allen and Unwin.

Whipp, R. (1987), '"A time to every purpose": an essay on time and work', in P. Joyce (ed.), *The Historical Meanings of Work*, Cambridge: Cambridge University Press.

Yurchak, A. (1997), 'The cynical reason of late capitalism: power, pretense and the *Anekdot*', *Public Culture* 9: 161, 188.

Part IV
Countering the Metanarratives

–10–

Quartering Sheep at Carnival in Sud Lípez, Bolivia
Maggie Bolton

Carnival celebrations immediately before the start of Lent in the Christian calendar are a feature of the Andean region and form an obvious focus for examining the significant timing of things in that context. This place in the calendar suggests a colonial origin and hence a possible link to structures of political power, and also, somewhat contradictorily, to the anarchic Carnival celebrations of mediaeval Europe. However, it is also for Andeans a seasonal festival linked to the agricultural calendar. February marks the end of the rainy season and the reaping of the first fruits of the harvest, and it is highly probable that the European festival swallowed up pre-conquest rites held at a similar time of the year.[1]

Anthropological writing about Carnival has tended to have two foci: seasonality and political power. Works addressing both have drawn heavily on historical material. Olivia Harris (1982), for example, writing about the Laymi of northern Potosí, explains how the souls of the dead arrive in the land of the living at the start of November for the festival of All Saints and All Souls. This is the time of year when the rains are held to commence and the dead are associated with the coming of the rains and with the fertility of the land (although not with human fertility).[2] Marking the end of the rainy season, Carnival is also for the Laymi the time when the dead are sent packing whence they came. The two festivals of the dead, All Saints and Carnival, thus divide the year in two, possibly echoing the experiences attributed to the dead of Qullasuyu, the south-eastern quarter of the Inca realm, by the sixteenth-century provincial Andean nobleman, Felipe Guaman Poma de Ayala (1993 [1613]: 221) who recounts how each year they experience six months of hard labour and suffering followed by six months of feasting.

Rasnake (1988: 255–9) takes up the theme of political power in his discussion of Carnival among the Yura in the south of Potosí department. He sees this as a time when political power is negotiated between the rural social group (*ayllu*) and the nation-state. Carnival is a celebration that emphasizes both internal organization and external relations, and is also a time of dialogue between *ayllu* and state – when the people of Yura define state control as an inevitable element of social life, and propitiation of the state is necessary in order to ensure their continued access to lands. Visits to the *ayllu* boundaries reaffirm the salience of a pact understood to exist between state and *ayllu*,[3] while the focus of attention in the centre of *ayllu* territory is a stone of ambiguous symbolism – it is both a symbol of the overall unity of Yura and also a symbol of Spanish colonial rule (and by extension the imposition of state power).

Social Memory and the Andes

The ethnographic works cited above all have as a central assumption that, in the Andean region, forms from the past persist into the present and that features of the present can be elucidated by reference to the past. The use of the past as a means of elucidating what is found in the present has long been a defining feature of Andean studies and a fruitful means of proceeding – those studying the region have long argued that it is impossible to understand it without reference to its colonial history and many have looked further back through accounts written in the early years of colonization to the times of the Inca empire.[4] This sort of reliance on the past brings to mind questions about structures – early works in Andean anthropology were concerned with identifying structures that could be taken as characteristic of Andean society – and also culture.[5] As Bloch (1996) has pointed out, the concept of culture inevitably raises questions about memory, and one definition of 'culture' would equate it with the knowledge or memories that different members of a society share: that is, with the elusive idea of social memory.

Various anthropologists have concurred in the idea that memory is not just an individual faculty, but is also something that is social or collective. Maurice Halbwachs (1950), a student of Durkheim, went so far as to state that the act of remembering was always social: what is recalled, however personal that may be, exists in relationship with the assemblage of notions that many others possess – with the whole material and moral life of the societies in which we live. Memories are constructed through a process of interaction and accommodation.

Halbwachs's ideas have been taken up by Connerton (1989) who writes principally about Western European society although his intention is to propose an idea that is much more general. His claim is that images and recollected knowledge of the past are conveyed and sustained through more-or-less ritual performances. Drawing on examples as diverse as Revolutionary France, Nazi Germany and rituals of the Catholic Church, he identifies commemorative ceremonies and certain bodily practices as sites of social memory.

However, there is to my mind a certain tension in Connerton's work. On the one hand, he seems to be saying that in commemorative ceremonies certain events and/or persons are remembered, and that it is possible to convey and sustain them through rituals. Commemorative ceremonies thus become acts of transmission for historical 'deposits' (Connerton's term) of memory. In the case of bodily practices, his emphasis is on how the past contextualizes the present and what is remembered might loosely be glossed as 'culture'. On the other hand, however, he emphasizes the performative nature of both commemorative ceremonies and bodily practices, although for him they are performative only in that they are acts that convey information. This emphasis on performativity, nonetheless, suggests something more subtle and more dynamic, that Connerton seems to avoid. This could suggest that the past not only shapes the present, but also that through ceremonies of commemoration and bodily practices, the present also shapes what is remembered of the past.

Ingold (2000: 138) taking most of his examples from hunter-gatherer societies, cautions against our tendency to think of memory as some sort of box in which information is stored, and of remembering as a matter of retrieval from storage. He emphasizes that objects of memory do not precede activities of remembering. On the contrary, it is through activities of remembering that memories are forged (ibid.: 148). He thus takes away the distinction between what is remembered and how it is remembered. Acts of transmission are replaced by activities of remembering, through which memories are generated. In hunter-gatherer societies, journeying forward along a path or a trail may also take one back to places imbued with the presence of the ancestors. In this model, emphasis is taken away from the replication and transmission of past events as activities of remembering may involve a good measure of improvization.

In the context of Andean studies, Abercrombie (1998: 130) has proposed something of a similar nature. He cites Connerton on social memory when he contends that in the Andes most forms of social memory are not construed, or even construable, through verbal narrative. His idea is that memories take the form not of narrative but of pathways through the Andean landscape – they are to be found in the landscape, in the pilgrimages that take place in it, in the libations that are poured onto it, and in the way people live in it. Here Abercrombie appears to be suggesting something much closer to Ingold's idea – that acts of pilgrimage, of pouring libations, and so on, are activities of remembering through which memories may be generated. However, while Ingold tends towards a presentist perspective, Abercrombie is well aware that the present is only experienced in specific historical and social circumstances – and hence juxtaposes ethnographic and ethnohistorical material.

This chapter looks at some ritual acts that take place in San Pablo de López as Carnival draws to a close. People there do not verbalize much about the ceremony in question, but archival documents and ethnohistorical evidence suggest a link between it and the payment of tribute to the Bolivian state in the nineteenth century. Here, I am concerned with the dynamics between past and present – with how it is that activities that generate (non-verbal) memories of the past are also acts of doing that effect something in the present and involve agency. Ceremonies that occur at the same point in the calendar each year, separated by qualitatively similar intervals of time, make space for politics as they intersect with the time of happenings in the region and of political changes at the level of the nation-state.

The Ethnographic Setting

San Pablo de Lípez is a small town in the extreme southwest of Bolivia and, although it has only around 300 inhabitants, is the capital of Sud Lípez province in Potosí department. This status as a provincial capital is significant for the identity of the present-day population of San Pablo. Sud Lípez is a sparsely populated province where much of the land is high *puna* (rough pastureland) in excess of 4000 metres above sea level. Unlike many communities in the Andes where anthropologists have worked, the local population is no longer organized into *ayllus*, the traditional unit of communal land ownership. That the *ayllus* disappeared in the 1950s is the latest round in the history of negotiations and contestations of identity in which local people have engaged with external powers (Spanish colonial regime and Bolivian nation-state). It is difficult to apply labels such as *mestizo* (of mixed descent) or Indian to the people of San Pablo and I have argued elsewhere (Bolton 2000) that they actively adopt a strategy of indeterminacy with regard to labels that others would put upon them.

Today local people herd llamas and a few still make annual journeys with llama caravans to the warmer valleys of Tupiza and Tarija to exchange salt for maize, although for most waged labour is also an important means of support. There are sometimes opportunities for paid work in the area, and many people migrate for periods of different duration to find jobs in Bolivia's larger towns and cities. The region is also rich in minerals: the area around San Pablo and neighbouring San Antonio de Lípez formed an important mining centre in the seventeenth century, when the silver mines of Lípez for a brief time rivalled those of the city of Potosí. Today there remains a limited amount of small-scale mining in the area and, from time to time, large international mining companies arrive to take mineral samples and to explore for gold deposits.

Bringing Carnival to a Close in San Pablo: Quartering Sheep at the *Kacharpaya*

Carnival celebrations in San Pablo last for about a week. The festival is brought to a close in a ceremony called a *kacharpaya* (from Quechua *kacharpariy* – to bid farewell) held on the Thursday of Carnival week and sponsored by a member of the community, which involves the playing of local music, dancing and the consumption of a communal meal.[6] An important feature of the *kacharpaya* is that two sheep, slaughtered before the event, are quartered. The idea is that the carcasses are pulled apart by dancing men, each man taking hold of one leg of the dead animal. In practice, the carcasses are slit in half longitudinally before the ceremony, and when the halves do not tear readily, someone intervenes with a sharp knife.

Carnival is a time when normal activities are suspended and people drink, play local music, dance and, if they remain sufficiently sober, visit the far-flung homesteads belonging to other community members. It seems at first sight to be a time when the local community sets aside its claim to be part of the Bolivian nation-state and forgets the involvement of its members in *mestizo* activities like waged labour and commerce. It is a time when its people appear more like the members of *ayllus* in other areas than like the market vendors and labourers of Bolivia's cities. A more considered view, however, shows Carnival to be more complex and to involve an interplay or dialogue between local and national identities.

The sections that follow examine how the ritual of quartering sheep at carnival recalls through a ritual act the organization of the *ayllus* by which the local population was organized and through which its people paid tribute in colonial and early republican times. However, rather than simply look at the ceremony as a relic from the past, I want to look at its salience for the present and to explore how the ritual makes space for politics – for actively contesting, negotiating and affirming internal relations and relations with outside entities.

Quadripartition

Quadripartition has long been considered an important motif in Andean social organization (Rivière 1983, Platt 1986). The Inca empire was divided into quarters – it was known as Tawantinsuyu, which can be glossed as 'The Land of the Four Quarters' or 'the Four Quarters Together' (the Quechua suffix *–ntin* indicating togetherness). Quadripartite models abound also in accounts of the social organization of present-day Andean communities. Platt (1986: 235–7) for example, writing of the Macha of northern Potosí comes up with a quadripartite model which results from the cross-cutting of two principles of dual organization: Ayllu Macha is divided into two moieties, Aransaya and Urinsaya, and is further divided in a way that cross cuts this division by an ecological division between *puna* (the highland area in which potatoes are grown and llamas herded) and valley (lower lying land where maize is cultivated). This quadripartition is further reproduced for the Macha at the level of the household through patterns of marriage. The quartering of sheep in the Carnival could thus recall some model of quadripartition by which some former *ayllu* of the area may have been organized.

Payment of Tribute in the Nineteenth Century

An Andean preoccupation with quadripartition may account for the quartering of one sheep at Carnival, but not for the two that are quartered at the *karcharpaya*. On this point, however, archival research proves illuminating, especially on the matter of the tribute paid by Indian *ayllus* to the Republican government in the nineteenth century. Tribute was paid by 'Indians' to the Spanish crown throughout the colonial era. Then, it has been argued (Saignes 1995) being 'Indian' was more a fiscal than it was a racial category – Indians were people who paid tribute, while Spaniards and *mestizos* paid tithes and a sort of value-added-tax (*alcabalas*). After Independence from Spain, in the early nineteenth century, tribute payments by Indians were retained by the republican government, in spite of the newly formed nation-state's intention to make all people within its bounds into Bolivian 'citizens', since these payments provided a large and important portion of state revenues.

During the period of the mid-to-late nineteenth century, the *ayllus* of the then much larger Lípez province paid their annual tribute in two instalments, and were charged as *agregados* (incomers rather than natives – a status that had been the source of contestation in earlier eras (Bolton 2000). This meant that each contributor paid three and a half pesos for the six-month period. The two instalments were due at Christmas and at the feast of San Juan in June. However, the calendar of activities of the *ayllus* – which involved periods of cash paid employment, whereby coinage for tribute payment could be earned, and annual journeys to the valley regions to exchange highland for valley produce – led to the tribute due at Christmas actually being paid at Carnival and that due at San Juan being paid in August.[7]

Censuses *(revisitas)* were taken from time to time in order to enumerate the tribute paying population. Those taken for the region in the mid-nineteenth century show that of the five *ayllus* in the south of the province, two paid their tribute in the cantonal capital of San Pablo. These were Ayllu Pululus and Ayllu Santa Isabel. It is tempting to speculate that these two *ayllus* may have been the halves of some larger entity of social organization. I want, however, to suggest therefore that the ritual held to mark the end of Carnival in San Pablo is from one perspective an activity of remembering that recalls this tribute-paying event, through remembering the structure of the *ayllus* involved, even though local people do not articulate this in words. Further, it may be suggested that the sheep-quartering ceremony recalls not only the internal divisions of the *ayllus* that organized the area but also the relationship between those *ayllus* and the nation-state that the payment of tribute implied.

Rather than see the sheep-quartering as simply a relic of the past – a representation of a mode of social organization, or of particular events that took place in the past – I understand the ceremony as also a performative act whereby memories are generated and where simultaneously something else is effected in the present: relations both internal and external to the local group are sorted out and affirmed. It is this activity of sorting out and affirming relations that makes Carnival celebrations salient and makes relevant the activity of remembering the sorting out of relations that took place in the past. I begin by examining the symbolism of dividing animals and birds in the Andes.

Dividing Animals and Sorting Out Relations

The ritual division of sheep in San Pablo recalls Platt's (1988) discussion of an Inca rite of conquest related by the sixteenth-century chronicler and extirpator of idolatries, Cristóbal de Albornoz. Albornos wrote of a ceremony in which the Inca (or his local representative) and the chieftain of a newly conquered people each took hold of the wing of a live falcon and pulled until the bird was torn asunder. Inca and chieftain would each retain his half of the bird. This appears to have been, in effect, an oath of loyalty by the chieftain to the Inca, signifying that, henceforth, Inca and chieftain would have to remain as closely linked as the two halves of the bird (Platt 1988: 413).

Platt sees the Incaic falcon-dividing ceremony as a rite of conquest that expressed new relations of power within the Inca state, but which was based upon a cultural logic shared by both local chieftain and Inca: a logic that involves the ambiguous inequality of symmetry or 'light disequilibrium'. This is also exhibited by the two moieties of an *ayllu*, that are symmetrical although one moiety takes precedence over the other, or between the two halves of a married couple, where man and woman are complementary, but where the man takes precedence at least in the public sphere.[8] Thus, a conquered people could understand their relationship with the conquering Cuzqueño regime as balanced, but with a slight disequilibrium that legitimized the supremacy of the Inca (ibid: 414). A conquered people would henceforth owe 'tribute' to the Inca in the form of services, usually work in the fields belonging to the state or to the solar cult, and in return would continue to enjoy access to their own lands.

In further works, Platt (1982, 1984) has explored the indigenous conceptualization of the relationship between tribute-paying *ayllus* and colonial and republican regimes. His interpretation is along similar lines to that set out above for the relationship between Inca state and conquered group. An *ayllu* paid its tribute in money to the state as part of a 'pact of reciprocity', which in turn guaranteed it access to its lands. Platt (1984) documents the unrest that followed Republican attempts in the nineteenth century to make 'Indians' into private landholders,[9] and Rasnake (1988) suggests that in Yura this relationship with the state, conceived as a state-*ayllu* pact was an underlying factor behind the group retaining the *ayllu* as their unit of social organization.

Hence, the sheep-quartering ceremony at Carnival may not only recall the *ayllus* that once organized the population in the area, but also the relationship between these groups and the tribute-collecting state and the sorting out of this relationship. The sections that follow explore how Carnival today is still a sorting out and affirmation of relationships.

Sorting Out Internal Relations at Carnival

In many areas of the Andes Carnival is known as *pujllay*, the Quechua term for 'play' (Allen 1988: 182–9, Flores Ochoa 1979: 90). According to Allen, in the Peruvian community in which she worked, it is a time for boisterous sexual play and ritual fighting. In this area of Peru, the latter is now reduced to competitive dance, but formerly real fighting between different *ayllus* or between the divisions within an *ayllu* took place with stones and slings, and could lead to deaths. Platt (1988) writing about the ritual battles (*tinkus*) between the moieties of Ayllu Macha similarly describes them as *pujllay*, but also sees them as serving to ritualize existing conflicts, along with providing a means to their resolution. He compares them also with the Incaic falcon-dividing ceremony described above and with a present-day rite in Macha, in which a hen or duck is cut in half and divided between the representatives of the two moieties of the *ayllu* following a game of tug-of-war. The hen-dividing rite appears related to the *tinkus*, in that it is concerned with the internal relations of the *ayllu*, while the Inca ritual was concerned with relations with an outside entity. Carnival can be seen as a time for sorting out relations between the various internal divisions of a group or for equilibrating relations between them through extraordinary behaviour that is classified as play.

One feature of Carnival week in San Pablo is that one is expected to be 'bad' (*malo*). In the Andes, 'bad' can mean bad in the sense of evil or nasty, but it can also mean 'powerful' and some combination of the two meanings is implied here. Carnival week in 1996 was one of the most difficult periods of my fieldwork, as my host, who was the sponsor for the *karcharpaya*, and who usually treated me with polite respect, spent most of the week drunk and being abusive to me, to other members of the community and to his family.

Drunkenness is an important feature of Andean festivities: as Harvey (1991: 12) has noted, being drunk beyond a state of controlled animation is necessary to engage fully with the powers achieved through drink and to animate the powers of the landscape. Drunks, she notes (ibid: 8), are also not held to be responsible for what they do or say. They do not remember what has happened while they were drunk, and distance themselves from it by the use of the reportative suffix (*-sqa*) in Quechua and by claiming that it is the drink that speaks rather than the imbiber.

In San Pablo the immunity conferred by drink and by the occasion of a festival in which the normal order of things is suspended – when people are exhorted to be 'bad' – was used by some San Pableños as an excuse to air their grievances and to 'have a go' at people they would normally treat with respect. This recalls Bakhtin's understanding of the Carnivals of mediaeval Europe, when festive behaviour could be used as a sanction to inflict a severe punishment on one's foes or settle accounts with them, and when there was no clear dividing line between what was play and what was life (Bakhtin 1984: 263–8). In other words, through drinking, being drunk and behaving badly at Carnival, San Pableños sort out relations among themselves.

Sorting out External Relations

As suggested above, a close examination of the Carnival celebration in San Pablo shows a complex interplay of local and national identities. Visits to the boundaries of a community are a feature of Carnival in many Andean communities: Harris (1982) notes that visits to outlying hamlets are a feature of the Laymi festival, and Rasnake (1988) describes the same to the boundaries of Ayllu Yura. Rasnake also interprets these visits as a reaffirmation of the state-*ayllu* pact, guaranteeing the rural group access to its lands. In theory, something similar is supposed to take place in San Pablo. Most families in the area own a house in the town, where, if there are children of school age, the family stays during the school term, and an outlying homestead (*estancia* or *campo wasi*). This is where their herds of llamas graze, often under the supervision of an elderly relative who is not responsible for bringing-up children. Some of these homesteads are 10 kilometres or more from the town itself. Carnival in San Pablo should involve visits to all of these outlying properties, and these visits are a feature that San Pableños will mention if asked about the celebration. As in Yura, the idea of reaffirming the extent of the territory of the community seems to be present.[10]

Carnival music is another site of dialogue between locality and state. Throughout Carnival week, male musicians play long wooden flutes (*flautas*) and small drums (*cajas*). Women are supposed to sing, but did not do so on the occasion when I was present, and they dance waving small white flags during the *karcharpaya*. The music played is particular to the festival and the intrusion of other sorts of music is not appreciated (although the cooperative miners at a nearby mine did listen to brass band music from the urban celebration in Oruro, on the radio).[11] One of my worst *faux pas* during fieldwork was to play urban music on my *charango*[12] during the festival – as explained below.

Although the music played at Carnival was undeniably local, the costumes worn by the male musicians playing at the *karcharpaya* juxtaposed local and wider identities. In recognition of the seasonal aspect of the festival, the men playing flutes and drums were adorned with various bits of greenery taken from the patios of those few people in San Pablo who take the trouble to cultivate anything.[13] They also wore two woven bags – a small *ch'uspa* for coca and a larger *talega* for barley – and were covered with confetti and streamers. However, along with the greenery, they also wore the blue fleece-lined caps with earflaps and safety spectacles that were issued by a US owned mining company that had set up its headquarters in the town. The company was prospecting for gold deposits, and had engaged many of the men of San Pablo for temporary work.

National and local identities are further juxtaposed in the events that take place after the sheep are quartered. The sheep-quartering ceremony itself is held in the courtyard of the festival sponsor's house. Once it is over, all the participants leave the town for the flat open space on its eastern edge. Carnival music and dancing continues there for a while, becoming more and more frantic and reaching a climax when the women dancers start to chase the male musicians and to hit them with stems of barley. Some run chasing and being chased far out into the countryside, where the women 'bring carnival to the men'. When they eventually come to a halt, they pour libations – a final action by which San Pableños say Carnival is released. The tenor of the festival changes at this point, and all of a sudden the flutes and drums of Carnival are cast aside. This was the point at which I realized my earlier mistake with the *charango* music, for suddenly people were asking me to get my instrument and telling me that the time had come when I could play.

After going down on their knees to ask pardon for their bad behaviour of Carnival week, San Pableños continue to celebrate for one final night. On this occasion, however, the flutes of Carnival, which have been cast aside until the following year, are replaced with taped *cumbia* music, the popular music of the nation (and of much of Latin America) played on ghetto blasters powered by car batteries. Thus music of the nation took over from music of the locality as if to affirm the relationship between San Pablo and the nation-state.

I am suggesting that Carnival is a time when the relationship between San Pablo and the larger nation-state is not set aside, as might initially be the impression, but is renegotiated and affirmed. This sort of renegotiation and affirmation may be necessary because of San Pablo's ambiguous status *vis à vis* the wider nation. It is a provincial capital and therefore has a real claim to a position in the structure of the nation. However, it is also a small rural village of only 300 people, and hence has nothing like the facilities that other towns with the same status enjoy – the capital of neighbouring Sud Chichas province is a much larger town with over 30,000 inhabitants. It is common to hear politically minded San Pableños complain that theirs is the forgotten province of the forgotten department of Bolivia. However, like the Chinese of West Hunan of whom Mary Rack (this volume) writes, they do not seek to set their province apart from the wider nation.

As noted, the disappearance of the *ayllus* of the Sud Lípez area was the latest round in a history of negotiations and contestations of identity in which local people have engaged with external powers. Although the *ayllus* have disappeared, the people of San Pablo still require access to pastureland that is held in common by the community and hence still need to negotiate and reaffirm their status with the nation-state. The situation of rural groups in relation to the nation-state is dependent on the policy-making decisions of the national government. Governments of the past sought to create a homogeneous Bolivian nation – nineteenth-century attempts to make 'Indians' into private landholding citizens have already been mentioned and, following the National Revolution of 1952, rural groups including *ayllus* were encouraged to register themselves as peasant unions (Albó 2002), which, I am told, the *ayllus* of Sud Lípez did in 1956. However, in 1994 new legislation was introduced which aimed to recognize the plurality of the Bolivian nation-state and the rights of indigenous peoples. This gave certain advantages to those who could demonstrate the persistence of traditional forms of organization in the countryside (e.g. through the presence of *ayllus*) particularly in relation to 'original' communally-held lands (Tierras Comunitarias de Origen, or TCOs). Thus, changes in state legislation make it still relevant to groups in the Bolivian countryside to reaffirm the boundaries of their land and to sort out their relationship with the state. For the people of San Pablo, this negotiation continues since they have to date been unable to register their communally-held lands as they told me they 'cannot remember' the *ayllus* and have no documentary or other reliable evidence of their boundaries. My contention here is that Carnival celebrations form one site through which negotiations continue and tensions and contradictions are played out, although, of course, at Carnival the state is represented only minimally, and does not participate in the symbolic negotiation.

Conclusions

In this chapter, I have attempted to explore the dynamics between past and present that operate in a rural Bolivian celebration of Carnival. The discussion bears some similarity to that presented by Rasnake for *Ayllu Yura*. However, while he sees Carnival as a time of dialogue between *ayllu* and state, he also sees it ultimately as the affirmation of the inevitability of state power. Here I have placed more emphasis on elements of active contestation and negotiation. Our different emphases originate in part from differences between the situations of San Pablo and Yura – while the latter has retained its *ayllu*, through which it has acquired titles to its land (Bigenho 2002) and thus a relatively stable relationship with the state, in the case of San Pablo the relationship with the state has still to be resolved. In one respect San Pableños have lost out by failing to retain a recognizable traditional form of social organization, although in another they may have gained in the power stakes through appearing less Indian than other rural populations.

The sheep-quartering ceremony of San Pablo's Carnival remembers the past, but is not simply a representation of it; it is a performative act through which present political concerns and frustrations are resolved symbolically. As in the situation that Dilley (this volume) describes, the presence of the past in the present does not function here simply to generate ideological knowledge in support of existing hierarchies, but instead makes space for agency and dissent. It is through the presence of the past in the present that ritual opens up a space for politics. Perhaps those charged with registering 'original' communally-held lands should visit San Pablo during Carnival for, so long as the sheep-quartering ceremony continues, it should not be said that present-day San Pableños do not remember their *ayllus*.

Notes

1. In his thousand-page letter to the King of Spain, Felipe Guaman Poma de Ayala notes that February was a month when the Inca and all his realm would sacrifice gold, silver and livestock to the sun, moon and other important deities, noting also that this was a time of hunger before the harvest. (Poma de Ayala 1993 [1614]: vol. 1, 180).
2. The association of the dead with the rains is widespread throughout the Andean region. See, for example, Gose (1994), Bolton (2002).
3. Here Rasnake cites Tristan Platt's (1982, 1984) work on tribute payments in the nineteenth century. Platt sees payment of tribute by *ayllus* to the Republican government, from the point of view of the indigenous communities, as the fulfilment of their side of a reciprocal pact with the state guaranteeing them access to their lands.
4. In this respect Andeanist anthropology, possibly as a result of its roots in the cultural anthropology tradition, has suffered from the reverse of the 'presentism' that Fardon (this volume) identifies as a feature of British and European social anthropology of the mid twentieth century. Rather than conceive of the past solely as a resource to be mobilized in present processes, some Andeanists have perhaps relied too heavily on the sixteenth century as a resource for explaining present phenomema.

5. See, for example Zuidema and Quispe (1973: 361).
6. In San Pablo there is no formal system or rota for festival sponsorship. Sponsorship relies on someone in the community feeling motivated to provide sponsorship, which is a considerable economic burden.
7. See Platt (1995), Bolton (2000).
8. See Harris (1978, 1994) for discussions of the relationships between men and women in Andean households.
9. In his discussion of the unrest, Platt (1984) notes how ritual made space for active resistance to the legislation. Both the sites of ritual action and the calendar of ritual events were mobilised in threats of violent action. Enraged Indians threatened to put government officials to death at ritual sites that, from their point of view, guaranteed the existing order and the provincial authorities prepared to withstand a revolt on the 6 May, the Festival of the Cross, the occasion on which membership of rural groups was consolidated and corresponding rights over land were affirmed.
10. In 1996, when I was present for Carnival in San Pablo, the town authorities of San Pablo posted a timetabled list of homesteads to be visited on the Tuesday of the week of celebrations. However, that year revellers got off to such a good start visiting houses within San Pablo (being served with corn beer and alcohol in each) that they did not get beyond the town itself.
11. I understood this as an affirmation of the identity of those concerned as part of a wider community of Bolivian miners which took precedence over their belonging to the locality.
12. A small instrument with ten strings, similar to a guitar.
13. Cold temperatures, lack of rainfall and searing winds ensure that no more serious cultivation takes place in this part of Sud Lípez.

References

Abercrombie, Thomas (1998), *Pathways of Memory and Power: Ethnography and History among an Andean People*, Madison: University of Wisconsin Press.

Albó, Xavier (2002), 'Bolivia: from Indian and Campesino leaders to Councillors and Parliamentary Deputies', in Rachel Sieder (ed.), *Multiculturalism in Latin America*, Institute of Latin American Studies Series, Basingstoke: Palgrave Macmillan.

Allen, Catherine (1988), *The Hold Life Has: Coca and Cultural Identity in an Andean Community*, Washington: Smithsonion Institution.

Bakhtin, Mikhail M. (1984), *Rabelais and His World*, trs. Hélène Iswolsky, Bloomington: Indiana University Press.

Bigenho, Michelle (2002), *Sounding Indigenous: Authenticity in Bolivian Musical Performance*, Basingstoke: Palgrave Macmillan.

Bloch, Maurice (1996), 'Memory', in A. Barnard and J. Spencer (eds), *Encyclopedia of Social and Cultural Anthropology*, London and New York: Routledge.

Bolton, Margaret (2000), 'Between the Ayllu and the Nation-State: Intertextuality and Ambiguities of Identity in San Pablo de López', Ph.D. thesis, University of St. Andrews.

——(2002), 'Doing *Waki* in San Pablo de López: reciprocity between the living and the dead', *Anthropos* 97: 379–96.

Connerton, Paul (1989), *How Societies Remember*, Cambridge: Cambridge University Press.

Flores Ochoa, Jorge A. (1979), *Pastoralists of the Andes*, trs. Ralph Bolton, Philadelphia: Institute for the Study of Human Issues.

Gose, Peter (1994), *Deathly Waters and Hungry Mountains: Agrarian Ritual and Class Formation in an Andean Town*, Toronto: University of Toronto Press.

Halbwachs, Maurice (1950), *La Mémoire collective*, Paris: Presses Universitaire de France.

Harris, Olivia (1982), 'The dead and the devils among the Bolivian Laymi', in Maurice Bloch and Jonathan Parry (eds), *Death and the Regeneration of Life*, Cambridge: Cambridge University Press.

Harvey, Penelope (1991), 'Drunken speech and the construction of meaning: bilingual competence in the Southern Peruvian Andes', *Language and Society*, 20: (1) 1–35.

Ingold, Tim (2000), *The Perception of the Environment: Essays in Livelihood, Dwelling and Skill*, London: Routledge.

Platt, Tristan (1982), *Estado boliviano y ayllu andino*, Lima: Instituto de Estudios Peruanos.

——(1984), 'Liberalism and ethnocide in the Southern Andes', *History Workshop Journal*, 17, 3–18.

——(1986), 'Mirrors and maize: the concept of *Yanantin* among the Macha of Bolivia', in N. Wachtel, J. Murra and J. Revel (eds.), *Anthropological History of Andean Polities*, Cambridge: Cambridge University Press.

——(1988), 'Pensamiento politico Aymara', in Xavier Albó (ed.), *Raíces de América: El Mundo Aymara*, Madrid: Alianza Editorial/ UNESCO, 365–450.

——(1995), 'Ethnic calendars and market interventions among the *Ayllus* of López during the nineteenth century', in Brooke Larson and Olivia Harris (eds), *Ethnicity, Markets and Migration in the Andes: At the Crossroads of History and Anthropology*, Durham and London: Duke University Press.

Poma de Ayala, Felipe Guaman (1993 [1614]), *Nueva corónica y buen gobierno*, Edición y prologo de Franklin Pease, Vocabulario y traducciones de Jan Szeminski, Mexico, Berlin and Lima: Fondo de Cultura Económica 3 vols.

Rasnake, Roger (1988), *Domination and Cultural Resistance: Authority and Power among an Andean People*, Durham: Duke University Press.

Rivière, Giles (1983), 'Quadripartition et ideologie dans les communautés aymaras de Carangas', in *Bulletin de l'Institut Français d'Etudes Andines*, 12 (3–4), 41–62.

Saignes, Thierry (1995), 'Indian Migration and Social Change in 17th-Century Charcas', in Brooke Larson and Olivia Harris (eds), *Ethnicity, Markets and Migration in the Andes: At the Crossroads of History and Anthropology*, Durham and London: Duke University Press.

Zuidema, R. Tom and U. Quispe (1973), 'A visit to God: the account and interpretation of a religious experience in the Peruvian community of Choque-Huarcaya', in D.R. Gross (ed.), *Peoples and Cultures of Native South America*, Garden City: Natural History Press.

–11–

Bandits and Heroes: Time and Place in Central China
Mary Rack

This chapter is concerned with stories of bandits and heroes in a mountainous area of south central China known as West Hunan. The research on which it is based took place in the city of Jishou and nearby villages.[1] Its aim is to look at accounts of the past which are not concerned with the progression of 'discrete periods of time' (Jordanova 2000). I am influenced in this by James, who writes that the disjunctures resulting from colonialism have been over-emphasized in the writing of the history of Africa and calls for a difference of emphasis (1998). The periodization so central to nationalist history can also be over-emphasized and there is a need to consider carefully the alternative views on time and place which appear in demotic accounts.

The writing of history in Communist states has been concerned to show Communism as 'the inevitable and glorious outcome of a discernable historical purpose' (Watson 1994: 1). In China an important aspect of this was the telling of the creation of a New China (*Xin Zhongguo*), radically different from what had gone before. For example, stories of the suppression of the bandits of West Hunan were well known throughout China in the 1960s when they were used to demonstrate the legitimacy of Communist Party rule. They show how, with the help of the Peoples' Liberation Army (PLA), the Communists effected a sharp break with feudal China, absorbing remote, bandit-run enclaves into a unified nation and beginning the process of modern development and progress. It proved impossible, however, to stifle all other forms of memory and in this chapter I consider how two kinds of demotic stories of the past undermine ideas of a progressive New China. Both are oppositional but their approaches are very different. First, this chapter examines the stories of bandits which are used by educated West Hunan people to question the legitimacy of the Communists' narrative of the building of a New China. Following on are the stories of heroes which are not contextualized within national history at all. These, too, challenge the legitimacy of government actions, but through an alternative perspective on time and place. By considering and distinguishing between the two approaches it is possible to look beyond nationalist approaches to time and place which all too often inform studies in

Mary Rack

anthropology (compare Karakasidou 2000: 416, Kahn 1989: 22) and Chinese history (Duara 1996).

James and Mills, in their introduction to this volume, describe how ceremonial events can 'shift the representation and ... enactment of time' thus opening up space for politics and even violence (p. 2). Ceremonial is a powerful way in which alternative forms of historicization are expressed in China, often through the cults of territorial deities (compare Feuchtwang 1992: 5–6). This chapter considers how stories of heroes that may be associated with birthplace, home or grave, provide a way of seeing how 're-structured' or differently structured time may be referred to at any point in the ceremonial calendar.

The Bandits of West Hunan: Legitimization and Resistance in Recounting the Past

After the Communists took power in 1949 they needed to present themselves as the leaders of a new, unified nation. They used stories of the suppression of the bandits of West Hunan to show themselves successfully replacing the feudal attitudes of the past. Stark contrasts were drawn between heroic PLA soldiers and the bandits, who were portrayed as cruel, superstitious landowners, interested only in defending their own interests. The fact that many of these bandits had held out into the 1950s added urgency to this message. West Hunan was a place that threatened the unity and cohesiveness of the nation, where elements of pre-liberation China within the new nation were eventually overcome. The bandit stories attempted to illustrate what has been described as the impossible unity of the nation narrated in both time and space (Balibar 1991, Bhabha 1990).

These stories have their origin in West Hunan's particular situation. The region has long been inhabited by a people known in Chinese as the 'Miao' and it was not fully incorporated into the Chinese state until the seventeenth century. It then became a form of military colony, known as the *tun* system, in which both Han Chinese and lowland Miao peasants bore arms to protect their area against rebellious elements, usually described as Miao rebellions. As the *tun* system began to break down in the early twentieth century, many local figures took advantage of the militarization of the region to take up arms on their own account and so-called bandits (*tufei*) became particularly numerous. The terrain of West Hunan must also have been a contributory factor since the mountains and the large number of caves provided hiding places for people and weapons and the *tun* blockhouses themselves could easily become rebel strongholds (Shi 1986: 206). Some of the rebels were 'social bandits' who championed the peasant cause in a manner described in Europe and elsewhere (Hobsbawm 1963: 14). In other cases, however, it is hard to distinguish between bandits and local militia, since the violence of the former was matched by that of the latter, many of whom deserted to become bandits themselves (Vance 1925: 213, Kinkley 1977: 93–4).

Stories of the West Hunan bandits became part of the school curriculum all over China and were, as a local schoolteacher told me, the only interesting thing one learned at school during the years of the Cultural Revolution. The best known was Long Yunfei, a former army captain who built up a following based on the village of Shanjiang. Official sources claim that he asserted that he was a Miao King,[2] had imperial pretensions and specialized in various forms of torture (Ceng and Hou 1993: 485). Rewi Alley, who travelled through the area during the late 1960s, writes that he 'typified all that was worst in a rotten society' (1974: 23). Most famous is the treatment of his tailor. According to official stories Long demanded a cloak in imperial style. When the tailor failed to deliver this, Long 'had him stripped, nailed to a young forked tree with big nails and slowly had him skinned alive, each bit of skinning being done at half hour intervals' (ibid.: 24). During the Cultural Revolution, visitors were taken to the site where these events were said to have taken place, just outside the village. Political study sessions were held comparing the evils of the feudal past with progressive and enlightened policies of the Communists.

The Continuing Fascination of the Bandit Stories

Though no longer a subject for political education, stories of the West Hunan bandits continued to catch the imagination during the 1990s, as I discovered during my fieldwork. The focus of interest was not on the suppression of the bandits but on the extraordinary, charismatic qualities of their lives. This is illustrated by the fact that one person suggested to me that I write a whole book about bandits, since everyone found them interesting. Another held that the local government was mistaken in attempting to base a tourism industry on the attractions of the Miao minority. If it were up to him he would build a theme-hotel in the form of a bandit's stronghold; this would be far more popular. This fascination was not confined to West Hunan. In the 1980s the struggles between bandits and the PLA had been retold in highly popular film and television versions and students arriving to study in West Hunan confessed to being afraid that bandits might still roam the region.

Many people attribute to these figures an almost superhuman quality that gives them a 'charismatic authority' and legitimacy (compare Weber 1948: 295) and these stories become a means of criticizing the current Chinese government. For many, including those in professional jobs, the 1990s were a time of increasing dissatisfaction. Many had lost the benefits, such as free housing and medical care, which they had previously enjoyed and unlike the booming coastal areas, West Hunan provided few opportunities for supplementing their salaries. Criticisms were not directly and publicly voiced but, as in other socialist countries, were expressed through 'alternative representations of the past' (Watson 1994: 19). As Hobsbawm (1963) noted for Europe, bandits have the capacity to become local, protective heroes, and in West Hunan this was especially the case since alternative versions of their stories were coming to light.

It was through a group of teachers at a nearby middle school that I first heard of these other bandit stories. Miss Long came from Long Yunfei's ancestral village of Shanjiang and soon after I arrived she invited me to visit it: this was one of the first times I had travelled out of the small administrative city of Jishou where I was based. We were accompanied by some of her colleagues, who were also keen to visit Long's home. We left the city, where the concrete buildings sprawled up a narrow valley, and drove for two hours through a landscape of limestone mountains and dramatic views. Shanjiang itself was a mix of mud-brick, wooden and concrete buildings, surrounded by steep rice terraces, speckled with newly transplanted rice seedlings. After having lunch at Miss Long's home, we were joined by her uncle, a middle-aged man who said that he would show us Long's old home. He took us over to the old part of the village, where a large brick house stood, dominating the village. Although obviously long empty and largely ruined, it still retained a thick protective outer wall with gunlocks and watchtowers. It was getting dark as we entered the compound and there was no-one else about. We went through an arch into an inner courtyard and Miss Long's uncle pointed out to us the old living accommodation and the stables. After a while, another member of the Long family, who had seen us walk through the village to the house, came over to join us. The teachers were curious and asked the two men a lot of questions. It emerged that the first man had been Long Yunfei's bodyguard for a while.

Like the visitors who came during the Cultural Revolution, we had come to Shanjiang to interpret the past, but we were told that the well known stories told about Long Yunfei were untrue, and that he had never aspired to an imperial robe. His tailor had been tortured for disloyalty and Long had killed him to put him out of his suffering. These men described Long as a protective figure. During his time of power he had kept the area peaceful, protecting it from outside attack and ensuring that the water supply worked well. He had also been a patriot whose intentions had been to mass forces to fight in the anti-Japanese war (in which both Guomingdang and Communist forces were involved). He had never intended to fight the PLA but had been persuaded to do so by his nephew. However, the men conceded that because he had to provide for his troops he had plundered outlying (*waidi*) places.

A Critique of the Present

The man who had been Long's bodyguard did not, therefore, view him as a cruel remnant of China's feudal past and his description of the stability of the area under Long's influence was in direct contradiction to official accounts of West Hunan as an unruly and threatening place. Long Yunfei's relatives also spoke of him as a charismatic figure whose authority had a legitimacy that is not generally attributed to current local government. Indeed, it almost seemed as if his presence could still be felt; we spoke in hushed voices among the empty remains of his house. At one point somebody asked, 'What did he look like?' and the guide replied that he had been rather short and rather fat. 'Like him' he said, pointing at one of the teachers who was walking back towards us through the darkening courtyard. There was a nervous moment when we all turned to look at him, then everyone laughed. As we walked back to the school minibus the teachers were keen to make sure that I had understood that the official stories about Long were not true.[3] To them, the story of Long Yunfei was a way of questioning the legitimacy of the current government, by questioning an element of their own foundation myth. If Long had not been a feudal despot with secessionist aims (as implied by his imperial pretensions) then the Communists' claims to have initiated a new, progressive and unified China, through suppressing his kind, must also be suspect.

Deities and Heroes: West Hunan Perspectives on Place and Time

The place of memory and the retelling of the past has become an important aspect of the study of what has become known as post-socialism (Watson 1994). Nonetheless, retelling the events of the founding of the Peoples' Republic of China (and the concept of post-socialism itself) does not move us away from the idea of a history based on a succession of 'discrete periods'. In the case I have just described, the teachers themselves did not question that a break had occurred; they had after all studied and taught within this political discourse for most of their lives. What they disputed was the nature of the break. If we are to move beyond accounts of the past informed by nationalist periodizations, we need to be open to other kinds of accounts.

The story of Long Yunfei can also be seen as part of another tradition of stories, one which does not depend on ideas of a break or of successive periods of time. In this section the way that ideas of social memory have been applied to stories of heroes is examined, although it is an approach which I find useful but ultimately limiting. When researchers come across stories of the past which differ greatly from those found in written histories, discussion of them is often framed in terms of social memory. While historical reconstructions are intended to determine what actually took place at a past time, social memory is often concerned with 'how this type of memory bears on contemporary aspects of social life or social relations' (Collard 1991: 89). Work on social memory shows how accounts of the past are influenced both by the experience of the individual and by what is shared by the people around, since 'the narrative of one's life is part of an interconnecting set of narratives; it is embedded in the story of those groups from which individuals derive their identity' (Connerton 1989: 21). Social memory may also have a bodily aspect, enacted through ritual experience.

Ideas of social memory have been applied to stories of heroic/bandit figures in Southern Europe. They show that it is mainly certain local deeds which are retold, not the 'great events' on which academic and nationalist periodizations of history are based (Jordanova 2000: 118). So for example, Fentress and Wickham describe how in the 1960s, French rural people in Protestant areas of Cevennes could tell detailed stories of the Camisards, an early eighteenth-century Protestant rebel movement (1992: 93–5). It is these figures who are remembered, rather than historical events such as the French Revolution because 'the "Great Events" of the past are designated as such by people external to most local societies' (ibid.: 96). Collard describes how Greek villagers recall the Ottoman empire as a time 'of freedom fighters (and brigands), of national resistance, of patriotism and heroic deeds' rather than of oppression (1991: 96). Often memories of a particular period appear to have wiped out other aspects of the past. In this context both Connerton (1989: 20) and Fentress and Wickham cite Carlo Levi, who observed that in southern Italy during the 1930s, 'the peasants of Gagliano were indifferent to the conquest of Abyssinia, and they neither remembered the World War nor spoke of its dead, but one war was close to their hearts and constantly on their tongues; it was already a fable, a legend, a myth, an epic story. This was the war of the brigands' (Levi 1948: 137, cited in Fentress and Wickham 1992: 87). In all these cases writers argue that a local history based on a particular period of the past is retold because of its resonances with present-day concerns.

The stories I heard in West Hunan had many similarities with these accounts from Southern Europe. Personal histories apart, almost all accounts of the past were concerned with the lives of protective, larger-than-life military heroes who protected and/or brought renown to the region. Though the details of these stories might, incidentally, situate them in particular dynastic reigns the past, they did not dwell on historical periodicity. Aspects such as the Miao rebellions and the creation of the *tun* (military colony) system, by which academic histories are periodized, went unmentioned. And they were directly, contrastively, relevant to the current situation. They told of a past when West Hunan was protected whereas today it is perceived as lagging behind.

Other Localized Heroes

Long Yunfei is only one of a number of heroic figures who are recalled in this way. Another, called Luo Daren was born in Yaxi, a village on the outskirts of Jishou. Once a place of importance in its own right, it commands some of the very scarce flat arable land in the region. A friend of mine called Mrs Yang, one of the custodians at Yaxi's temple, first told me about this hero. Luo had been a great fighter of enormous stature, she said, stretching out her hands to show how broad his legs had been. There had been a huge grave mound to him, situated on the hill above the village, but, she said in a reference to the Cultural Revolution, 'we pulled it down'. Another local heroic figure, Yang Guangbo, also had supernormal power and it was said that he could not die, even under gunfire. When his grave was dug up, his body was found undecayed in its official robes.

Other local, protective, military figures were the deities at Yaxi's temple, where Mrs Yang worked. Their story was well known in Yaxi and was told to anyone who visited the temple and its main points are as follows:

> The Tian Wang were born to a local woman and the Dragon King, who lived in one of Yaxi's wells.[4] When they reached manhood they were enormously strong. At this time West Hunan was attacked and the three brothers killed seven thousand enemies in its defence. They went to the emperor to report what they had done. At first they were afraid to tell him the truth because they thought he might become jealous of their power. Instead they told him that thirty six people had killed the seven thousand. Later they told him the truth. Because the emperor was afraid of them he gave them a gift of poisoned alcohol, telling them not to drink it until they got home. But they stopped before they got to Yaxi and they were thirsty. The first brother drank a little of the alcohol and he died. The second brother saw this but he thought that he was stronger than the first brother so he drank some of the alcohol. He drank more than the first brother, his face turned dark red and he died. The third brother thought that he was stronger than the first brother and the second brother so he drank even more of the alcohol and he died, his face turning black. But the emperor's victory was not complete. The three brothers became the Tian Wang (Celestial Kings), deities of great power.

The deities' images with their white, red and black faces are found in a number of temples in West Hunan, but the most important is in Yaxi where they are regarded as particularly responsive to the requests of their supplicants and generally protective of the area. The site at Yaxi has been the subject of an ongoing struggle between villagers and the local authorities over the rebuilding and running of the temple.

Heroes Become Deities

Similarities between local strongmen and local deities in China have been widely noted. Both are in some ways superhuman individuals, whose authority is based on charisma and strength. There is an association of temples with martial arts bands (Feuchtwang 1992: 83, Jordan 1972: 48–9) and writers on Chinese religion have drawn explicit parallels between military deities and bandits. For example, Seaman writes,

> These are spirits that are worshipped as gods though they are thought not to have been appointed by the Jade Emperor. They are specifically likened to the semi-independent 'country-kings' (*Kuo-Wang*) of historical China, who, although formally acknowledging the suzerainty of the Chinese Emperor, actually ran their own territories as they saw fit. It is thus not unexpected that many of these 'god-kings' are thought to have been terrible pirates or powerful robber chieftains. (Seaman 1978: 55)

A similar point is made by Weller who describes military deities in Guangxi province who 'acted like the local strongmen who sometimes usurped state authority and ran their own little empires where the state grew weak' (1994: 253).

As well as the protective military nature of their heroes, there are other common themes between these stories. Both Luo Daren and the Tian Wang are closely connected with water and images of fertility. When the Tian Wang died, the water in Yaxi flowed backwards; when Luo Daren died, a well in Yaxi churned up silt. When the father of the Tian Wang came to earth he turned back into a dragon if touched by water and once this was known, he had to return to the well. When Luo Daren washed (according to the local story) he turned into a fish and when this was witnessed by his servant it resulted in Luo Daren's death.

Alternative Views of Time and Place

While the themes of water and fertility are no longer much discussed (efficient irrigation systems are a legacy of Communist rule), the themes of military prowess and protection recall a time when West Hunan was better served than it is today. It is not just the professional classes who have grievances, though the wider population puts the blame on local government and corrupt cadres rather than national level politics. Local complaints were illustrated by a widow who lived in a village not far from Jishou who bitterly listed examples of disorder and government neglect. People came and stole things from her with impunity, including her chickens and some of her clothes. Young people in the area got into fights and several times people had been killed but little attempt was made to bring them to justice. In one case a murderer had been set free after a fine of only 5,000 yuan. Even leaving the area brought no relief. One of her sons had been to the eastern city of Ningbo to take up casual work in a factory and had been cheated out of his wages, a common experience among people from the area. In recalling a past where great men protected West Hunan and the people who lived there, these stories express a telling contrast.

While the approaches used in social memory provide a useful alternative to those used by historians, they present certain problems. Noting that certain accounts of the past are not based on ideas of national, or 'great events' history does not in itself query assumptions of historical periodicity. It simply defines the stories by their lack of it. Suggesting that a certain period is recalled, to the exclusion of others, likewise reinforces the idea that periodization is crucial. Where accounts from West Hunan are concerned, it is useful to think instead in terms of a different sense of the past, where certain themes repeat themselves regardless of the century. Furthermore, to characterize certain stories as expressing *local* concerns would simply reinforce the dichotomy between national and local that was found in official bandit stories, where bandit enclaves were portrayed as a threat to the unity of the nation. What such an approach would fail to do is to present a distinctive, West Hunan based view of time and place. As Bolton demonstrates in her chapter (this volume), a celebration of locality may also be a reminder of the accommodation which has to be made with the state.

First it is worth considering what the stories of West Hunan's bandits have to say about locality. Demotic accounts of West Hunan's past do not, of course, present the region as a threatening pocket of pre-nationalist, feudal times, but nor do they present loyalty to the region as an oppositional stance and an alternative to being Chinese. The heroic figures may gain authority locally because central authority is weak, but the stories do not call for differently drawn boundaries, such as the secession of West Hunan. Far from representing a dichotomy between local and national interest, local heroes are shown as the greatest patriots of all. So, while official stories present Long Yunfei as a rebel counterpoised against the central state, and a figure with aspirations to be emperor, the stories we heard had quite a different emphasis. Long Yunfei's main concern was to protect his locality but he was also loyal to China and planned to mobilize his forces in the war against the Japanese. Similarly, in the stories told at the Yaxi temple, the Tian Wang heroically defended West Hunan but suffered precisely because of their loyalty to the emperor. The emperor here, as in the oral Cantonese tradition described by Watson, might be 'the villain of the piece' and a leader who is 'remote, unapproachable, and extremely jealous of his power' (1991: 171, 173) but nonetheless, the Tian Wang openly reported their deeds to him.

The combination of being a local hero and Chinese patriot is achieved more successfully by Luo Daren and Yang Guangbo. Both of them had been great patriots, I was told. Luo had fought against the British and Yang against the Japanese in Taiwan.[5] Nevertheless, recalling them today is regarded as a threat by local government. Mrs Yang, the temple custodian, said that some of Luo's descendants had applied to built a temple in memory of him but had been turned down by the local government, and told that this would have been a form of superstition – therefore not appropriate. All these stories tell of an uneasy balance between local and China-wide loyalties which has been the experience of West Hunan since pre-nationalist times. Thus, rather than describing a specifically local point of view what they give is a West Hunanese perspective on being Chinese. It is the (temporary) successes of these figures in achieving this balance that gives them their authority whilst their deaths are reminders that those who work for the Chinese state cannot be trusted.

An Unending Time Frame

I have suggested that stories of West Hunan's heroes also express a particular view of time. This is evident in the lack of reference to historical periodicity and the 'great events' of national history. But it can also be seen in the way that the heroes seem to inhabit a repetitive time where the same dilemmas recur regardless of the century in which they are set. Themes of loyalty and place continue to repeat themselves as the tensions between protecting West Hunan and loyalty to China, between local charisma and central authority, are worked over. Like the heroes of the golden age, described by Hubert (1999), they are set apart, in a time that is different from the ordinary time of mortals. Hubert describes heroes who belong to mythic time which differs from ours in that it precedes it. West Hunan's heroes, however, inhabit a repetitive time that is once again different from everyday experience and one that is usually recalled at sites connected to their extraordinary lives. Although these stories do not confront the legitimating narrative of the Communist New China, they are threatening to the government in a rather different way: they do not make reference to national history, since time in these stories is not linear and the past cannot be learned from and left behind. But the ongoing recurrence of events itself challenges the idea of socialist progress and the possibility of a break with the feudalist past.

Heroes from the Past Commenting on the Present

The heroes of the past become most challenging to local government when they make themselves known directly in the present. Their appearance in the present recalls the collapsing of time, which Dilley (this volume) describes, when Senegalese praise singers have direct contact with the people they sing of. But it could more accurately be seen as a logical outcome of the repetitive nature of the time which these heroes inhabit. We experienced a suggestion that past heroes exist in the present at Long Yunfei's house, when Long seemed to appear in the figure of one of the teachers. People in West Hunan communicate with past heroes more effectively at the temple of the Tian Wang, where offerings are made to the deities and custodians call on them in a confident but conversational tone[6] asking them to answer supplicants' requests. Indeed it is the heroic aspect of these deities' former lives which allows them to transcend everyday distinctions between past and present. They have, as Feuchtwang puts it, 'something uncanny – *ling* [responsive] – something besides the present but with the power to transgress the division into past and present' (Feuchtwang 1992: 21). The deities may also make themselves known through bodily possession. This may be a passing experience, as when a custodian at a minor shrine to the Tian Wang told me that the deities came over from the main temple at Yaxi when she called on them and she felt them tingling (*ma*) in her body. More long term was the experience of spirit mediumship, when women became possessed by the Tian Wang or the mother of the warriors, and spoke directly in their voices or hers. In this way they could make direct and highly authoritative criticisms of local policies.

A Medium for the Tian Wang

It was some time before I met a medium, since spirit possession was considered to be highly superstitious, but eventually I was introduced to one by the same Mrs Yang who had told me about Luo Daren. The medium we visited had migrated to Jishou from the countryside to look for temporary work and she said that Chairman Mao had told her to build the temple there. She had set herself up in a small two room stone building on cultivated land on the outskirts of Jishou.[7] One room of the temple, which was open on one side to the elements, contained a wooden table that held some pieces of old-fashioned blue and white china, including a bowl in which sticks of incense were burning. Behind this were posters of Chairman Mao and the other former leaders, Zhou Enlai, Zhu De and the West-Hunan born former 'bandit', He Long. (Such posters were still available at a low price in state-run bookshops.) Mrs Yang was on very friendly terms with the medium and spent some time recounting to her the difficulties of her own life. She did not ask the medium to go into a trance since there was no need. What the medium learned from her possession by the Tian Wang meant that she had healing skills but also that she knew their views on the current situation in Jishou.

The Tian Wang had made a number of pronouncements through this woman that directly challenged local government actions. They said that a new road junction in Jishou, where several people had been killed, was inhabited by the ghosts of those who had died there. They had also told her that the new road past Yaxi village had disrupted the *fengshui* of the area. In the past the village itself had been prosperous (as Mrs Yang explained it to me later, 'we were on the back of the dragon, we produced people like Luo Daren') but now the village was lagging behind. More controversially the medium said that the Tian Wang had left their temple at Yaxi and moved to inhabit another place. They had done this in protest at the way local government had taken over running the temple and set it up as tourist site and cultural relic.

Such communications from the Tian Wang about the local government's use of land were not unusual. On another occasion I witnessed a consultation between a medium and the parents of a child who had died young. After contacting the child and establishing that she was unhappy in the underworld, menaced by other figures who took away her belongings, the medium was possessed by one of the Tian Wang who again stated that the problem was with the building of a road. It was too close to the grave and the *feng shui* was being disturbed.

Such criticisms from the Tian Wang on present-day issues are highly threatening to the local government in West Hunan. These are legendary heroes whose past actions have accorded them a legitimacy to power in the region, which the current all too human government lacks. Statements from the Tian Wang carry a particular authority and, in criticizing the government's appropriation of land for road building and at the temple, they give expression to some of the most resented ways in which government affects everyday lives. Like most people in Jishou, I rarely met with spirit mediums and even more rarely heard them actually pronounce statements critical of local government. But their messages from the heroes circulated widely in the conversations of others, giving focus for a the more general concern with disorder and poverty.

Conclusion

As Davis (1991) writes that there are different views on history, and those produced in the academy can be distinguished from other forms of thought. He suggests further that different kinds of recall of the past have different effects on present and future: 'We construe our times in different ways, in different idioms, with different rhetorics and ... these are consequential' (ibid.: 19). Since the views of the academy tend to overlap in a number of ways with those of the nation I have taken particular care to examine these other forms of thought. In suggesting that stories of bandits in West Hunan are told in different ways, that is, in terms of a national past or a local past, I make a point similar to Feuchtwang and Wang's when they write that 'millenarian movements and charisma conjoin historical narrative and a mythic or messianic time' (2001: 20). Such stories have been used to underline the legitimacy of the People's Republic of China, the break with feudalism and the unification of the nation. They are also used to challenge this legitimacy, as in the retelling of the story of Long Yunfei by his relatives and by the teachers. But to leave an examination of these stories at this point simply reinforces ideas of historical periodicity and a national/local dichotomy. The story of Long Yunfei must also be seen as part of a wider tradition of local hero stories in which the same themes keep repeating without reference to historical period, where local protectors are also patriots.

Both kinds of stories have potential consequences. The first type reinforces the notion of historical periodicity and a national break with the past, whether or not they support the legitimacy of the Communists. The second presents an alternative perspective which does not address ideas of national history but which nonetheless powerfully questions the legitimacy of mundane, central authorities. The threat represented by these heroes can be seen in the struggles which occur over the sites associated with them. These may take the form of conflicts with local government, such as over the temple of the Tian Wang and the grave of Luo Daren but less overtly, they influence feelings, as in the avoidance of Long's tree in preference for the ruins of his house.

Notes

1. This research was made possible by an ESRC studentship.
2. *Miao wang* (Miao King) is a Chinese term for messianic leaders who arose periodically among the highland population of Southwest China. It is beyond the scope of this chapter to deal in detail with the implications of this but I note here that it was the official versions of stories of bandits and local heroes which had an ethnic dimension. When I asked about Long Yunfei I was told that he numbered Miao and Han among his followers. Written versions of the Tian Wang (discussed later in the chapter) hold that they put down a Miao rebellion. However demotic versions of these stories make no mention of ethnic difference. For more detailed discussions of ethnicity in West Hunan see Sutton 2000, Rack (forthcoming).
3. Two PLA soldiers, Ceng Fanhua and Hou Jianfei, collected a number of other stories of bandits who are warmly remembered as local protectors, in their 1993 book Dang Fei Dan Xiangi Chaofei (Suppressing the Bandits of Greater West Hunan) (in Chinese). I am grateful to Liang Zhaohui for his excellent translations of the Chinese texts quoted in this chapter.

Mary Rack

4. Their mother, Mu Yi, is said to have been dragged into the well while washing clothes. Stories of young women who become impregnated in this way and give birth to dragons or fish are common in South China and have been evident since at least the Tang dynasty. These stories are often considered to be derived from pre-Han cultures (Eberhard 1968: 38, 232, 242, Schaefer 1967: 255).
5. These appear to be references to the Opium war of 1840 and the Sino-Japanese war of 1895.
6. This is similar to interactions with Chinese deities which Hansen describes from medieval times (1987: 71–2).
7. Spirit mediums (*xian niang*, lit. fairy women), were quite numerous in the Jishou area and were people who were said to be able to communicate with the spirits of the dead and with the deities. As has been described in other parts of the world (cf. Lewis 1971: 59), in West Hunan, a spirit medium's career would begin with an initial possession, which was involuntary, and took the form of a period of illness. As a result, the woman concerned would accede to the deity or spirit who possessed her and would communicate with him or her, and other figures, at regular intervals. New mediums might seek the advice of another medium and develop their skills so that they could enter a trance when asked to do so, but they would also be susceptible to continuing episodes of involuntary possession. All the mediums I knew of were rural women. Some women are possessed by Chairman Mao and I was told of one woman, who lived on the campus of Jishou University, and was frequently possessed: she walked around scolding all and sundry for the disorder (*luan*) apparent in society today.

References

Alley, R. (1974), *Travels in China 1966–1973*, Beijing: New World Press
Balibar, E. (1991), 'The Nation Form: History and Ideology', in E. Balibar and I. Wallerstein (eds), *Race, Nation, Class: Ambiguous Identities*, London: Verso.
Bhabha, H. K. (1990), 'Introduction: narrating the nation' in *Nation and Narration* H.K. Bhabha (ed.) London: Routledge.
Ceng Fanhua and Hou Jianfei (1993), *Dang Fei Da Xiangxi: Xiangxi Chaofei Jishi* ('Suppressing the Bandits of Greater West Hunan: A Record of the Bandit Lairs of West Hunan'), Changsha: Hunan Arts Publishing House (Chinese text).
Collard, A. (1991), ' Investigating social memory in a Greek context', in E. Tonkin, M. McDonald and D. Chapman (eds), *History and Ethnicity*, London: Routledge.
Connerton, P. (1989), *How Societies Remember*, Cambridge: Cambridge University Press.
Davis, J. (1991), *Times and Identities: Inaugural Lecture*, Oxford: Oxford University Press.

Duara, P. (1996) *Rescuing History from the Nation: Questioning Narratives of Modern China*, Chicago: Chicago University Press.

Eberhard, W. (1968), *Local Cultures of South and East China,* trs. A. Eberhard, Leiden: E.J. Brill.

Fentress, J. and C. Wickham, (1992), *Social Memory*, Blackwell: London

Feuchtwang, S. (1992), *The Imperial Metaphor,* London: Routledge.

Feuchtwang, S. and M. Wang (2001), *Grassroots Charisma: Four Local Leaders in China,* London: Routledge.

Hansen, V. (1987), *Popular Deities and Social Change in the Southern Song Period (1127–1276),* PhD dissertation, University of Pennsylvania.

Hobsbawm, E.J. (1963), *Primitive Rebels, Studies in Archaic Forms of Social Movement in the 19th and 20th Centuries*, New York: Praeger.

Hubert, H. (1999 [1905]), *Essay on Time: A Brief Study of the Representation of Time in Religion and Magic,* trs. R. Parkin and J. Redding, Oxford: Durkheim Press; Oxford/New York: Berghahn Books.

James, W. (1998), 'Mauss in Africa: on time, history and politics', in W. James and N.J. Allen (eds), *Marcel Mauss: A Centenary Tribute*, Oxford: Berghahn Books.

Jordan, D.K. (1972), *Gods, Ghosts and Ancestors: Folk Religion in a Taiwanese Village*, Berkeley: University of California Press.

Jordanova, L. (2000), *History in Practice*, London: Arnold.

Kahn, J.S. (1989), 'Culture: demise or resurrection?' *Critique of Anthropology* 9: 5–22.

Karakasidou, A. (2000), 'Essential differences: national homogeneity and cultural representation in four recent works on Greek Macedonia', *Current Anthropology* 41 (3): 415-25.

Kinkley, J. (1977), *Shen Ts'ung-wen's Vision of a Republican China*, PhD dissertation, Harvard University.

Lewis, I.M. (1971), *Ecstatic Religion: A Study in Shamanism and Spirit Possession*, London: Routledge.

Murray, K. (1925), 'The missionary of Kienyang' *The Sign: A National Catholic Magazine* 4 (9): 389–92.

Rack, M. (forthcoming), *Ethnic Distinctions, Local Meanings, Negotiating Cultural Identities in China*, London: Pluto Press.

Schaefer, E.H. (1967), *The Vermilion Bird: T'ang Images of the South*, Berkeley: University of California Press.

Seaman, G. (1978), *Temple Organisation in a Chinese Village*, Taipei: The Orient Cultural Service.

Shi Qigui (1986), *Xiangxi Miaozu Shidi Diaocha Baogao (Report of a First hand Investigation of the West Hunan Miao)* Changsha: Hunan Peoples' Press (Chinese text).

Sutton, D.S. (2000), 'Myth making on an ethnic frontier: the cult of the Heavenly Kings of West Hunan, 1715–1996', *Modern China* 26 (4): 448–99.

Vance, R. (1925), 'Paotsing Progress', *The Sign*: *A National Catholic Magazine* 5 (5): 211–15.

Watson, J. (1991), 'Waking the Dragon: visions of the Chinese Imperial State in local myth', in H. Baker and S. Feuchtwang (eds), *An Old State in New Setting: Studies in the Social Anthropology of China in Memory of Maurice Freedman*, Oxford: *Journal of the Anthropological Society of Oxford*.

Watson, R.S. (1994), 'Memory, history and opposition under state socialism: an introduction', in R. S. Watson (ed.), *Memory, History and Opposition under State Socialism*, Santa Fe: School of American Research Press.

Weber, M. (1948), *From Max Weber: Essays in Sociology*, tr. H.H. Gerth and C.W. Mills, London: Routledge.

Weller, R.P. (1994), 'Capitalism, Community and the Rise of Amoral Cults in Taiwan', in L. Kendall, C. F. Keyes and H. Hardacre (eds), *Asian Visions of Authority*, Honolulu: University of Hawaii Press.

——(1996), 'Matricidal magistrates and gambling Gods', in M. Shahar and R.P. Weller (eds), *Unruly Gods: Divinity and Society in China*, Hawaii: University of Hawaii Press.

–12–

The Persistence of Multiple-religious Practices in South-west Ethiopia
Wolde Gossa Tadesse

This study focuses on Gamo peoples of Southern Ethiopia. Gamo people are mountain cultivators and number over 750,000. Gamo and other Omotic areas such as Wolaita and Kore were part of an old Ethiopian Christian area. The only written document which acknowledges this fact is Bahrey's seventeenth-century *History of the Galla* (1954). This book gives accounts of the military organization of the expanding Oromo and the devastation that resulted from waves of migration. Bahrey lived in what is known as Birbira. Following his account, historians referred to his material as evidence of Christian practices in the sixteenth century in Gamo. It is possible that the churches were of a much earlier period. The history of the clans in the region, the multiplicity of small mountain kingdoms, names of political titles, the history of crops and of initiations of seasonal activities, all indicate the existence and coexistence of a far older Christian and pre-Christian tradition in Gamo than is commonly believed. Both Christian and non-Christian populations survived waves of devastation in pockets of safe mountain terrain cut off from contact with one another following the devastation of conquest by Emperor Menelik II in 1895. In the south, Christian celebrations in this part of the country have not been homogenized along Ethiopian Orthodox Church lines as has been the case in other areas of Ethiopia. It is noticeable that some features of the celebrations contrast with Ethiopian Orthodox practices.

My aim in this chapter is to show how groups of Gamo who subscribe to different religious traditions with divergent histories share space and time and perpetuate themselves not so much by gains they have made but by giving meaning to losses they have suffered and by forging a new sense of being. I illustrate my point by outlining a celebration at Ele in Gamo country, of the archangel Gabriel's day, where followers of all religious groups in Gamo take part. Here I indicate the unique mix of practices including songs, dances and horse races and how practices of the Old Gamo Rules (OGR) and of the pre-conquest Christian practices dominate the present-day Ethiopian Orthodox Church celebrations in this region.[1] I outline variation in the practice of acts of faith in the traditions and in those of the modern Orthodox Church. I then focus on the emphasis on traditional and modern religious authority and the timelessness of space, which is demonstrated by the temporal merging of leaders, followers, and the symbolic ark of the archangel on the sacred landscape of the assembly place. As in everyday life, all religious groups share the sacred landscape in the emotional non-secular moment.

In the second part of the chapter, I address the past when the OGRs and Christianity as it was known before conquest were practised. I deal with the period of confrontation between the powerful and the vanquished in appropriating religious symbols and how, despite the ordeal of exile and the humiliating loss of autonomy, Gamo guardians of religion struggled to maintain their version of the faith. At the same time I illustrate how a rebellious religious movement emerged under the leadership of the Gamo prophet Essa (c. 1835–1915), who was exiled in Addis Ababa together with wise men from all over the newly conquered territories, and was later released and sent home due to the respect he won, for his wisdom and the prophetic knowledge which he demonstrated to his captors. He was exiled in the palace of Addis Ababa during the reign of Empress Zawditu, Menelik's daughter. To this day he remains a popular religious leader in Gamo. His followers and those with physical and emotional trouble visit his home in Lisha in Zad'a. Recently, his teachings were circulated on recorded cassettes in Ethiopia, as discussed further in this essay.

The chapter shows how Gamo religious groups (Followers of Old Gamo Rules and Old Christianity as practised in Gamo before the conquest) confronted the introduction of Ethiopian Orthodox teachings at the same time as sharing space and social memory with them and with one another, portraying themselves as Gamo and underplaying differences and avoiding all that which sours the meaning they give to life as a group, as they went forward into the future. All four religious traditions coexist and share sacred landscape as well as memories of the past. Each of the religious groups has apparently large followings and has sacred sites. All of them have religious calendars regulating times for worship, celebrations, sacrifices and for initiating various activities. There is, however, an important calendrical and spatial overlap in which the various groups realize the above activities together and moments in time when annually, or in much shorter intervals all of them merge for one or more of these moments. This shared time and the particular moment which these groups capture in some sacred sites and the sense they make of it, is the focus of this study.

To illustrate my point I take a case from a mountain sacred place dedicated to the archangel Gabriel. The site is located in Ele, a settlement on the steep escarpment of the Western Gamo highlands, at the foot of Mount Gughe (3568 metres) in South-west Ethiopia. Here, the symbolic ark of Gabriel had been kept in caves for generations until the arrival in the late 1890s of Menelik's forces. *Qeso*, senior members of the Amara clan, were the hereditary caretakers of the symbolic ark.

For many generations to the present the archangel's day is celebrated annually on 27 December as well as in the month of August. The celebration in December is the biggest and will be described below. It coincides with the greening of mountain crops and harvest preparations. December marks the end of the rainy season and both fields and pastures provide sufficient greens for families and fodder for domestic animals. The azure sky and the morning sunshine of the month add beauty to the grandeur of the mountain landscape.

Observing Gabriel's Day: the Fusion of Religious Traditions

The celebration of the archangel in Ele has not been much discussed in the literature. Jacques Bureau (1976) observed the celebration in Ele in the seventies, and myself in 1991 and in 1995. I first travelled to attend the celebrations in Ele on foot from Arba Minch, through Bonke and Kacha past Mount Gughe, thence descending to Ele. On the second occasion I travelled by car from Arba Minch to Chencha and spent a night in Doko. I then joined friends from Doko and we trekked together southwards along the watershed, viewing the escarpments on both sides of the mountain. We went over to Dita and Gughe, then turning right and descending to Ele. In what follows I comment on what I was able to observe outside the church building on these two occasions.

Annually, hundreds of pilgrims wearing white cotton blankets form white human chains and lines along the numerous mountain paths that thread their way over the green Gamo Mountains. From a height I saw them wind like streams of milk down the escarpment to reach Ele where they formed a huge, luminous crowd in the yard and the meadows surrounding the church of the archangel Gabriel. Participants of the celebrations in Ele identify themselves as followers of Old Gamo Rules (OGR), as followers of the teachings of prophet Essa, and as Christians in the way that they were known in Gamo before the conquest in the times of the Old Christianity. Followers of the OGRs viewed the celebration in Ele generally as their own occasion and expressed their enjoyment in attending this annual event. They saw prostration before the symbolic ark and before a *Qeso* priest[2] as a serious act of faith. They thought of much of the activities of the celebration such as making confessions, receiving blessings[3] and singing collective praises of Gabriel as acts of faith. They were in Ele to be grateful for all the good that the archangel had provided for them. They say that sprinkling holy water on their bodies is therapeutic and gave them energy, as is true of other groups who took part in all of the activities listed above. None of the activities of the event were discriminated against by participants for being characteristic of a particular religious group. A visit to a diviner known as Otsa Na, in a yard connected to the sacred assembly place and the church is also considered part of the event. Otsa Na, like the *Qeso* is member of the Amara clan. Followers of Essa who came from Zad'a and other places said they attended the celebrations as they have always done, but the main reason for one group that I met to visit Ele this time was to celebrate the return of a soldier who had been reported missing in the Eritrean war and to thank the archangel for his safe return. Ethiopian Orthodox Church followers from towns such Awasa, Sodo, Arba Minch or Gofa attend Ele annually and take part in most activities. Their reason this time was mainly for baptizing their newborn babies, born with the archangel's blessing. They said that they had in the past vowed to Gabriel to witness this moment and as they now have babies, it was necessary to pay tribute. Among the people I have spoken to there were many other reasons for coming to Ele. For young Ethiopian Orthodox Church members from Arba Minch it was an act of faith but also a test of prowess so that they could talk about trekking there and back in the shortest possible time. Others went to seek Gabriel's assistance in their education. Young girls and boys from the local districts (*deres*) around went there in their best dresses to worship and to sing and dance. Other young men went with their horses to mime war, to give colour to the celebration and escort the symbolic ark (*tabot*) of Gabriel.[4]

It was evident that people were very much at ease with one another. Condensed experiences of such moments over the years build closeness and intimacy between people and create a relaxed atmosphere. Whatever their religious backgrounds, people join other pilgrims with whom they would under normal circumstances not identify or associate, and do not react to others' unusual practices. It is not the sequence of details or the manner of the celebrations but rather the moment in which people of various beliefs congregate that is of greatest experiential value.

In Ethiopian Orthodox celebrations elsewhere, for example, a *tabot* wrapped in glittery garments is carried on a priest's head, whereas in Ele wrapped *tabots* are put in the arms of a descendant of *Qeso* ordained by the Ethiopian Orthodox Church In the south, celebrations in this part of the country have not been homogenized along EOC lines as has been the case in other areas of Ethiopia. It is noticeable that some features of the celebrations contrast with Ethiopian Orthodox practices. In other Ethiopian churches during such celebrations priests carrying the *tabot* go around the church building three times. In Ele priests carrying *tabots* in their arms carry them out of the yard altogether and bring them back later. In other Ethiopian Orthodox Churches pilgrims sing praises in Amharic, in Ele they sing in Gamo. The symbolic ark *tabots* of Ethiopian Orthodox Churches are not linked to senior figures of specific hereditary clans. In Ele they are connected to *Qeso* of the Amara clan. In general animal votive offerings are rarely made but in Ele, calves, oxen and cows are driven down a steep hill into the church grounds. Votive offerings in other Ethiopian Orthodox Churches are given in the form of cash, wax candles, embroidered garments, icons, raisins, incense, sandalwood sticks, etc. In Ele they consist of first butter, first milk, the first harvest of grains, honey, coffee, etc and some other items such as incense and raisins. One could further expand this list of variations.

When the celebrations began after mass two priests carried out two *tabots* wrapped in colourful garments in their arms. Pilgrims prostrated themselves at first sight of the *tabot* and started singing *woze*[5] prayers and praises loudly. The procession left the churchyard and moved diagonally across the meadow outside past the edge of the sacred assembly place[6] towards the holy spring where the priests entered a small bamboo enclosure covered in coloured garments.[7] In the middle of a meadow next to the holy spring thousands of people sang praises to the archangel, and fighting was mimed by people riding horses. In the rest of Ethiopia such practice is performed during Epiphany, in the Eastern Orthodox sense. The *tabots* stayed in the enclosure for about an hour during which time the hill above the meadow was completely covered by pilgrims wearing white. From here they had a good view of the horse race, war mime, dancers and singers without difficulty.

After pausing at the spring, priests emerged from the enclosure carrying the *tabots*, but now on their heads. Pilgrims sang loudly and ululated in unison during the procession and moved in great numbers behind the priests. Armed police formed a protective ring around the priests and pushed pilgrims aside to make way for the priests and deacons who followed the *tabot* holding colourful umbrellas and ringing bells. When the procession moved to pause at the Amara assembly place of Ele, Amara clan members holding ceremonial staves formed a line to receive the *tabot*, while the priest carrying it took his place at the head of the formation. Together, they faced thousands of pilgrims who stood on the meadow below singing praise of the archangel in the Gamo language. It was an extraordinary moment, hearing the ululation and song of praise echo in the whole valley and the mountains above. It was a powerful moment: I have not heard of any Ethiopian Orthodox Church religious celebration where praises are sung other than in the Amharic language. The *tabot*'s pause at the assembly place with members of the Amara clan in the background reaffirmed the historical link between the *tabot*, the Amara clan ranged behind him and the assembly place. The clan has provided *Qesos* in the service of Gabriel for many generations and has contributed to leadership in Ele. The pause here reaffirmed the sanctity and timelessness of the assembly place as the site where justice is done and where truth is upheld, and at which even the archangel paused in acknowledgement. The pose of the Amara against this background reconfirmed their seniority in the constellation of Ele 'fathers of the land'[8] and the seniority of their assembly place in relation to other similar venues. The *tabot* of Gabriel itself appeared to be a clan member of the Amara in the way it posed with them before the public. This pose enacted and re-legitimized the sanctity not only of the assembly place, but everything connected to it including the yard of the diviner, the meadow and all the pilgrims who were in attendance. Interestingly, this composition of people and places included every group, present and past. Many generations back, before the arrival of Gabriel, the churchyard and the sacred forest grove on which it is built was a sacred place of the OGR followers, and this is acknowledged by all groups as sacred and ancient. At this moment of climax, all categories dissolved and more importantly, certain moments appeared to merge: the timelessness of the Old Rules, the indispensability of Old Christianity and the present celebration.

Such mixing of times and religious orientations, experienced in varying degree at different sanctuaries bring together communities who more often experience themselves as quite distinct from one another. The Ethiopian Orthodox Church normally distances itself from others outside. But when time is shared, as during the celebration in Ele, it benefits largely from the wisdom of the *Qeso* and the timelessness of the link between Gabriel and these ancient assembly places. Such captured moments shape new rhythms in the move towards the future.

Amid piercing ululations and songs of praise the *tabots* were finally carried to the churchyard. The armed police escort took different positions at one moment between *tabot* and the Amara and at another behind the Amara and the swarming people. As the priests entered the churchyard and posed in front of the church doors facing the public, many rams were sacrificed. Once the *tabots* were taken inside the church, pilgrims prostrated themselves and sang praises very loudly. Those who had sacrificed rams rubbed the blood on the church door; others anointed it with butter while gunfire echoed from the valley below in an extraordinary display of heightened emotion.

Offerings that are brought to Gabriel are supposed to express a kind of kinship between pilgrims and the angel. In Gamo secular contexts, the same sort of objects are offered to fathers, elder brothers, clan seniors, and diviners. Such gifts are prescribed by the OGR. First fruits are given to living fathers, elder brothers, to spirits of ancestors. Gabriel is viewed as one in the constellation of kin who have power over a person. The colour and sex of animals (bulls, heifers, rams) given to Gabriel are also prescribed. Wheat and barley grains, milk, honey, coffee, butter, bulls, heifers and rams are also offered. Cash gifts are brought, and newly-born children were dedicated to Gabriel, so that he may be their Godfather. All offerings, however, are no longer dealt with by the traditional caretakers, the *Qeso*s, but are handled by a committee and an armed police unit.

Both on the eve and the day of the celebration pilgrims took their children to the holy spring to be baptized without church formalities. Parents splashed water onto their children and brought them to the churchyard to be blessed by a *Qeso*. Then they set off for their homes in the mountains directly after prostrating themselves on the meadow inside the churchyard and mumbling a few prayers.[9] This practice is unusual. The power of the holy water, the devotion of the parents, their physical presence in the churchyard and the blessing received from the *Qeso* were all thought to be as good as formal baptism. Formal baptism in the tradition of the Ethiopian Orthodox Church was also held before the mass, inside the church.

Otsa Na, the diviner mentioned earlier, was busy throughout the day, counselling couples, single people, the young and old who were haunted by fear of taboos they had breached. As one of the senior Amara, his position was hereditary and visits to his yard were part of the celebration. Visitors sat on the meadow in front of his house to make confession to him; he gave them instruction for self cleansing and blessed them. For others, he gave direction that he was simply not the right person with proper seniority to deal with their problem and referred them to the sons of Nare, in Ezo, North Gamo who are the most senior in power for averting misfortunes that arise from other kinds of transgression of taboos.[10] Finally, all his visitors left feeling greatly relieved. Others went to places where they were served water pipes and ember for smoking tobacco while still others went into temporary shelters where food was served for money. In open spaces between the shelters, young men and women who have come together from various Gamo *deres* sang and danced their respective *dere* songs in many smaller circles. The mass service which is part of the celebration in Ele was held in Amharic and Geez and there was no common linguistic medium between the majority of pilgrims and the officially acknowledged clergy leading the celebration. Among the pilgrims are young men, the majority descendants of the Amara who were to be ordained as priests.[11] The point I want to make here is that the celebrations described above can be seen as based on the cooperation of some three distinct groups which at certain moments come to share sacred objects, physical space and time.

Although the moment of celebration is shared by all participants, their ease with the unusual and extraordinary circumstances of the celebration appears to arise from their knowledge of their past in which the traditions of each group are seen to be intertwined with one another in time. Each group knows of a series of moments in its history over the years which it invokes to form a common past with the other groups. The understanding across the groups is based on this intertwining of the past. Followers of the Old Gamo Rules are at ease with the assembly places, the praises and the songs and have provided sanctuary to Gabriel's *tabot* and the Amara who brought it with them and have cared for it for many generations. They know how these traditions merged and how they were operational until the period of conquest and later. After the conquest additional elements, specifically those of the recent Ethiopian Orthodox Church were added to these older traditions. The later addition of Essa's teachings in response to the conquest also followed the same traditions.

Since the time of conquest the rules of the Ethiopian church are said to have been operational and to have taken priority over the Old Gamo Rules although this is not borne out in practice as I indicated above. The real contact in time between places such as Ele and the Ethiopian Orthodox Church is only during such celebrations and that one focus of the contact appears to be the channelling of funds to the Ethiopian Orthodox Church.[12]

Background to Christianity in Gamo, South Ethiopia

Christianity has been practised in the Gamo Mountains for over five centuries. Bahrey's (1954) manuscript written in Birbira is the main reference for such a claim but the assumption that Christianity might well have been professed much earlier can also argued for. Some manuscripts, the symbolic ark *tabots*, some crosses and other ecclesiastical objects, and the existence of the Amara clan link to the symbolic arks testify the possibility (Azais and Chambard 1931; Caquot 1955 (Kraus reprint 1975); Bureau 1976). For reasons that so far have not been sufficiently explained, Gamo Christianity remained isolated but intertwined with the practices of OGRs referred to as *Beni Woga* (literally traditions of long time ago). In January 1895 after the fall of Wolaita, Menelik's officer, Ras Wolde Ghiorghis proceeded to Gamo where the conquerors demanded the surrender of the *tabots*, manuscripts and other ecclesiastical objects (Vanderheym 1896; *Qeso* Kabiso Kasto of Doina and Assafa Albe of Birbira January 1992, pers. comm.). The *Qeso* of the Amara clan, one of over a hundred such clans in Gamo, were the keepers of these sacred objects, which were handed down to elder sons by rules of primogeniture that were recalled by means of deep genealogy.[13] The sections of Gamo where these items were concentrated were Ele, Doina, Birbira and Dorze.[14] The keepers, senior members of the Amara clan, also formed part of the politico-religious leadership of these areas and had influence over the political affairs of their territories and of other Gamo sections. Furthermore, their religious influence extended well beyond Gamo territory; pilgrims gathered at their churches for annual celebrations. When the surrender of these items was demanded the Amara *Qeso* and the population as a whole were angry. The Amara refused to hand them over and expressed their fear of doing so, with good cause. There are many accounts of the military actions and atrocities of the conquest period (Vanderheym 1896; Harrison 1901; Maud 1904; Gwynn 1911; Smith 1969; Darley 1969; Dilebo 1974; Donham and James 1986; Bulatovich, 1993; Donham and James 1979).

Resistance against the conquering power could not be shown too openly as the late Kasto Kabiso (of Doina Kidane Mihret), one of the descendants of those who encountered Emperor Menelik's men, recounted. Elders who understood the devastating effect of the initial conquest days agreed to the demands on one condition. The Gamo proposed that the *tabot* be taken to the Emperor but only in the hands of the *Qeso*. They stressed the importance that no one else was entitled to have access to the tabot and the dangers involved if this rule were transgressed. The symbolic ark was then brought to Addis Ababa on these terms.

The elders of Birbira regretted showing their *tabot* to Menelik's men when they ceremonially carried it out to receive the arriving soldiers. The news of Wolaita's bloody and brutal defeat had already terrified them and they brought out the *tabot* as a sign of their common faith and in the hope of minimizing casualties. *Qeso*s who had hidden their symbolic arks in caves were prepared to travel to Addis Ababa carrying crosses and manuscripts as a proof of their professed faith and in the hope of being allowed to practise their tradition without fear. The symbolic ark of Ele and various objects that belonged to it were detained in a garrison town named Qara. In Dorze, Ghiorghis was kept in a cave and the Dorze did not suffer until much later after their incorporation into Menelik's empire. The symbolic ark of Kidane Mihret in Doina too was kept in a secret cave and the *Qeso* carried only books and a cross to petition Emperor Menelik.

Conquest soldiers were happy to take plenty of 'religious' trophies but were also fearful of the religious power of the symbolic arks and of the *Qeso*s. *Qeso* Kabiso explained to me that for his father, the act of denying others access to the ark was a religious act and a way of honouring their age-old tradition as servants of their faith. Only these servants held the privilege of being allowed to look at a *tabot* and to feel it with their hands. They believed that were it to be seen and held by others, the honour of the arks would be tainted, resulting in a catastrophe befalling the *Qeso* in the first place and the land in the second.

In Addis Ababa the symbolic arks and *Qeso*s were kept in the palace together with many other exiles who came from the newly conquered lands. The *Qeso*s lived there for two years and waited for the release of the symbolic ark impatiently. They reported a chaotic situation in Addis. Dysentery epidemics and famine raged in the capital and strong winds blew away houses. Two of the exiles from Gamo died of smallpox but the others survived.[15] All this was attributed to the anger of Mariam's symbolic ark, which had been taken from Birbira: the exiled *tabot* was punishing Menelik for making the land of Gamo a land of suffering. Famine and smallpox also ravaged Gamo country, and similar explanations arose except that here Gamo people were blamed for their failure to protect their symbolic ark from strangers.

The Gamo attributed their well-being, their continuity as a group and their past victories over their enemies who had crossed Lake Abbaya, to Mariam. They saw no future without bringing her back to the land where she belonged, and which belonged to her. The conquerors on the other hand saw no reason for leaving the symbolic ark of Mariam in Gamo in the hands of people they referred to as 'Galla', people who consumed tobacco – the worst of sins in the Ethiopian Orthodox practice – and were considered 'heathen'.

Indeed, *Qeso*s did smoke tobacco and did not recite conventional prayers. Words of prayer were transmitted orally from generation to generation and over time had come to deviate from the prayers recognized by Menelik's orthodox priests.

Though Gamo people were illiterate they had kept holy books for generations. They had memorized prayers that were a blend of the ancient church language of Geez and Gamo words. In the eyes of the Abyssinians, Gamo handling of the *tabot* was inappropriate. Gamo wrapped the ark tablets in homespun cotton blankets and anointed them with the blood of sacrificed rams. This was extremely difficult to accept from the orthodox point of view represented by Menelik's forces.

Back in Gamo elders exerted strong pressure on Menelik's officers to return the symbolic ark from exile, to avert looming danger. The resilience of the group was considered to depend on the symbolic ark's physical presence in Gamo. Meanwhile disease and famine reigned in the mountains.

According to Kabiso, the late *Qeso* of Doina, only the miracle of Mariam brought to an end the period of exile in Addis Ababa. Initially Menelik did not understand Mariam's anger until his own life was threatened. One night, it is said, Mariam was revealed to a *bahitawi* monk[16] in his dreams. According to the revelations Menelik was to be given divine instruction to release and let go the ark and the *Qeso* who had stayed in his custody. When the monk failed to bring this message to Menelik's attention, Mariam appeared in his dreams for the second time and warned that his life as well as the life of his sovereign was in danger if he did not relay the divine message. Threatened by this the monk visited the emperor and informed him of the revelations. Menelik acknowledged the truth of the case and released the *Qeso*s and the three remaining Amara of Doina. He also wrote a letter to his subordinates in Gamo instructing them to release the symbolic ark of Gabriel of Ele and its sacred objects from exile in the garrison town of Kamba in Qara. When the *Qeso*s took leave of the emperor he exempted them from *gabbar* duty[17] and recognized the symbolic arks of Gamo. He then provided the *Qeso*s with sufficient supplies to reach home and provided armed escorts to honour the symbolic ark of Mariam and to protect them from brigands. He urged the Amara to be baptized and to send their children to the new churches he was proposing to set up in their country. The return of Mariam and of the *Qeso* to Gamo was the occasion for great celebrations, for mourning the two *Qeso*s who had died of smallpox in Addis and marked the beginning of a new life.

In telling me this history Kabiso and Assafa were passing on their own memories of their father's narrated memories of these events. They take pride in these histories and the role they play in their communities. They often tell these stories around fire places at night when neighbours assemble for evening chats and to smoke water pipes. They also narrate them more carefully when they meet state officials.

With the appointment of Ethiopian Orthodox Church conquest-time priests to head these ancient churches the *Qeso*s underwent shocking experiences when most of the books and other objects began to disappear (Azais and Chambard 1931; Caquot 1955; Bureau 1976). In one case, the symbolic ark of Doina, Kidane

Mihret, was stolen by a priest and was retrieved after the case was taken to Menelik's court in Chencha. This was a test of the legitimacy of the *Qeso*s, to the Christian past of the Gamo and the intertwined tradition built on the framework of the OGR.

To understand the framework of the OGR it might help to understand Gamo territorial and social organization. The region is made up of some fifty-five autonomous units known as *dere*, each made up of a number of sections which are ordered in ritual seniority and have autonomous assemblies led by fathers. Each assembly is led by a *halaqa* man who serves for a given period. After feeding the fathers of the assembly, he is initiated, joining their ranks to decide on all matters of a *dere*. Each *dere* also has an hereditary king referred to as a *kao* whose role complements that of the assembly in mainly ritual and sacrificial spheres. *Deres* share market networks, some assembly places, diviners, rainmakers, and holy sites. The authority of persons commanding divine power goes well beyond *dere* territories although they remain *dere* members.[18] Regardless of their position as diviners, kings, or ordinary residents all males together with their wives or mothers initiate individually as *halaqa* and serve the assembly.

Persistence of the Old Rules

Many factors may have helped the Old Gamo Rules to endure. Its egalitarian political system appears to be a major factor: Gamo assemblies operated on consensus and its leadership maintained its position after incorporation into the state of Ethiopia. The fact that conquest soldiers resided in isolated mountain outposts rather than among the Gamo may well have meant that the smooth functioning of the assemblies was left undisturbed, but the inability of conquerors to engage in matters beyond conquest and self-maintenance also needs to be taken into account. Some Gamo kings became corrupt after accumulating wealth and power in their capacity as mediators between the state and their own people. In a majority of cases, however, assemblies of fathers have been able to control the situation by nominating junior brothers of their kings to take those intermediary roles when required by the state. Thus they have been able to secure ritual power which was normally supposed to be in the hands of elder brothers. This enabled communities to tap with ease into ritual efficacy from their kings whom tradition obliged to maintain complementary relations with the assemblies of fathers.

Resistance to conquest soon emerged but targeted sacrificers and the sacrificial system rather than the power and operation of assemblies. Dissent against the new rulers was led by Prophet Essa (also referred to as king in Gamo). His exile was the result of the great fear during the conquest that he could mobilize the people. On his return, he was greeted by enormous crowds – it is said that it rained at every stopping-place on his journey home. In his teachings, he introduced a new form of sacrifice and enhanced the sacrificial cycle by changing the calendar of the OGR. Essa embraced craft workers whom the OGR excluded and hence he introduced a new set of rules known as Words of Essa (Essa *Qala*). His 'words' or sayings rearranged and redefined post-conquest Gamo society along two political-religious lines. Today Essa's teaching has a large following in the mountains and beyond.[19] Consequently the assembly in Gamo remains a common platform for followers of the OGR, for Orthodox Christians as well as for followers of Essa. The assembly's autonomy and endurance helped to stabilize life in Gamo which had been disrupted by the operations of the conquest state.

To this day political and ritual authority is marked by costumes, dreadlock hair, the use of ceremonial staffs and by the position of one's seat in the assembly. A yearly ritual calendar indicates initiatory sacrifices to be performed across the landscape, on mountain pastures, on streams, on fields, on sacred groves and in each homestead. The landscape is parcelled into numerous sacrificial units. Certain times are assigned in the calendar for heads of families to perform rituals on specified sites. An attempt is made to harmonize human activities with the seasonal cycle. On the top rung of the sacrificial ladder is a king who sacrifices for the wellbeing of his section of Gamo.[20] This is true of followers of the OGR as well as Ethiopian Orthodox farmers in Gamo.

The post-conquest situation put some kings in the service of the state and their descendants were considered to be corrupt. The state was often violent and its agents looked down on the people. Much later, in the 1970s the people took revenge. Delinquent kings were chased out of their respective sections during the revolution in 1974 (Bureau 1980; Donham and James 1979).

Those who remained loyal to their tradition and accepted change, mediating it through mild pressure without fundamentally disrupting Gamo life, were protected and people rely on them to the present day. The Amara *Qesos* happened to be such people and were at the forefront of those who resisted the disruptive situation that befell their country.

Followers of the OGR, and of Essa the Prophet have bittersweet memories passed down from the generation of the conquest period. Exiled *Qesos* contributed to the resilience of their people, although it cost them dearly at the time. This was how the memories of people who lived in the 1890s have survived, contributing to a social memory of a shared past of suffering and resilience. Each one of these teachings in its own way shares practices and places in the present particularly with regard to sanctuaries such as Ele, where they collectively thank (Gamo *woze, galata*) the archangel for their people's endurance and pray for their perpetuation into the future.

When elders talk about the past they are keen to mention the visit of Emperor Haile Sellasie to honour the archangel Gabriel in Ele. He presented the church with a golden ceremonial cross and the *Qeso*s of Ele presented him with the oldest manuscript in their possession. His pilgrimage to Ele reinforced the power of their sanctuary and they were greatly astonished to see their sovereign prostrate himself before the archangel's symbolic ark. That moment was captured in memory and its retention in the social memory of Gamo groups contributes to the way in which they define themselves as distinct from central Ethiopians. The taking of leave from Emperor Menelik which ended the period of exile is also retained in social memory and is retold time and again not as the epitome of suffering and misery but as the gateway to survival, freedom and honour.

Conclusion

The Gamo feel that their religious practices have persisted, even when some of their *tabot*s, their sacred books and religious symbols have been appropriated by the Ethiopian Orthodox Church, by conquest soldiers and by Italian forces during the war. Just as the OGR have persisted so Gamo people as a whole have also retained their sense of distinctive identity. The process of persistence, however, is a process of relinquishing symbols, of capturing certain historic moments of loss and recasting one's state of being through new ideas and new symbols. In the process of interaction with others something is lost: a religious symbol, a manuscript, autonomy, sacred grove, honour and prestige, property. What persists is a sense of identity, which does not focus on loss, however great, but rather on a new state of being. What has persisted over time is in fact the very sense of collective identity shared between the different religious traditions, experienced, expressed and reinforced during shared ritual moments that occur at regular intervals throughout the Gamo ceremonial cycle.

Notes

1. Lately various Christian denominations have begun to flourish in Gamo but they do not feature in this study. However, their members do attend celebrations in Ele.
2. Hereditary priests of the pre-conquest Gamo church, members of Amara clan.
3. Blessings are central in Gamo religious practice as well as in many south Ethiopian groups. See Tadesse (1999: 222–60) for contexts and cases of Prayers, Blessings and Cursing among the Hor/Arbore Pastoralists of Ethiopia.

4. There is more than one *tabot,* the first belonging to the archangel Gabriel, and others (known as *debbal)* lodged with this one for protection, as happens in other locations. When it is the day of Gabriel, as at Ele, all sheltered there will be carried out in public for the celebrations.

5. *Woze* prayers are sung in unison; they are a mixture of song and invocation to Gabriel, Saint Mary and St George, Tsos – God – all called on to guarantee the well-being of the people, the land, and to ask for rain.

6. Sacred assembly places are ubiquitous in Gamo. They are named and are taken care of by families that inherit the responsibilities along senior lines. See Tadesse (1991) on some Gamo and Konso sacred assembly places.

7. The temporary sheltering of the *tabot* in the enclosure is said to make the holy water potent both for baptism and for curing the sick who bathe in the water.

8. A number of initiated men, who take part in assemblies of a *dere.* Their oratorical skills, truthfulness and their power to bless make them like fathers to the *deres* whom they are considered to 'herd'. They are thought to be particularly virile males and thus capable of reproducing the community.

9. The *Qeso* prayer according to the late Zuma of Ele goes something like *Basmam; sededekan; duyan duyan; taw Tsos, Gergesa, Gabrela; ta dere naga.* ('In the name of the father, I repudiate satan; *duyan, duyan,* lord, Saint George, Angel Gabriel, watch my land.')

10. Sperber (1980) explains the management of misfortune in nearby Dorze in an elaborate way. He does not however show its link to a regional network of diviners.

11. To reclaim their lost position taken by north Ethiopian clergy descendants of *Qeso*s were ordained into the priesthood.

12. In 1995 alone the Ethiopian Orthodox Church collected forty-five thousand Birr, approx. £4500-worth of votive offering for a single day during the celebration.

13. Kasto of Doina, a hereditary priest and a member of the Amara clan is a descendant of Kabiso, Ashko, Albiso, Ch'ala, Gogisa, Genno, Mariye, Zadab, Sutuel... Kasto gave birth to Kabbada and Kabbada to Aabba. In Ele Gabrela in the same manner Zuma who is of the same clan (but a junior in the lineage of priests) is a descendant of Zulla, Chabakko, Onch'a, Ordaye, Otsa, Halcho, Zinne.

14. Ofa and Yakima in Wolaita and the Yero Mountain top in Kore country, east of Arba Minch, are also said to be ancient Christian sanctuaries.

15. The *Qeso*'s account of the situation in Addis is similar to the account by Garretson (2000).

16. A celibate world-renouncing monk.

17. *Gabbar* duties involved extraction of physical labour and essential supplies by conquest soldiers.
18. In some cases a constellation of *deres* form a confederation and have more than a single main assembly. Qogo in north Gamo is one such unit with two assemblies at Zozo and Dorbo.
19. See Abélès (1980) for a brief discussion of Essa's teachings in Gamo. Essa was taken prisoner to the court of Empress Zawditu and later died in his homeland after being freed from exile. His teaching was considered a threat to the conquest forces. Today the relation of Essa's followers with OGR adherents is healthy and there has not been any confrontation since the days of Essa. Early attacks on OGR were a result of its failure to lead people effectively against the conquest.
20. Bolada Boqa of Otchollo (a former Kao-sacrificer) told me that he had made thirteen major sacrifices in various parts of Otchollo in a single day before he gave up his position.

References

Abélès, M. (1980), 'Religions, traditional beliefs: interaction and changes in a Southern Ethiopian society: Ochollo (Gamu-Gofa)', in Donald Donham and Wendy James (eds), 'Working Papers on Society and History in Imperial Ethiopia: The Southern Periphery from the 1880s to 1974', Cambridge: African Studies Centre.

Azais, F. and R. Chambard (1931), *Cinq années de recherches archéologiques en Èthiopie*, Paris: Paul Guethener.

Bahrey (1954), 'History of the Galla', in C.F. Beckingham and G.W.B. Huntingford (eds), *Some Records of Ethiopia (1553–1646)*, London: Hakluyt Society.

Bulatovich, A. (1993), *Ethiopia through Russian Eyes: An Eye-Witness Account of the End of an Era, 1896–1898.* Consisting of two Books, *From Entoto to River Baro* (1987) and *With the Armies of Menelik II* (1900). Electronic source translated and produced by Richard Seltzer, 2003.

Bureau, J. (1976), 'Note Sur Les Eglises Du Gamo', *Annales d'Ethiopie* 10: 295–301.

—— (1980), 'A diachronic study of two Gamo titles', in Donald Donham and Wendy James (eds), 'Working Papers On Society and History in Imperial Ethiopia: The Southern Periphery from the 1880s to 1974', Cambridge: African Studies Centre.

Caquot, A. (1975 [1955]), 'Note on Berber Maryam', *Annales d'Ethiopie* I: 109–16.

Darley, H. (1969 [1935]), *Slaves and Ivory in Abyssinia: A Record of Adventure and Exploration among Ethiopian Slavers*, New York: Negro University Press.

Dilebo, G.L. (1974), 'Emperor Menelik's Ethiopia, 1865–1916: National Unification or Amhara Communal Domination?' PhD dissertation, Howard University.

Donham, D.L. and W. James (1979), 'Working Papers on Society and History in Imperial Ethiopia: The Southern Periphery From the 1880s to 1974', Cambridge: African Studies Centre.

Donham, D. and W. James (eds), (1986), *The Southern Marches of Imperial Ethiopia: Essays in History and Social Anthropology*, Cambridge: Cambridge University Press. African Studies series, 51.

Garretson, P.P. (2000), *A History of Addis Abäba from its Foundation in 1886 to 1910*, Wiesbaden: Harrassowitz Verlag.

Gwynn, M.C.W. (1911), 'A journey in Southern Abyssinia', *Geographical Journal* 38: 113–39.

Harrison, J.J. (1901), 'A journey from Zeila to Lake Rudolf', *Geographical Journal* 18: 258–75.

Maud, C.P. (1904), 'Exploration in the Southern Borderland of Abyssinia', *Geographical Journal* 23: 257–88.

Smith, D.A. (1969 [1897]), *Through Unknown African Countries: The First Expedition from Somaliland to Lake Lamu*, New York: Greenwood Press.

Sperber, D. (1980), *The Management of Misfortune Among the Dorze*, Chicago: Fifth International Conference on Ethiopian Studies.

Tadesse, W.G. (1991), *Social and Ritual Function of Some Gamo and Konso Public Places*, XIth International Ethiopian Studies Conference, Addis Ababa: Addis Ababa University Press.

——(1999), 'Warfare and Fertility: A Study of the Hor (Arbore) of Southern Ethiopia'. PhD thesis, Department of Anthropology, London School of Economics.

——(2003), 'The postsocialist agrarian situation in Southern Ethiopia', in C. Hann and the Property Relations Group (eds), *The Postsocialist Agrarian Question: Property Relations and the Rural Condition*, Halle: Lit.

Vanderheym J.G. (1896), *Une éxpédition avec le Negus Menelik*, Paris.

–13–

Time-shapes and Cultural Agency among West African Craft Specialists
Roy Dilley

This chapter engages with a series of issues regarding the cultural representation of time and of history that are well established in the anthropological literature (see, for example, Adams 1997, Leach 1961, Bloch 1977, Gell 1992). I derive the phrase 'time-shapes' from our editors' Introduction to this volume and from their introductory conference presentation 'Giving Shape to Time' (see also James 1998 on Mauss's approach to time and history in Africa). It covers very broadly the types of concern encompassed by the conventional concept of cultural representation of time and history:[1] within different cultures the notion of time and a sense of the past can take on different shapes or be represented by specific forms that are particular to a social community (see, for example, Davis 1989). Furthermore, I employ this phrase because it suggests other layers of significance. The argument here is not simply that 'a culture' might possess a single representation of time or 'time-shape'.[2] Indeed, part of the thrust of this chapter is to argue against this one-dimensional approach to the anthropology of time, by highlighting the multiplicity of time-shapes amongst specific West African craftsmen and how this diversity engenders a variety of forms of cultural agency and of experience of personal identity.

In their Introduction, James and Mills highlight a range of perspectives on time that characterize the diverse body of writing by social and cultural anthropologists, and others, on the topic. This present analysis takes its initial direction from what might be described as a Durkheimian perspective towards time, namely that 'social time is structured through collective discourses of language and ritual practice'. In this respect, ritual practice is suggestive of collective forms of the representation of time. From this initial insight, however, I wish to pursue further layers of significance by linking my analysis to local understandings of individual subjectivities and personal identities, and to suggest a more phenomenological approach to human experience and imagination in the consideration of how time-shapes, and their associated forms of ritual and mystical practice, coalesce to provide the cultural grounding for particular kinds of human and spiritual agency.

Roy Dilley

The ethnographic focus of this chapter is what are frequently described as 'caste' groups among Haalpulaaren in Senegal.[3] The putative lines of ancestry of these groups not only trace a sense of historical origin – a perspective on the past, and form of social memory – but are also genealogies of power which can be invoked in the present-day. Time can be ruptured, folded back upon itself, or moreover the past can be summoned for social effect within the present.[4] The presence of the past in the present is linked to the social experience of time and agency by specialist practitioners, and is not necessarily connected with the construction of ideology to bolster existing hierarchies, as Bloch might argue (Bloch 1977 and 1985). Indeed, 'caste' groups are marginal to the structures of power and domination in Haalpulaar communities, and so the connection that Bloch makes between the ideological constructions of ritual time and political authority do not grant much purchase in this case. As Martin Mills points out in his chapter 'Living in Time's Shadow', Bloch has criticized Geertz for confusing ideologies of ritual time with cognition and neglecting power (p. 349). Mills goes on to advocate a position wherein the singular ascription to one time-shape of the label 'ideological' misses crucial aspects of the problem, namely 'the examination of time *as a system of power in itself*'. He continues: '"Time anthropology" therefore involves two linked considerations: firstly, a more or less abstract examination of *why people represent time in a particular way* (and who might benefit from them doing so); and secondly, an examination of the *embodied practices by which people do time* – how they orientate themselves towards particular temporal/calendrical ideologies' (original emphasis, p. 350).

The representation of time and the social praxis of time – how 'people do time' – are thus embraced in my use of the phrase 'time-shape' and are linked to forms of cultural agency and notions of personhood, a point that Mills also raises in his chapter. This chapter argues that 'non-linear' representations of past and present are crucial to the workings of certain forms of magic and mysticism, and to the experience of such practitioners. Magic and mysticism constitute a very specific kind of social context in which particular time-shapes occur. These shapes can be contrasted with those pertinent in other areas of life, such as in the round of Muslim festivals and feasts in the lunar calendar. This social representation of time is cyclical and overlays, but does not match, similar time-shapes in the solar and agricultural annual cycles. For specialist practitioners, it is not so much that events repeat themselves by virtue of a circular conception of time or history, but rather that the 'mythical' past and 'mythical' persons, as a form of 'genealogical time' (Davis 1991), become synchronous with the present. Personal identities are transformed, and forms of human and spiritual agency are made possible. Furthermore, investigation of Davis' concept of 'genealogical time' suggests that genealogy can be used to form different time-shapes in relation to the different forms of social organization in which they are found. In Davis' case of the Zuwaya of Libya, genealogical representations of the past – a form of 'precedental history' (Davis 1992) – collapse time by virtue of their function within a segmentary lineage society. My argument below is that genealogical time has a different role in a society characterized by caste-like distinctions rather than segmentary lineages.

Haalpulaar Ethnography

The recital of genealogies of leading ruling families and of important Muslim religious leaders by professional praise-singers and others is a feature of many Senegambian societies (see, for example, Diop 1995, Irvine 1978, Kane and Robinson 1984, Wright 1989). Among Haalpulaaren from Fuuta Toro in northern Senegal, the social category of Islamic clerics, who seized power in the late eighteenth century, constructed putative lines of descent that trace their origins to Arab-Berber populations to the north in the Maghreb. These lines extend further to Middle Eastern ancestors, who are often linked with the Prophet, his family, or one of his companions. By means of these pedigrees, members of cleric families can claim for themselves a privileged cultural identity and an exclusive form of social status (see Dilley 2000, 2004).

The historical social processes that brought about the construction of these putative lines of descent are connected with the emergence and rise to dominance of the clerics as a major political and religious force during the eighteenth century. It is intriguing that the clerics seem to have mimicked a form of social exclusivity adopted by the so-called 'despised and scorned' 'castes' of craftsmen, musicians and praise-singers – and who also produce pedigrees but of a different sort – from whom they were trying to distance themselves.

These hereditary specialist craft and artisan groups also concoct putative lines of descent (sg. *asko*) that connect present-day practitioners of specialist trades to specific points of origin. These are often traced to powers residing in the bush, to forms of spirit forces that, through accident or design, became harnessed by the first specialist craftsmen. Such is the case of the weavers, whose founding ancestor was the offspring of a spirit mother and a human father. This mythical figure discovered by accident a group of spirits weaving in the bush, and took from them the secrets and skills of the trade and introduced them to human society. The pedigrees of each of the distinct hereditary specialized craft groups are as much genealogies of culturally defined forms of power as they are strict lines of blood descent. Made up of strings of names, predominantly of male forebears, the pedigrees eventually reach back to the inscrutable sources of spiritual power. These pedigrees, constituting a form of social memory, are construed by the craftsmen specialists who recite them, as well as by those in whose praise they are sung, as a source of knowledge about people and events now long past, as a testament to a contemporary form of social and cultural identity linked to membership of an exclusive 'caste' category, and as a claim to sources of power that lie outside the remit of the dominant Islamic cleric group. Here, a genealogy of blood and shared substance is fused with a genealogy of power.[5]

By contrast, the Islamic clerics appear not to have fused these two aspects quite so rigidly. Having concocted putative lines of ancestry in earlier historical periods, that connect them with the paths of diffusion of the Muslim faith from the Middle East to West Africa, they also hold dear the idea of separate chains of learning and the transmission of mystical power. In a Sufi Islamic tradition, these chains (*silsila*) represent the persons through whom the litany (*wird*) of a brotherhood has been passed from the founding Shaikh of an order. They also represent the transmission of spiritual grace or *baraka*, a quality that can be passed from father to son, or more often from Islamic teacher or holy man to disciple by means of 'breath' or 'saliva' (Schmitz 2000). A genealogy of power is to some extent hived off from a genealogy of blood in the case of the Islamic clerics.

Rhythms of Social Life and the Punctuation of Time

It is important to examine some of the rhythms that social life takes on and the way in which time and the daily round are punctuated, before examining the pedigrees of craftsmen in more detail. Many of these rhythms and punctuation points are derived from the Muslim calendar of activities, and its round of celebrations and rituals. Islam is the dominant religion among Haapulaaren, and forms the contours for many of the time-shapes they experience, whether these individuals be clerics or craftsmen. While craftsmen and women have had a more ambivalent relationship to local Islam than the cleric groups (who have been one of its main driving forces in the whole Senegal valley), the former still consider themselves part of the Muslim community and conform to its established patterns.

One of the most salient forms of time punctuation is the pattern of five prayer times in the day. Many routine activities are organized to accommodate these times: work ceases, domestic tasks are suspended or travel interrupted for short moments, during which prayers are offered either by individuals praying separately, or by persons assembled as a group. The five prayer times are significant events in the day, which is punctuated by the sound of the muezzin's calls to prayer ringing out across towns, cities and villages. They guide activities, the co-ordination of tasks, the meeting of people or the arranging of affairs. ('We'll meet after *asri*, the second afternoon prayer.') The five prayers are known locally as: *fajiri*, the first prayer before sunrise; *sallifana* or *tisbar*, the first afternoon prayer (around 2 p.m. clock-time, but strictly when the shadow of an object is equal in length to the object itself); *asri* or *takusan*, the second afternoon prayer (around 4 p.m. but more strictly when the sun starts to yellow (*alaasara* is the name in Pulaar given to this period between three and five o'clock in the afternoon); *futuro* or *timis* is at sunset, or at least the period during which the sun begins to set and until the red disappears from the sky; and finally, *isha* or *esa'i* (*geuye* in Wolof), the last prayer held after darkness has fallen.

Another important dimension for the punctuation of time is the Muslim calendar, the twelve lunar months of twenty-nine or thirty days. Each strictly begins once the new moon is actually sighted, so the same month might start at slightly different times in different places. Together these comprise the Muslim year, eleven days shorter than the solar cycle. Each of these months is named, and some of them are associated with specific Muslim rituals or with particular historical events deemed to be significant in the development of the religion of Islam. For example, *Muharran*, the first month of the year, corresponds to the period in CE 680 during which Hussain, the son of Ali and Fatima, and grandson of the Prophet, confronted the Umayyad dynasty, the first caliphal dynasty. The third month of the year, *Rabi al Awwal* is the month in which Mohammed is believed to have been born, on the twelfth day (the same date on which he died), and this occasion is celebrated in the *Mawlud*, remembered as the Prophet's birthday. Other significant rituals are enacted in the ninth, tenth and twelfth months of the year. These are *Ramadan*, the period of fasting and the holiest month of the Muslim calendar during which it is believed that the Quran was revealed to Mohammed. The end of this month is signalled by the sighting of the new moon which brings an end to fasting and the start of the feast *'id al-fitr*, the 'feast of the moon'. If this celebration is also known as the 'little festival', then *'id al-kabir* is the 'great festival', performed in the twelfth month of *Dhu'l Hijja*, the period to go on the *Hajj*, to make the pilgrimage to Mecca. It concludes with the sacrifice of a ram, in memory of Abraham's readiness to give up his son for Allah, and is marked by a feast known locally as *Tabaski*.

The daily round and the yearly cycle are marked by activities and events closely associated with Islam.[6] Furthermore, the Muslim calendar also marks historical, or supposedly historical events, and thus the nature of the year is at once cyclical and repetitive, as well as being chronological (in that it marks historical distance from the date of the *Hijra*, the flight of Mohammed and his followers from Mecca to Medina in CE 622. A social memory of these early events in Muslim history is also reflected in the significance attached to the individual months of the year.

While Islam defines a circular shape for time in its annual cycle, it also defines a past in terms of a teleological conception of historical time embodied in religious thought suggesting that the design of and purpose to the material world consists in the growth of the Muslim community. The representation of history within Islam has further significance, for Muslim religious thought, art and science are dependent to a large extent on a conception of history. The role of history is supported by various genres of writing about the past, such as the Hadith, the purported sayings and actions of the Prophet Mohammed, and Tarikh, a form of reporting on the past in annals or chronicles that might give details, for example, of a dynasty or ruler organized chronologically. Among Haalpulaaren, this genre also encompasses stories to do with the origins of social groups, and the movements of people from one place to another over time, and so forth.

The time-shapes derived from Muslim thought and practice are part of a common stock of representations of the past and of the location of events within the present that are shared by most Haapulaaren – cleric and craftsman alike. The notion of pastness and its representation in various forms, as well as the notion of circularity of time, will be seen again in the following section, which focuses more exclusively on craftsmen and their activities.

Past and Present of Pedigrees

The pedigrees of craftsmen can be viewed from at least two perspectives. The first is that they can be used to situate historical events that took place in Fuuta Toro. A particular link in a chain of ancestors might be identified as a specific person who had a role in a historic event that is remembered as significant by a local community. This might be, for example, the repulsing of a raid by Moors from Mauritania on the north bank of a river and the protection of a river crossing point vital to local people on the south bank. Such events occurred particularly in the late eighteenth and early nineteenth centuries during the establishment of Almamate Islamic polity in the Senegal river valley.

Second, the recital of pedigrees and their connections to past events could be called the 'collapsing of time', in that the past and the present are brought together in a moment of simultaneity. For that moment the past becomes synchronous with the present. This can be illustrated by the claims of a weaver praise-singer with whom I worked, named Seydon Guisse, whose praise-songs (*dille,* sg. *dillere*) were performed on occasions such as the weddings of fellow weavers. In one example,[7] he recited the lines of incantations inserted into the main body of the song, which was performed by his younger brother, who recited the lines of ancestry of significant figures, and would occasionally pause in his rendition to consider the deeds of particular ancestors associated with noteworthy past events. The second singer, as a statement of his own powers and abilities, frequently associated himself too with these deeds of courage, temerity or endurance. Not only that, but a constant refrain throughout these passages was the following: 'at that time I was with...' (*oon sahaa mido wondi e...*) referring to one of the praise-worthy individuals who featured in the song. There was a strong theme of identification between the singer and the time and space of the cultural heroes in the praise-song. The singer's claims could be seen as a form of poetic licence which allowed him to make statements about himself, his identity and his personal charismatic powers. Through a form of metonymic association with other persons and their deeds, the singer enhanced his own reputation in an act of shameless self-aggrandisement.

But there might be further levels of significance to examine. The collapsing of time may not just be a trope or a literary device through which metonymic connections are established. There might be a more literal understanding we have to consider, a closer identification that operates at the level of personal being. This might be seen with reference to the experience of the singer himself. While the singer acknowledged that the persons he sang about had lived in the past and were now dead, there remained a sense in which he himself re-lived and re-animated that past through his own actions. Indeed, some forms of agency he claimed for himself were based precisely upon the collapsing of time, and the synchronous presence of himself and other persons from the past. In the case of the identification in song, it is the singer who, as it were, projects himself back into the time and space of cultural heroes, whereas in other contexts he might be seen to summon figures from the past into the present.

The praise-singer, Seydon Guisse, had been a practising weaver but at the time of fieldwork (early 1980s and mid-1990s), he concentrated more upon singing and performing. During discussions we had about both aspects of this craft, we touched upon ideas about creativity and inspiration in his trade. What we might call 'individual creativity' in craft industries is a quality attributed among Haalpulaaren to a more general form of inspiration that comes from spirit powers associated with the craft. These spirits (jinn) visit weavers with new ideas, designs or words for songs and so forth. Such visitations and forms of inspiration frequently occur at night in dreams (cf. Dilley 1992).

Seydou Guisse claimed that when he was a practising weaver, novel combinations of threads, new techniques or words in the form of magical incantations to be used in weaving would come to him in dreams and spirit-inspired visitations. In particular, he claimed that the weavers' mythical ancestor, Juntel Jabaali, half-man half-spirit, frequently spoke to him, communicating magical verses, lines of poetry and inspiration for songs. This was a relatively common occurrence, something that might happen more than once or twice a week during particular periods of innovation. Thus, agents external to the individual person of the weaver were seen to be the cause of his own creative acts, as we might label them. He saw himself more as a conduit through which such forces operated than as an individual agent in the pursuit of power and knowledge.

Seydou admitted that Juntel had lived in the past and was now in a bodily sense dead. However, his spirit continued as a contemporary force, and this force was the foundation of specific forms of social action and craft practice that he undertook.

The genealogical (and temporal) distance between contemporary living persons and a mythical ancestor was, therefore, foreshortened. Pedigrees that might also be read as 'genealogies of power' possessed a simultaneity and synchronicity that betrayed their pretensions as historical texts. Pedigrees as genealogies of power undermined the very temporal distance they seemed to indicate when considered as lines of forebears.

The Practice of *Nyengo*

The connection between an individual person and a spirit aid is also seen developed in a nefarious form of 'magic' or 'sorcery' called *nyengo* that can be practised by anyone irrespective of caste origins. However, craftsmen in particular are thought to have a special affinity with it. The practice involves an individual striking up a deal with a spirit helper, who will assist the person achieve his or her aims. These aims usually include the theft of other people's property by means of the spirit helper, who carries away desired items. The price of this relationship for the practitioner is high, for there is a Faustian quality to the pact between human and spirit: the petitioner must agree to sacrifice a part of him or herself or one of their family to acquire the spirit's services. After drawing up this pact, the petitioner may lose a finger in an accident or a child in the family might die or be killed accidentally. The forces associated with this form of agency are often named spirits who live in a timeless realm which nonetheless belongs to this world. They are a feature of an earthly human existence, ever-present, encompassing practitioners past and present.

Discussion

I have briefly outlined above various time-shapes among Haalpulaaren. One of these is the Muslim calendar that represents time in a cyclical and repetitive, although not necessarily a reversible, frame. This frame constitutes the means by which ordinary folk can co-ordinate themselves and their daily activities. A second time-shape is 'genealogical time' that sets up a frame of persons and events set in the more distant past, although it is not cemented to a strict chronological reckoning of history. While there are some differences between cleric and craftsmen's genealogies, I argue they both constitute similar sorts of time-frame. A third set of considerations dealt with above comprises how specialist practitioners – singers and *nyengo* experts – operate within different time-shapes that collapse chronological and indeed genealogical time in particular ways. I have focused specifically on craft specialists, although a similar case could have been made for Muslim grand marabouts (*sirruyanke* or 'masters of secrets') whose specialized procedures imply time-shapes not dissimilar to those of craftsmen. An indulgence in the arts of 'time-warping' marks out both types of specialist from ordinary folk in the community.

The three types of 'caste' being and identity examined in this chapter are the 'precedental history' of genealogy (Davis 1992), the collapsing of time in poetry and song, and the collapsing of time in the operation of certain forms of ritual activity that involve spiritual agency. In these latter processes, individual personal identities become fused with figures who are located in the past but who may be summoned in a simultaneous present. Such an identification provides the dynamic for very particular and powerful forms of agency in the world. It is also the foundation for certain types of social practice and craft activity.

Many years ago, Maurice Bloch (1977, 1985) suggested that in ritual a special form of ritual time may be represented whereby the presence of the past in the present indicates one means by which ideological knowledge is generated as a support for hierarchical social formations. If what I have described is a form of ideological knowledge (although requiring a more encompassing view of ideology is necessary rather than the dichotomous approach Bloch adopts), then it is certainly not used to support those in positions of dominance or political power. What I have described is a feature of marginal, despised and scorned craft groups, where in contrast, representations of past and present are crucial to the workings of certain forms of spiritual agency and mysticism. Indeed, a parallel could be drawn here with the operations of local Islamic, cleric-dominated forms of mystical and spiritual practice. Moreover, such representations are crucial to the individual experience of the practitioners, to the phenomenology of specific types of social action. It is not so much that events are construed to repeat themselves by virtue of a circular conception of time or history, but rather that a 'mythical' past and 'mythical' persons become synchronous with the present. The personal identities of those involved in such practices are thus transformed, and they are experienced in ways feared by most ordinary Haalpulaaren. Moreover, forms of human and spiritual agency are made possible by means of these collapsings of time. To be a conjurer of time is a dangerous and even morally dubious type of social behaviour.

Haalpulaaren have numerous forms of representing time or 'time-shapes'; there are no doubt other forms that have not been covered here. The idea of differing conceptions of social time and historical time should serve not to separate 'us' from 'them', the West from the rest, but serve instead to point to forms of continuity in the range of representation and indeed human experience of time. The opposition between, say, continuous linear time, on the one hand, and repetitive pendulum time and cyclical time, on the other, has been overplayed in earlier bodies of anthropological writing. In them, such oppositions were used as a tool to distinguish one kind of society from another. Adams (1997) has argued that

Western categories of time are multiple and various, and this idea undermines the notion of social exclusivity of representations of time. James (1998) articulates a similar idea: 'From this perspective, the notion of culturally exclusive time worlds disappears...'; and again: 'The distinction between "traditional" and "modern" time ... collapses into the history which has produced it' (ibid.: 226). Adams's idea of the multiplicity of human temporal experience has to be extended elsewhere to other places, beyond the West, in order to appreciate something of the subtlety of the use of differing 'time-shapes' in different social contexts.[8]

In this chapter, I have chosen to focus on two cultural representations of time that are central to the social activities and experience of one Haalpulaar social rank of people, namely craftsmen, musicians, poets and singers. The first was the representation of a historical past by means of genealogy, that is chains of purported begetters and their begotten. Davis (1992) calls such a construction 'precedental history' based on a particular conception of time. The second is the representation of time in spiritual and mystical practice, wherein social time past and present collapses in a simultaneity that in turn enables particular styles of human and spiritual agency. Adams (1997) talks of 'time-transcending practices', and perhaps what I refer to as 'collapsed time' might be included under her rubric. These two forms of representation can be considered further.

John Davis (1989) argues that genealogy in segmentary lineage societies is a means of giving structure to a person's world and their place within it. Historical events are also structured by genealogy: 'Narratives of feuds and peaces, of battles and defeats grew out of genealogical recitation' (1989: 108). Zuwaya poets addressed the history of their social group and they sang of past events with reference to genealogy: 'They [poets] were concerned with the higher reaches of genealogy: they spoke of origins...' (1989: fn. 118). These ideas could be imported to a Haalpulaar social context without too much strain in cultural translation, for genealogy and historical event are linked in a similar way.

Davis goes on to argue that 'the chief effect of genealogy was to eliminate time', that 'a genealogy collapses time' (ibid.: 108). This argument hinges on such ideas as the alternation of names between generations, implying the sense that a man named after another is in some respects that man himself. Another pivotal idea is the use by Zuwaya of the names of childless kin to name one's own children, thereby perpetuating an aspect of the childless person. Genealogical history is cast in the mould of 'precedental history', since Zuwaya history 'was a tale of the working principles in an essentially timeless world' (ibid.: 110); an idealized image of the past that was essentially static and had little content of change or progress (ibid.: 111).

Here my views diverge from those of Davis for the following reasons. Davis' argument is assembled in the context of segmentary lineage societies in which genealogy is the property of each group, and it is the means for expressing alliances and enmities. The Haalpulaar situation is one in which lineages in the classical sense have little bearing on social organization, and caste-like distinctions are the main social feature. While Zuwaya genealogies point to a common point of origin in the form of a distant ancestor of the collectivity, Haalpulaar genealogies serve to point out not commonality but separation into caste-like divisions by reference to very different points of social origin and culturally-defined realms of power (see Dilley 2000 and 2004). These points of origin recede into a mythical past that can be accessed by means of 'genealogies of power' that reach back to the beginnings of human activities as they emerged over time. In both ethnographic cases, however, genealogies have social values, being used as cultural tools in the social definition of contested cultural identities.

A Haalpulaar version of genealogical or precedental history is, I argue, not timeless nor do genealogies collapse time. Instead, they set up a time-frame not structured by chains of cause and effect, or by a sense of duration commensurable with calendars and time-reckoning schemes with objective points of reference such as numerical dates. The time-frame of genealogy floats free from a historical grounding and might be considered analogous to 'chronicle history', a representation of the past that is non-consequential without the narrative structure of conventional academic historiography. Genealogical history is claimed by its local narrators to be a source of knowledge about the past. But it also has contemporary uses with respect to distinguishing cultural differences between caste-like social groups, and with respect to the claims made by their members to tap very distinct sources of power that are held to be in competition with each other.

Davis states in *Times and Identities* that 'humans have different notions of time, and that consequently they have different ideas about what their identities are' (1991: 1). This argument is clearly reflected in the Haalpulaar conception and use of genealogical history in a social organization comprising opposed caste-like categories. But this important insight is also applicable to the second form of representation of time considered above – the collapse of time in spiritual and mystical practices. Moreover, the very same persons, who narrate genealogies with a view to express a form of cultural identity centred around the precedental history of their social category or 'caste', are also those who engage, at other times, in time-transcending practices of certain kinds of ritual activity.

Differing time-shapes and representations of time are connected to different kinds of human experience and consequently forms of social practice. Genealogical time provides a frame for the articulation of indigenous forms of cultural difference, how one stock of humankind is construed as different from another. The collapsing of time in song and magical practice provides a time-shape that transcends genealogical or other forms of time representation. Indeed, these different time-frames seem to operate in different sorts of social context.

It could be argued that different social contexts are defined with reference to the particular concepts of time upon which they are founded.[9] People have the ability to switch between one social context and another, between one time-frame and another; and hence they experience different forms of identity or even aspects of their own personhood. Not only that, but the switch from one social context to another allows people to construe and experience for themselves different forms of human and spiritual agency. Particular conceptions of time specific to distinct, socially recognized contexts provide the conditions of possibility for construing human and spiritual agency in different ways. A magician encounters the efficacy of his own practices through his ability to identify with and tap into the powers of beings unrelated to himself in time and space.

Just as John Davis attempts to show how differences in representing the past make a difference in social practice, and that they are consequential (1991); so too have I attempted to examine the idea that differences in representing time have consequences for how people construe the effects they may have upon the world; indeed, the ways in which they might react in relation to the world.

Notes

1. I do not mean to reify this concept of time-shape, for I am aware of Collingwood's warning concerning metaphors of time: 'all statements ordinarily made about time seem to imply that time is something which we know it is not, and make assumptions about it which we know to be untrue' (1926: 138).
2. Note also A. Blok's critique of anthropologists who completely culturalize notions of history, calling instead for a revised concept of a more rounded historical anthropology (Blok 1992). See the chapters by Stack and Fardon in this volume for an attempt to move in this direction. On the problem of history Collingwood's distinction between the present (social) memory of a past event (e.g. a car accident), and the present and future effects of a past event (having only one leg) is useful (Collingwood 1926).
3. Haalpulaaren, 'the speakers of Pulaar' are also referred to in much of the literature as 'Tukulor'.
4. On the role of the past in the present see also the chapters by Bolton and Rack, as well as others in Part II of this volume.
5. The metaphor of blood draws on a local idiom, for it is conceived as a substance that passes down the male line specifically; by contrast, milk is referred to as the substance common to links of ancestry through women.

6. The Muslim yearly cycle does not of course correspond with seasonal change and agricultural practices. The Islamic year shifts back eleven days with respect to the solar year and hence the agricultural calendar.

7. An example of such a song is presented and analysed is an earlier publication (Dilley 1992) and this song is the basis of what follows.

   This spelling of 'Guisse' conforms to the orthography in official French language-based documents (such as a *carte d'identité*), but would be rendered as 'Gisse' using the recognised conventions for Haalpulaar orthography.

8. A number of other contributors to this volume make similar points regarding multiple time-shapes within specific cultural settings; see, for example, the chapters by Bolton on the ritual activities of members of an Andean community, by Heintz on Romanian urban dwellers who are increasingly integrated into a capitalist economy that entails a notion of time as a commodified value.

9. See Hubert (1999) on the relationship between time and magical practices, and how this is connected with the definition of social contexts of a particular kind – an issue referred to also in James' and Mills' Introduction to this volume.

References

Adams, B.E. (1997), 'Perceptions of time', in T. Ingold (ed.), *Companion Encyclopedia of Anthropology: Humanity, Culture and Social Life*, London: Routledge, 503–26.

Bloch, M. (1977), 'The past and the present in the present', *Man*, 12: 278–92.

—— (1985), 'From cognition to ideology', in R. Fardon (ed.), *Knowledge and Power*, Edinburgh: Scottish Academic Press.

Blok, A. (1992), 'Reflections on "Making History"', in K. Hastrup (ed.), *Other Histories,* London: Routledge.

Collingwood, R.G. (1926), 'Some perplexities about time: with an attempted solution', *Proceedings of the Aristotelian Society*, N.S. 26: 135–50.

Davis, J. (1989), 'The social relations of the production of history', in E. Tonkin et al. (eds), *History and Ethnicity*, London: Routledge, ASA Monograph 27.

—— (1991), *Times and Identities. An Inaugural Lecture*, Oxford: Clarendon Press.

—— (1992), 'History and the people without Europe', in K Hastrup (ed.), *Other Histories*, London: Routledge.

Dilley, R.M. (1992), 'Dreams, inspiration and craftwork among Tukolor weavers', in M.C. Jedrej and R. Shaw (eds), *Dreaming, Religion and Society in Africa,* Leiden: E.J. Brill.

—— (2000), 'The question of caste in West Africa, with special reference to Tukulor craftsmen', *Anthropos*, 95: 149–65.

—— (2004), *Between Mosque and Termite Mound: Islamic and Caste Knowledge Practices among Haalpulaaren, Senegal*, Edinburgh: Edinburgh University Press, for the International Africa Institute, London.

Diop, S. (1995), *The Oral History and Literature of the Wolof People of Waalo, Northern Senegal: the Master of the Word (Griot) in the Wolof Tradition*, New York: Mellen.

Gell, A. (1992), *The Anthropology of Time: Cultural Constructions of Temporal Maps and Images*, Oxford: Berg.

Hubert, H. (1999 [1905]), *Essay on Time: A Brief Study of the Representation of Time in Religion and Magic,* Oxford: Berghahn Books.

Irvine, J.T. (1978), 'When is genealogy history? Wolof genealogies in comparative perspective', *American Ethnologist*, 5 (4): 651–74.

James, W. (1998), 'Mauss in Africa: on time, history and politics', in W. James and N. Allen (eds), *Marcel Mauss: A Centenary Tribute*, Oxford: Berghahn Books.

Kane, M. and D. Robinson (1984), *The Islamic Regime of Fuuta Tooro: An Anthology of Oral Tradition Transcribed in Pulaar and Translated into English*, Michigan: African Studies Center, Michigan State University.

Leach, E. (1961), 'Two Essays on Time', in *Rethinking Anthropology*, London: Athlone Press.

Schmitz, J. (2000), 'Le souffle de la parenté: mariage et transmission de la baraka chez des clercs musulmans de la vallée du Sénégal', *L'Homme*, 154: 241–78.

Wright, B. (1989), 'The power of articulation' in W. Arens and I. Karp (eds), *Creativity of Power: Cosmology and Action in African Societies,* Washington: Smithsonian Institution.

Part V
Cosmologies and the Making of History

The 'Rounds' of Time: Time, History and Society in Borana Oromo

Gemetchu Megerssa and *Aneesa Kassam*

In their essay on time, Hubert and Mauss (1909: 210) affirm the philosophical view that duration is not only measured *quantitatively*, but that its cognition is experienced *qualitatively*. In anthropological terms, they surmise that these qualitative aspects of time form part of the collective representations of society, of its cosmology and world-view, hence that they are essentially magico-religious in origin.

Among the Oromo of east and northeast Africa, this qualitative nature of time is rendered by the religious and philosophical concept of *ayyaana*. This is a difficult term to translate, but basically it stands for the nature of time, for the way it behaves and for the manner in which it mystically influences the outcome of all events. Like the Maya notion of *kinh* 'sun-day-time', which also connotes destiny (León-Portilla 1988: 17, 20), *ayyaana* 'day-time-fate' is a sacred concept. It is a manifestation of the Creator, which is incarnated in all aspects of creation (Bartels 1983; Megerssa 1993; Van de Loo 1991). On a *pars pro toto* basis, it designates time itself. Like *kinh*, *ayyaana* is said to be at the origin and centre of the universe. It is more than a causal principle. In a complex way, *ayyaana* becomes that which it has caused; it is both the character of something and its cause (Knutsson 1967; Megerssa 1993). In Oromo, as in Maya, time is 'cyclical'. In Oromo, however, cycles are open-ended, like spirals; they make concentric 'rounds'. A cyclic event never repeats itself in exactly the same way. These temporal cycles, which occur at different levels, are linked to symbolic numbers. The work of the sages in both societies was to record these recurrent patterns and to interpret the destinies contained in them. Like *kinh* for the Maya, *ayyaana* represents a primal symbol or key trait of the Oromo culture. It was the cultural template through which the Oromo traditionally viewed the world (Megerssa 1993). It was a system of classification, a device for putting order into things and for structuring experience. Like *kinh* for the Maya, *ayyaana* encapsulated the Oromo philosophy of time and history and formed part of its system of knowledge.

While the concept of *ayyaana* can be found in almost all the sub-groups of the Oromo, it is the Borana Oromo or the Borana, of southern Ethiopia and northern

Kenya, who have probably retained its original significance. In many parts of Oromo country, due to the encounter with Christianity and Islam, this ancient concept has come to be associated with a possession cult known by the same name (Knutsson 1967; Lewis 1989; Morton 1975). The cult also occurs among the Borana. Elsewhere, however, the core meanings of the concept have been obscured through social change.

This chapter will describe the view of time and history of the Oromo as it is still exists today in traditional Borana society. As Hubert and Mauss (1909: 204–8) indicate, in preliterate societies, the parts of time were represented as being equivalent, creating homologous relations between its different aspects. In Borana, time and history are seen as two levels of the same phenomenon that are articulated through the concept of *ayyaana*. The concept provides the time-reckoners and historians with the same underlying rules for interpreting the recurrent patterns that occur both in nature and culture. The structures of time, history and society can, therefore, be seen as replications of the same classificatory principles. We will attempt to describe how the concept of time forms the basis of the Borana politico-religious institutions, is used to organize the lives of the people and to understand the working of history.[1]

The Borana Oromo

The Borana, who are the southernmost group of the Oromo, number some half a million people.[2] They practise cattle nomadism, but have never been 'pure' pastoralists. Since their great sixteenth-century migrations, they have inhabited the regions of Liiban and Dirree in southern Ethiopia, which are associated with their ritual sites. They are divided into two moieties, the Sabbo and Gona, which represent the temporal and spatial division of the group. At the end of the nineteenth century, the Oromo were incorporated into the empire state of Abyssinia. A number of Borana took refuge in Kenya, where they had one of their dry-season pastures, and were allowed to settle in the Northern Frontier District, bordering Ethiopia. In the early 1930s, due to conflicts over pasture and water with the Somali, British administrators moved a group of Borana to Isiolo District. Today, these different sub-groups are known by their localities.

The traditional religion of the Borana was based on the worship of a monotheistic Deity (*Waaqa*). Its adherents still perform the associated rituals, despite the impact of mainstream religions like Christianity and Islam on their way of life. For practical reasons, Borana have adopted the local Ethiopian or Swahili names of days, but retain their own calendar for ceremonial purposes.

The Borana of southern Ethiopia consider themselves to be descendants of the first-born sons (*hangafa*) of Horo, the epynomous ancestor of the Oromo. They regard themselves to be 'purer' than other Oromo groups, such as the territorially adjacent Gabra, whom they consider to be descendants of the younger sons (*manda*). They view this social distinction as a 'natural' one, based on order of birth. This temporal priority carries both rights and responsibilities, which endow the eldest male child with greater spiritual wisdom. Hence, they see themselves as practitioners and custodians of the original culture, its institutions, laws and customs. These practices include adherence to the values of the traditional politico-religious institution *Gada*, which is still practised today.

The *Gada-Qaalluu* Institution

Gada is a complex system of temporal differentiation through which all the male members of society undergo a series of initiations and are socialized into the social, political, legal and religious roles that they will fulfil in the course of the life cycle (Baxter and Almagor 1978; Legesse 1973).[3] In the past, it also had military functions. As Legesse (ibid.: 81) notes, the term *gada* is a multi-referential one and designates both the system as a whole (generally capitalized), as well its component parts, a common linguistic device. Like *ayyaana*, it is not a univocal concept. The system is said to be of ancient origin, and to have undergone a number of modifications since its inception. Oral historians attribute the current version to a leader named Gadayo Galgallo in the middle of the fifteenth century and indicate that minor structural modification has continued since this time. *Gada* is based on two crosscutting systems of classifying males according to both age (*hariyyaa*) and generation (*luba*).

The *luba* system divides all the male members of society into a number of generation 'sets' (Baxter and Almagor 1978: 151) or 'classes' (Legesse 1963: 2).[4] Females belong to the same class as their husbands after they marry. Membership in the class is prescriptive and life-long. This group of individuals moves through the ten grades (or eleven, depending on the way they are counted) that make up the hypothetical life cycle, normally at intervals of eight years, and perform the associated rituals together. These grades are as follows: *dabballee, gammee didiqqoo, gammee gugurdoo, kuusa, raba didiqqaa, raba gugurdaa, gada, yuba*, divided into three stages, and *gadamojjii* (Legesse 1973: 52–105). The system is a 'generational' one, in that a boy is always separated from his father by five classes; his class succeeds that of his father after forty years. Hence, a generation span is forty years. What complicates matters, is that the grade the boy enters at birth is dependent on that occupied by his father. The boy may not, therefore, move through all the grades chronologically. Consequently, the age gap between the youngest and oldest members of the class may exceed forty years. Those children who enter the class at exactly the 'right' time in the first grade (*dabballee*) when their fathers are in the fifth grade (*raba*) are relatively few in number (cf. Bassi 1978: 68; Legesse 1973: 133). They occupy a special place in the society in terms of knowledge and leadership, and are known as sons of the first born (*ilmaan kormaa*).[4] Those children born 'out of time' (to adopt the Shakepearean phrase to which Martin Mills draws attention, this volume), are known as the 'sons of the aged' (*ilmaan jarsaa*) and are not allowed to hold the highest positions of authority. They can, however, perform the necessary rituals, but separately. Waata hunter-gatherers could be entrusted with bringing up the first-born sons of members of the warrior class (*raba*) and acted as their surrogate parents for the first eight years of their lives (Baxter and Almagor 1978: 172). They also adopted those children who had been 'abandoned' outside the settlements by their parents in the token practice of infanticide. The generations of grandfathers, fathers and sons succeed each other by patri-filiation, forming a 'set-line' (ibid.: 158) or a 'patriclass' (Legesse 1973: 189). There are five such patriclasses (*gogessa shanaan*) between which power rotates. The generation classes are points on these lines, so that fathers and sons belong to the same *gogessa*, but to different *luba*.

The age-set (*hariyyaa*), on the other hand, has nothing to do with generation or genealogy, but is based on actual age. It is formed in the third grade and consists of all males born during the eight-year period between the initiations of the retiring elders (*gadamojjii*). The group is given a generic name which is qualified by that of its leader. The men will belong to the set for the rest of their lives. In the past, its main function was to undertake offensive and defensive wars and to lead cattle raids on other ethnic groups.

Political leadership is exercised during the sixth grade, also known as *gada*. The patriclass in power has an elected leader, who becomes its social 'father' (*abba gadaa*). The class is named after this leader, who rules for eight years. This period of rule is also played out in space, during which the leader circumscribes the territory (*goro marmara*) and performs sacrifices at all the major ritual sites for the successful outcome of his term of office and for the well being of the society at large (cf. Hinnant 1978: 207–43 on the Gujjii Oromo). Each of the years that constitute this spatio-temporal cycle is named according to the particular politico-religious activity undertaken by the assembly (Kassam 1999). These movements also enable the *abba gadaa* and the members of his governing assembly (*yaa*) to establish direct contact with the people and to deal with any legal or other problems arising. During his term of office, the leader is the custodian of the communal law. The confirmation of existing laws and legislation of new ones pertinent to current reality are performed in presence of the 'assembly of the multitudes' (*Gummii Gayyoo*), which is attended by representative members of the society as a whole.

Religious authority is vested in the *Qaalluu*, who represent each of the moieties. Their origins are shrouded in myth. The First *Qaalluu* is said to have brought the sacred objects and substances used in ritual when he 'descended' from heaven. The position is an hereditary one. The *Qaalluu* sanction all political appointments and confirm new laws enacted. Members of the class perform a pilgrimage (*muda*) to the homelands of the senior *Qaalluu* in every eight-year cycle of power for the wellbeing of the society.

This term of office represents one period of historical time and constitutes one of the most important methods of dating events. The current *abba gadaa* is Jaldessa Liiban (2000–2008). Each of these *gada* periods is also qualified by one of the seven class names (*maqabassa torbaan*) that cycle through the five patriclasses (see below). The patriclass in power inherits the name, which is a 'bearer' of the good or bad fate that will characterize its period of rule.[6] The name represents the *ayyaana* of that historical period, which is a replication of that of an earlier period. The present g*ada* is qualified by the class name *moggissa*, which is linked to the effects of both war and peace on pastoral production.[7] Following the chronology established by Legesse (1973: 190–1), this name first occurred in the *gada* of Sora Daddacha (1730–1737) and is thus cyclically linked to this period. On assuming power, part of the responsibility of the leader is to deflect any disasters or to enhance the positive aspects contained in the return of the name to his patriclass. This introduces the notion of agency in history. Genealogical pedigree is thus an important criterion in the nomination of a leader. He is charged with carrying the burden of time associated with his patriclass for a particular period of history. Through his skill, knowledge, and the proper performance of ritual, he can partially reverse a cycle of disaster, or at least diffuse some of its negative impact. This intervention is, however, fairly limited (see below). The succession of the leaders, the name associated with their period of rule, the events that marked it and the manner in which the *abba gadaa* dealt with the cyclical return of any fortune or misfortune, represent key elements in Borana oral historiography.

The division of the society into five patriclasses, the rotation of power between them every eight years, the forty-year generation span, the life cycle of eighty years made up of ten initiation grades of approximately eight years, the return of the seven names to the patriclasses every two hundred and eighty years, and the three hundred and sixty year life cycle of the system itself, represent interlocking periods of social time, the nature and duration of which are determined by *ayyaana*.

Ayyaana, Day-Time-Fate

Like the Maya, the Oromo identified time (*yo'a*) as a governing principle of the universe, and sought to understand its nature and behaviour (*ayyaana*), by observing the movements of the sun, moon, stars and other heavenly bodies. Their view of time and history was constructed on the cycles that they discerned in Nature.

The etymology of the word is uncertain. Haberland (1963: 584) suggests that it could be traced to the Arabic root word *an*, or comes from *ayyam*, 'days', but it is probably of more ancient origin. The term has a complex semantic structure and is made up of a cluster of interlinked meanings, the interpretation of which is dependent on the specific context in which the word is used (cf. Bartels 1983: 112–19; Knutsson 1967: 53–55; Megerssa 1993; Van de Loo 1991: 145ff). It stands for a number of related ideas.

In its primary sense, *ayyaana* denotes one unit of time, the day, in the Borana permutation calendar, which combines stellar, lunar and solar observations (Bassi 1988; Legesse 1973; Tablino 1994; 1999). More precisely, it designates a stellar day, whose *ayyaana* is 'born' at dawn. Secondly, it is the bundle of twenty-seven names that are used to denote each of the days. Thirdly, it represents the causal principle through which all things come into being, change, and pass away. It is both the primary motive cause of something and its resulting nature. Fourthly, it refers to the destiny, luck, fate, or presiding spirit that gives the day its particular nature and spiritual quality. Fifthly, it is a manifestation of the divine, an emanation of the creative power of the Supreme Deity, which is found in all things. In an abstract sense, it represents the very essence of time, its inner nature, and the ways in which it unfolds. Hence, *ayyaana* is simultaneously day-time-fate.

Every person, people and place is said to possess their own particular character and destiny, linked to the day on which they came into being. *Ayyaana* connects one's personal fate to that of a family, lineage, clan, nation or country and epoch. People are generally named according to the day on which they were born, to some quality or event associated with it, or to their birth status. A person's name encodes his or her character and identity and links him or her subjectively to time. As in the case of the cyclical names, rites can be performed to reverse any misfortune contained in the day of birth. Time also determines the outcome of all activities undertaken. It is important, therefore, to select the propitious day for all transactions, such as going on a journey, buying, selling or loaning property, performing life-cycle rituals, and in particular marriage ceremonies.

The names of the twenty-seven *ayyaana* and their astrological and ceremonial meanings are described below. Some of the names are paired or tripled. Since the names cycle, there is no first name. It is the order that is important. There is no complete agreement between the mentors on the significance of the days. Our description is based primarily on Megerssa (1993), which differs from that of Leus (1995) and of Bagaja and Harsama (1996). It thus represents one variant of the data set.

Bita qaraa and *bita balla*: *bita* means 'left'. These *ayyaana* designate the stars Sheraton and Hamal (*lammii*) in the constellation Aries (Bassi 1988). *Bita qaraa* is one of the most important in the series for establishing the lunar calendar (Bassi 1988; Beyene 1995). They pertain to the senior, Sabbo moiety, which celebrates its rituals on these days. *Sorsa* refers to Aldebaran. It is also known as *ejjaa-bule*, 'standing all night', as it is said to be a very bright star that is visible in the sky from evening to morning. It can be seen all year round, but appears at different times in each season. It represents the collective *ayyaana* of all stars. A person born on this day may have the power to decipher the mysteries of the stars. *Algajima* denotes Bellatrix. It is the *ayyaana* of stones and represents that which is old, barren or infertile. *Arba* designate the stars delta, epsilon, and zeta Orionis, and is associated with the elephant. It depicts that which is steadfast and heavy. A woman married on this day will keep running away from her husband.[8] *Walla*, which designates Saipha, is the day of the *Qaalluu*. It is associated with peace and holiness. *Bassa qaraa* and *bassa balla* stand for women and the qualities of kindness and compassion. A person who is born on this day will show sympathy for the sick and hungry. *Chaaraa* is the *ayyaana* of the moon. It is that which shines in the dark. It is linked to the origins and end of lunar time. It is also associated with war. A person born on this day will feel helpless, like a victim in war. *Maganetti jaaraa* and *maganetti biritii* belong to the retiring elders. Their rituals are celebrated on these two days. *Salbana qaraa*, *salbana balla* and *salbana dullacha* refer to a sequence of good or bad luck. They also designate the flow of people making their pilgrimage to the *Qaalluu*. *Gardaduma* is the *ayyaana* of the horse. A person born on this day will be a good cavalryman and brave warrior. A woman who marries on this day will be clumsy and break her household utensils. *Sonsa* is derived from the word for 'wasp'. It is associated with the Waata hunter-gatherers, and with aiming with precision. *Ruruma* is related to the hyena. A person born on this day will have a difficult early life, but will succeed in the latter part of his life. *Lumasa* is linked to the lion and has the same attributes as this animal. A person born on this day will be strong and healthy, but his strength will decline in old age. It is the opposite of the day of the hyena. It also corresponds to a day in the cycle of the moon, when heavenly bodies are in a specific relationship to one another, especially at dawn. *Gidada* indicates a state of disorder and confusion, and the break down of social order. A man born on this day will be unruly and lawless. *Ruuda* is the day of the sheep, linked to the *Qaalluu* and to peace. *Arerri dura* and *arerri ballo*: *arreera* is the mixture of milk and water. The two days pertain to milk cows and to cattle wealth. A person born on one of these days will be a good husbandman and his cattle will multiply. The second concerns rituals of hair shaving in which the milk/water mixture is used. *Addula duraa* and *addula ballo* indicate the origins of the sun (*addu*). It stands for authority. *Gada* officials are normally elected on these two days. A person born on this day may have the gift of leadership, but this quality may not be realized. *Garba qaraa*, *garba balla*, and *garba dullacha*: *garba* designates a body of stagnant water. It stands for the junior,

Gona moiety, and for the *Qaalluu* of the Odituu clan. All Gona moiety prayers are held on these days.

Time specialists, *ayyaantu*, establish the order of the days at the beginning of every month. They use three different methods in their calculations: *baha*, *dhaha* and *mara*. *Baha* relates to the rising of the moon with a star or set of stars. *Dhaha* relates to the conjunction of the moon with seven or eight groups of stars, known as the *urji dhahaa*, 'stars in which the moon shows itself' (Tablino 1994: 194). *Mara* deals with the cyclical nature of this process and with its cumulative differences and effects (*saglii*). The names of the twelve months (*ji'a*, 'moon'), which correspond more or less to the Gregorian ones, and the day-names attributed (in brackets) are: *abraasa* (*areerrii duraa* or *areerri bala*); *ammajjii* (*adula duraa* or *areerri balla*), *guraandala* (*garba balla, garba dullacha,* or *garba duraa*[?]), *bitotessa* (*bita qaraa* and *bita balla*), *ch'aamsa* (*sorsa* or *algajima*), *buufaa* (*arba* or *walla*), *woch'abajjii* (*basa qaraa* or *basa balla*), *obora gudda* (*maganettii jaara* or *maganettii biritii*), *obora diqaa* (*salbaan balla, salbaan dullacha* or *salbaan dura* [?]), *birra* (*gardaduma* or *sonsa*), *chiqa* (*ruruma* or *lumasa*), *sadaasa* (*gidaada* or *ruda*) (Tablino 1994: 193).[9] The paired day-names serve to accommodate the difference between the stellar (27.3 days) and lunar (29.5 days) calendars. The new moon is said to occur when it becomes visible, a day or two after its astronomical appearance. According to Tablino (1994: 200), the first name is used when the lunation is twenty-nine days (*turkudde*) long, and the second when it is thirty days (*faraade*) in length. The expert whom he consulted did not use stellar conjunctions to determine these names. The expert with whom Bassi (1988) worked, however, charted the moon over eight consecutive nights in relation to the group of stars, which form a more or less straight line in the sky, on a north-east/south-west axis. The names of these constellations are: *lammii* (Aries), *busaan* (Pleiades), *sorsa* (Aldebaran), *algajimma* (Bellatrix), *arba guddaa* (Orion), *walla* (Saiph), *bassa guddoo* (Sirius), *bassa diqqoo* (Procyon) (ibid.: 621). To accommodate the difference between the lunar (354 days) and solar (365 days) year, the experts use accurate astronomic observations to determine the conjunction of the moon with these constellations. This adjustment is achieved by intercalating an extra month every three years (Bassi 1988: 623–4). The experts say that this repetition can only occur in two months, *gurrandala* or *obora diqqa,* when a gap (*maqaama*) occurs between the star and the moon (Tablino 1994: 197). This correction means that the seasonal calendar remains constant.[10] These calculations are formulaically encoded, and serve as a mnemonic device (ibid.: 196). With these observations, the experts are able not only to establish the ceremonial calendar, but also to forecast the weather, which is crucial for the pastoral production system.

From the above, it is clear that the Borana developed a sophisticated way of calculating time, using a number of different units and methods: the twenty-four hour solar day, which begins and ends at sunset; a lunar month of twenty-nine or thirty days, a stellar month of twenty-seven days which forms the basis of their ceremonial calendar and astrological predictions; a lunar year consisting of twelve months; and a solar year of three hundred and sixty-five days, the basis of their seasonal calendar. They dealt with the differences in the lunar and solar calendars by adding an intercalary month every three years. They did not use weeks, but the seven nomenclatures (*maqabassa torbaan*) correspond to this temporal unit at the level of the *Gada* historical chronology.[11]

The Historical 'Cycles' (*Mara*)

History is designated by the expression *argaa dhageettii*, 'things that have been seen and heard'. The acts of seeing and hearing are a re-enactment of the past in the present. This encompasses knowledge of the customs (*aadaa*), laws (*seera*), the cyclical nature of events (*mara* 'rounds') and involves prediction of the patterns of positive and negative change (*saglii*) contained in these cycles. The cycles are thought to recur at many different levels (*sabbaqa*, 'fold'), and to affect kin groups, all societies and the world at large, according to their particular *ayyaana*. As in the case of the *ayyaantu*, the work of historians (*warra argaa dhageettii*) is to record, memorize and advise on these historical cycles using different methods. The cycles of history are composed of different units, which correspond to those of time, and are similarly interconnected.

    Gada, the eight-year period of power, in which the leader performs the ceremonial circuit (*goro*), represents the basic unit of historical time computation (*mara gadaa*). It is used for dating each of the years in the cycle and the 'regnum' as a whole. This period of history corresponds to the one-day unit of time. Each of these intervals is named, which qualifies it and links it cyclically to a previous *gada*. The name is the bearer of the *ayyaana* or 'fate' of that *gada*. The seven names will move in a complex way between the five other patriclasses, which will each hold power for eight years, before returning seven generations later to the same line (Legesse 1973: 192–3). The epicyclical movement between classes takes fifty-six years (7×8) and the movement within classes takes two hundred and eighty years (7×40). As our teacher, Dabassa Guyyo, puts it, the *maqabassa* will 'sleep outside' and will come back and 'face' the patriclass after this period has elapsed. It will come back with something old and something new. Together with the *gada* chronology, it represents one of the main methods through which history is recorded.

    The seven *maqabassa* and their meanings are as follows. Since the names have a cyclic order, the sequence can begin at any point. *Moggissa*, the name associated with the present *gada*, is characterized by both war and plenitude (*qufa*) of food and pasture, but only where custom and law prevail. *Sabbaqa* heralds rain, peace and contains all good things. *Libasa* brings about disagreements, confrontations, and conflict. *Fullasa* is a time of prosperity, when livestock multiplies. *Mardida*, which literally means that which stops the cycle from turning around, indicates that something will come to an end. *Darara* is that which flowers, and is also linked to peace and prosperity. *Makula* will be neither good nor bad; it both builds and destroys things. These cyclical destinies do not move between the patriclasses, only within them.

The forty-year generation cycle (*afuurtama abboottii*) represents the second unit of historical time computation. It is the equivalent of a month, during which one complete cycle of time through the five classes is completed. The epicyclical movement of the *maqabassa* through the forty years corresponds to that of the *ayyaana* through the stellar and solar months.

It is believed that the plus or minus three days, difference between lunar and solar cycles creates an effect of unpredictability at different levels of time and history, which Borana refer to as *saglii*, the word for the number nine. There are only nine 'true' counting numbers. Nine marks the end of the cardinal series and ten begins a new, higher level in the 'rounds' (*mara*) of numbers. It represents the concept of zero. In historical time reckoning, nine is linked to patterns of change. *Saglii* relates to the uncertainties contained in the transition between cycles of time. It is the second method used by historians, which is based on both observation and calculation. The historians consult the *ayyaantu* for signs in the stars that will reveal the nature of the changes for a particular period of time. Eclipses and comets play a significant role in this respect (cf. Legesse 1979). The historians also look for signs in Nature: changes in weather patterns; in insect, animal or bird life and in vegetation growth.

The concept of *dacci*, or repetition, is the equivalent of *saglii* at the genealogical level. It moves within the 'bones' or bloodlines of families, clans and lineages. It is linked to recurrent misfortune or pattern of good fortune. It complements the *gada-maqabassa* methods in predicting the outcome of a particular leader's rule.

The third unit of historical time is the cycle of three hundred and sixty years (*jaatama*). This occurs when forty generations repeat themselves nine times ($9 \times 40 = 360$). It marks the end of an era of time. This closure is brought about through the cumulative effect of the *saglii* as it moves between cycles. It causes the breakdown of social order, necessitating a radical new beginning. The last days of an era are marked by chaos and confusion in all aspects of life, including disease, war, and ecological catastrophe. In the greater cycle, this happens not only at the societal, but also at the global level. It brings about a civilizational change. The *saglii* of the era can also be linked to the reversal of fortune, in a positive or negative sense. This depends on the *ayyaana* of each society or nation.

Our teacher indicates that the era of the Borana came to an end in about 1990–1. Due to the plus/minus three factor, however, it has now entered into a transitional phase of twenty-seven years (9×3; also the twenty-seven *ayyaana*), and will undergo a major transformation after this period. The historians state that eight other related groups, who have now disappeared, been reabsorbed or displaced, preceded the Borana. One of these groups, the Suftuu, who can be dated by extrapolation to about 161 BC–191 AD, are said to have been the master builders of the complex of nine deep wells (*tulla saglaan*) of the region. The Borana took over control of the wells from the Wardai or Orma, who, it was deemed, were no longer upholding the customs and laws of the land.

At the institutional level, *gada* is also said to end after three hundred and sixty years (*gada hin jaatamme*), to enter into a transitional phase, and cease in its prevalent form. Only the historians know the duration of this transitional phase.

Apart from this long-range cycle (*saglii deertuu* or *guddittii*) of three hundred and sixty years, the Borana also distinguish short-range cycles (*saglii gababduu*) of fifty years and medium-range cycles (*saglii jidgareettii*) of ninety years. Each of these cycles carries a 'load' or 'burden' (*baa*). When a cycle deposits part of the load that it is carrying, this marks an end, known as *chinn*. Historically, the most well known is that of the 'time of the black flies' (*chinn tiittee gurraacha*), corresponding to the rinderpest pandemic of the 1890s. However, a cycle may not 'off-load' its burden, but will take it forward to the larger cycle above it. The cycles are thus interconnected. Borana elders state that there have been nine such major disasters.

These cycles also influence *gada* rule. In some cases, it is possible for a leader to intervene to reverse a cycle of crisis, but this may cause the disaster to regress and return at a later time with greater intensity. In oral history, this regressive tendency is termed 'coming back on its hands, feet kicking backwards' (*harkaan tarkaan fattee, lukaan dhittee*). Such a regression is said to have taken place in 1991. The impact of such crises can be minimized through ritual performance. Prophets (*raaga*), who are said to 'hear the whisper of *Waaqa*', generally instruct people and leaders in the types of rites they should perform.

Conclusion

Our data confirm the thesis of Hubert and Mauss (1909) that time is a religious concept and that there exists a homology between its parts.

Ayyaana, 'day-time-fate', is a philosophic and religious concept that provides the cognitive framework or grid through which the Borana view the world and interpret events. It accounts for the origin of all things. For the Borana, everything comes into being in and through time. Time is not only the 'first cause' of all things; it also determines what something will become. It gives things their essential qualities and attributes. It encodes their destiny. It also programmes the manner of their becoming. All things follow a cyclical pattern of growth, based on the vegetal metaphor, but this cycle is an open-ended one. Each ending contains the seeds of a new beginning. Time is a manifestation of *Waaqa*. All things that exist in time are thus refractions of the Creator. Hence there is an underlying unity in the apparent diversity of things. Everything contains the divine principle, but develops independently of Him, according to its own inner logic, telic purpose and direction. In this metaphysical view, the Creator transcends his Creation. Only He, through prayer and ritual supplication, can reverse the inexorable cycle of time.

The ancient Borana thinkers modelled their society on the patterns that they discerned in Nature. They applied the concept of the life cycle to their social, political and religious institutions. Time thus represents the basic epistemological principle for ordering things. The body politic reflects the dualities in Nature. The five social groupings reflect the divisions found on the human body. The twenty-seven parts of time, with its three 'hidden' aspects, are prefigured on the male and female bodies. All those that are 'first-born' in the social and natural realms are symbolically equivalent, share higher attributes and are accorded priority. There thus exist homologous relations between the component parts of the interconnected whole. The same methods can, therefore, be used for understanding phenomena at different levels. In the system of knowledge, this principle of replication is known as 'that which applies to the centre applies to the peripheries' (*waan qarri qabbu, qaraari qaba*).

Historical events follow the same cyclical and numerical patterns. Oral historians and time-reckoners employ a limited number of procedures for recording and predicting these events. These include the rising and setting of stars and their lunar conjunctions (*dhaha* and *baha*), observation of the phases of the moon, knowledge of the 'rounds' (*mara*) of time, based on short, medium and long-range cycles, knowing the 'burdens' carried by the bearers (*maqabassa*) of time for each power cycle (*mara gadaa*) and the specific events marking each regnum, crises (*saglii*) that occur at the societal level and recurrent misfortunes at the genealogical level (*dac'c'ii*), and natural signs. Through these methods, the oral historians are able to account for both the predictable and unpredictable aspects of time and for reversals in the cycles of time. Their purpose is to understand the inner meanings of history of an era (*jaatama*) of time and to look for the patterns that connect events at different levels.

Time is ritually inscribed into space and creates the sacred geography of the land. These politico-ritual cycles also enabled the Borana to record ecological and climatic data that were critical to their survival in a marginal environment. It allowed them to predict drought and other periodic disasters and to take appropriate measures. In comparison to Gabra, little research has been conducted on this aspect of history in Borana. Further research needs to be done on the *gada* chronology as a whole.

The Borana do not appear to have embodied their conception of time in material forms, like the Maya. The question of whether or not an 'archaeo-astronomical' site found at Namoratunga in northern Kenya and dated to 300 BC by Lynch and Robins (1978) can be attributed to the ancestors of the Borana remains a matter of academic debate (Soper 1982). More work needs to be done on this topic, as well as on the complex of nine wells and on the burial mounds that form part of the ancestral 'megalithic' culture of the Borana.

Notes

1. This chapter draws on teachings given to Megerssa (1993) on the concept of *ayyaana* by his mentors in different parts of Oromo country. Where a citation is not attributed, it refers to his doctoral thesis. It is also based on a 'lesson' on Borana historical cycles given to Kassam in November and December 2002 by one of these teachers, Dabassa Guyyo, who is exiled in Kenya. This discussion was transcribed and translated by Dr. Hussein Isaak of the National Museums of Kenya. Mr. Feyisso Bedhaso assisted with further questions that arose on the topic. We express our deepest appreciation to all three for their help. We would also like to express our gratitude to the British Academy, the Department of Anthropology (University of Durham) and the Ford Foundation respectively for funding our attendance of the Association of Social Anthropologists' conference in Arusha, Tanzania in April 2002, where a preliminary version of this chapter was presented.
2. The Ethiopian population and housing census of 1994 provides a figure of 250,000 for the Borana. The 1999 Kenya national census does not disaggregate the data by ethnic group. Tablino (1999: 19), based on his work on household data collected by the Catholic Church in 1989, estimated the Borana in Marsabit District at 200,000. An estimated 50,000 live in Isiolo District.
3. This section draws mainly on Legesse (1973), who has described the main features of *Gada*.
4. In this chapter, the term 'class' is used to designate the generation classes (*luba*) formed every forty years, and patriclass, to designate the patri-filiated classes (*gogessa*).
5. The translation of *ilmaan kormaa* as 'sons of bulls' in many ethnographic descriptions does not capture its intrinsic meaning, which relates to being born at the 'right' time, in the sense of being 'true' born. See also Bassi (1978, 1988).

6. The term 'bearer' of fate is borrowed from the Maya literature (cf. León-Portilla 1988). This usage is justified in that Dabassa Guyyo describes the different cycles as bearing 'burdens' or 'loads' which they have to throw off, or carry forward to the next cycle. He also describes cycles as appearing with new 'faces', as in Maya.
7. This qualification appears to correspond to the current reality: Borana has been spared the famine that is devastating many other parts of Oromo country in Ethiopia, yet at the same time the historians are expecting the outbreak of wars on a world-wide scale.
8. Women acquire their *ayyaana* at marriage, not birth.
9. Tablino (1994: 193) states that the names with question marks cannot be used. The data of Tablino, Bassi and Legesse vary.
10. Tablino (2000) confirms that such a correction was made by *ayyaantu* in Kenya in 1996 and 2000, when the name *gurrandala* was repeated.
11. The Islamized Gabra use the days of the week to name the cycle of eight years, which forms the basis of their historical computation (Robinson 1985; Tablino 1999).

References

Bagaja, J. and K. Harsama (1996), 'The Boorana *ayyaana* and their horoscopic significance'. Marsabit, mss.

Bartels, L. (1983), *Oromo Religion. Myths and Rites of the Western Oromo of Ethiopia – An Attempt to Understand*, Berlin: Dietrich Reimer Verlag.

Bassi, M. (1988), 'On the Borana calendrical system: a preliminary field report', *Current Anthropology* 29 (4): 619–24.

—— (1978), *I Borana. Una società asembleare dell'Etiopia*, Milan: Franco Angeli.

Baxter, P.T.W. and U. Almagor (1978) (eds), *Age, Generation and Time. Some Features of East African Age Organisations*, London: C. Hurst & Co.

Beyene, A. (1995), 'Oromo calendar: the significance of Bita Qara', *Journal of Oromo Studies* 2 (1–2): 58–64.

Haberland, E. (1963), *Galla Süd-Äthiopiens*, Stuttgart: W. Kohlhammer Verlag.

Hinnant, J. (1978), 'The Guji: Gada as a ritual system', in P.T.W. Baxter and U. Almagor (eds), *Age, Generation and Time. Some Features of East African Age Organisations*, London: C. Hurst & Co., 207–43.

Hubert, H. and M. Mauss. 1909. 'Etude sommaire de la représentation du temps dans la religion et la magie', in *Mélanges d'histoires des religions*. Paris: F. Alcan.

Kassam, A. (1999), 'Ritual and classification. A study of the Booran Oromo terminal sacred grade rites of passage', *Bulletin of the School of Oriental and African Studies* 62 (3): 484–503.

Knutsson, K.E. (1967), *Authority and Change. A Study of the Kallu Institution among the Macha Galla of Ethiopia*, Gothenburg: Etnografiska Museet.

Legesse, A. (1963), 'Class systems based on time', *Journal of Ethiopian Studies* 1: 1–19.

——(1973), *Gada. Three Approaches to the Study of African Society*, New York: Free Press.

——(1979), 'La mort du soleil: signes naturels, tabous et autorité politique', in G. Francillon and P. Menget (eds), *Soleil est mort. L'éclipse totale du soleil du 30 juin 1973*, Nanterre: Laboratoire d'Ethnologie et de Sociologie Comparative, 245–76.

León-Portilla, M. (1988 [1968]), *Time and Reality in the Thought of the Maya*, Norman: University of Oklahoma Press.

Leus, T. (1995), *Borana Dictionary*, Schijndel: W.S.D. Grafisch Centrum.

Lynch, B.M. and L.H. Robbins (1978), 'Namoratunga: the first archaeo-astronomical evidence in sub-Saharan Africa', *Science* 200: 766–8.

Lewis, I.M. (1989 [1971]), *Ecstatic Religion*, London: Routledge.

Megerssa, G. (1993), 'Knowledge, identity and the colonizing structure. The case of the Oromo of East and Northeast Africa', Ph.D. thesis, University of London, School of African and Oriental Studies.

Morton, A.M. (1975), 'Mystical advocates. Explanation and spirit sanctioned adjudication in the Shoa Galla ayana cult', in H.G. Marcus (ed.), *Proceedings of the First United States Conference on Ethiopian Studies*, East Lansing: Michigan State University, 73–89.

Robinson, P.W. (1985), 'Gabbra nomadic pastoralism in the nineteenth and twentieth century northern Kenya', Ph.D. thesis, Northwestern University.

Soper, R. (1982), 'Archaeo-astronomical Cushites: some comments', *Azania* 17: 145–62.

Tablino, P. (1994), 'The reckoning of time by the Borana *Hayyantu*', *Rassegna di Studi Etiopici* 39: 191–205.

——(1999), *The Gabra. Camel Nomads of Northern Kenya*, Nairobi: Paulines Publications.

——(2000), 'Borana and Gabra calendars at Marsabit, northern Kenya'. Paper presented at the XIVth International Ethiopian Studies Conference, Addis Ababa, 6–11 November.

Van de Loo, J. (1991), *Guji Oromo Culture in Southern Ethiopia*, Berlin: Dietrich Reimer Verlag.

–15–

Cutting Time: Beads, Sex and Songs in the Making of Samburu Memory
Bilinda Straight

Maasai associate cuts in an ornament with natural and cultural phenomena like slashes in a piece of roasting meat, breaks in a line of cattle or people, or the short interruption when a Maasai woman fills a cup by pouring a little milk, stopping, and then pouring again to fill it up. A general cultural attitude unites these different 'cuts': nothing should be continuous and unbroken. Maasai deliberately 'cut' beadwork patterns and activities such as pouring, because to create pure colour fields or a continuous milk flow would seem to claim the purity and power attributed only to God (Kratz and Pido 2000: 53).

In this essay,[1] I will describe some of the cuts that the Maasai's 'cultural cousins,' the northern Kenyan Samburu, make in time, beadwork, and song. Congratulating Kratz and Pido for the insightfulness of their observation, my examination of Samburu cuts goes beyond suggesting these as belonging to a 'general cultural attitude', to elucidating them as an organizing framework for a Samburu consciousness that is always an historical consciousness – a consciousness over and through time – and a gathering point for social memory.

Within anthropology, studies focusing on memory have become popular in recent years (e.g., Antze and Lambek 1996; Borofsky 2000; Fabian 1996, 1999, 2002; Malkki 1995). Although this scholarship is diverse in topic and approach, the tendency has not been to question in the most basic sense, just what memory is.[2] This is not to suggest that these works are not critical in their approach. Fabian (2002) for example, focuses on forgetting rather than remembering, or rather, on how forgetting is implicated in the selective process of remembering. Moreover, the attention many of these scholars give to 'collective' or 'social' memory suggests sensitivity to the problem of Eurocentric notions of unitary, individual selves implied by the term.[3]

Michael and Susan Whyte's grappling with the issue of structural versus biological, historical, or intersubjective time demonstrates the vexing assumptions at the intersection of memory and time as they have long surfaced in anthropology. Whyte and Whyte want to attend to the intersection of historical time – the time of large-scale social transformations – and the lifeworlds of social actors, which exist in the *intersubjective time* of shared biographies and common experience (Whyte and Whyte 2002: 1). Their discussion of different kinds of time suggest a fundamental difficulty within Western philosophy of conceiving of memory apart from notions of individual selves, and conversely, of time and history as anything apart from objects that humans observe as external to themselves. The unmarked category for time has often been 'linear'. Quite related to this phenomenologically, the unmarked category for memory, as used particularly in the neurobiological and psychological sciences, is individual or personal memory – just where notions of unitary selfhood emerge.[4] Any other type of memory must be qualified, just as any time other than linear, chronological time must be qualified.[5]

In her discussion of Mauss' work on Africa, Wendy James has illuminated Mauss' sensitivity to broad regional systems comprising a number of societies sharing 'common features which have a connected history', that is, sharing a wide range of phenomena that are 'essentially international, extranational' (1998: 242). Mauss' conception of civilization, in other words, was supple enough to encourage examination of socially-embedded time and inherently dynamic, historical, and complexly regional forms of consciousness. Attending to a specific dimension of such a time-consciousness sense, Martin A. Mills (this volume, p. 350) looks to understanding 'time *as a system of power in itself* – as a means of actively integrating individual experience into social time.' Through his examination of Buddhist Ladakh, Mills attempts simultaneously to describe some of the 'embodied practices by which people *do* time' and question 'why people *represent* time in a particular way,' ultimately relocating the focus of time-anthropology from time to the construction of personhood.

Keeping these issues in view, I will examine a particular instantiation of consciousness moving across time and space. For Samburu, that movement must be accompanied by a 'cutting' (*aduŋ*) that maintains proper divisions both of social space and social memory. Samburu adornment and song cut the generations of the present and create parameters for structuring future remembering. Thus, while Samburu adornment and song might seem well-positioned to become the foci of analyses of 'timeless tradition' against, for example, the novel vicissitudes of colonialism and global capitalism, Samburu *aduŋ* demands a different reading. Thus, when we consider colonial phenomena with respect to Samburu cutting, it is possible to see bead and song transformations not as colonially induced in any simple sense, but rather, to see the ways that colonial forms, events, and processes became *embedded* in Samburu ways of cutting time and structuring memory. Here, the complicated nexus of space, time, memory, and consciousness is of necessity *about* particular ways and moments of becoming (and un-becoming), a person moving within a dense fabric of local, regional, and global hierarchies.

The Samburu of Northern Kenya

The Samburu inhabit northern Kenya's semi-arid lands, raising cattle, some camels, and goats and sheep. A dominant feature of Samburu social organization is the *age-set* system, whereby a group of young men (*lmurran*) is set apart from the rest of society, forming a collective for warfare and defence. Young men become *lmurran* in an inititation ceremony marked by the cut of circumcision that divides them from their boyhood. Circumcision for both girls and boys is the quintessential cut that creates them as Samburu persons in a highly structured social space. Throughout their lifecycle, men are divided into the age-grades of boy, unmarried young man (*lmurran*), and married elder. These age-grades through which every Samburu male must pass form a cyclical periodicity. In contrast, membership in a particular *age-set* (a new age-set forms approximately every fourteen years) is lifelong, so that individual age-sets comprise temporally coeval generations. Each new age-set of freshly initiated unmarried young men is given a name, the previous age-set become junior elders, and so on.

Although not as formal as the men's age-set system, women likewise pass through stages, each of which forms an interdependent counterpart to men's. Thus, 'uncut', uncircumcised girls are the girlfriends and singing partners of *lmurran*, just as 'cut' married women are the interdependent, if politically unequal, counterparts of their husbands. Besides the various cuts of initiation (including the cut of circumcision itself), the cuts of Samburu age-gender categories are further marked by rules of comportment, productive and reproductive labour forms, clothing and adornment styles, song and performance styles, and other practices. And each of these in turn, is marked by its own internal cuts.

While the majority of Samburu live in rural areas and continue to rely on the herding economy, the intertwining factors of colonialism, drought, development, and Christian missionization have led many Samburu into wage labour, petty hawking, agriculture, and livestock trade (Fratkin 1991; Holtzman 1996, 2003; Sperling 1987; Straight 1997a,b, 2000). These and other changes affecting the Samburu have had a variety of implications for their understandings of themselves, and the Samburu 'wear' such changes. Samburu adornment styles refer to a broad range of social memories and are likewise an increasingly contested site of cultural transformation. Thus, the proliferation of clothing and adornment options has led to immense visual variety – with many in town adopting Western styles in contrast to rural Samburu who wear a range of so-called 'traditional' cloth and bead styles or dress in points in between. Yet adornment is a salient feature of Samburu consciousness, and changes in such practices are duly noted and even lamented. Indeed, adornment can become so morally charged as to be the focus of divine prescriptions by ritual specialists.

Cutting Time

The British presence in Kenya coincided with the availability of beads on an unprecedented scale. As the British established themselves in northern Kenya, colonial officers used beads and other imported goods to incorporate the Samburu into the cash economy. While beads were a desirable stimulus to cash-use for the colonial government and highly prized by Samburu women and men for their adornment potential, they quickly led both sides into a quandary as well. The trouble for the Samburu had already started by the 1860s – in the pre-colonial era when beads came into Samburu hands from Somali and other sources.[6]

The legend of the *Leisa* girls is famous even now, in the early years of the new millennium. By current Samburu oral accounts, Leisa were the first Samburu girls notable for their beaded ornaments, which they called *lomito*, worn in combination with little metal chains that hung down and tinkled as they walked.[7] Leisa were the daughters of the *Lkipeku*, the generation of men circumcised in the 1830s and 40s. These girls danced with *Ltarigirig lmurran*, circumcised in the 1860s and 70s, and the oldest among them married *Ltarigirig* as well, once the *Lmarikon* began to be circumcised in 1879. In the years before the Leisa girls married, they enjoyed their unfettered and uncircumcised youth dancing and flirting with their Ltarigirig boyfriends in a time of plenty. As Samburu elders relate it, in the early years of the Ltarigirig generation there was no famine, no livestock diseases, and milk flowed plentifully. This wealth and abundance had its counterpart in the beaded adornment and beauty of the Leisa girls. As one elder related, these girls were so proud they sometimes shunned people who visited them: 'What is in the house? And the other girls answer: *Nkobei* (a post).' If someone should ask a Leisa girl for milk, she responded rudely, 'Just let them talk with *nchongorro* (a type of calabash).' Leisa girls' pride went beyond vanity; their refusal to speak to and share with hungry people – particularly their elders – was a manifestation of Leisa girls' subversion of the all-important cuts that organized social existence and maintained the moral order itself. Some Samburu go so far as to suggest that Leisa girls even violated avoidance cuts/norms, standing too close to elders of their father's age-set and by implication, perhaps having affairs with them as well.

Inevitably, Leisa girls' pride and their Ltarigirig *lmurran* boyfriends' love for these girls with their beautiful beads, was the undoing of two generations. By the time *Lmarikon* were being circumcised in 1879, war, disease, and famine had either already come or were on the horizon. Historians of East Africa and Samburu themselves agree that one problem followed another, from the 1870s *Laikipiak* inter-ethnic wars up to the smallpox and rinderpest epidemics that decimated people and cattle populations in the 1880s and 90s (see also Waller 1988). It was not until the early years of the British colonial administration at the turn of the twentieth century that the Samburu began to recover.

While the *Leisa* legend is the quintessential cautionary tale, the years a Samburu girl spends dancing with *lmurran* is the right time to amass an abundance of brightly coloured beads. First her family gives her beads to help her attract a boyfriend, and then if all goes well, a boyfriend will give her enormous quantities as well, whether he has to raid cattle or engage in wage labour in order to acquire them. Every generation of 'warriors' and girls has their own song and bead styles – the beads making the women beautiful as they bounce their heads to reveal necks as long as ostriches' and the promise of beauty and (sexual) relationships is enough to prompt young men to earn girls' praise and the wherewithal to buy beads. Stretching across individual and collective Samburu biographies in multitudinous ways, beads serve as colourful testimonies of important moments for both individuals and entire generations.[8]

While beads are tangible reminders of youth however, it is the songs sung by and between *lmurran* and their girlfriends that bring beads, sexuality, and youthful exploits together in performances that will be remembered.[9] During these performances, girls wear their full collection of beads and smear themselves with animal fat and red ochre. *Lmurran* do likewise, and song competitions between them often break off into romantic trysts later.

As they sing, individual *lmurran* boast their accomplishments about the cattle raiding known for attracting and beading girls in unique song lines (*rrepeta*)[10] cut (literally) with collective verses/choruses (*ngirukoto e singolio*)[11] in a set structure they sing with members of their own clan and generation. In 1994 for example, a Lmooli *lmurran* sang these lines between other verses that alternated individual and collective accomplishments: 'I will tell you what I did/I slept without food for three consecutive months/I guided my colleagues [fellow *lmurran*] and I lost self-control' (recorded at Ngare Narok 1994). This *lmurrani* boasted that he was strong enough to face deprivation and to 'lose his temper' or 'self-control' sufficiently so that he could steal cattle. Then the song continues in a collective voice: 'We still follow along raiding cattle/*Lmurran* have long necks adapted for singing and for the girl who says she will not go home unless in the company of *lmurran*'.

Women's songs may cut within cuts, cutting *lmurran* collective deeds with individual love lines as *rrepeta* that are in turn, cut with chorus lines, or they may simply cut *lmurran* deeds with love lines. Thus, a woman who danced with her *Lkishili* boyfriend in the 1960s alternates sexually explicit lyrics ('you'll get a big *lorien*')[12] with these collective lines: 'Oh my friend who gives me milk, we killed the Somalis until the end of them was seen/We stayed in Seiya, we never packed/And the ones we danced with had long hair and red eyes [a sign of bravery]' (recorded at Lpartuk, 14 February 2002). Subsequent generations may keep the tune and chorus of earlier songs, but will add their own verses incrementally, continuing to merge individual and collective memories until only *rrepeta* boasting a generation's greatest accomplishments and most famous names remain. When the last member of an age-set dies, so does the corpus of his or her generation's songs. Yet, old men and women will weave some songs and famous lines of old songs into narrative features or *rrepeta* of oral histories and songs of memory.

Besides this cutting of chorus lines with unique lines, and collective with individual deeds, in the earliest years of the colonial period young men and women began to merge Euro-American cultural forms and administrative rules with songs otherwise focused on love and bravery. Samburu *lmurran* and their girlfriends achieved the blending in two ways: first, they sang of the colonial rules and practices affecting them as a song's setting. In this, they followed a classic Samburu song form that is visible in today's songs and also in fragments sung in songs originally composed before British colonization of northern Kenya. Second, they fashioned Euro-American cultural forms into new, often whimsical metaphors. The latter method is visible in some of the lines sung by a woman who had performed with her Lmekuri boyfriend in the 1930s and 40s. She sang just a fragment from one of her old songs, that will probably never be heard in its entirety after her death: 'My boyfriend is tall with eyes like a car's headlights so that he can see clearly in the forest at night' (recorded at Lpartuk, 14 February 2002).

Both methods of merging colonial events and cultural forms into Samburu songs appear in another example, from a woman who danced with Lkishili *lmurran* in the 1960s. First, she interrupted herself to tell me that when she sang this song, she was a young girl just starting to mature. She was competing with *lmurran* in dancing and singing, and no *lmurran*i could challenge her. Then she sang about meeting her boyfriend at a shop, noting that the fifty-cent piece had just been introduced and it seemed like everything cost fifty cents as a result. This brief description of her song's setting places us very particularly in Samburu generational – and colonial – time. It is cut however, by a description of her love for an *lmurran*i that is a Samburu archetype: 'If I love you in my heart, how will it be in my stomach [emotions originate in the stomach] . . . God, don't kill me before I see a warrior with fat in his body.'[13] Then, again, she returns to a setting that places us in a linear temporality: 'Someone in our home was caught with a flag [spear]/We paid a cow [fine] as all families have/How many good things have you seen from the person given that cow?' Following this critique of the implications of colonial rule – including taxation and fines whose implementation was uneven or even capricious, she returns to a love that quintessentially belongs to girlhood and *lmurran*-hood. This time, she uses a Euro-American object playfully: 'We let *lmurran* touch our hips/I put my boyfriend between telephones [metaphor for thighs]' (14) (recorded at Lpartuk 14 February 2002).

As this woman and others explained to me, songs to lovers were sung in *Ltimayo*, or code:[15] 'So we'll pick Ltimayo/Let's talk in low tones, so our mothers won't know' (recorded at Lpartuk 14 February 2002). Plans were made and sung in

Ltimayo, and sexually explicit words were concealed by it. Importantly however, mothers were not the only authority figures requiring clever ruses. On the one hand, an *lmurran*i might sing 'I'll break my glass on my mother's bed' – a sexual code meant to deceive mothers.[16] On the other, by the 1930s, *lmurran* and their girlfriends found that their celebrations could get them in trouble with the colonial government as well. The boastful songs of *lmurran* and their girlfriends are said to have led the government to suspect that Lkileku warriors had killed a young British settler in 1931. That event, following upon numerous other reminders of the unruliness of *lmurran*, played a determining role in the government's decision to ban precisely those songs and beads sung and used by warriors and their girlfriends.

By the time of Lmekuri, the colonial government's attempts to control Samburu *lmurran* led to the banning of other accoutrements of the age-grade as well, such as spears and red ochre. The Samburu response was twofold: *Lmurran* sang of their exploits in code, pointing up what they perceived as the stupidity of colonial restrictions by singing of the dogs rather than the lions they had killed, and of the colours rather than the names of the beads they gave to their girlfriends. The girls in their turn kept their banned *soomi* beads, but hid them under their other beads. The banning of beads and spears was a dramatic moment for the Samburu, memorialized immediately in songs and stories. Moreover, the bitterness of the overall events surrounding the death of the British settler continues to be keenly felt by both male and female surviving members of the Lkileku generation. In contrast to their usual eagerness to sing old songs, it is a rare person who will sing the song that culminated in members of the Lkileku age-set being tried for murder, even though the colonial ban has of course long since passed. The poignancy of the events is still evident, as in these lines from one of the songs sung in the event's aftermath: 'Tell my mother, tell my father, look for a bowl, the one you'll put tears in/I'll go to be hanged… My shadow is pink/Good-bye my dear/My brother, I'll go to hang' (recorded at Lpartuk 12 February 2002).

In the aftermath of the ban on certain beads and songs, *lmurran* and their girlfriends sang in code and even transformed entire song forms. Again – as with Ltimayo – the practice of changing song forms was not invented specifically for the colonial government. It was (and continues to be) simultaneously, a conscious means of cutting generations apart from one another and a common method for keeping secrets from parents. In many ways, from the point of view of young people, the government merely colluded with parents who were already wary of the *lmurran*'s excesses. As the colonial government soon learned – often from *lmurran*'s own elder generations – the young warriors raided cattle and killed people when necessary in order to prove themselves to their girlfriends and acquire the means to buy the latter many beads. Thus, even when beads are not mentioned explicitly, they form the backdrop for youthful exploits. As such, as I noted early in this essay, beads have been a site of ambivalence for a long time. Parents themselves buy beads for their daughters because they want them to attract boyfriends. Yet at the same time, they are ever wary that a line will be crossed – through excessive raiding and excessive beads.

Cutting Moral Personhood

The story of the *Leisa* girls not only exemplifies the danger that pride can have for the Samburu community; the story signals the critical importance of adornment in making the cuts that relate to the Samburu moral order and the centrality of adornment generally to the organization of consciousness. Beads and cloth are crucial in making necessary distinctions between men and women, men and boys, women and girls. Beads follow Samburu from birth to death, whether figuring in significant ceremonies or simply forming a part of daily attire. Thus, the green or blue beads worn around the waists and necks of infants and small boys and girls do not merely signify bodily well-being; they *are* a prayer for health, just as blue beads hung at the house door are a prayer for the entire household.

By late childhood, the importance of beads expands beyond health to sexual matters. It is helpful here to distinguish between sexual transgressions that require ritual cleansing and those that are not particularly serious, though they may lead to violence perpetrated by offended partners and divine sanction if Nkai becomes offended. Boys, who should wear the simplest beads, are not supposed to engage in any sexual activity at all.[17] However, to have sex with unmarried girls is not a serious moral transgression, although it can result in beatings by the *lmurran* for 'stealing' their girls. For boys to have sex with married women is a grievous moral offence, however, which must be ritually cleansed if it occurs – which is rare.

In contrast to boys' simple beads and highly limited sexuality, *lmurran* and their uncircumcised girlfriends have a fair amount of sexual freedom, matched by extravagant adornment styles. *Lmurran* are normatively permitted to engage in sexual relations with the unmarried, uncircumcised girls in their clan, and unlike married women, girls are free to end relationships completely by removing any beads a boyfriend has given, or simply breaking up verbally if no beads were exchanged. Unmarried girls are normatively prohibited from engaging in sex with married men however, and the offence is even more serious if the girl's father belongs to her sexual partner's age-set, in which case it constitutes incest. In any case, a relationship between an uncircumcised girl and a married man brings shame, particularly upon the man. In contrast, *lmurran* frequently exceed the sexual boundaries prescribed for them by having affairs with married women, risking violence if caught by the women's husbands but not transgressing serious taboos. Thus, of all age and gender categories, the *lmurran*, with their flamboyant beads and other decorations, have the greatest sexual latitude, followed by uncircumcised girls.

Competing Histories

While Samburu flagrantly violated colonial rules, calling beads by other names and singing songs in code, the government had of course upset their moral universe on a wide scale. While Samburu had encouraged the beauty of their girls and the wild bravery of their young men – to a point that is, the colonial government attempted to utterly ban beauty *and* bravery. If Samburu attempted to keep clear the cuts/distinctions between married and unmarried men and women, colonial officials' attention to such prescriptions and taboos was manifested in efforts to erase distinctions and rush young men from boyhood to sober married life. Yet the failure of such attempts is witnessed in the Lmekuri song, 'If they refuse *saen lpusi* (multi-coloured beads – code for *soomi*) we will give *ntuntwa*.' The 'they' in this case is the government, which Samburu were careful to avoid mentioning by name.

Returning to issues I raised at the beginning of this essay, what *should* we mean by personal memory, biographical memory, or social memory? What should we mean by consciousness when we use it to refer to a range of cultural practices? Noting the tendency of psychological and neurobiological notions of consciousness to be unambiguously based in individual cognitive processes, it would seem prudent to take care that anthropologists' laudable attempts to extend consciousness to embrace macro-processes do not become a reinvigoration of culture as personality writ large. Similarly, while a term like social memory appears to subvert *a priori* Eurocentric understandings of memory as individual and personal, we might ask what precisely is being accomplished in that subversion. Is there a vernacular term we would translate as memory or social memory in the communities in which we work? More pointedly, is social memory the same as historical consciousness? I pose this question because it would seem synonymous, at least when we use both terms together without distinguishing them.[18]

Clearly, we are struggling to formulate new terms in the face of post-modern critiques and the fact of post-coloniality. Nevertheless, we need to take care to subject new terms, or old terms put to novel use, to the same scrutiny as the old ones. When consciousness is used in contexts in which culture might previously have been used, we may be implying 'core' consciousness. When social memory and historical consciousness are used, we may be alleviating that problem without specifying precisely what historical consciousness is. Is it one 'core' consciousness continually giving way to the next? When we attend to border crossings, what is it exactly that is crossing borders? Are we examining the diffusion of culture traits? It would seem that if something travels, it has a recognizable form at the point of departure, even if that form becomes transformed *en route*. Or does it have a recognizable form? What are we describing in these travels across space and time?

When the Leisa girls proudly wore their *lomito*, refusing to talk to anyone but their *Ltarigirig* boyfriends, the Samburu did not exist as a distinct ethnic group, but rather as a loose collection of clans. By 1888, when the European explorer Count Teleki passed through northern Kenya, this group of clans referred to themselves as *Loiborkineji*, 'People of the White Goats' (Von Hohnel 1894). As Samburu assert today, both clan membership and identity as Loiborkineji were fluid at that time, and intermarriage with and adoption from other groups was frequent (see also Spear 1993; Waller and Sobania 1994). The Dassanetch and Rendille were among their marriage and trading partners, though the colonial administration successfully put an end to the Dassanetch connection (Sobania 1991). Did the occasional Somali caravans passing through northern Kenya and southern Ethiopia influence Samburu epistemology and consciousness? Did the Dassanetch and Rendille whom they frequently married and adopted do so? What about the Laikipiak, whose members they likewise adopted and assimilated, particularly after they were defeated by the Samburu in a series of wars beginning in the 1870s? Even to the extent that we might attempt to disentangle a 'core' identity with recognizable features of consciousness – a problematic notion in itself – we are still left with the admission that those features themselves have transformed over time and continue to do so. Given this political-economic and cultural dynamism, to suggest that colonial domination and encompassment by the West represent a more dramatic, even radical break with what came before does not fully resolve the dilemma.

Particularly when cross-checked against written documents and archaeological sources, Samburu oral traditions are probably the richest and most reliable resources we have for the elusive task of reconciling historically contextualized cultural forms and something we might refer to as continually transforming forms of consciousness.[19] As with our own scholastic tradition however, Samburu oral history is likewise told and interpreted through the Samburu present so that the past itself is continually transformed. Yet, holding their grandmother's beads in their hands, men and women are very credible witnesses to lost or enduring elements of past consciousness as they appear for them in the present. In following just a slender thread of Samburu social memory, I have found adornment and related narratives to be significant, to persist, and to be integrally related to Samburu understandings of themselves on the one hand, and of what I take to be Samburu forms of consciousness on the other.

What I find particularly significant in this regard is that Samburu individual biographies always turn directly to collective historical narratives and that indeed, songs based on individual exploits tend to coalesce into songs of collective experience, through the enduring structure of cutting and collective chorus lines with individual (*rrepeta*) or praise lines. Here, Kondo's (1990) suggestion that the individual is fragmentary and contradictory rather than a unified essence assumes an added dimension. Individual biographies are moulded into collective, *generational* histories like those of the *Leisa* girls, and it is these narratives of brave young men and beautiful girls that offer people discrete reminders of what they have been over time. Moreover, it is the practice of cutting Samburu into recurring age grades with named and distinctive *age-sets* that creates Samburu individuals who move in a dense crossroads of synchronic and diachronic social space/time. Adornment and song styles act to recreate the hierarchical divisions in here-and-now social space even as unique generational adornment styles and song lines cut Samburu in time, creating a framework for social memory.

Conclusion

Before tartan blankets imported from Pakistan became Samburu elders' favourite attire, men and women alike scraped hides with painstaking care, after which the women sewed them into clothing and baby slings. As of 2002 women still prepare skins for skirts and wedding attire; however, it is unusual to see an elder working leather for clothing these days unless his wife has died and he is left to make skirts for his girls. If the materials used to cover the bodies of married men have changed the most dramatically with the availability of imported cloth, contemporary Samburu claim that at least some of the cultural practices associated with those changing materials have endured. Like their leatherwear before, men's tartan blankets can still be used to end violence between people. Thus, married elders can divide the space between disputing parties by placing their walking sticks (*sobua*) and/or blankets on the ground between two fighting sides. Few would dare to step across the blankets that Samburu elders have pulled off their own bodies, and death in some form will visit the person who does.

There is perhaps no better example to illustrate the categorical distinctions integral to Samburu consciousness than the *sobua* walking sticks and blankets carried by elders. These men are at the apex of the Samburu political hierarchy: it is they who divide people and animals in the daily management of the settlement; it is they who settle disputes; and it is also they who can divide people when quarrels turn into violence. Nkai likewise supports these distinctions, with death the potential penalty for defying categorical rules and subverting the moral order, as the Leisa girls and succeeding generations have learned to their peril. Samburu memories, housed in clothing and adornment forms worn by generations of men and women and narrated through story and song, are simultaneously biographical and historical, individual and collective. They embody and narrate individual exploits enjoyed collectively, group experiences transformed into morality lessons.

I am engaged in a delicate task here, tempted to use my pen like a *sobua* to cut/divide colonial from 'traditional', capitalist from 'non-capitalist', cosmopolitan from local forms of consciousness. Perhaps, like any good Samburu, I could then be seen as placing lines across threatening chaos, constructing divisions to create and maintain order – and power. What I see instead is a concatenation of objects pulled from near and far, put to use and thought about in ways that Samburu assert are their own. Similarly, I hear stories and songs in which colonial memories or contemporary global economies and cultural forms shift between being undeniable or subtle, but which always mark cultural remembering for the Samburu. I am not iterating here another example of the global in the local (e.g., Appadurai 1996; Miller 1994, 1995), nor of encompassment. And I am not highlighting the increasingly submerged features of Samburu consciousness. Rather, I have been looking for that part which is still visible, for the 'Samburu-in-the-Samburu', of the past as it endures and is understood in the present, of objects and memories that Samburu are still prepared to talk about. In this respect, I have to agree with Michael Jackson that 'the domain of knowledge is inseparable from the world in which people actually live and act' (1996: 4). Our focus is necessarily ever on the present, on a world that is never finished, on lives made understandable in the continual acts of reflecting and narrating. Or, as one wise elder once told me: That life now . . . He cannot remember the real life of *lmurran*-hood he led. He would just say for the sake of it, 'When we were *lmurran*, no one dared us,' or 'We used to really sing there.' You cannot remember. It is just this present one you are leading that you are in touch with/remember (Lekelele interview 1994).[20] I think Lekelele would agree that as long as there are living people, together with the people and things they hold dear, there will be memories to be re-cast into the stories that organize the unruliness of Samburu existence. In turn, the daily experiences on which this truism is based are the stuff out of which ethnographers organize their own memories into narrative form. And we too, can only say that we really used to sing there, and that our ancestors, people like Durkheim, Mauss, and Mead, generously provided us with the grist to reflect on the sins of previous generations.

Notes

1. The research for this paper was generously supported by grants from Fulbright IIE, Ford Foundation/University of Michigan Center for Afro-American and

African Studies, University of Michigan's Rackham School of Graduate Studies, and Western Michigan's Department of Anthropology. I would like to thank the University of Nairobi Institute of African Studies for affiliation and the Office of the President and Kenya Ministry of Education for permission to conduct field research in 1992–4 and 2001–2. I would like to express my extreme gratitude to Jon Holtzman, Musa Letuaa, Timothy Loishopoko, and all of the Samburu who have befriended and hosted me over the years. Finally, because I initially wrote this essay in the field with only the memory of my library to hand, I would like to apologize to anyone whom I have shamelessly failed to cite in my references.

2. See Strathern 1997 for an exception. Strathern questions what we mean by memory, going on to suggest that memory is embodied.

3. This includes Connerton's 1989 'personal memory' in conjunction with his 'habit memory' and 'cognitive memory,' underscoring the problematics of Eurocentric approaches to memory as individually biographical while at the same time attempting to account for collective and intersubjective forms of memory.

4. Recent research in psychology and neuroscience is also destabilizing the self, suggesting that there is no 'real' self, but rather continuities in the process of cognition that facilitate the formation of a 'narrative' of self, with memory serving to construct the fiction rather than storing a reality. However, fictional or no, a singular self remains (see Nelson 2000). These studies do suggest that fictional selves are fundamentally embedded in cultural understandings of personhood (Eakin 2000).

5. More radical notions of time and self such as philosopher Henri Louis Bergson's (1971) and mathematician L.E.J. Brouwer's (1975) suggest that humans experience a continuous flow of time in the process of being and perceiving. We base our understandings of time and mathematics on that 'private duration' (Tasic 2001). Yet even these 'radical' notions are based on a sweeping notion of individualism and choice and an implicit notion of disembodied mind experiencing time in the process of cognition, but not space in the midst of being in the world.

6. See Sobania 1991; Nelson 1993; Jargstorf 1995; Straight 2002.

7. The interdependence of *lmurran* and their girlfriends is demonstrated by contemporary Samburu assertions that Ltarigirig warriors took their name from their girlfriends' tinkling ornaments (*ntarag'ragi* – an onomatopeic term). *Lomito* were beaded ornaments generously embellished with *ntarag'ragi* – shiny metal disks about 1cm. in diameter – attached to the bottoms of chains (*nkaiwal*) hanging from the *lomito*.

8. No one has *lomito* anymore, but the *soomi* of the *Lkileku* (circumcised 1921) are still around, and so are the *ntuntwai* of the *Lmekuri* (circumcised 1936);

the *nkipiren* of the *Lkimaniki* (circumcised 1948), and the *saen rongen* (among others) of the *Lkishili* (circumcised 1960), which persists with slight variations through the *Lkiroro* (circumcised 1976) and current *Lmooli* (circumcised 1990) generations.

9. See also Spencer 1965, 1985. On song performances among the culturally similar Maasai and Okiek, see Kratz 1993, 1994. On the symbolic significance of beads among Maasai and Okiek, see also Kratz and Klumpp 1993, Kratz and Pido 2000.

10. The noun *rrepeta* derives from the verb *'arrep'*, to praise.

11. *Ngirukoto* derives from the verb *'airuko'*, 'to follow after' (respond) in speech.

12. This is sexually explicit because it alludes to the strength/health/vitality/luck (*lorien*) of a boyfriend during love-making. It is in contrast to the lover 'with green veins who cannot make a well for watering cattle'. The latter is sung to insult other people's boyfriends.

13. This mention of fat is another allusion to a young man's health and vitality – characteristics crucial for good lovemaking.

14. The codes are so bound to particular communities and age-set generations that some younger Samburu suggested that the telephones were breasts, while the *Lkishili* who had been a part of the song's performance argued with conviction that the telephones were thighs.

15. *Ltimayo* is the word for code for older generations like *Mekuri*. Although the practice of encoding is seen in songs from *Lkileku* and even earlier, the term for this encoding changes. The term for 'code' itself is *nkutuk oo lkite* ('twisting of the mouth').

16. This expression uses a code word for bed and means that an *lmurrani* intends to have sex with his girlfriend. Other codes can refer to planned meeting places as well. In some cases it is clear that parents would indeed be deceived if they did not know the code, while in others, it would appear that using the code avoids too sexually-explicit means of expression in front of elder men and women.

17. That boys should not engage in sexual activity is not as obvious as it appears. Any uncircumcised male is categorically a 'boy', even if he is eighteen years old and eagerly awaiting circumcision and initiation into the next age-set. And indeed, in practice, boys are known to transgress the rule of celibacy.

18. See Moore and Sanders (2001: 16) for an example of this tendency.

19. I agree with Donald Donham (2001) and Michael Jackson (1996) here and throughout this essay that the narratives of those with whom we work must be incorporated into our ethnographies. See also Donham (1999); Ferguson (1999).

20. Lekelele is a pseudonym.

References

Antze, Paul and Michael Lambek (eds), (1996), *Tense Past: Cultural Essays in Trauma and Memory,* New York: Routledge.

Appadurai, Arjun (1996), *Modernity At Large: Cultural Dimensions of Globalization,* Minneapolis, MN: University of Minnesota Press.

Bergson, Henri (1971), *Time and Free Will,* New York: Humanities.

Borofsky, Robert (2000), *Remembrance of Pacific Pasts: An Invitation to Remake History,* Honolulu, HI: University of Hawaii Press.

Brouwer, L.E.J. (1975), *Collected Works,* A. Heyting (ed.), Amsterdam: North-Holland Press.

Connerton, Paul (1989), *How Societies Remember*, Cambridge: Cambridge University Press.

Donham, Donald L. (2001), 'Thinking temporally or modernizing anthropology', *American Anthropologist* 103(1): 134–49.

——(1999), *Marxist Modern: An Ethnographic History of the Ethiopian Revolution,* Berkeley: University of California Press.

Eakin, Paul John (2000), 'Autobiography, identity, and the fictions of memory', in Daniel L. Schacter and Elaine Scarry (eds), *Memory, Brain, and Belief*, Cambridge: Harvard University Press.

Fabian, Johannes (1996), *Remembering the Present: Painting and Popular History in Zaire*, Berkeley: University of California Press.

——(1999) 'Remembering the other: knowledge and recognition in the exploration of Central Africa, *Critical Inquiry*, 26:49–69.

——(2002), 'Forgetting Africa', *Journal of Romance Studies,* 1 (3); 9–20.

Ferguson, James (1999), *Expectations of Modernity: Myths and Meanings of Urban Life on the Zambian Copperbelt*, Berkeley: University of California Press.

Fratkin, Elliott (1991), 'The Loibon as sorcerer: A Samburu loibon among the Ariaal Rendille, 1973–87', *Africa* 61(3): 318–33.

Holtzman, Jon (2003), 'Age, masculinity and migration: gender and wage labour among Samburu pastoralists in Northern Kenya', in Gracia Clark, (ed.), *Gender and Economic Life*, SEA Monographs, USA: University Press of America.

——(1996), 'The Transformation of Samburu Domestic Economy', Ph.D dissertation, University of Michigan.

Jackson, Michael (1996), 'Introduction: phenomenology, radical empiricism, and anthropological critique', in Michael Jackson, (ed.), *Things as They Are: New Directions in Phenomenological Anthropology*, Bloomington: Indiana University Press.

James, Wendy (1998), 'Mauss in Africa: on time, history, and politics', in Wendy James and N.J. Allen (eds.), *Marcel Mauss: A Centenary Tribute*, New York: Berghahn Books.

Jargstorf, Sibylle (1995), *Glass Beads from Europe*, Atglen, PA: Schiffer, Ltd.

Kondo, Dorinne (1990), *Crafting Selves: Power, Gender, and Discourses of Identity in a Japanese Workplace,* Chicago: University of Chicago Press.

Kratz, Corinne A. (1993), '"We've always done it like this"... except for a few details: "Tradition" and "Innovation" in Okiek ceremonies', *Comparative Studies in Society and History* 35(1): 30–65.

—— (1994), *Affecting Performance,* Washington, D.C.: Smithsonian Institution Press.

—— and D. Klumpp (1993) 'Aesthetics, expertise, and ethnicity: Okiek and Maasai perspectives on personal ornament', in T. Spear and R. Waller (eds), *Being Maasai: Ethnicity and Identity in East Africa*, London: James Currey.

—— and Donna Pido (2000), 'Gender, ethnicity, and social aesthetics in Maasai and Okiek beadwork', in Dorothy Hodgson (ed.), *Rethinking Pastoralism in Africa*, Oxford: James Currey.

LiPuma, Edward (2000), *Encompassing Others: The Magic of Modernity in Melanesia*, Ann Arbor, MI: University of Michigan Press.

Malkki, Liisa (1995), *Purity and Exile: Violence, Memory and National Cosmology Among Hutu Refugees in Tanzania*, Chicago, IL: Chicago University Press.

Miller, Daniel (1995), 'Introduction: anthropology, modernity and consumption', in Daniel Miller, (ed.), *Worlds Apart: Modernity Through the Prism of the Local.* London: Routledge 1–22.

——(1994), *Modernity: An Ethnographic Approach*, Oxford: Berg.

Moore, Henrietta L. and Todd Sanders (2001), 'Magical interpretations and material realities: an introduction', in Henrietta L. Moore and Todd Sanders (eds), *Magical Interpretation, Material Realities: Modernity, Witchcraft and the Occult in Postcolonial Africa*, London: Routledge.

Nelson, Charles M. (1993), 'Evidence for early trade between the coast and interior of East Africa', Paper for the WAC Mombassa Intercongress Conference Volume, Available at http://cag-www.lcs.mit.edu/~hacrat/TRADE.HTM.

Nelson, Katherine (2000), 'Memory and belief in development', in Daniel L. Schacter and Elaine Scarry (eds), *Memory, Brain, and Belief*, Cambridge, MASS: Harvard University Press.

Sobania, Neal (1991), 'Feasts, famines and friends: nineteenth century exchange and ethnicity in the Eastern Lake Turkana region', in John G. Galaty and Pierre Bonte (eds), *Herders, Warriors, and Traders: Pastoralism in East Africa*, San Francisco: Westview Press.

Spear, Thomas (1993), 'Being "Maasai", but not "People of Cattle": Arusha agricultural Maasai in the nineteenth century', in T. Spear and R. Waller (eds), *Being Maasai: Ethnicity and Identity in East Africa*, London: James Currey.

Spencer, Paul (1965), *Samburu: A Study of Gerontocracy in a Nomadic Tribe.* Berkeley, CA: University of California Press.

—— (1985) (ed.) *Society and the Dance*, Cambridge: Cambridge University Press.

Sperling, Louise (1987), 'Wage employment among Samburu pastoralists of Northcentral Kenya', *Research in Economic Anthropology* 9: 167–90.

Strathern, Andrew (1997), *Body Thoughts,* Ann Arbor, MI: University of Michigan Press.

Straight, Bilinda (1997a), 'Altered Landscapes, Shifting Strategies: The Politics of Location in the Constitution of Gender, Belief, and Identity Among Samburu Pastoralists in Northern Kenya', PhD dissertation, University of Michigan.

—— (1997b) 'Gender, work, and change among Samburu pastoralists of Northern Kenya', *Research in Economic Anthropology* 18: 65–91.

—— (2000), 'Development ideologies and local knowledge among Samburu women in Northern Kenya', in Dorothy Hodgson (ed.), *Rethinking Pastoralism in Africa: Gender, Culture, and the Myth of the Patriarchal Pastoralist*, Oxford: James Currey.

—— (2002) 'From Samburu heirloom to New Age artifact: the cross-cultural consumption of Mporo marriage beads', *American Anthropologist* 104(1): 1–15.

Tasic, Vladimir (2001), *Mathematics and the Roots of Postmodern Thought*, Oxford: Oxford University Press.

Von Hohnel, Ludwig (1894), *Discovery of Lakes Rudolph and Stephanie: A Narrative of Count Samuel Teleki's Exploring and Hunting Expedition in Eastern Equatorial Africa in 1887 and 1888*, 2 vols., London: Longmans, Green, & Co.

Waller, Richard (1988), 'Emutai: crisis and Response in Maasailand, 1883–1902' in Douglas Johnson and David Anderson (eds), *The Ecology of Survival: Case Studies from Northeast African History*, Boulder, CO: Westview, 72–112.

—— and Neal W. Sobania (1994), 'Pastoralism in historical perspective', in Elliot Fratkin, Kathleen A. Galvin, and Eric Abella Roth (eds), *African Pastoralist Systems: An Integrated Approach*, London: Lynne Rienner Publishers, 45–68.

Whyte, Michael and Susan Whyte (2002), 'Children's Children: Rethinking Relationships Between Alternate Generations in Eastern Uganda', Paper presented at the Annual Meeting for Association of Social Anthropologists of the United Kingdom and the Commonwealth, 8–12 April 2002. Arusha, Tanzania.

Wolf, Eric (1982), *Europe and the People Without History*, Berkeley: University of California Press.

–16–

Old System, New Conflicts: Age, Generation and Discord among the Meru, Kenya
Anne-Marie Peatrik

Age and generation systems of Eastern Africa offer an unusual opportunity in anthropology to think over the plurality of time, its combination and discord, the tensions between the dynamics of the society and the becoming of the individual; and the question of the *longue durée* and history, of event and historical consciousness (cf. Spencer 1990). This saturation with meanings reflects an unusual situation. Not only is time defined on common patterns, as in any other society, but the passing of time systematizes the society and its reproduction. In short, this slippery abstract notion, time, has been used by these people since a remote past as a constitutive principle. Well known but partial implementations of this principle are evident in monarchies whose time is punctuated by unequal lengths of the successive reigns, or the democratic regimes where elections are held at regular intervals. In both cases, the anticipation of the renewal of authority concerns the political body of the society; but in these Eastern African societies, the whole population, within each group, is set in motion at predictable intervals. When a new class of Fathers is endowed with authority, the preceding and the following classes reach new positions. Hence the concept of system is used, since when one part is moving, the whole is affected.

Men are distributed into successive generation classes. At any time, one class is invested with power and authority which will be handed over to the succeeding generation in due course (depending upon the system this may be every 8 years, 15–20, 30–40 or even 50 years and more). But men of a generation called 'A' do not beget children at the same time or for the same period of time; in class 'B' their children will be of different ages; and in class 'C' the ages of their grandchildren will be increasingly different. Generation after generation, the overlapping of the successive classes increases, and it becomes impossible to distinguish people according to their generational position. If it is not contained in one way or another, this demographic drift of successive generation classes brings a rapid end to the working of the system because of the increasing number of 'overaged' and 'underaged' people, that is, those who are born too early or too late to pass through the same grades as their peers. Because of this recurring tension, 'age-setting or generation-setting ... is an unwieldy, almost bizarre mode of social organization' (Baxter and Almagor 1978: 2). Since the 1950s, numerous field investigations conducted in different groups have elicited the variety of models and heterogeneity of rules as well as their wide geographical distribution in this part of Africa.[1] Despite the continuity of debate about their nature and workings and the enlargement of the theoretical perspectives, 'definitive answers to the big questions remain elusive' (Waller 1999: 139).

My research among the Meru in Kenya was carried out among the Tigania-Igembe, two Meru groups settled on the Nyambeni Hills located north-east of Mount Kenya. I tackled the classic question 'How do their age and generation systems work?': whether we consider the framework of their socio-political organization or the locus of mere categories. More specific issues directed this choice. I intended to conduct field research among Bantu speakers to address the received idea of whether Bantu-speaking people had borrowed the principles of age and generation classes from Cushitic or Nilotic speakers; in this view their classes were regarded as not genuine, and their societies loosely structured. But a careful reading of the available ethnography, however incomplete, challenged this diffusionist assumption as well as its lack of sociological focus, as for example in H. E. Lambert's synthesis (1956) on the Eastern Bantu speakers of Mount Kenya (the former Kikuyu Land Unit) and B. Bernardi's monograph (1959) on the *mûgwe* of the Meru.[2]

To deal with the multiplicity of time within the scope of a paper, I will explain how, during my fieldwork, I had to disentangle part of this plurality before resuming further enquiries and how this difficulty helped disclose relevant aspects of the question.[3]

Discrepancies in Structural Time and in the Longue Durée

At the beginning of my fieldwork in October 1986, I was completely baffled when people gave me very different explanations and contradictory judgements on the rules of the classes and their importance (either persisting, disappearing or vanished entirely). Generations (*nthukî*) as a political organization no longer operated. Most of the rituals did not seem to be performed any more. Opinions varied greatly, ranging from denigration ('*nthukî* are nothing') to advice ('take care, it is dangerous to study initiation'). I nearly decided that it would wiser to choose another topic.

As a way to resolve the problem, I thought it would be useful to engage in a kind of census of a sub-location to check the kinship patterns, the domestic and territorial arrangements and the possible distribution of the people into the generation classes. Then I discovered that the naming system, based on the principle of eight revolving names, was and still is operating. Everybody knows the name of his or her generation, of their parents' and grand parents', of their brothers' and sisters' and in laws'. At least my research topic was not irrelevant. After six months of inquiries with the help of a research assistant, I began to understand that the different versions of the rules, and the different judgements on them were not mere idiosyncrasy but related to the generation and the sex of the informant – whether he/she is old, middle age or young, or whether he/she belongs to a powerful or a plain family. Biographical researches had an unexpected outcome in that they brought to the fore the importance – up to the 1950s – of the prescribed stages of the life cycle which are age-grades combined with generation classes, called in Kimeru *etaalia* (pl. *mataalia*), or 'steps for measuring' a plot of land or another length; this local concept of age and ageing conveys a mixture of quantitative and qualitative aspects.

The rules of recruitment are simple, at least for the informants if not for the researcher. I use the past tense to summarize them but – and this is precisely the main issue (cf. Davis 1992) – some of them are still working, and part of the past is in the present. A person entered a grade and all successive ones together with his or her class. For instance, if a man belonged to class 2, identified by one of the eight revolving names, his sons could not be incorporated before class 4; sons of class 2 were in class 4 or 5, sometimes in 6, but less frequently so. Sons were recruited every four or five years, at the time of their initiation which is performed in public. After the completion of their initiation, they entered the first grade of 'warriors'. Each class was divided into three sub-classes, known by the ordinal names *ndinguri*, *kobia*, and *kaberia*. After the recruitment of the last sub-class, a new class had to be opened while the former closed. When a new class was opened every fifteen to twenty years, all the classes ascended into a new age-grade. For men, there were four age-grades: warrior, young father, Father of the country, Accomplished person (*mwariki*).

Classes were distributed alternately in two streams (*gîtiba*), named Kiruka and Ntiba in Tigania, or Ntangi and Mbaine in Igembe, all symbolically associated with the sun or with the rain. Each stream held power and authority in turn. As the ruling class, the 'Fathers of the country' governed the society through councils (*kiama*); they also controlled the class of the warriors which often included their own sons, as long as this class was recruiting.

Women too were classified, following other principles based on rules of affinity, not only on descent. It was said that a daughter could not marry a man of her father's class (for example class 1) but could married either in class 2 or 3; after her marriage, she joined the class of the spouses of her husband's class. Women also held power and authority through women's councils (*kiama kia aka*) and a symbolic item called *kaaria* which was handed over in due time between successive classes of spouses. There were three age-grades for women: young mother, Mother of *kaaria*, and Accomplished person (*mwariki*).

Moreover, each class in power had a kind of religious dignitary (*mûgwe*), well known from Bernardi's monograph (1959) and Needham's analysis (1960). The *mûgwe's* function was to bless the acting class of warriors with his left hand, also the generation classes of men and women, and to protect the country from *mûgiro*, a state of ritual impurity brought about by the exercise of power. In the Nyambeni Hills, there were three *mûgwe*, one for the Igembe, two for the Mwiko jwa Ngaa (former name of the Tigania). At the time of the colonial conquest there was one system of classes and a common tempo of recruitment for a population of about 90,000 inhabitants of the region.

My findings were that the Meru Tigania-Igembe society was not loosely structured. Its generation system was a multi-purpose principle of organization. As the framework for an integrated political system, it bore an expression of sovereignty although the polity was acephalous and the authority diffused, or more precisely, collective. Generation classes organized kinship and affinity, the domestic cycle, the life course of men and of women alike. It took time to become a person; social and psychological maturation were lengthy processes. People were considered as grown-ups when they reached the last stage of life called *mwariki*. *Nthukî*, the generation system of the Meru, is a kind of *'fait social total'* following Marcel Mauss' 'vague but suggestive concept' (Gofman 1998). Political and social rules cannot be separated, nor the symbolic and moral values embedded in them; *nthukî* was the frame of reference of an original religion, an unusual *Weltanschauung*.

The significance of this issue emerged during the handing over of power and authority between retiring Fathers and incoming Fathers of the country, called *ntuiko*, or 'breaking of the rule'. This signifies a recurrent state of crisis and transgression due to the fact that the Fathers had clung to power: even if they were no more able to keep the peace (*thîîri*), they were not ready to put an end to their mandate and so had to be pushed away. Disobedience and misbehaviour were triggered by the inconsistency in status brought by the demographic drift of the generations: older uninitiated boys, sons of the future ruling Fathers, were eagerly waiting for their initiation into the proper class, that is, two classes after their own fathers, at the very time when many younger boys have been initiated. Older boys began to struggle with younger, initiated sons, and their fathers started to behave badly, roaming about the country.

This inconsistency illustrates that combination and discord of time are always at stake in any age and generation system. This is true for any form of social group, but in this case, this structural feature differentiates a generation system from descent groups, which, for example, convey different patterns of time and of reproduction in the long run. Several questions arise. How the individual time fit or not fit with the time of the classes? How are the various devices, social, ritual and so forth used to cope with this recurring tension elicited? What happens if they fail? A generation system is not only a formal way to classify people. It is a process depending upon social actors, and the reproduction of the classes lies in their hands. Not unconscious of the nature of their actions, such actors are aware of the social principles. Up until the 1940s, elders of the ruling set used to know the demographic state of the classes by checking at the level of each territorial section, the numbers of boys staying in the huts for non-initiates, and the numbers of warriors in the barracks (*gaaru*); this was the way by which elders, or delegates from the different territorial sections, decided whether it was the right time for the recruitment of a new sub-class or the opening of a new class. In short, it was not an automatic procedure but was decided at sight and implemented through conflicts and negotiations. Elders had a good knowledge of the rationale behind the rules of the system, expressed for example through the naming of the sub-sets in each class: the first one called *ndinguri* meaning 'the ones who waited because it was closed' refers to 'overaged' warriors; and the last one *kaberia* meaning 'the smaller ones who are before [the older]' refers to 'underaged' warriors. Elders tried to keep the proper balance between the classes because as long as war was an issue, they had to recruit enough warriors in an appropriate physical condition to protect the polity. But if this aim ceased to be at stake, the rules could be modified.

This situation can be extrapolated to the regional level of Eastern Africa. Age and generation systems are very widespread principles and are found in different populations, whatever their language (Bantu, Cushitic or Nilotic) and whatever their economic organization. A striking feature is the great variety of rules of recruitment and of their functioning.[4] This response to changing conditions – very often the relationship between demography and territory – illustrates the problem of history and historicity in two ways. It can be regarded as a clue to the antiquity of this principle in this part of Africa and also indicates a kind of historical concern. People were not isolated from other groups; interaction in peace or in war, or exchanges of every kind occurred.[5] Here Lévi-Strauss's (1973, 1993) distinction between *sociétés froides* and *sociétés chaudes*, between *histoire stationnaire* and *histoire cumulative* is rather misleading. It would be better to speak of a generational paradigm, with different scales of time, ranging from wide levels to local and individual viewpoints. The larger one is Braudel's scale of the *longue durée* (1958); the reproduction of generation classes needs *at least* three generations before becoming a system, an institution. The best documented examples of generation classes in the *longue durée* are found in the histories of the Karimojong cluster, of the Maa speakers and of the Oromo. At present ethnographic knowledge of the Bantu systems is rather blurred since the history of the migrations of the Bantu speakers is still a matter of debate and research (Ehret 1998; Peatrik 1994, 2003).

The smaller scale is the local level and the focus is on the individual becoming. For instance, sons who are waiting too long for their initiation may decide to leave their fathers and build a new society on their own; in this case, tension is eased by their departure. This issue, only one among many others, is a new illustration of the combination and the discord of time, of the fitting of individual time within the time of the classes.

Events

Another heuristic muddle emerged during my inquiries. Differences of opinion appeared also to be related to historical events, mainly to the deep crisis and lasting conflict that developed during the 1930s–1950s between the colonial administration and the Meru people, and also among the Meru themselves. Time and historical consciousness embedded in age and generation sets is not a new topic of research. Very early ethnographers noticed that the naming system and the duration of the classes were clues to the time depth and the chronology of the society, a correct observation as long as the data are carefully contextualized.[6] Nevertheless other aspects came to light during my fieldwork. Since the colonial conquest, people have maintained a certain knowledge of the chronology by associating the timing of initiations and the revolving names of classes with major events, international and national, such as the Great War, the Mau Mau struggle, or the death of Jomo Kenyatta. As I was trying to collect a more accurate calendar of events, one of my best informants, a former sub-chief of Ithalie generation (initiated after the Great War), added an unexpected twist to my work by encouraging me to consult *baruga thirikari* (the colonial archives). For good reasons the colonial archives of the Meru District are full of information. I was able to match up oral data with written sources and to understand the key role played by H. E. Lambert both as District Commissioner and as anthropologist in his official and private papers.

After twenty years of colonial administration (the conquest of Meru took place in 1908), the Meru District was in a state of disorder and disobedience. Hut and poll taxes were not really paid, while many people were not ready to look for employment in the White Highlands. The Councils (*Kiama*) of Fathers had lost their influence and were unable to judge an increasing number of cases. Accusations of 'witchcraft' – a colonial catchword for all kinds of actions – was also on the increase. Former warriors, disarmed and without purpose, roamed the country; their interaction with non-initiated girls was beyond control and led to unwanted pregnancies. A basic rule persisted: any child conceived by a non-initiated girl as called a *kitheega* and was regarded with the utmost horror as a kind of freak, a danger to society and its people. Any pregnancy in a non-initiated girl resulted in abortion or to the abandonment of the child in the bush – cases of infanticide increased. The colonial administration resorted first to repression, without result, then Lambert was posted in Meru – a man with a knowledge of anthropology. He carried on the research of his predecessors, analysing the classes in particular, and concluded that the main problem was the late initiation of both men and women.

Being performed up to the age of twenty-five years for women and up to the age of forty for men, late initiation was deeply influential on the working of the generation system, its value and its symbolism. There was a strong belief that on the initiation of a male or female first-born, parents ought to stop reproduction. Initiation was regarded as the first step towards the reproductive role of the next generation, and such activity in adjacent generations endangered the younger generation and created a state of *mûgiro* that jeopardized everybody. A man whose first child has been initiated was allowed to take another younger wife, but generally polygamy was not highly valued and monogamy prevailed, providing the main motive for parents to postpone the initiation of their first born. At the level of the family and of the domestic cycle, how the individual came of age kept pace with the recruitment of the classes, as a way to counteract overageing (which is more disturbing than underageing). Thus the prevalence of monogamy is also part of this story.

The lowering of the age of initiation became a major recommendation of the Government. The colonial administration, and in particular Lambert decided to enforce the measure because of the improvements it would bring: earlier initiation would put an end to infanticide; it would promote marriage at a younger age and the growth of the fecundity rate; it would also increase the number of the warriors ready for employment, since as long as men were not initiated, they were not allowed to leave the Nyambeni Hills. But the enforcement of the measure worsened the crisis among the Meru. Only some of the elders agreed with the reform. The majority of women – namely women of Ithalie and of Michubu – refused it for different and linked causes: the overlapping of the generations brought by the lowering of the age of initiation challenged their domestic and their kinship status as well as the hierarchy of women's classes and the authority of women's councils. Their opposition also revealed the ontological aspect of the issue. Lambert was aware of their opposition but he was unable to give an explanation, hoping only that a female anthropologist would conduct researches on this matter in the future. (This came to pass, but fifty years later!) However, Lambert had powers as acting District Commissioner: to deal with the opposition he enforced another reform based on a distorted analysis of the ethnographic data (either on purpose or through ignorance). He concluded that the genuine *kiama-* council of the Meru was the *njuri ncheke*.

The *njuri ncheke* was a tribal council whose duty was the arrest of murderers and the carrying out of the death sentence, decided in the case of established witchcraft through trial, and in the case of parricide (father and mother, either in the family or in the polity). *Njuri ncheke* elders were a minority of men who underwent a special initiation, performed at the grade of young father, that made them able to endure the mortal pollution of 'bad death'. Very violent and costly, the initiation was performed in secret – elders of *njuri ncheke* were really feared. Furthermore, the *njuri ncheke*, as an institution recruiting secretly, had been less affected by the colonial regime than the Councils (*kiama*) of Fathers of the country. Lambert implemented a kind of indirect rule in the Meru District. Any elder who wanted to be appointed at any level of the local administration had to belong to the *njuri ncheke*. The numbers of initiates increased: part of the men of Ithalie and of Michubu generations entered the secret company. The *njuri ncheke* elders became the new local rulers; for a while the situation improved, from the viewpoint of the colonial administration and the *njuri* elders alike. Backed by the colonial administration, these elders enforced the lowering of the age of initiation through the control of its organization. As the opposition of the women persisted, they prohibited the women's councils, the handing-over between women's classes[7] and finally, the initiation of the women themselves. This entailed the modification of the rules of kinship and the vanishing of the rules of affinity. The position of the women in Meru society was thus completely modified; from a rather equal status with the men – a feature related to the working and the spirit of the political system and to the linked rules of affinity – their status was lowered and women lost influence in the process of decision-making, whether in the family or in the society.[8] Following the lowering of the age of initiation, which really took effect after the Second World War, at the time of the initiation of the Ratanya, the old demographic regime gave way to new demographic trends resulting in an increase of the fertility rate and a baby-boom.[9] This went together with economic development based on coffee production, the diffusion of schooling, a growing 'land consciousness' as well as unprecedented land pressure.

The crisis of the 1930s to 1950s enlarged the question of time to encompass structure, history, new life courses and expectations. The conflicting power and authority between the new tribal council and the former ruling Fathers was attributed to the new (at that time) paradigm of modernity *versus* tradition and backwardness. Rivalries and competition occurred between old and new ways of initiation, between the usual age-grades with their prescribed statuses *versus* the achieved (and costly) standing of the *njuri ncheke*. The crisis triggered the rise of Mau Mau in the Nyambeni Hills (see Kamunchulu 1975) and ended only partly after independence. The cause was thought to lie in growing and enduring socio-economic inequalities, but this explanation is insufficient. Rivalries illustrate also the ontological aspect of the question. Either in the old way or in the new, a man has to be initiated to become a person. Once again, this statement could be generalized to the other age and generation systems in Eastern Africa; what happened in the Tigania-Igembe in modern circumstances probably occurred for many other reasons many times in the past. Neo-initiations, either achieved or ascribed, weave a kind of syncretism which is an efficient way to cope with the uncertainty and new meanings brought by changing events.

Contemporary Trends

Nowadays[10] in Tigania-Igembe, few people are newly initiated into the *njuri ncheke*; it has lost influence except in conflicts over land demarcation, but this does not mean that it will disappear indefinitely. The revival and re-invention of such institutions that recruit on secret oath-taking can never be discounted. The generation system is both defunct and working, a contradictory statement that explains my initial difficulties in understanding its role. As a system the generation classes no longer function but their ethos and certain linked rules, implicit or expressed, persist. The collective initiation of boys, albeit in a very simplified version, is always performed in public under the supervision of the *lamalle* – older initiates who have chosen for a while to deal with this matter and act as 'warriors'. They organize the whole process of the sessions which generally take place during the national holidays of Christmas.[11] At the end of December, it is not uncommon to run into processions of hundreds of newly initiated boys led by the *mugaa wa ntaane*, a jester dressed up as a cow. They celebrate the end of the seclusion period before resuming school a few days later.

Boys are recruited into the proper generation. This gives the initiate a unique sense of identity in relation to younger boys, his peers and his parents. Henceforth, as a *muthaka* (an initiate boy), he is allowed to look for sexual intercourse with girls of the proper category. But boys are initiated at a younger and younger age because of the humiliations they endure and the rivalries which break out between initiates and non-initiates, formerly only in secondary schools, but nowadays in primary schools too. Parents try to resist the early initiation of their sons. In the past, this *rite de passage* was a protracted ordeal performed on grown-ups; it took nearly two years to complete the cycle of the circumcision proper. When performed at a younger age, in a condensed way, this ritual can become a painful event bringing psychological and physical disorders as well as behavioural problems. Initiation also means more autonomy in relation to parents. Some boys avoid their parents' opposition by running away to be initiated in other places.

Generation classes have become generation categories, but the prohibition on sexual intercourse and marriage of a girl with a man of her father's category is always enforced. The same holds true for a boy with a woman of his mother's category, for this is regarded as a kind of incest different from the family incest. Anyone guilty of such a transgression is called *kioncho* ('runt', 'premature', 'untimely'), a very derogatory term conveying that the culprit has been expelled from his/her generation as if he/she has not been properly conceived.[12] During preliminaries to any sexual relation, a boy and girl let each other know which generation their parents belong to, in order to avoid being *kioncho*; the corollary is that initiated boys may have the feeling that any girl of an authorized category belongs to them.

The rule of opening and closing the successive generations is always carried out; through the theoretical device of the eight revolving names of the generations and of the three sub-sets in each generation, everybody knows which generation will come next. At the inception of my field-work, the sons of Ratanya were still being recruited into Miriti; at the end of 1993, the following generation, the sons of Lubeeta sons called Gwantai had started to be recruited. I was not aware at that time of this incoming transgressive state of 'breaking the rule' (*ntuiko*) which partly explains, no doubt, the reluctance of my interlocutors to speak about generations. The handing-over and its associated state of *ntuiko* has become more a way of speaking than acting. During the national election in 1988, with the introduction of the 'queueing system' in the KANU (Kenyan African National Union), and in 1992 when multi-partyism was introduced for the first time in Kenya, candidates used the *nthukî* idiom in a joking and boasting way, claiming that the time of Ratanya as Ruling Fathers was over and that it was the time of Lubeeta in the running of the country. It is a fact that in 1992 all the newly elected members of the Parliament from Tigania-Igembe belonged to the Lubeeta generation. And in a different connection, it is not mere chance than the tragedy of St Kizito occurred in July 1991.[13]

In St Kizito mixed secondary boarding school (Tigania division), on the night of Saturday 13 July 1991, many schoolboys ran amok and attacked a dormitory where 270 girls had locked themselves in to escape the marauding boys. The invading boys assaulted and raped seventy-one girls; in the melée they caused the deaths of nineteen girls, and more than a hundred were injured. The school boys, who numbered 306 in all, had decided to stage a strike against the school headmaster, but the girls had refused to join in. The raid was planned by a core group of the boys in retaliation. They had allegedly taken *bhang* (cannabis) and *chang'aa* (sugar cane alcohol) earlier in the day.

A combination of pressures caused the strike and the tragedy: long simmering tensions over the organization of schooling, poor conditions of leave, and gender violence in a patriarchal society (see Steeves 1997). But the retaliation against the girls signifies more precise causes which surfaced in the testimony of the three school watchmen (reported in *Daily Nation* 11 December 1991). They claimed that the boys had stoned and insulted them, singing traditional songs and saying – in the words of the watchmen – 'We were too old for the girls'. The boys demanded to know why these men were preventing them from meeting their 'wives'. It was also widespread knowledge that some male teachers had had love affairs with the girls. In 1989, one girl had become pregnant and had been obliged to leave the school. After her baby was born, she completed her education in another school and then returned to St Kizito early in 1991 to run a kiosk inside the school compound, a 'privilege' given as compensation. The boys resented this and had demanded her removal; the kiosk was one of the issues which the students wanted to discuss with the headmaster, but every time it was raised he brushed it aside.

Everything happened as if this school acted as a stage for a traditional generation class performance which turned into a modern generational nightmare. After all, there is an acknowledged continuity between any age or generation system and a school organization. Given the persistence of some rules of the old generation system, the attitude of the initiated boys (today they are all initiated at the level of secondary school) becomes more transparent. Teachers, 'too old for the girls', were behaving as *kioncho* – that is in an 'untimely', 'abominable', and virtually as 'incestuous monsters' towards girls whom the boys regarded as 'theirs'. The girls' refusal to join the strike increased the tension as they denied the boys precisely the right to appropriate their persons. Sexual competition and reversal of statuses were all the more resented since the precedence of age and the generational affiliation seemed blurred by the on-going state of limbo, between the closing of a generation and the opening of a new one. This period of uncertainty fuelled the boys' emotional expectations. They reacted to the breaking of the rules by the teachers by breaking other rules on their own initiative. Local circumstances rekindled the defunct scenario of the *ntuiko*.[14]

Apart from the revolving names and the linked rules of sexual prohibition, the persistence of the generational rhythm is also rooted in the conception of life and death that is typical of the generational paradigm. One becomes an 'Accomplished person' (*mwariki*) while alive and not in any after-world. Everything must be done at the proper time. There is a proper time for initiation, for marriage and parenthood, a proper time for grand-parenthood and ritual duties – and a proper time for ending a life. In Meru conception, there is no belief in life after death; there are no ancestors, no ancestor worship, no genealogical mentality, a state of things that fits well with the absence of descent groups. This is the reason why the corpses of people who have died before the completion of the life cycle are so feared. And the different death rituals were, and still are, performed according to the age of the dead person (Peatrik 1991). Perpetuation is achieved through grandchildren, by the gift of a grandparent's name to a grandchild of the same sex, and through the orderly flow of the generations. This itself originates in the paramount principle of Ngaï (Nilotic) or Murungu (Bantu), a very abstract deity that resembles the Biblical God, although this analogy has led to misleading interpretations. Ngaï is a kind of energy (in Kimeru *inya*) that brings life through the rituals performed at the appropriate time, and through the blessings of the appropriate persons: the blessing of the grand parents, of the *mûgwe*, of any senior to their junior, of any individual more advanced in initiation towards one coming after.

This enduring attitude towards death and life throws light on two matters. With the exception of people of the old classes (Ithalie and Michubu) who are vanishing, Meru people today are not aware of the events of the 1930s–1950s, a history that in part explains the *anomie* of contemporary Meru society. Actors and victims in this history do not elaborate, unless they are asked to by a researcher. Despite the drastic changes in the initiation process, boys are still prepared to think that they are following the way of their fathers. Their fathers and mothers know it is not true but they make no comment and there is no transmission of this history.[15] The way in which the tradition is believed to continue addresses the question of contemporary historical consciousness. With a blank past, it is difficult to imagine a future. Contrary to the Kikuyu, for example (Lonsdale 2002), there are no 'organic intellectuals' within Meru society, except the few who are concentrating on the meaning of the myth of Mbwaa and the question of the Meru origins (M'Imanyara 1992). This quest for origins and the related construction of an ethnicity are ways to enter the political arena and to take part in the sharing of the 'national cake', but Mbwaa is also a story about initiation and bears the repeated signification that life is *now* and in the incoming cycle of generations. The necessity of initiation is so much embedded in the mind of the people that it is at the root of conversion to Christianity and the independent churches. This is taking place at an increasing rate nowadays,[16] and could be the arena of a new syncretism where the generational paradigm might flourish.

Given the state of their society and the questions I had in mind, my ethnographic encounter with the Meru Tigania-Igembe could have come to a sudden end if I had confined myself to a classic approach. The untangling of the plurality of time became essential for further research; as a feed-back effect, the combination and the discord of time led me to address the unusual epistemological questions raised by the age and generation systems in Eastern Africa. The understanding of these complex societies has to go beyond the limits inherited from different schools of thought. As Asmarom Legesse (1973) foresaw, what is needed is a multi-faceted approach, taking into account structural, demographic, religious, local and global, synchronic and diachronic aspects. Together with the pursuit of the question of time, these systems can still open up new kinds of analysis in anthropology.

Notes

1. The literature is far too large to cite comprehensively; see syntheses by Stewart (1977) and by Bernardi (1985) and collective editions by Baxter and Almagor (1978) and Kurimoto and Simonse (1998).

2. This essay would be incomplete if I failed to note that my interest in Eastern Africa arose in the 1980s from working with Serge Tornay, then lecturer at the University of Nanterre-Paris X, who carried out research among the generation system of the Nyangatom, Karimojong speakers located in the south-west of Ethiopia (Tornay 2001).

3. All the data used in the following presentation are taken from my monograph (Peatrik 1999).

4. Variations revolve nevertheless around two main generational models (Peatrik 1995).

5. This question was first approached in Kurimoto and Simonse (1998).

6. Lack of sociological interest has often led to misinterpretation by over-interpretation; the analysis given by a historian of the myth of Mbwaa, the story of the migration of the proto-Meru, is a good illustration (Peatrik 1999: 381–425).

7. Women's classes handed over *kaaria* (the right to smear oneself with a type of white clay reputed dangerous, together with the right to display female weapons); both symbolized their authority. At rituals performed on consecrated spots, women of the incoming set had to bring baskets with as much grain as possible and to give them to the women of the retiring set in exchange for the *kaaria*. This was achieved through dances where younger women defied and insulted the older women. It took hours and many conflicts before the completion of the handing-over, which ended in a kind of raid on unititated mature girls by the set of women in power. *Njuri* elders prohibited the *kaaria* on the plea of witchcraft.

8. The question of abortion and infanticide in Meru District has been recently studied by the historian L. M.Thomas (1998). Her analysis of the colonial politics looks sound but the use of the ethnographic data is less convincing; she probably underestimated the differences between the so-called Meru tribes and the difficulties raised by the analysis of the generation systems, which is understandable.

9. This point has interested historians and demographers since it reveals unsuspected dynamics of fertility in Africa (Cordell 2000).

10. Nowadays refers specifically to the period 1986–1993 during which I conducted three different periods of field-work.

11. Individual circumcision in clinics does exist. Nicknamed '*kiswahili*' and regarded as non-*kimeru*, it is regarded with disapproval.

12. During my fieldwork, I met only one elder regarded as a *kioncho*; he was defying public opinion by living with a mistress, past child-bearing age, of the same generation as his mother. But this man used to behave provocatively in other circumstances.

13. At that time, I was in France. I went back to Kenya in December 1991 but was not allowed to get even a provisional research permit from the Office of the President. I carried out a last field stay during the first semester of 1993.

14. This point was touched on at the trial: 'At the close of the much-publicized St Kizito trial last month, the District probation officer, Machira Appolos, spoke of localized factors that may have given rise to the tragedy; "the same immorality, traditions and the Tigania sub-culture remain; the loose tempers, circumcision rites and brewing of traditional liquor around the new St Cyprian school remain" ... in light of the inherent sub-culture, it was a mistake to have boys and girls learning under the same roof' (*The Sunday Nation* 21 June 1992).

15. The lack of transmission of historical events is not a 'traditional' feature. In the past, the knowledge of events was useful, such as knowledge of the years of famine whose nicknames are still remembered by old people, or knowledge of the causes and issues of war and raids, knowledge of the various cases judged by the *Kiama* that served as a basis for new cases. Nowadays the customary channels of oral history no longer operate. Except for land disputes, *Kiama* no longer act as a judicial body. Within the family, apart from parents and their children who are 'avoiding' each other, grandparents and grandchildren are free to speak together but the old people think that their knowledge is useless for the young. Moreover the events of the 1930s–1950s is a tragic, complex story that is still difficult to explain. To keep silent is easier and better than to remember.

16. Since the 1950s, conversion to Christianity has been a women's concern; they have found a kind of compensation for their loss of position in society. However, more and more men are joining churches at present.

References

Baxter, P.T.W. and U. Almagor (eds) (1978), *Age, Time and Generation. Some Features of East African Organizations*, London: Hurst & Co.
Bernardi, B. (1959), *The Mûgwe, a Failing Prophet. A Study of a Religious and Public Dignitary of the Meru of Kenya*, London: Oxford University Press.
——(1985), *Age Class Systems. Social Institutions and Polities based on Age*, Cambridge: Cambridge University Press.
Braudel, F. (1958), 'La Longue durée', *Annales E. S. C.*, 4: 725–53.
Cordell, D.D. (2000), 'African historical demography in the years since Edinburgh', *History in Africa*, 27: 61–89.
Davis, J. (1992), 'Tense in ethnography: some practical considerations', in J. Okely and H. Callaway (eds), *Anthropology and Autobiography*, London and New York: Routledge.

Ehret, C. (1998), *An African Classical Age. Eastern and Southern Africa in World History, 1000 B.C. to A.D. 400*, Charlottesville and Oxford: University Press of Virginia–James Currey.

Gofman, A. (1998), 'A vague but suggestive concept: the "total social fact"', in W. James and N. J. Allen (eds), *Marcel Mauss, A Centenary Tribute*, New York: Berghahn Books.

Kamunchulu, J.T. (1975), 'The Meru participation in Mau Mau', *Kenya Historical Review*, 193–216.

Kurimoto, E. and Simons, S. (eds) (1998), *Conflict, Age and Power in North East Africa. Age Systems in Transition*, Oxford: James Currey.

Lambert, H.E. (1956), *Kikuyu Social and Political Institutions*, London: Oxford University Press.

Legesse, A. (1973), *Gada: Three Approaches to the Study of African Society*, New York: The Free Press.

Lévi-Strauss, C. (1973), 'Race et histoire', in *Anthropologie structurale deux*, Paris: Plon, 377–422.

——(1993), 'Un autre regard', in *L'Homme*, special issue of *La Remontée de l'Amazone*, 7–10, 126–128.

Lonsdale, J. (2002), 'Contests of time: Kikuyu historiography, old and new', in Axel Harneit-Sievers (ed.), *A Place in the World: New local historiographies from Africa and South Asia*, Leiden: Brill.

M'Imanyara, Alfred (1992), *The Restatement of Bantu Origin and Meru history*, Nairobi: Longman Kenya.

Needham, R. (1960), 'The left hand of the Mugwe: an analytical note on the structure of Meru symbolism', *Africa*, 30 (1): 20–33.

Peatrik, A-M. (1991), 'Le Chant des hyènes tristes. Essai sur les rites funéraires des Meru et des peuples apparentés', *Systèmes de pensée en Afrique noire*, 11: 103–30.

——(1994), 'Un Système composite: l'organisation d'âge et de génération des Kikuyu pré-coloniaux', *Journal des Africanistes*, 64 (1): 3–36.

——(1995), 'La Règle et le nombre: les systèmes d'âge et de génération d'Afrique orientale', *L'Homme* 134 (2): 13–49.

——(1999), *La Vie à pas contés. Génération, âge et société dans les hautes terres du Kénya (Meru Tigania-Igembe, Kénya)*, Nanterre: Société d'ethnologie.

——(2003), 'Arrangements générationnels. Le cas inattendu des Gusii (Kenya), *L'Homme* 167–8 (3–4): 209–34.

Spencer, P. (ed.), (1990), *Anthropology and the Riddle of the Sphinx. Paradoxes of Change in the Life Course*, London: Routledge, ASA Monographs 28.

Steeves, H.L. (1997), *Gender Violence and the Press: The St. Kizito Story*, Athens: Ohio University Centre for International Studies.

Stewart, F.H. (1977), *Fundamentals of Age-Group Systems*, New York: Academic Press.

Thomas, L.M. (1998), 'Imperial concerns with women's affairs: state efforts to regulate clitoridectomy and eradicate abortion in Meru District, Kenya, c. 1910–1950', *The Journal of African History*, 39 (1): 121–45.

Tornay, S. (2001), *Les Fusils jaunes. Générations et politique en pays Nyangatom (Ethiopie)*, Nanterre: Société d'ethnologie.

Waller, R. (1999), 'Age and ethnography', *Azania*, 39: 135–44.

–17–

The Kanungu Fire: Millenarianism and the Millennium in South-western Uganda

Richard Vokes

On 17 March 2000, a fire in the church headquarters of The Movement for the Restoration of the Ten Commandments of God (MRTC) killed several hundred members of this sect, in the small town of Kanungu, South-western Uganda. Six days afterwards, the Ugandan police discovered a pit grave containing 153 bodies at another of the sect's compounds, in the nearby village of Buhunga. Two days later, a further 155 fresh corpses were pulled out of a cellar at the home of one of the sect's leaders, Fr. Dominic Kataribaabo. Subsequent discoveries unearthed a further 136 bodies, and during my research on the incident I discovered a number of additional graves, suggesting that the final death toll may exceed these figures. These latest discoveries of these additional graves threw doubt on the original conclusion, propagated by the world's media, that the fire itself had been an instance of mass suicide, and pointed instead to the conclusion that the sect had been involved in some bizarre form of mass murder. It is not my intention here to address the question of whether the Kanungu fire is best understood as suicide or murder. Instead, this chapter is concerned with the sect's 'millenarianism', evidence of which had led to the initial interpretation of the Kanungu fire as a suicide.[1]

Originating in Persian Zoroastrianism, millenarianism *per se* is today most widely associated with Roman Catholic doctrine.[2] As revealed to St John the Divine, the concept describes a coming Kingdom of God on earth to be ruled over by Jesus himself for a period of a thousand years. It marks an end point of historical time, and the beginning of a new, 'final' age, which will culminate in a final judgement and a final redemption for the chosen. Although today somewhat marginal to mainstream Christian theology, expectations of this coming end of the world continue to be harboured by numerous Christian (and other) groups throughout the world.[3] Since at least the early 1960s, the anthropological study of these organizations has sought to understand the specific social and economic contexts in which they emerge.[4] In this regard, the study of millenarian movements has also become a study of social change, or more accurately, people's attempts to negotiate that change. The will to an ultimate, collective salvation has been found to be usually a response to the onset of a new social order (colonial, global, economic etc.) and the demands created by that order. In such contexts 'prophets surface with messages that reveal an impending millennium ... and they prescribe what people must do in order to sweep away the present, debased political and economic orders' (Lindstrom, 1996: 372). For a number of Marxist historians, millenarianism is, in this way, a form of nascent class struggle.[5] However, it is in this context that the millenarianism of the MRTC in Kanungu appears somewhat anomalous. As I will argue below, the group did not emerge as a millenarian movement in response to any particular social change. Rather, the sect existed as a coherent organization before its adoption of a millenarian outlook. The MRTC's millenarianism was not, in other words, reflective of structural tensions and disruptions, but instead derived simply from the worldwide hype about the coming year 2000, which the group took as gospel.

Messages from Heaven

In 1991 the MRTC published a book outlining their key beliefs and practices, reprinted in 1994 and 1996. In both English and Runyankore/Rukiga editions of 1996, the versions to which I have had access, the book is rather ominously entitled *A Timely Message from Heaven: The End of the Present Times*. From the time of its first reprinting, in 1994, until the Kanungu fire, this text was central to the ritual life of the MRTC. The informal prayer meetings used to recruit new members to the group centred around readings from the book. The sect's week-long induction for new members involved, in practice, little more than study of the text. And daily prayer at the compounds also drew heavily on the book.[6] It should also be noted that throughout this period, this text also constituted the only 'public face' of the sect. In almost all other ways highly secretive, the MRTC went to great lengths to circulate their book as widely as possible.[7] Most importantly, the book provides insight into the sect's thinking about, and use of, millenarian ideas.

Due to a number of its textual features, the MRTC's book in fact enables us to trace, with a good degree of accuracy, the evolution of the group's millenarian thinking. Primary among these features is the fact that the book is set out in chronological order.[8] Ten of the book's sixteen chapters concern the visions (*kworekwa*) of the Virgin Mary and Jesus that had been received by senior members of the sect. Each details the vision received by one of the group's leaders. Usefully, a majority of these ten sections record the exact date on which the particular vision was received. Reading by these dates, one can ascertain that the visions are recorded in the book in sequence. The first chapter details a vision of March 1981, the second a visitation of 14 June 1989, the third one of 25 June 1989, and so on.[9] This set of dates also matches what we know about the timing of various leaders' entry into the sect.

Origins of the Sect

The MRTC came into existence in April 1984, when the Virgin Mother appeared to Joseph Kibweteere, commanding him to work towards the restoration of the biblical ten commandments which the world had forgotten. However, the Movement only gathered momentum after June 1989, following Kibweteere's recruitment of Ceredonia Mwerinde to his group. Mwerinde was already one of the most renowned Marian visionaries in South-western Uganda, the Virgin having appeared to her regularly since at least 1981. Mwerinde's sister Ursula Komuhangi, another Marian visionary, also joined at the same time. In 1991, the ranks of the MRTC leadership swelled still further with the entry into the group of three visionary Roman Catholic priests, Frs. Dominic Kataribaabo, Paul Ikazire, and Joseph Kasapuraari.[10] The first two men were at that time the parish priests of Rugazi RC parish, and had invited Kibweteere's group to come and preach in their church. Of significance for my argument here, the MRTC book recounts the visions of these individuals in order of their entry into the sect. Thus the first three chapters of the book concern the visions of Kibweteere, Mwerinde and Komuhangi, with the visions of Kataribaabo, Ikazire, and Kasapuraari following in later chapters. In the case of Kataribaabo and Kasapuraari, the specific dates of the visions coincide with the timing of their entry into the sect.

The fact that the visions are recounted in chronological order enables us to use them to trace the development of the sect's millenarianist thinking. The first point to be made here is that the end of the world is not a primary, or even a predominant issue in *any* of the visions. All implore the faithful to return to a life based on the biblical ten commandments, and each details one way in which people's behaviour may be in contravention of this legal code. For example, the vision of Ursula Komuhangi (chapter three) outlines the ways in which pre-marital sex tends to contravene the seventh commandment, 'thou shalt not commit adultery'. The vision of one Byarugaba (chapter six) details the way in which drunken behaviour leads to the contravention of the seventh and eighth commandments. And the vision of John Kamagara (chapter seven) explains the many ways in which people break the fourth commandment, 'thou shalt respect the Sabbath'. Several of the visions, including those of Kibweteere, Mwerinde, and Fr Kasapuraari (chapters two, one and ten respectively), describe in great depth the ways in which 'modern' behaviours contravene *all* ten commandments. Within this context, the end of the world is only ever mentioned in passing, although all of the chapters do make *some* reference to a final judgement.

Despite this fact, the visions offer some insight into the development of the sect's millenarianism. In particular, it suggests a shift from judgement day as inchoate future possibility, to impending event. In the earliest visions, such as that of Joseph Kibweteere, the rhetoric of a final judgement is used in much the same way as it would be in any mainstream Catholic pedagogy. The 'final day' is a vague, even hypothetical, future event for which all people should nevertheless prepare. People should repent their sins and return to the true path (the ten commandments) 'before it is too late'. For example: 'the ten commandments are given by God to all men, and as such should be respected by all, because at the final hour of judgement, our Lord God will cast out all those who have broken them' (MRTC 1996: 19). It is nowhere stated exactly when this final hour will come. And similarly, in the vision of Ursula Komuhangi: 'I ask you to repent... I no longer do the aforementioned things because God has saved me, has saved me until the final day [of judgement]... You too can also join me on the righteous path, and we can run away from hell, and run instead towards heaven' (ibid.: 37–8). Again, no concept of timing is conveyed. In the vision of Henry Sempa (chapter five): 'It is here forewarned that all those failing to mend their ways will face God's wrath on the judgement day' (ibid.: 54–5). In all of these cases, reference to the end of the world seems to serve a purely rhetorical function. Nowhere is this clearer than in the vision of Byarugaba, which goes as far as to make fun of the idea (ibid.: 58). On the final day of judgement, this vision tells us, drunkards will have no chance of hiding their sinful behaviour. This is because the smell of stale alcohol and tobacco on their clothes will surely give them away!

In only one of the early visions is there a marked difference from this general pattern: Ceredonia Mwerinde's opens with a most extraordinary divine drama. As described to her by one of its characters, the Virgin Mary, the drama opens with an angry God. He has 'been scrutinizing the state of the world, and has found that people are no longer observing the ten commandments he gave them ... he has therefore decided, with great sorrow, that the people of today are not worthy to be called his children. As a result, he has decided to do the right thing, and destroy them all, one by one' (MRTC 1996: 1–2). Upon hearing these angry words, Mary knelt before God, begging him not to destroy humanity. She suggests that people might be persuaded to reform, if only she be allowed to go down among them. God is unmoved. Mary weeps uncontrollably, begging to be given this one chance. 'Out of maybe one thousand people, I might at least be able to save one or two' she pleads. Upon seeing the tears of his mother, Jesus is moved to also intervene on her behalf. He joins his mother in petitioning God to let her be sent down, and suggests that he could also assist her task by appearing to people in visions. God finally relents: 'I do have mercy, so you go down and tell them [of my anger], save them... The saved ones will be forgiven, and I will even delay the entire punishment as long as they all repent and turn back to me, by accepting my commandments' (ibid.: 2). In this case, the biblical end of the world is not an hypothetical future, but a postponed event. Still, it is an event which can remain postponed indefinitely, as long as people repent their sins, and turn back to the true path.

By the time of Kataribaabo, Ikazire, and Kasapuraari's visions, a shift had occurred. The biblical end of the world is no longer referred to as a hypothetical or postponed future, but instead as an imminent event, as clearly stated in the vision of Kataribaabo: 'You people, read your bibles where it states that "Jesus is to return, to judge the cases of both the living and the dead". Look around you at what is happening in the world, and you will see that what is written in this holy book is already being fulfilled. This proves that now is the time to be saved' (ibid.: 73). In the vision of Ikazire, a number of references are made to the world having already entered the 'period of punishments' which precedes the final judgement (ibid.: 68–9). And the vision of Kasapuraari opens with the ominous warning that 'the time is drawing near. God is very angry ... and the world will not now survive, unless it repents' (ibid.: 76). It later explains that 'all who have sinned against God cannot now stop the anger of his divine punishment... You people of the world, pray for yourselves. Do not fear the judgement of God, for his judgement in right... But remember that God is angry. My God and your God is angry. My children, repent as you reach the end' (ibid.: 85).

A certain progression over time in the MRTC's millenarianism is clear, and additional evidence from the book suggests that the group's apocalyptic thinking developed still further in the period following the last of the leaders' visions (8 June 1991). It is significant that chapter four appears to be a later addition to the book. Placed alongside all of the other chapters of the book, it appears anomalous in several ways, and is much longer than any of the other chapters. While each of the other chapters concerns a vision received by one of the sect's leaders, with the exception of final chapters of the book, chapter four recounts a single vision experienced by all of the MRTC leadership that is different from any of the individual visions. Declarations to this effect, one for each of the sect's leaders, are included towards the beginning of the chapter. Each of these declarations includes the given leader's full name, the date and place of his/her birth, and a formal statement of witness to the vision that is about to be recounted. The declarations resemble the witness statements of a legal document. But a crucial point is that if all of the leaders experienced this vision, yet none of them had mentioned it in their personal chapters, then it must have been received only after all of the other, individual visions had been written down. Given that the last of the individual visions (Kasapuraari) is dated 8 June 1991, the group vision must have been first experienced only after that date.

Further evidence to support this is the absence of Joseph Kibweteere's wife, Teresa, from the list of leaders bearing witness to the vision at the beginning of the chapter, although another chapter of the book is devoted to the revelations received by Mrs Kibweteere. This allows further inferences to be made about the timing of the group vision. Following Ceredonia Mwerinde's entry into the sect in the middle of 1989, the MRTC had been based at the Kibweteeres' family home in the village of Ruguma, Ntungamo District. Throughout the period of their stay, Teresa Kibweteere had, alongside her husband, been a leading figure in the organization. However, following a dispute with a number of the group's other leaders, sometime in mid-1992, Teresa and her son Giles Musiime decided to throw the entire sect (including husband and father, Joseph) out of the house. As the sect moved off to other of its premises, Teresa and Giles withdrew entirely from the group. The omission of Mrs Kibweteere's name in chapter four would further suggest that the vision was only received after she had left the group. This in turn suggests that the fourth chapter was probably added to the MRTC's book after its first edition in 1991.

By the time of the group vision, the impending apocalypse seems to have become an all-encompassing obsession for the MRTC leadership. While the visions of Kataribaabo, Ikazire and Kasapuraari had talked of the end of the world as an imminent event, their content was primarily concerned with other issues and so they differ little from other chapters in the book. By comparison, chapter four is much darker in tone, and is concerned exclusively with impending doom. It begins: '[this message] is to inform you of the misguided nature of the world, of the punishments that are going to be handed out to the wrongdoers, of the end of the current times, and of the three days of darkness. It outlines that which is to happen, and that which is already happening' (MRTC 1996: 39). The reader is left in little doubt as to the exact nature of these imminent events. 'There is going to be a lot of pain, more than people have ever previously experienced.' There will be a famine. 'People will be forced to eat their children. Those without children will steal their neighbours' children, and if they are strong enough, will eat their neighbours as well' (ibid.: 42). An animal 'as big as a mountain ... [will] swallow people whole' (ibid.: 43), and the earth will be covered with snakes, 'ten times the size of a lorry tyre' which will devour humans. There will be 'a heavy fog, snow storms, landslides, tidal waves on both lakes and seas, and huge earthquakes will shake the world' (ibid: 44).

Finally, Satan himself will come into the world. 'He will come up and rape people. His male followers will rape women, and his female followers will rape men... Satan will hunt all those who follow the ten commandments, and will kill all others' (ibid.: 45). The world will be plunged into an age of darkness, during which people will be transformed into animals. 'Women will produce deformed children whose eyes are on the backs of their heads, whose noses are on their chests, and whose buttocks are on their heads' (ibid.: 47). This age of darkness is a prelude to the final battle of good and evil. At that time, Jesus himself will come down into the world to do battle with Satan. Only a quarter of the people currently in the world will survive, as all those who have failed to repent are wiped out. For the survivors, however, a final, golden age of heaven on earth will prevail. 'A new world is promised to all those who are saved. Death, and the grave, will here be defeated. Satan will be completely imprisoned, together with all those who believed in him. He will never again be able to tempt the saved. The world and heaven will be one' (ibid.: 52). From the point of view of the MRTC leadership, at least, the end of the world was nigh.

This reading of the MRTC's central text allows certain conclusions to be drawn about the evolution of the sect's millenarianism. From the time the group was formed, in 1984, until Kataribaabo, Ikazire and Kasapuraari joined the sect in 1991, the MRTC seems to have held no particular commitment to the idea of a millennial 'end of the world'. Its various leaders did talk about a future 'judgement day', but this served a largely rhetorical function in their teaching. By simply talking about repentance 'before it is too late', these early writings are hardly distinguishable from any mainstream Catholic pedagogy. By 1991, the MRTC's thinking had changed and the group began to represent the biblical apocalypse as a real and imminent future. Between Mrs Kibweteere's departure from the sect in 1992 and the publication of the 1996 edition of the book, things changed again. The MRTC leadership seems to have become obsessed by the idea of the apocalypse. All other ideas were pushed aside as the group began to focus exclusively on the concept of the biblical end of the world, an event they perceived to have already started. It is only during this period, then, that the MRTC emerges as a truly millenarian movement.

The Marian Worldview

The MRTC did not come into existence as a millenarian movement. But how and why did it later come to take on such a profile? It is necessary to say something of the MRTC's method of recruitment during the early years of its existence. Significantly, Joseph Kibweteere first started the group following a vision from the Virgin Mary, and many of the sect's early leaders were also Marian visionaries. Such events have long played a central role in Catholic worship throughout South-western Uganda, especially for Catholic women. As I have argued elsewhere, this is largely explicable in terms of the fact that Holy Mary exists, for many local people, as a transformation of the historic Nyabingi spirit.[11]

Nyabingi is a feminine fertility spirit whose worship was introduced to the area some time in the eighteenth century. In times of trouble, women would receive visions from the spirit, to be later communicated to the public, advising them of the best response to the misfortune at hand. The European White Fathers who settled in South-western Uganda in 1923, were keen to gain converts for the Catholic church and put great energy into turning people away from Nyabingi worship.[12] In particular, the Europeans projected an image of Catholic theology in which the Virgin Mary was constructed as a divine female capable of addressing the same range of misfortunes as had previously been dealt with by Nyabingi. By design or otherwise, the missionaries incorporated much of the ritual practice and terminology of Nyabingi worship into their Catholic rites. As a result, local women began to receive visions from not Nyabingi, but Holy Mary. So widespread did Marian worship become in the local Catholic church, that throughout much of the colonial period the Legion of Mary group existed as what Kassimir has described as 'the exemplary Catholic lay association ... and the most pervasive mode of organized lay life outside the daily purview of the church, especially in rural communities' (1999: 258).[13]

A major change in the organization of the Catholic church in South-western Uganda started around the late 1960s, and was more or less concluded by the early 1990s: the gradual withdrawal of European missionary priests from dioceses in the area, and their replacement with indigenous clergy. It is interesting to note that the first ever Ugandan priest to be ordained in his own parish was none other than Fr Dominic Kataribaabo.[14] Perhaps more acutely aware of the significance of Holy Mary for local people than their former European colleagues, this new indigenous clergy sought to promote her worship still further. As a result, from the early 1990s onwards, enthusiasm for the Legion of Mary became greatly reinvigorated throughout the South-west. Throughout its early years, the MRTC recruited through this newly revived Legion. Mr and Mrs Kibweteere regularly attended the organization's meetings, through which they contacted Marian visionaries throughout the region and beyond.

As the most renowned seer in the South-west, Mwerinde's involvement in the MRTC attracted both other Marian visionaries, and members of the Legion to its ranks.[15] But another important factor was the group's apparently wide network of contacts with other Marian groups throughout the world. During his brief spell in national politics in the 1970s, Joseph Kibweteere had travelled abroad on a number of occasions and in 1979, he and his wife had visited Rome. A certificate commemorating the visit still hangs on the wall of their family home. It was during that visit that Mrs Kibweteere had made contact with a number of Marian groups in Italy, and these in turn had put her in touch with other such organizations around the world. By the mid-1980s, when she and her husband were beginning to contact visionaries throughout South-western Uganda, Mrs Kibweteere was receiving literature from Marian groups as far apart as England, Spain, Ghana, Japan and Australia. Thanks to Mrs Kibweteere's industriousness, the MRTC had access to books and pamphlets from a quite startling array of worldwide Marian organizations. However, the vast majority of the organizations were based in the USA: Vermont, New York, Massachusetts, Louisiana and Texas.[16]

The Influence of Marian Literature

The illusion these texts created of a global network, within which the MRTC was located, was key to the group's early expansion.[17] This was a time before print media and commercial radio became widely available in South-western Uganda, when people generally received very little information about the outside world. Within this context, the information contained in these Marian texts, emanating from the four corners of the earth, must have seemed extraordinary to the majority of the sect's membership. As Mrs Kibweteere now recalls, many people attended the group's meetings solely for purposes of hearing readings from the Marian literature. Throughout the period of their stay at her home, readings from, and interpretations of these texts formed the very basis of the MRTC's daily routine. And according to at least one former member, even after the sect left the Kibweteeres' home, copies of the material continued to be widely drawn upon by the sect's leadership in their preaching. This seems to have continued until the publication of the MRTC's 1994 edition, after which that text formed the basis of worship,[18] but by then, many of the Marian literature's key insights had already been incorporated into the MRTC's own cosmology.

Millenarianism and the Millennium

Again using the MRTC book as evidence, it is possible to trace growing influence of the Marian literature on the sect's thinking. As one would expect, in the very earliest vision of Mwerinde's (10 March 1981), one finds no reference at all to the Marian literature, since this vision was received several years before Mwerinde ever met Mrs Kibweteere. In the visions of 1989 (Kibweteere and Komuhangi's), no reference is made to this source either. By 1991, however, the leaders' visions were borrowing directly from the Marian texts. Although none of the visions directly reference the pamphlets, various ideas seem to have been lifted from them. Among these are Fr Kasapuraari's notions of cosmetic surgery, as well as his ideas about IVF treatments, whereby 'people have sex by way of injections for the purpose of conceiving children' (MRTC 1996: 76, 81, respectively).[19] But the clearest example of borrowing is found in the vision of Fr Ikazire, which is primarily concerned with the sacrament of the Eucharist, and in particular with a return to an older practice in which the host was placed directly on the tongue of the receiver, rather than laid in the communicant's palm (ibid.: 67–8). All of Ikazire's ideas on this issue are taken directly from a pamphlet entitled 'Communion in the Hand is a Sacrilege' written by the organization Our Lady of the Roses of New York city. This development coincided with the MRTC's serious consideration of the idea of an imminent end of the world. Aside from talk about cosmetic surgery, abortion and the sacraments, this was the key issue in the Marian texts received by the group at this period. Such a preoccupation was epically true of the literature of the American Marian organizations. In all cases quoted in their writings, this apocalypse had been predicted by Holy Mary, and was either imminent, or had already begun. As one pamphlet, from an organization based in Buffalo, N.Y.,

begins, 'Our Blessed Mother ... [has] said: '... Many of my children must change
their lives drastically, and soon! For time is SHORT [*sic*]; much shorter than
people think.' A booklet from the St. Paul's Guild of Vermont, quotes from a vision
received at Fatima, Spain. 'Our Lady has repeatedly told me: "Many nations are
going to disappear from the face of the earth, Godless nations will be picked up by
God as His scourge to punish the human race ... tell them, Father, that the Devil
is waging his decisive battle against Our Lady".' Another leaflet of the Marian
Workers of Atonement, of New South Wales, Australia, quotes a seer in Poland.
'At 12.30 pm... Holy Mary entered ... [she said] 'Turn back, for time is short.
You are living in the days where the signs are given in the sky and on the earth...
If the people do not turn to God, then will come down terrible continuous thunder
and lightening and the earth will start to crack.'

It is not necessary here to analyse this literature in depth. However, I would
note in passing that the texts often relate the predicted biblical end of the world to
the ongoing Cold War struggle (most of them were produced before the fall of the
Soviet Union). My aim here is simply to demonstrate the influence this literature
had on the development of the MRTC's own millenarianism. It is significant that
the visions of 1991, the first to borrow directly from the Marian texts, are also the
first to suggest that the end of the world is an imminent event. By the time of the
MRTC's group vision, however, the Marian literature's obsessive millenarianism
pervaded the sect's entire worldview. Chapter four leaves the reader in no doubt
that the MRTC's own millenarianism derives directly from this source. At the
very outset of the chapter, before the declarations of the MRTC leaders, the text
explicitly lists all those who have received this vision worldwide. It includes the
names of all of the seers mentioned in the various Marian texts (MRTC 1996:
40). Many of the details of the forthcoming apocalypse described in the MRTC's
book are taken directly from the pamphlets. At the end of the vision, details are
included of the specific fate awaiting various named countries, bearing a striking
resemblance to the countries named in the Marian literature. The nation that tops
the list, and the first to suffer the forthcoming apocalypse, is none other than
Russia.

A key question is why the MRTC's millenarianism did not fully develop until
some years after they had begun using the Marian texts Why, in other words, did
the end of the world become an obsession for them only after they had left the
Kibweteeres' home, at which time they had been in possession of the Marian
literature for almost four years? The key to this question is contained in the Marian
texts themselves. Perhaps for purposes of adding urgency to their prophecies of
doom, at several points in the various books and pamphlets the coming end of
the world is given a specific timing. Take, for example, the booklet from the St.
Paul's Guild. 'A great chastisement will come over all mankind; not today or
tomorrow but in the second half of the twentieth century... the great, great war

will come in the second half of the twentieth century.' Recall the opening of the vision of Fr Kasapuraari 'the time is drawing near...' (above). A brief passage at the beginning of chapter four of the MRTC's book states, in bold letters, that 'some of those who have received this vision have been told on what date it will be realized, others have not' (ibid.: 41). Still, the event cannot be far off. But also in that chapter another interpretation of the above passages in the Marian literature begins to emerge. This is the idea that the 'second half of the twentieth century' (quoted above) indicates that the end of the world will occur at the millennium, in the year 2000. 'Listen to this, people of the world. When the year 2000 A.D. comes to an end, there will be no 2001' (ibid.: 47). The urgency with which the MRTC now regarded the coming apocalypse stemmed directly from this interpretation of the event's timing. 'Count the time from when you hear these words until the year 2000 A.D. That is how much time you have remaining to get your affairs in order' (ibid.: 48).

By the time chapter four was written down, not everyone in the MRTC seems to have been convinced of the validity of this timing. Jumping ahead to the year 2000, it would seem that even by that time, some in the group were still in need of convincing on this point. Four days after the Kanungu fire, James Mujuni reported a letter, written in Runyankore, which had earlier been received by the New Vision's sister paper, the vernacular *Orumuri*, from Joseph Kibweteere. Written sometime in January 2000, the letter explicitly addresses an ongoing tension within the MRTC as to the exact date on which the end of the world was to occur. People in the group had apparently been receiving visions conveying different timings. But the letter clarifies: 'I Joseph Kibweteere, my boss Jesus Christ, has appeared to me and given me a message to all of you that there are some people arguing over the message that this generation ends on 1st January 2000. On the contrary, the generation ends at the end of the year 2000 and no other year will follow'.[20] This new vision of Kibweteere seems finally to have been accepted by all. When the MRTC handed in a report on their activities to the Ugandan Ministry of Internal Affairs, three days before the fire, it stated that 'their mission was coming to an end, and there would be no 2001. Instead, next year would be year number 1, starting with a new generation'.[21] As it turned out, for the majority of the MRTC membership, the world was due to end several months before that date.

Conclusion

The history of the MRTC challenges previously held assumptions about the sociology of millenarian movements. Rather than emerging as an apocalyptic movement locally in response to some major, concrete social change, the group's final millennial outlook was instead drawn from external sources. The key to understanding the organization's history lies not in its later millenarianism at all, but in the fact that it began as a branch of the Legion of Mary, itself a partial transformation of the old cult of Nyabingi. The group's eventual adoption of a millenarian world view was not an internally generated response to social tension and schism, but was taken up from the apocalyptic literature of other, international Marian organizations to which the group had access. Written for other (ostensibly political) purposes, this literature was interpreted by certain elements within the MRTC as referring to the coming apocalypse at the end of the year 2000. The urgency created by this timing then drove events, resulting in at least some tensions within the group. If the millennium had not occurred when it did, the MRTC would not have become a millenarian movement at all.

I began this chapter by arguing that uncertainties have continued to exist around the cause of the MRTC's ultimate fate. A significant point is that both the 'suicide' hypothesis' and the 'mass murder' alternative rely on an understanding of the sect as essentially millenarian in nature. The realization that this was only a later gloss challenges both of these explanations. The implication is that the ultimate fate of the MRTC may have been more complex than either of these views would suggest.

Notes

1. This chapter is based on part of my D.Phil thesis: 'The Kanungu Fire: Power, Patronage and Exchange in South-western Uganda', Oxford University 2004. The research was funded by the Economic and Social Research Council.
2. Although examples are of course found in both Judaism and Islam. I here use the word 'millenarianism' in its historical rather than typological sense.
3. See, for example, Stroup, 1945; Froom, 1946–54; Daniels, 1992.
4. The seminal anthropological work on millenarianism is Thrupp, 1962. See also Mair, 1959 and Wilson, 1963.
5. Notably Hobsbawm, 1959 and Lanternari, 1963.
6. Indeed, from the time of its first publication, study of this book replaced conventional biblical textual study. From 1991 onwards, bibles were effectively banned from all MRTC compounds.
7. The book's prologue lists all the people to whom the sect intended to send a copy. In addition to the Pope, it includes all of the country's religious, political and civil leaders.
8. Throughout this chapter, all of my references to the MRTC's book are to the 1996 Runyankore/Rukiga edition. All of the following quotes are based on my own translations of the original, which were aided by Mwombeki Rwabahima.

9. The last chapters of the book are exceptions because they address practical affairs.
10. Fr Ikazire left the group in 1994.
11. See for example my article in the *East African* 8–14 July 2002, available online at http: //www.nationaudio.com/News/EastAfrican/15072002/Features/Magazine6.html
12. See, in particular, Bessell, 1938 and Freedman, 1984.
13. He continues: ' the Catholic tradition of the veneration and intercession of Mary and the saints corresponded with pre-Christian appeals and sacrifices to ancestor spirits and local spirit cults' (1999: 258).
14. He was ordained in Rugazi Parish on 8 August 1965. Kataribaabo went on to a distinguished career in the church, winning a scholarship to a leading US Jesuit University, Loyola Marymount in Los Angeles, and later ran the largest Catholic Seminary in Uganda, at Kitabi.
15. As further evidence of the link between the 'old' Nyabingi and the Virgin Mary, it might be noted that Mwerinde's reputation derived from the fact that her visions of Mary had occurred in the village of Nyakishenyi. These caves had previously been the most auspicious site for Nyabingi worship.
16. I am extremely grateful to Mrs Kibweteere for allowing me to photocopy all of this literature. I thank her also for granting me a number of interviews on the subject of the MRTC.
17. The MRTC's leaders later claimed their sect to have a privileged position within this global network. As later sections of the book states, it is Uganda which is to be the 'new Israel' after the judgement (1996: 52–3).
18. The 1994 edition of the book had a much bigger print run than the first edition.
19. The latter, in particular, is a recurring theme in many of the pamphlets, which are often concerned with issues of abortion and new reproductive technologies.
20. *New Vision*, 21 March 2000. The letter is translated from Runyankore by Mujuni.
21. Report by Simon Kaheru in *New Vision* 21 March 2000.

References

Bessell, M.J. (1938), 'Nyabingi' *Uganda Journal* 2: 2.
Daniels, T. (1992), *Millenialism: An International Bibliography*, Connecticut: Garland.
Freedman, J. (1984), *Nyabingi: The Social History of an African Divinity* (Tervuren: Koninklijk Museum voor Midden-Africa.

Froom, Le Roy E. (1946–54), *The Prophetic Faith of our Fathers: The Historical Development of Prophetic Interpretation*, Washington: Review & Herald vols 3, 4.

Hobsbawm, E. (1959), *Primitive Rebels: Studies in Archaic Forms of Social Movements in the 19th and 20th Centuries,* New York: W. W. Norton & Co.

Kassimir, R. (1999), 'The politics of Popular Catholicism in Uganda', in Thomas Spear and Isaria N. Kimambo (eds), *East African Expressions of Christianity*, Oxford: James Currey.

Lanternari, V. (1963), *The Religions of the Oppressed: A Study of Modern Messianic Cults,* London: MacGibbon & Kee.

Lindstrom, L. (1996), 'Millennial movements, millennialism' in Alan Barnard and Jonathan Spencer (eds), *Encyclopedia of Social and Cultural Anthropology,* London: Routledge.

Mair, L.P. (1959), 'Independent religious movements in three continents' in *Comparative Studies in Society and History* 1: 113–6.

MRTC [Movement for the Restoration of the Ten Commandments of God] (1996), *Obutumwa bwaruga omu eiguru: okuhwaho kw'obusingye obu*, Rukungiri, Uganda. English version, *A Timely Message from Heaven: The End of the Present Times*, Rkunguri, Uganda.

Stroup, H.H. (1945), *The Jehovah's Witnesses*, New York: Columbia University Press.

Thrupp, S. (ed.) (1962), *Millennial Dreams in Action: Essays in Comparative Sociology*, The Hague: Mouton.

Wilson, B.R. (1963), 'Millennialism in comparative perspective', in *Comparative Studies in Society and History* 6: 93–114.

Part VI
Persons In and Out of Time

–18–

Life Made Strange: an Essay on the Re-inhabitation of Bodies and Landscapes

Andrew Irving

This chapter compares the way in which time is experienced and transformed within the changing social settings and circumstances of people's lives, by considering how the temporality and imagery of people's bodies becomes radically destabilized during and after illness.[1] If, as generally accepted, perceptions of time and space are generated through people's everyday activities, then the disruption caused by illness transforms pre-existing ways-of-being in time and place. The chapter begins with two extended 'ethnographic portraits' of people living with HIV/AIDS; the first a photographer from New York who finds himself blind; the second a mother from Kampala who 'digs' the land to feed her family. Although they inhabit different social, cultural and physical worlds both persons struggle to maintain bodily continuity amidst illness. The blind photographer wakes up after night and renegotiates the relationship between body and world by feeling around and re-orientating himself towards his house. The mother's day begins by walking around her living-room, attending to her body and obtaining a sense of herself in anticipation of working the land.

By comparing each person's attempt to maintain bodily continuity within different social settings I aim to consider the temporality of 'everyday life' in ways that displace the polarities of universality and difference. This follows Parkin's work on comparison in the search for continuity (1987). Only while Parkin considers everyday speech, cross-cultural etymology and semantics, I emphasize acts of dwelling and disruption in relation to once familiar social practices and landscapes and the declining bodies of people with HIV/AIDS.

The Tale of the New York Photographer

Back in the early 1990s John Dugdale was a renowned fashion photographer working in New York. Given his enjoyment of Manhattan's gay nightlife he was convinced he was HIV-positive and testing later confirmed this. Until then John had enjoyed a carefree existence, handsome, intelligent, successful. Although he was now HIV-positive he assumed he would be a 'long term survivor'.

John's skill behind the lens made people's garments look good and betrayed a distinctive aesthetic style that meant he was always in demand. His success allowed him to run an apartment in Greenwich Village and a farmhouse upstate. One morning he was at his farmhouse before travelling into New York for a photo-shoot. He had some tea, ate breakfast and left for the city. However after arriving John began to feel disorientated and then without further warning collapsed on the city's hardened concrete pavement. He'd undergone an HIV/AIDS related stroke and never made the appointment. Moreover from now on the world's surfaces and textures would become increasingly unfamiliar.

John was found in the street and taken to hospital where his condition steadily deteriorated. Also, because he was confined to bed he experienced a type of pain and fatigue that takes over when lying down for days on end. Of having one's habitual perpendicularity removed, of having one's flesh and bones continually press down on a soft bed, of blood flowing round horizontally and of being removed from routine body practices and movement. He had just turned thirty-three, a man supposedly in the prime of his life, who could not get out of bed, was too weak to piss into a pot unaided and had to be looked after by nursing staff and his family.

With his family's help came shame, humiliation and the resurfacing of memory. John was the eldest son and when he was young he used to help his mother by changing his infant brother's diapers. This 'long-forgotten' memory resurfaced: for his brother now comes into hospital and changes John's diapers. No-one could have anticipated the later significance of John's early actions, nor imagined the peculiar reversal of roles that confronted the two brothers – who as grown men now meditate on the strange contingencies and unlikely circumstances of the present. John's sister would also come into hospital and change his diapers, clean his ass, freshen him up. He found this disconcerting but nowhere near as difficult as when his mother changed his diapers. Feeling her warm hands on his wasting flesh was as disturbing than anything he'd experienced while living with HIV/AIDS. John recalls wishing he'd already died ... he was already in extreme pain and nearing death but why die with that playing on your mind? And what about his mother's feelings ... changing her sick son's diapers ... thirty years after the first time. Only now she found a son who was slowly decaying and approaching the end of life rather than opening up towards the future.

After a while John began noticing parts of his visual field were slowly disappearing. Where he once saw the world he now saw nothing while the remainder seemed covered by a heavy black-mottled veil. When the doctors investigated they discovered the HIV virus had begun eating away at the retina, something called CMV *retinitis and yet another ailment caused by HIV. John, who had learnt to see through his culture and profession, now had to use the weak awareness on the periphery of his visual field because the centre was blocked by blackness. He'd move his head and eyeballs as if to 'look around' the blackness, but blackness would follow and smother the object of his attention. Accordingly John had to learn a new way of co-ordinating eyes, head and world in order to see and interact within his environment.*

John had numerous operations to try to save his sight. After the last one he was sitting talking to a friend, and she went for some coffee. When she returned she noticed John bent over in the hospital corridor crying and draped herself over him. John had just been informed there was nothing more the surgeons could do and that his sight would deteriorate until he was blind. The months that followed were like a slow, continuous twilight. John existed in the gloaming ... and like a craftsman desperately trying to work at the end of day he tried to make the most of the remaining light. He scrutinized the world more intensely than he ever had as a photographer, drinking up colours, faces, patterns, textures, flowers and storing them up for when blind. John looked intensely at the face of his mother, her hairline, every slight discolouration and wrinkle, her mannerisms and expressions, her face while smiling, while talking and when returning her son's odd, fragmented gaze. He looked at his brother, his sister, at the woodiness of wood, at red and blue and the transparency of glass, at flowers, sky and the reflections on ceramic surfaces. In choosing where to look John undertook an active creation of memory, scrutinizing the present to create what he would remember in a blind future.

On recovering sufficiently to leave hospital John had lost most of his sight. He was able to see vague outlines and shapes, detect differences in colour and between light and dark, but not enough to understand what he was looking at. John's brother drove him up to the farmhouse and away from the traffic, speed, unlighted-chaos and intolerant pedestrians of New York's crowded streets and shops. This was where John was going to re-inhabit his body and renegotiate the world. It was now several months since he'd got up that fateful morning to leave for the city ... and still there in the living room remained the empty cup ... next to it was the plate and the remainder of the toast which had hardened over the months. Little could he have imagined when eating breakfast that morning that he'd return months later – almost blind, thin, severely weak, his once handsome features sucked into his face.

Unsurprisingly, John found the silence and creaks in the farmhouse disconcerting. The re-alignment of his senses while in the hospital had transformed how he related to the environment and even the once familiar sounds and surroundings of the house were made strange. He couldn't see things properly and increasingly began orientating himself by touch, texture, sound and smell. John's brother helped but eventually had to return to work. The first day alone John kept banging into things, barking his shins, bashing his face, falling over. He went outside where there was no furniture, but lost his balance on slopes and ditches, banged his head, got black-eyes and stumbled into a thorny unforgiving hedge. Scratched, bruised, bloody, covered in mud, he went back inside and headed to bed. As he could no longer read he decided to put a book over his face and lay there smelling the warm paper pages.

The Tale of the Ugandan Mother

The same year (1993), Yudaya Nassiswa and her four young children moved to Ndejje, an area of Kampala near Entebbe Road. Although Ndejje is in a city of two million, Yudaya still calls it her 'village' because until recently it was mostly bushland. Ndejje has since been transformed from bush to urban neighbourhood, and Yudaya's house is now surrounded by houses, a school, shopping-kiosks, a radio-mast and boda-boda cyclists touting for trade. Ndejje's rapid growth is not surprising for despite losing over a million people to HIV/AIDS, Uganda's population has increased by nearly sixty per cent to around twenty million over the past decade.

Yudaya moved after her husband Daniel died from AIDS in 1992. Daniel had three wives and many children who all shared the same compound. After his death, the wives went their separate ways. Daniel's property was claimed by the 'first-wife', although she too soon succumbed to AIDS. Afterwards her relatives moved in. Yudaya, as the 'second-wife' was made to leave the home and remained with little that was not already hers (she now regrets being so naïve). The 'third-wife' also left and soon died from AIDS. Some eight years later Yudaya still lives in amazement that she is still able to look after her children while Daniel and the other two wives succumbed to AIDS. As to how and why this happened, Yudaya does not know. Ask her one day how she survived and she will reflect at length on luck and chance; ask her another day and she says she must have a strong constitution. Ask Yudaya one further time and she thanks God, puts her faith in his benevolence and powerful will, and trusts the destiny he has planned for her family. These are not contradictions, just situational responses at different times to awkward questions.

Although Yudaya lost her home and husband she was fortunate to own a second-hand clothes stall in Owino Market that provided extra income for her children's education. Now with no home her priority was to find somewhere for her children and herself to live. She sold the stall and put the proceeds with a friend who was in a similar situation and together they bought some land in a cheap out-of-the-way place called Ndejje. But it was on a hill and covered in bush that needed to be cleared before work on the house could begin.

Yudaya frequently suffers opportunistic infections and last Christmas had her first ominous bout of tuberculosis, which is morbidly significant in Uganda where it is the primary cause of death amongst HIV-positive persons. That Yudaya came down with tuberculosis at Christmas was hugely significant for her children and herself – not because Yudaya, although born a Muslim, converted and raised her children as Christians but because her husband died on December 25th. In Uganda – where children are present to most that life offers – children get caught up in the voluminous atmosphere whenever there is a dying person in the house.

Every Christmas the atmosphere in Yudaya's house is thick with memories of Daniel's illness and death. This last Christmas was even worse as Yudaya's illness and tubercular breathing mixed with her children's anxieties about the future. The suffering and uncertainty caused by HIV/AIDS has a 'volume' that extends out from the person and fills up the entire room, house and even seeps out into the neighbourhood. If you ask Yudaya's children they will tell you how it felt to dwell in the midst of their father's death; they'll talk about how this atmosphere descends every Christmas and how this last Christmas they kept imagining their mother's impending death. They'll tell you they are worried about the future, about who will look after them and remind you how two of them have stopped attending school because of lack of money. They will talk about how they thought they were going to be orphans with no-one to pay their school fees and about their relief once their mother began to pull through. Now all the children hate Christmas.

The family home looks like many houses in Kampala. It is built from the same earth that it stands on. The earth is scooped up, mixed with straw, stones and water and moulded into large bricks fired in neighbourhood kilns. Wood and mud-plaster are added, while the ground from which the bricks were extracted creates a compact floor alongside the characteristic trenches found outside people's houses. Yudaya did not do the work herself but it is tangibly her place – a house mixed out of earth, straw and personal history – and which wouldn't exist without Yudaya or her husband's death from AIDS. The house is just two rooms with no windows or electricity. Water is fetched from the public tap and boiled on an open charcoal fire in the sitting room. The mud-plaster walls are decorated with children's drawings, calendars, magazine pictures, Man-United posters and old newspapers. Three beds take up all the space alongside everyone's shoes and clothes. Round the back is the vegetable plot, where Yudaya grows sweet potatoes, matoke, yams and other staples to feed the family. It used to be a wilderness but when Yudaya is well enough she makes an effort, and so do the children. Together they have enough to eat.

The house is halfway along a little slope just beyond the ridge of a long steeper hill. This is not unusual – everyone in Kampala lives up or down a slope. Hills and slopes are part of daily being, and Yudaya's existence is intertwined with certain slopes: the long steep hill that goes up to Makindye, the winding slope down to her friend Rebecca's house, the short steep hill near the main bus-park ... the hill she walks up to fetch water ... and lastly the slope that leads to the sweet-potato plants. Even this gentle path changes from day to day. We might go further and say that maybe all the world's surfaces, including the gentle slope up to sweet potatoes, wax and wane from moment to moment, for slopes and hills take time to climb and can seem very different when half-way along. The way Yudaya feels about herself and her situation when walking up the dusty path to the sweet-potato plot can differ radically from when she is on her sofa drinking tea. However, both these 'realities' can change again when she picks up the hoe and starts digging, sometimes her body betrays her and she establishes yet another sense of her self.

Accordingly the first thing Yudaya does when she wakes up is test out and 're-inhabit' her body by walking around the house and if she feels 'fine' she goes to dig the sweet potatoes, still checking her body step-by-step. When she picks up the hoe there are some days when Yudaya can hardly make out the difference between body and world, instead both come together in the task-at-hand. She digs all day and gets tired but this in itself becomes an index of health. On other days a radical discontinuity soon emerges between body and world, perhaps whilst still in the house, or walking along the path, or soon after digging. Either way the sweet potatoes go untended with all the accompanying consequences for her family. Most mornings Yudaya wakes up not knowing whether she can dig or not, and it takes her a while to feel part of the day, part of the world.

Discussion

John Dugdale and Yudaya Nassiswa, like everyone living with HIV/AIDS, were born into worlds already constituted by particular socio-cultural practices. Prior to diagnosis each incorporated specific ways of *using* and *imagining* their bodies, and post-diagnosis they interact through bodies that betray different gender identities, physical topographies, religious, cultural and temporal epistemologies. Although John and Yudaya are separated by very different ways-of-being, both face the daily struggle to maintain bodily continuity while living with HIV/AIDS. Their experiences are representative of how for HIV-positive persons, being a body-in-the-world ceases to be taken for granted but is disrupted and 'made strange'. People re-learn how to use their bodies, are made to re-negotiate the environment and begin to understand body processes in new, sometimes radically different ways.

Ordinarily an habitual unity of mind, body and world is forged through the skills and practices of 'everyday life' (Ingold 2000), whereby a continuity of person, body and action is maintained over time and within specific environments through a combination of culturally defined tasks and desires.[2] For people living with HIV/AIDS the sense of continuity becomes continually displaced as they have to repeatedly *re-inhabit* their bodies during and after the disruption of illness. Moreover the illness trajectory of HIV/AIDS is not one of gradual decline but of undulating cycles of illness and recovery that can persist for days, months or even years. Accordingly people learn to 'test out' their bodies at strategic times within different contexts for different purposes, thereby recalling the etymological origin of 'experience' wherein *ex* signifies 'out of' while *peira* means 'attempt, trial, test'. As Edward Casey suggests, 'places, like bodies and landscapes, are something we experience … and to have an experience is to make a trial, an experiment, out of living. It is to do something that requires the proof of the senses, and often of much else besides' (Casey 1993: 30).

Certain rhythms and temporalities of being emerge during seemingly simple, axiomatically 'universal' actions such as *walking* – where intentions, desires, eyes, lungs and legs coalesce into an unconscious habitual activity – or *drinking*, *eating* and *talking*, where words, ideas, lungs, mouth, tongue, lips, hands, air and sound-waves merge into seamless action. Here the body's image and temporality are already familiarized, naturalized and immersed in the practical activity of daily life in ways that are 'absent' to consciousness (Leder 1990, Parkin 1999). Frequently there are few conscious boundaries between 'person' and 'world' and it becomes uncertain where the person ends and the world begins. Instead there is an unbroken continuity, a moving-together, coherence or confluence of human action within the world (Parkin 1985).

However the undulating cycles of illness and recovery while living with HIV/AIDS means that being a body-in-the-world continually becomes disrupted and subject to self-conscious reflection. Even when there is minimal disruption people plan and legislate for the possibility of future physical decline. Thus, while HIV/AIDS is always culturally situated, it involves experiences and modes of action that are particular to persons in search of bodily continuity who are making trials out of the everyday circumstances of their being. For as Drew Leder says, '…the imagery of the body can be understood not only in reference to the cultural projects at play but as an articulation of certain phenomenological possibilities and pre-dispositions arising out of the lived body' (Leder 1990: 127).

Walking Fieldwork: with Francis

To this end I conducted a type of *walking fieldwork* as an ethnographic tactic whereby I accompanied people moving between places and witnessed those moments when their bodies – or the surrounding world – became 'present'. Walking is not a pre-cultural activity but changes in different contexts and historical periods (Ingold 2001) and is also a form of continuity over time and space, involving embodied memory and repetitive body movements. *Walking fieldwork,* meanwhile, attempts to reveal the temporality and specificity of walking practices by accompanying people on their journeys and asking them to narrate their experiences.

People would describe, in their own terms, an explicit awareness of their body in relation to their surroundings. They recalled the precise distances written into particular practices such as buying a newspaper or making tea, and demonstrated how distances and actions have to be worked at rather than assumed. When walking it became noticeable that the environment was rarely 'simply there' and how that physical character was forever constraining or enabling certain types of action and interaction. One soon establishes a sense of how seemingly 'passive' physical features of the environment – earth, paths, corridors, stairs, gradients, edges, concrete-pavements, hospital-wards – possess dynamic, transforming properties that outline the possibilities available in *this* body, in *this* time and *this* place. Furthermore such features possess different 'social densities' at different times (Parkin 1999) and my co-walkers were extremely sensitive to how crowds, lunch-times, rush-hours, weekends and so forth change the character, mood and possibility of each place.

A Friend in Kampala

His name was Francis Wasswa. He'd been ill and hadn't ventured outside for some time, but his weakness was overshadowed by the desire to walk around Kampala for one last time, before it became too late. So one fine equatorial day I accompanied Francis into the city. Slowly, with frequent rest intervals we walked down the slope to Entebbe Road. Francis worked out a way that he could cope with, setting a pace for both of us without either of us saying anything. The first hundred yards took around five minutes of painfully slow walking, then we stopped and watched the world for a few minutes before tackling the next short stretch. Our walk continued in this way until we reached the main road from where we decided to catch a matatu *to the art exhibition at the Gallery Café.*

By the time we reached the Gallery Café, Francis was too tired to view the exhibits so we sat down, ordered some African-tea, mandazi *and waited. After the tea came, things followed much the same pattern as our walking. Francis would take a sip of tea, bite the* mandazi *and then chew bit by bit, slowly, for a while, then stop and sit still for five minutes. Not wanting to rush Francis I did the same thing. We chatted in much the same way. We'd begin a subject and then leave it a while before continuing where we left off. The tempo didn't need to be stated and, like the silences, didn't feel awkward.*

Walking, talking, eating with Francis: the limits of his body became placed upon my actions and by doing these things in his company I partially inhabited Francis' world. By using my body as if constrained by his disease, a degraded and impoverished inter-corporeal realm was created between us. This was not formed through any commonality of bodily praxis because of the radically different bodily experiences that were being compared; and my bodily mimesis of a body with AIDS rarely, if ever, merged with Francis' own experience. Instead the discrepancies between our experiences of walking dissolved any assumed universality of the body, undermined any recourse to hermeneutic inter-subjectivity and simultaneously forced recognition of the otherness of Francis' lived experience.[3] Prior to walking my sense of Francis' experience of AIDS was based upon the stasis of his living room where he chatted relatively easily in his shabby chair. However this image immediately became dispersed outside the house, where Francis' every step seemed present to consciousness and where few words were exchanged even when resting.[4]

Here, a sense of body-image is formed between persons and places, within and through similarities and discontinuities in praxis and behaviour – or to recall the etymology of 'image' – through 'mime'. The word 'image' derives from the Latin *imago, imaginem,* and is related both to imagination and memory – thus placing the body in time – but if we trace the etymology further and we find that *imago* and *imaginem* derive from *mimos* or mime: 'a mime moves in space and portends more than he or she gestures. In this way miming – which is precisely *not* imitating in a strictly repetitive manner – *creates images*' (Casey 1991: 117 italics in original). Image it seems is *already* a bodily concept, something that is simultaneously seen and performed through time and space and thus to talk of 'body-image' is already to talk of the body-in-action. Walking always took much longer in Francis, John or Yudaya's company and it is through the recognition of such discrepancies that a sense of their experience was communicated. In other words comparing bodily praxis exposes the hermeneutic borders that exist between people's experience of time and space, and although people do not intend to communicate their experience, their every act is potentially left open to comparative interpretation. Maybe the walking body – this enacted mime – does not intentionally convey meaning, and its constitution as a sign is erroneous. Nevertheless it has the quality of a 'good error' and by sharing practices and using the body's mimetic potential it is possible to build a comparative – although not 'inter-subjective' – understanding of people's experiences.

The Syntax of Practices

Everyday practices such as *walking, eating* and *going-outside* have a 'language like' or syntactic quality. This is not to say their performance depends upon language or possesses a formal grammar, rather it is to use the sequential and situational (*even interruptive!*) qualities of language to understand the situational, procedural character of practice. In other words there is a *syntax* of practices that places the body in time, for example by situating the person in terms of habituated, embodied memory and by orientating them towards their future aims and desires. As illness progresses, once-routine practices become increasingly opaque in terms of how each constituent part is ordered into a syntactical chain of action (which is itself embedded in one's surroundings). To give an example, the fact that *brushing-teeth* involves walking to the bathroom is something rarely recognized as part of the practice. However whenever people enter periods of decline such features become increasingly explicit. It becomes apparent that brushing-teeth involves raising-one's-head-off-the-pillow, getting-out-of-bed, walking-to-the-bathroom, opening-the-door, standing, leaning-over-the-sink, administering-the-toothpaste, brushing, and walking-back. During illness, persons become more conscious of the entire chain of action involved in previously taken-for-granted practices. Simple tasks become fragmented and their constituent parts are made present by an inability to perform, revealing facets and temporalities that were previously hidden in an embodied memory once naturalized through practice but now degraded through disruption.[5]

The syntactic chain can be modified and some parts discarded according to current physical condition but some facets must be retained. The ability to perform a task may lie with a single component and if this cannot be re-negotiated the practice is jeopardized regardless of its importance or pragmatic need. On the days when Yudaya was unable to walk up the slope to the sweet potatoes, she remained in the house. When John was in the hospital he had no option other than stay in bed, Francis was able to walk into the city on that particular morning but shortly afterwards became restricted to his immediate locale.

The syntax of bodily practices has further implications for the way people experience and imagine time. For as being and time are not merely coterminous but are fundamentally constitutive of each other; different temporalities emerge through our immersion within different forms of everyday practical activity (see Heidegger 1962, McInerney 1991, Sartre 1996). Different practices – *walking, cooking, talking, reading, washing-clothes, watching-the-neighbourhood, shopping, listening-to-radio* – create or transform the way people experience time (see Wendy James and David Mills' Introduction to this volume). However, the rhythms and temporalities of different practices themselves become transformed by cycles of illness and recovery. When living with HIV/AIDS, periods of illness and fatigue interrupt pre-existing ways-of-being and disrupt temporal structures that have long been ingrained into people's bodies through practice. Thus HIV/AIDS not only disrupts time and makes strange the rhythms of habit but also establishes new ways of experiencing and being in time and place.

John Dugdale, Yudaya Nassiswa and Francis Wasswa's experiences of being *inside* and then going *outside*, exemplifies how time and reality are transformed between places. A provisional reality emerges within their living-rooms that incorporates their past, in terms of sedimented or habitual practices, and the future, in terms of the tasks and experiences awaiting them outside the house. If Yudaya is to feed her family she must leave the house to work in her field however her body 'bites'; and her inability to dig after reaching the field retrospectively orders her earlier experience of wellbeing while walking around the house. It is an inability that is transformed from a provisional perspective to something tantamount to her true 'state'. For her inability overshadows her recent experiences in the house and recalls William James' notion of how the truth of an idea 'is not a stagnant property inherent in it. Truth happens to an idea. It becomes true, is made true by events. Its verity is in fact an event, a process' (1978: 97).

Coda

Bodies, like landscapes, are inhabited, re-inhabited and re-evaluated over time. In this brief essay I have tried to emphasize how the temporality and imagery of people's bodies are constituted mid-stream between the culturally ingrained habits of the past, their immersion in the tasks 'at-hand' and a reality that always lies 'further-on'. Thus I would suggest that people's continual re-evaluations of body-image while living with HIV/AIDS are an extreme example of what Merleau-Ponty terms 'the experience of dis-illusion, wherein precisely we learn to know the fragility of the "real"' (1968: 40); whereby reality is continually transformed through time and movement:

> The destruction of the first appearance does not authorise me to define henceforth the 'real' as a simple probable, since *they are only another name for the new apparition,* which must therefore figure in our analysis of the *dis-illusion.* The dis-illusion is the loss of one evidence only because it is the acquisition of *another evidence...* Perhaps 'reality' does not belong definitively to any particular perception, that in this sense it lies *always further on.* (Merleau-Ponty 1968: 40, italics in original)

John Dugdale still wakes every morning and tests out the relative position of his body by moving around the house before going outside. Nowadays he has come to an arrangement between himself and the environment whereby he cedes to its power each morning before reclaiming part of the day for himself. On some mornings Yudaya attends to her body within the house but realizes working the land is beyond her. Later that same morning although it is far too hot for work, she feels well enough to leave the house and then decides whether to 'foot' it down the long hill to Entebbe Road or spend 500 shillings on a boda-boda.

Notes

1. First and foremost my gratitude must be extended to John, Yudaya, Francis and their families, who by sharing their lives made this chapter possible. It is dedicated to Francis who died in 2001. Thank you also to Hospice Uganda, National Community of Women Living with HIV/AIDS, Visual AIDS and last but not least the Economic and Social Research Council and the School of Oriental and African Studies for funding this research.
2. As Merleau-Ponty says, 'Is my body a thing, is it an idea? It is neither' (1968: 152), which is to suggest how people's bodies are a synthesis of time, imagination and materiality forged through specific purposes and practices within specific environments.
3. A process that thus questions the validity of Bloch's (1977) argument for the universal perception of time.
4. Likewise John Dugdale has learnt to move around his house quite gracefully but becomes noticeably more self-conscious and awkward whenever he goes outside.
5. Obviously different syntactic chains exist in each location. For example ablutions and brushing teeth are differentiated by the fact that people in New York don't fetch water from wells whereas many people in Kampala do.

References

Bloch, M. (1977), 'The past in the present and the past', *Man* 12: 278–92.

Casey, E. (1991), *Spirit and Soul: Essays in Philosophical Psychology*, Dallas: Spring Publications.

—— (1993), *Getting Back into Place: Toward a New Understanding of the Place-World*, Bloomington and Indiana: University of Indiana Press.

Heidegger, M. (1962), *Being and Time*, New York: Harper Row.

Ingold, T. (2000), *The Perception of the Environment: Essays on Livelihood, Dwelling and Skill*, London: Routledge.

Ingold, T. (2001), 'Evolving skills', in S. Rose and H. Rose (eds), *Alas Poor Darwin*, London: Vintage.

James, W. (1978 [1907]), *Pragmatism*, Cambridge, Mass.: Harvard University Press.

Leder, D. (1990), *The Absent Body*, Chicago: University of Chicago Press.

McInerney, P. (1991), *Time and Experience*, Philadelphia: Temple University Press.

Merleau Ponty, M. (1968), *The Visible and the Invisible*, Evanston: North-western University Press.

——(1992 [1962]), *The Phenomenology of Perception*, London: Routledge.

Parkin, D. (1985), 'Reason, emotion and the embodiment of power' in J. Overing (ed.), *Reason and Morality*, London: Tavistock.

——(1987), 'Comparison in the search for continuity', in L. Holy (ed.), *Comparative Anthropology*, Oxford: Blackwell.

——(1999), 'Suffer many healers', in J. Hinnells and R. Porter (eds), *Religion, Health and Suffering*, London and New York: Kegan Paul International.

Sartre, J.P. (1996 [1958]), *Being and Nothingness*, London: Routledge.

–19–

Embodied Memories: Displacements in Time and Space[1]
Julia Powles

There was a vigorous shout. The older women lifted their skirts mischievously and then, with an emphatic clap of their hands, they brought the song to an end. Almost immediately somebody's voice rang out with the first line of another popular Meheba melody; the drummers shifted their rhythm slightly and the circle of dancers set off again.

Sapasa of Road 67 was entering his sons into the circumcision camp (*mukanda*).[2] His mother, Kashala, had encouraged me to come, but now in the semi-darkness, amidst the smoke of the huge fires around the homestead, and disorientated by the press of people, I couldn't find her. Eventually I discovered her dancing near Sapasa's thatched kitchen. She was bent forward, her arms open wide as if holding something large. Her feet side-stepped swiftly across the ground so that her body followed an invisible line, back and forth. She appeared to be completely absorbed but then she glanced over her shoulder and saw my puzzled face. '*Nguna kuswinga*', 'I'm fishing'.

During the last four decades many thousands of refugees have fled Angola for neighbouring countries, initially on account of the liberation war and then as a consequence of the civil war between the MPLA Government and the UNITA movement.[3] Of those arriving in Zambia many Luvale from the Eastern part of Angola were taken to live in an official government settlement scheme called Meheba. I began research in this community in 1992.[4] One question that has always concerned me is 'How do the refugees remember Angola?' and it is this which I shall be discussing here.

Liisa Malkki has described how Hutu refugees in a settlement scheme in Tanzania consistently arrange their memories of Burundi into a collective narrative that focuses on violence (1995). Brinkman has reported a similar social memory of violence amongst Angolan refugees in a settlement in Namibia (2000). I have found that this pattern is not repeated for the Luvale in Meheba. Perhaps surprisingly, it is memories of catching and eating fish, and not the violence of war, that are collectivized during the process of on-going social life in the settlement.

In Angola these people were fishermen and women. Their lives were organized around seasonal changes in the waters of the Zambezi River and its tributaries.

When they were forced to flee, many tried to settle in Zambian villages just across the border, where their hosts largely followed the familiar annual rhythm. Some succeeded in staying in these villages, others were forced to move to Meheba. The settlement is in a slightly different ecological zone and so the latter were no longer able to pursue their past way of life. It can be argued that such relocation was at least as significant an interruption to the pattern of their existence as civil war or displacement, and so it becomes less surprising that catching and eating fish are the subject of social memory.

This social memory of catching and eating fish is I suggest, primarily embodied rather than narrated; it is the sediment, to use Paul Connerton's evocative word (1989), of past sensory experiences of different fishing techniques and the tastes and textures of the various species of fish they used to enjoy. As I shall explain, it is intimately linked with Luvale history, social organization and cultural identity.

In recent years there has been a great deal of discussion about embodiment within anthropology. Andrew Strathern suggests that one of the strengths of this new emphasis is that, 'embodiment ... reminds us of the concrete, the here and now presence of people to one another, and the full complement of senses and feelings through which they communicate with one another' (1996: 2). A number of extremely rich ethnographies have been produced, such as Paul Stoller's *The Taste of Ethnographic Things* (1989). These ethnographies have been effective because the anthropologist has been able and willing to share and take seriously the sensory experiences of those with whom he or she is working (as does Irving for example, in this volume). But how can one come to understand and appreciate embodied *memories*? Nadia Serematakis, in her study of sensory memory among modern Greeks (1994), was fortunate to be able to draw on her own childhood memories. While carrying out research with the elderly in rural France, Judith Okely (1994) was able to seek out opportunities to participate herself in the activities to which the old men and women's memories referred. I do not pretend to have had either of these advantages in my discussion of the Angolans' embodied memories of catching and eating fish. It has been a matter of being attentive to, as Judith Okely puts it, the 'distilled clues'(ibid.: 48) of this largely unspoken part of their experience, to the remarks overheard, to song and dance; and of writing in expectation, that one day, when the refugees return to Angola, I will be able to go down to the river to fish with them and later savour those 'wonderful tiger-fish, bream and barbel'.

Meheba Refugee Settlement

Meheba is in the North-western Province of Zambia, one hundred and fifty miles from the nearest border point with Angola. Since the first influxes of refugees in the 1960s the Zambian Government policy has been that they should be resident in officially designated settlement schemes. Despite this the majority have preferred to settle in border villages and only the minority have gone to Meheba, often against their will.

By the time of my research in Meheba in the mid 1990s the Angolan population had reached approximately 27,000, of whom about 8,000 were Luvale. The settlement fell into two main areas, the original 'Old Meheba' established in 1971, where the refugees were mostly Ovimbundu, Luchazi, Mbundu and Chokwe from the interior of Angola, and supporters of UNITA; and then the 'New Extension' opened in 1987, where they tended to be Luvale and Lunda from Eastern Angola, and supporters of the MPLA. I worked almost entirely within the New Extension.

There is one river running through the settlement, the Meheba. However, because of the forced dispersal of the refugees along so-called 'roads' (a series of numbered parallel tracks accessed by a main gravel thoroughfare) many live several kilometres away from it. Moreover, on account of the high density of the population, the Meheba River is now almost devoid of fish. Dried fish are available in the market but many refugees do not have the money to buy them on a regular basis.

Refugees are entitled to a food ration for the first two years after arriving in the settlement. This ration consists of maize, beans, cooking oil, salt and sometimes sugar. The maize is ground and made into a staple food called *shima*, a stiff porridge that is always eaten with one or more side dishes. After the first two years the authorities assume that refugees will have established crops on their 2.5 hectares plot and cease their rations, unless they fall into a 'vulnerable' category. People grow maize, cassava and a white sweet potato called *chingovwa*, the latter in part as a cash crop. They also grow a variety of vegetables.

Memories of Fishing

For the Luvale refugees the geography of the settlement has forced them to shift their energies away from fishing towards agriculture. In Angola fishing had been, for most men and women, an important occupation, one that they had managed to maintain despite the exigencies of the Portuguese colonial period and the civil war that followed Angolan independence in 1975.

There was in Angola a clear annual fishing cycle which began with the spawning run (*musuza*) of the mud barbel (*vambuli, clarias sp.*) at the onset of the rains in November. A middle aged refugee called Pedro Kakoma recalls:

The fish swim up from the large rivers to spawn on the flood plains ... people know that at this season the fish will come and they wait for them at the fishing camps. The fish arrive squirming and wriggling into the grass and curling around [the depressions are quite shallow]. It is the middle of the night. The people hear *pe pe pe* [the sound of the fish thrashing about] and they know its time. They kill them with axes and knives, or beat them with sticks. When they hear the cock crowing, that's when everyone comes out of the water to warm up by the fire.

The spawning run only lasted a few days. Little further fishing was possible until the floods started to recede again in April (*kakweji wakambamba*). Then weirs (*walilo*) were built across the streams to catch the fish moving with the receding water. Johnnie Lukama was a regular fisherman at this time:

Many of us would go – to Mbwela or Koto or Mukolweji. We would put up some small grass huts and then build the fish-weir. We used to make a really large fish trap (*likinga*) out of grass called cow-grass (*ngombe*). When we set the trap [on the downstream side of the weir] it would catch all sorts of fish (*vandembe, vatohwu, misoji, misuta, vambuli*)... We used to dry them on mats, high up on a rack, for they would have rotted on the ground. The barbel we would flatten out first. In May when it is cold, they would dry quickly. Then we would pack them up and carry them home, either by boat, or bicycle or motor vehicle. Sometimes we brought them to sell here in Zambia.

By the beginning of the hot season (*kasukwe*) all that was left on the plains of the earlier floods were large pools of water (*vyoze*). These were amenable to various forms of fishing. The smaller ones were fished by men with spears (*kusohwa*) or together with women, by bailing (*kusuhwa*); the larger ones were fished, again jointly, using poisons (*kusukila*) (although there were various restrictions on this practice). Pedro's recollection is again vivid, this time of spear fishing:

The men get some metal and use it to forge fishing spears. When they have finished they set off. There needs to be a crowd of thirty or forty men for one pool. They start to spear the fish. They stir up the water with their feet, *kuvu kuvu kuvu*. There are animals in the pools too. If they see a monitor lizard they thrust their spear at it and kill it, or a snake or a crocodile, and then drag it onto the shore. There are so many people and there is always a lot of fun. And there are strings and strings (*mazeze*), bunches and bunches (*masunga*) of fish to take home – all mud barbel, nothing else.

The end of the hot season brought the rain and so the fishing cycle would begin again. There was one additional method of fishing that was the preserve of women alone, basket fishing (*kuswinga*). This was sometimes done in large groups in the hot season pools but also in smaller, more intimate groups in the rivers and streams. Nyachipango describes what they used to do:

Next month, at the beginning of the hot season, we would make the fishing baskets (*mayanga*). Assuming you were family, then you and I, the two of us, would go down to the stream. You would carry a calabash (*kumbu*) and I would carry the fishing basket. When we reached the stream we would lower the basket *tu!* onto the ground and take off our clothes and put them on the ground too. Then we would enter the water and you would go down the stream a bit. From there you would start coming towards me, pounding the water, pounding it with your hands. Meanwhile I would drag the basket upwards and then, using a small club, I would kill any fish inside and put them into the calabash. When we finished doing this, then we would take the basket together, you on one side and I on the other, and draw it again and again through the water, killing any fish and putting them into the calabash. If a fish jumped out I would tease you and say 'Look, you let one jump out,' and you would say, 'No, he did it by himself.'

When we had completely finished, when it was getting late, then we would climb out of the water and scale the fish, scale all of them and put them back in the calabash. After that we would throw ourselves into the river once more and wash with some soap. When we were clean and fresh, then the one who had brought the basket would take the calabash, and the one who had brought the calabash would take the basket, and we would go home… The next day we would eat the fish with *shima*.

It is evident from these descriptions that the sequence of fishing activities gave a human pattern to the changing of the seasons. This is not to say that the passing of time was only ever considered in terms of these activities,[5] but that they gave a shape and significance to the gradual shifts in the weather and consequent changes in environmental conditions. And yet I suspect the fishing cycle was less a conceptual framework for the passing of time than a rhythm that was lived through: 'Time', as Christopher Gosden puts it, 'is not simply a mental ordering device, but an aspect of bodily involvement with the world' (1994: 7). And pursuing this phenomenological interpretation, we might say that the temporal movement from spawning run to weir fishing to fishing the pools of standing water and so on, became incorporated through its annual repetition, in an unconscious way, into the individual and collective body. Moreover the particular fishing practices themselves had their own rhythms, which likewise through frequent repetition were incorporated into people's very being.

The descriptions from Pedro, Johnnie and NyaChipango related above were in response to the enquiries of two individuals who had not had the opportunity to observe fishing in Angola, or at least who could not remember it: myself and a young man called Nelitu, who fled to Zambia as a small child. In the course of normal daily life it was actually quite unusual to hear people recalling their experiences of fishing in this way. The reason for this may be that people's memories of fishing were less easily narrated than embodied (although even in these descriptions one does have a sense of Pedro remembering the sensation of lifting his feet in the water, *kuvu, kuvu, kuvu* or NyaChipango pounding the water with her hands). The throwaway remark, the brief song or the distinctive dance pointed to the existence of these embodied memories. For example one August morning in 1996 I was chatting to a woman called Anna. As a sudden gust of wind scuttled across the dusty homestead, she drew her shawl more tightly around her shoulders and said, 'In Angola this is when we used to fish the pools (*kusuhwa*).' Or there is the following song. The words are simple but it is their unusually rapid repetition and the accompanying breathlessness that evokes the act of basket fishing so beautifully:

Tuvaswingenu, tuvaswingenu	Let's catch them, let's catch them
Ishi mukava	Follow that fish
Tuvaswingenu, tuvaswingenu	Let's catch them, let's catch them
Ishi mukava	Follow that fish
Mba	There we are [implies satisfaction]
Tuvanonenu, tuvanonenu	Let's collect them up, let's collect them up.

And then of course there is Kashala's dance with which I began; for her, fishing was indeed a very bodily memory, one that surfaced on the occasion of her grandson's circumcision, in ritual performance.

Memories of Eating Fish

Mention Angola and invariably any Luvale who is able to remember the country will respond along these lines, 'Angola is a wonderful country, you wouldn't believe the fish!' And they will go on to speak enthusiastically of how plentiful, varied and tasty the fish are. Mealtimes similarly tend to elicit a process of recollection: 'Ah, in Angola we used to eat fish every day,' and then if it was vegetables for lunch they would say, 'We just had these things for a change,' or if beans, 'We used to eat these with a spoon as a snack' (in other words they were never used as a relish to eat *shima* and not treated very seriously).

According to White, who wrote extensively about the Luvale in the 1950s and 60s, they have an exceptional knowledge of the many species of fish that are available on the upper Zambezi and its tributaries (1956: 75). This is no doubt true: I was myself impressed by the refugees' ability to look through a pile of assorted dried fish and distinguish between the many, very similar looking, species. They would often do this in order to pick out for example a tiny *musoji* (a young mud barbel), either because they did not like the taste (some feel that *musoji* are too pungent, *kuyekemena*), or because they were under a ritual taboo (see below). Individual preferences are common, so that amongst the fish that Johnnie Lukama used to catch, he particularly liked the taste (*kuyema*) of tiger fish (*pungu*) and bream (*kundu*); however best of all he liked the mature mud barbel (*mbuli*): 'In the rains you can get barbel this size [he clasps his thigh to show just how big they

Figure 16 Remembering Angola: a land of fresh fish. Photos: Julia Powles

are] and they are so tasty, the oil in your stomach … [from his expression it was evidently very enjoyable].'

The oiliness of fish was often commented on in these sort of animated tones. In fact according to the Luvale dictionary, the Luvale word for oil or fat, *maji*, is thought to derive from the same root as the word for good or agreeable, *mwaza*; and if oil is by definition a good thing then my observation in Meheba is that fish oil more so than vegetable oil and certainly more so than pig fat. Apparently when a large mud barbel was cooked, two and a half litres of oil could be skimmed off.

The positive recollection of fish in Angola was often in direct contrast to the perception of food in Meheba, Joseph Kaumba[6] expresses this very clearly:

> In Angola I used to go fishing with a hook and line, I would come back with some fish, everyone would eat and they were happy. The women would go fishing with their baskets, they would come back with some fish, everyone would eat and they were happy. Nowadays here [in Meheba] there are just sweet potato leaves (*kalembwila*), that's it! And when they reach your stomach its really painful, it churns and churns and churns around, and then you get horrible diarrhoea.

Nor do the leaves look and taste very pleasant; they are boiled briefly to make a dark green, rather slimy relish, which unlike the naturally oily fish sauce does not help *shima* to slip down the throat.

According to the settlement's agricultural officer, the sweet potato plant (*chingovwa*) was only introduced to Meheba in 1989, but by the mid-1990s it had already become a major cash crop. In 1994/5 it was estimated that the settlement had produced a total of 615,000 25 kg bags of sweet potatoes for sale. The potatoes, as well as the leaves just described, have also become a key supplement to the daily diet during the harvest period of March to September. They will usually be used as breakfast and/or for an evening meal; but in March, before the maize harvest is dry enough for grinding, a family may eat only sweet potatoes for several days. This may happen again in the cold season when there is a shortage of vegetable relishes for accompanying *shima*. Unfortunately sweet potatoes do not leave the stomach with the satisfying heavy fullness of *shima*; instead they cause an uncomfortable gaseous bloating. A popular song plays humorously upon this physical effect: a young woman travels to the district hospital in Solwezi thinking that her old lover has made her pregnant, and instead she discovers that she is 'with sweet potatoes':

Lunga lyami wamwaka	My old lover
Nanguhane lijimo lyamwana	Has made me pregnant
Shikaho kufuma kuno kuMaheba	So I went from Meheba
kuya kuSolwezi	to Solwezi [hospital]

Vanangupimi ngwavo	They examined me and said,
'uli nachingovwa'.	'You are with sweet potatoes'.

There are dried fish available in Meheba but the contrast with Angola is still a negative one, for dried (*vaumu*) fish are a poor version of the fresh (*vautute*) fish they once were, in addition to which, the better dried fish, such as the barbel or bream, are for many refugees unaffordable. For the majority the only dried fish that they can manage to buy are the tiny species sold by the cupful, such as *vasese*; these almost translucent minnows, as much eyes as body, are rather papery and really need the addition of expensive cooking oil to have any taste at all. They come from the lakes in Northern Zambia, and at least one man calls them *tusese* [literally 'a joke'] rather than their proper name of *vasese*. Moreover the occasional purchase of dried fish from the market only serves to underscore the burden of eating sweet potato leaves the next day – and the day after – and the day after that.

Are these memories of catching and eating fish just so much nostalgia? The comparisons of a plentiful Angola with an unforthcoming Meheba are almost relentless. Brinkman (1998) describes how Angolan refugees in Namibia similarly contrast positive images of Angola, a 'garden of Eden', with negative images of Namibia, a dry and arid land; and she does indeed refer to this as their 'nostalgic framework'. I think the difficulty in using the word 'nostalgia' is that we tend to associate with it a rather sentimental, disembodied and backward-looking process of remembrance. If we are going to use it then perhaps we need to claim for it the stronger Greek sense of the word, a desire or longing to journey back that is, emotionally and bodily, acutely painful (Serematakis 1994: 4). And we need to remember that, as Battaglia argues, the practice of nostalgia is not simply mimetic but poetic: in dwelling on the past, experience of the present is altered (1995: 93).

Embodied Memories: History, Society and Cultural Identity

In her discussion of the impact of modernity on Greek life, Serematakis argues that certain foods, in particular a peach called the 'breast of Aphrodite', alluded to the past in a way that newly introduced foods cannot. People's ability to replicate their cultural identity was embedded in these foods, in their colours, textures, tastes and smells. As they have disappeared it has become an increasing struggle to find meaning, and whole epochs have taken on the quality of 'tastelessness' (1994). I want to suggest that fish are similarly entangled with Luvale history, society and cultural identity, in part explaining the force of the refugees' embodied memories of catching and eating them.

The Luvale are descended from the Mwaant Yafwa kingdom in what is now the Democratic Republic of Congo. In the early seventeenth century there was a migration southwards of members of the Nama Kungu chiefly clan, amongst them a man called Chinyama cha Mukwamayi. On reaching the Upper Zambezi region he subjugated the various autochthonous populations, including the Mbwela and the Humbu, giving rise over time to 'the Luvale' as a distinct ethnicity (Papstein 1989). In Luvale tradition the practice of fishing underscores the continuity from Chinyama up to the present; in the words of the Luvale historian Moses Sangambo, 'Our chieftainship ... brought improved fishing techniques into the region – the same techniques we use today' (1982: 69). By the nineteenth century the Luvale already identified themselves, and were identified by others, primarily as fishermen (Oppen 1994: 186), and so today.

Both the act of fishing and the exchange of fish helped to shape social relationships. It was clear from the descriptions of fishing which I related above that many of the techniques necessitate the participation of large numbers of people. Luvale are principally matrilineal, but according to White fishing often called upon a wider set of ties: for example he says, 'the builders of a *walilo* [dam] may be linked matrilineally, patrilineally, by marriage or merely by a close friendship' (1959: 11). Fish were an important medium for reciprocal exchange between man and wife, brother and sister, in-laws, and so on, as well as between local neighbours. The more intensive techniques that men employed meant they had access to greater quantities of fish. Women meanwhile took more of the responsibility for cassava cultivation, but both products were essential for a satisfying diet (Oppen 1994).

It is particularly in the realm of ritual that we see fish – in all their rich sensual variety – linked to collective and individual vitality. Boys all undergo a circumcision ritual (*mukanda*), nowadays usually at about the age of eight or nine and as part of a small group. The operation is followed by a period of seclusion of some weeks or months at a site away from the village, inaccessible to women and uncircumcised men. The *mukanda* is a rite of passage that severs the close ties between a boy and his mother and prepares him for manhood. Girls are also initiated, although the ritual (*wali*) is carried out individually at the onset of a girl's first menstruation. Likewise the girl is secluded, either in a special hut (*litungu*) at the edge of the homestead or in the kitchen. A woman, often her father's sister (*tata-pwevo*), is appointed to give her medicines (*vitumbo*) and appropriate instruction whilst she is in seclusion. Some of the medicines are intended to make her more sexually attractive to men, and are put into the vagina to make it 'hot' and 'dry', whilst others are meant to enhance her fertility.[7] A girl who has not been an *mwali* and not had these medicines would, I was told, be 'incompletely made' (*himwatenguka*).

Crucial to the *mukanda* and the *mwali* rituals are a set of food taboos, including prohibitions on certain species of fish. These taboos are associated with a particular material characteristic of a fish that makes it inappropriate for consumption during the ritual. For example *kundu* (*Tilapia melanopeura*) is avoided by the boys at the *mukanda* because it has a red chest, which is symbolic of blood. *Chikanya, mbuli* and *chivende* (*Clarias sp.*) are all avoided because they have smooth slimy skins and symbolize difficulty in the healing of the scar. Similarly *mukunga* (*Sarcodaces sp.*) and *pungu* (*Hydrocyon sp.*) are avoided because they have sharp teeth and symbolize painful after-effects of the operation (White 1961: 6, footnote 19). Girls undergoing *wali* are also prohibited from eating *kundu* because of its red colour, in this case because it will cause prolonged menstruation. They too must not eat the smooth-skinned, slippery species, as they could precipitate an excess of vaginal secretions (White 1962: 7 and Wele 1993: 47).

There is one further set of rituals which are relevant here, those performed when somebody has been afflicted by *mahamba*, spirits associated with a matrilineal ancestor. During the curative rites of *mahamba*, all black species are avoided. One woman told me that if she saw a black fish on her plate whilst she was undergoing these rites for repeated miscarriage, she would pick it out; it was a 'thief' (*wiji*) – it wanted 'to eat the child'. Through its colour the fish was associated with witchcraft.

We saw above how in the absence of foods like the special peach, Greeks struggle to find meaning in their lives. What then for the Luvale in Meheba? The following, taken from a conversation with a middle-aged man called Sangambo, is very suggestive:

In the past [in Angola] if I had caught something I would share it with [my neighbour] and he would share what he caught with me. Nowadays everything is about money: you can be dying of hunger and you still have to pay; your child can die of hunger if you don't have any money. This is the problem that we are experiencing and we can't sleep at night. I fathered beautiful children. When I was still fishing they were healthy but now look at how their cheeks have become swollen.

We give them these greens and they refuse to eat them: 'not sweet potato leaves' they say. And this month even the sweet potato leaves are dried up. How are we supposed to survive? Shall we go and eat grass like animals? At least animals can search for the best grass before they eat, but what about us, people created by God? This is what we are grieving about. In the past we could provide for ourselves but not anymore... They tell us [at the clinic] that the children don't have any blood and that we should prepare avocadoes for them. But blood comes from food, those wonderful fish: tiger-fish, bream and barbel.

[He mimes now] You fill the pot – up to the top! Haa [its ready]. Then *twee* [he pulls off a small piece of *shima*] and here [he moulds it] a tiny cup. Then scoop the cup into the fish sauce and *waha mwana*! [he puts it in the child's mouth knowing that he will like it].[8]

Sangambo's enactment of eating *shima* underscores once more the very embodied character of people's memories of fish – of course *shima* is eaten with the hands and so the texture of the experience is very tangible.

However, what Sangambo speaks of is not only fish in and of themselves, but a whole social world gone awry in their absence. He and his neighbour used to share what they caught; but nowadays there are no fresh fish to bring home, and 'everything is about money'. It is commonly held that people are more selfish in the settlement than they were in Angola. There may be a variety of reasons for this. The difficulty of establishing neighbourly networks in a new place is surely one, exacerbated by the fact that extended families who would have lived nearby and co-operated together in Angola are dispersed along different roads in the settlement. But the want of a clear medium for reciprocation must also be important. In Angola there had been little need for money; during the colonial period they had been able to exchange their produce directly with Portuguese traders as well as with fellow Luvale, the former accepting fish, cassava, honey and so on in return for fabric, clothes, salt and other commodities. The only specific requirement for money had been taxation. This did not change a great deal during the post-colonial period: under UNITA administration in the latter years of the civil war, even taxation was in kind rather than in cash.[9] But in Meheba money is essential. Some of the younger generation of refugees have become profitable businessmen and women but there are many who struggle, especially amongst the elderly, infirm and those living alone. They can try to sell a few sacks of sweet potatoes, do piecework, or for the women there is the possibility of distilling a potent whisky (*lituku*) for sale. And yet none of these activities earns enough to supply the relish and other things they need on a regular basis.

The absence of fishing opportunities within the settlement emphasizes its bounded nature: 'At least animals can search for the best grass before they eat, but what about us, people created by God?' Thus the memory of fish becomes a form of political critique. In the words of another refugee, 'In Angola we ate well, we used to eat good things like fresh fish, and nice meat, either fresh or dried, and you would find a person was fat and healthy. Here we have *shima* but no relish. There is no good relish, and there is nowhere we can go to find it, since we live in this wire fence' (Sangambo 1999: 8). The Zambian Government policy of providing agricultural schemes for refugees was, in part, designed for their material welfare (Hansen 1979); but Meheba is nonetheless experienced by a number of its would-be beneficiaries as a constraint, a 'wire fence'.

As already mentioned, the majority of those fleeing Eastern Angola since the 1960s have preferred to settle in villages along the border. Many were able to find not only fellow Luvale or Lunda speakers to host them, but actual kin; when the border was demarcated in 1905 the Portuguese and British colonial governments took no notice of the ties of language and kinship between people on the ground.

Life in the border villages was certainly difficult initially, but of those who managed to avoid detection by the authorities, most had fully integrated within a few years (Spring 1979; Hansen 1986; Bakewell 1997). Settling in Meheba is, by comparison, a bureaucratic process; the allocation of a 'plot' to live on and cultivate is usually random and subsequent assistance, 'a ration', does not depend on any personal relationship. Refugees may try to reframe this bureaucratic process so that they describe UNHCR as their 'mother and father'; however the language of kinship is, practically speaking, meaningless in this context. By definition those in Meheba are refugees and cannot become locally integrated. As Sangambo went on to say, 'We have nowhere to go, we are tied up like animals, quiet... And there is no one we can fight with' (in other words, no one to whom they can address their concerns).[10]

For Sangambo a world without fish is a world in which a crucial source of vitality is gone. He is experiencing a form of atrophy (a word Serematakis uses in her analysis). When he speaks of his children 'having no blood' because of the impoverished diet in Meheba, this is more than the accidental repetition of a bio-medical diagnosis. For Luvale and Lunda the human person begins with blood, the coagulation (*kulikela*) of female blood and male semen, which is thought of as a form of blood (Turner 1967: 75). It is blood that unites the children of a woman's womb (*lijimo*), and more broadly all matrilineal kin. If a sorcerer wishes to make a familiar, such as a *lilomba* or *likishi*, he must animate it with substances drawn from his own body-self, in particular his blood. It is in drinking the blood of their victims, as well as eating their flesh, that witches gain their strength and satisfaction.[11] So when Sangambo says that he 'has no blood', he is indicating a wasting of the core being, and an inability to locate himself in the social world. It also suggests that he is experiencing an external assault upon the integrity of his person.

And Sangambo is not alone when he describes his children as having no blood. During the infinite series of greetings that punctuate each day I often heard people say, 'I'm not well – they have told me, I have no blood.' Alternatively they might respond to the question 'How are you?' with, 'I'm not well, look how thin I have become,' followed by a sigh and the one word most emblematic of life in the settlement, '*kalembwila*', sweet potato leaves.

Going Home?

My focus has been on the over-arching shared memory of catching and eating fish amongst the Luvale-speaking refugees in Meheba. My observation was that this social memory took on a new vitality whilst preparations were being made for a mass voluntary repatriation following the signing of a peace agreement between the Angolan Government and UNITA in Lusaka in November 1994. The joint recollection of delicious fresh fish certainly lent momentum to the process. Perhaps the most popular song during this turbulent time was the one below. The refugees identify themselves with the fish they so long for: the baby minnows have been carried by the current to a pool and are now stranded, where they await the floods to release them.

Twapwile tuvana vasenge	Like baby minnows
Twejile namuta	We came with the current
Nge livaji lineza	When the floods come
Natukahiluka	We shall return
Nge jita yinakumu	When the war ends
Natukahiluka	We shall return.

Before this period refugees rarely talked about their memories of war and violence as part of the process of on-going social life.[12] Faced with the possibility of a return 'home' they began to speak more frequently about the events that had brought about their displacement, but these memories still did not take the sort of standardized form described by Malkki for the Burundians in Tanzania (1995), or Brinkman for the Angolans in Namibia (2000). There was a sense in which the social memory of fish eclipsed these more individual, and often fragmentary, memories of war and violence. For while the refugees were focusing on how much better their lives had been, and would be again when there were fish available, it was easier for them to put aside their past experiences during the long history of conflict, and the very real possibility that the peace would not last (as indeed it did not). For many it appeared almost as if fish were alone enough reason to return to Angola. In the poignant words of one young man, left as a note on a tree to his brother when he decided to make his own way ahead of the UNHCR repatriation: 'It is nothing you have done, I am just going home to eat fish.'

Notes

1. I would like to thank the Government of the Republic of Zambia for granting me permission to carry out research in the refugee settlement, the ESRC for funding this research and the British Academy for enabling me to attend the conference in Arusha. I would also like to thank Sonia Silva, Inge Brinkman and Veronica Lassailly-Jacobs for their comments on an earlier draft of this paper, as well as the editors of this volume.

2. As described by C.M.N. White (1961) and Victor Turner (1967).
3. MPLA refers to the Popular Movement for the Liberation of Angola and UNITA to the National Union for the Total Independence of Angola.
4. Field research was carried out from 1992–3, 1994–6, and in July 1998 and July 2002.
5. The names of the months in Luvale refer to the natural changes and crop development as well as fishing activities (White 1959: 4). For related discussion see Evans-Pritchard 1940: Chapter III.
6. Taken from interview material collected for the book, *Vihande vyamu Meheba navyamu Angola* (Sangambo 1999). This is a collection of testimonies recorded by students at the Meheba D basic school. The project was fed by, and in turn has fed into, my research.
7. Anita Spring (1976) has shown that these medicines often have the opposite effect and cause infertility.
8. Taken from material collected for *Vihande* (Sangambo 1999).
9. UNITA took control of the Eastern salient during the 1980s, gaining Cazombo town in 1983. My comments regarding the penetration of the cash economy require further research.
10. The refugees from Eastern Angola come from a peasant background; they have shown little direct resistance to either relocation or the regime in Meheba. They did participate in the 'food riots' in 1994 but these had been initiated by a group of newly arrived Zairean refugees.
11. De Boeck (1994) contains a fascinating discussion of the symbolic meanings of blood for the Aluund in Zaire, not dissimilar to those I describe.
12. Michael Barrett makes the same observation for the period after the postponement of the repatriation (1998).

References

Bakewell, Oliver (1997), 'The prospect of peace in Angola: Bringing solutions to Mwinilunga's non-existent refugee problem?' (Paper presented at UNZA, October 1997).

Barrett, Michael (1998), 'Tuvosena: "Let's Go Everybody"': identity and ambition among Angolan refugees in Zambia', University of Uppsala: Department of Anthropology, Working Papers in Cultural Anthropology, 8.

Battaglia, Debbora (1995), 'On practical nostalgia: self-prospecting among urban Trobrianders', in D. Battaglia (ed.), *Rhetorics of Self-making*, Berkeley CA.: University of California Press.

Brinkman, Inge (1998), 'Landscape and nostalgia: refugees' remembrance of south-eastern Angola', Paper presented at 'Landscape and settlement patterns' workshop, Cologne, October 1998.

——(2000), 'Ways of death: accounts of terror from Angolan refugees in Namibia', *Africa* 70, 1–24.

Connerton, Paul (1989), *How Societies Remember*, Cambridge: Cambridge University Press.

De Boeck, Filip (1994), '"When hunger goes around the land": hunger and food among the Aluund of Zaire', *Man* 29: 257–82.

Evans-Pritchard, E.E. (1940), *The Nuer: A Description of the Modes of Livelihood and Political Institutions of a Nilotic People*, Oxford: Oxford University Press.

Fabian, Johannes (1983), *Time and the Other: How Anthropology Makes its Object*, New York: Columbia University Press.

Gosden, Christopher (1994), *Social Being and Time*, Oxford: Blackwell.

Hansen, Art (1979), 'Managing refugees: Zambia's response to Angolan refugees', *Disasters* 3 (4): 375–80.

——(1986), 'Refugee dynamics: Angolans in Zambia 1966 to 1972', *International Migration Review*, 15 (1): 175–94.

Malkki, Liisa (1995), *Purity in Exile: Violence, Memory and National Cosmology Among Hutu Refugees in Tanzania*, Chicago: Chicago University Press.

Okely, Judith (1994), 'Vicarious and sensory knowledge of chronology and change: ageing in rural France', in K. Hastrup and P. Hervik (eds), *Social Experience and Anthropological Knowledge*, London: Routledge.

Oppen, Achim von (1994), *Terms of Trade and Terms of Trust: The History and Contexts of Pre-colonial Market Production Around the Upper Zambezi and Kasai*, Munster and Hamburg: Lit Verlag.

Papstein, Robert (1989), 'From ethnic identity to tribalism: the Upper Zambezi region of Zambia, 1830–1981' in L. Vail (ed.), *The Creation of Tribalism in Central Africa*, London and Berkeley: James Currey and University of California Press.

Powles, Julia (2000), 'Road 65: A narrative ethnography of a refugee settlement in Zambia', D.Phil thesis, University of Oxford.

Sangambo, Charity (1999), *Vihande vyamu Meheba navyamu Angola*, Lusaka: Panos Southern Africa.

Sangambo, Mose (c. 1982), *The History of the Luvale People and Their Chieftainship*, Zambezi: Mize Palace.

Serematakis, Nadia (1994), 'The memory of the senses, part I: Marks of the transitory' in C.N. Serematakis (ed.), *The Senses Still: Perception and Memory as Material Culture in Modernity*, Chicago: Chicago University Press.

Silva, Sonia (1999), 'Vicarious selves: divination baskets and Angolan refugees in Zambia', Ph.D. thesis, University of Indiana.

Spring, Anita (1979), 'Women and men as refugees: differential assimilation of Angolan refugees in Zambia', *Disasters* 3(4): 423–8.

——(1976), 'Women's rituals and natality among the Luvale of Zambia', Ph.D. dissertation, Cornell University New York.

Stoller, Paul (1989), *The Taste of Ethnographic Things: The Senses in Anthropology*, Philadelphia: University of Pennsylvania Press.

Strathern, Andrew (1996), *Body Thoughts*, Michigan University Press.

Turner, Victor (1967), *The Forest of Symbols: Aspects of Ndembu Ritual*, New York: Cornell University Press.

Wele, Patrick (1993), *Likumbi Lya Mize and Other Luvale Traditional Ceremonies*, Lusaka: Zambia Educational Publishing House.

White, Charles. M.N. (1956), 'The role of hunting and fishing in Luvale society', *African Studies* 15(2) 75–86.

——(1959), 'A preliminary survey of Luvale rural economy', *Rhodes-Livingstone Papers* 29: 1–57.

——(1961), 'Elements in Luvale beliefs and rituals', *Rhodes Livingstone Papers* 32: xvii–73.

——(1962), 'Tradition and change in Luvale marriage', *Rhodes Livingstone Papers* 34: 1–38.

–20–

Living in Time's Shadow: Pollution, Purification and Fractured Temporalities in Buddhist Ladakh

Martin A. Mills

> The time is out of joint: O cursed spite,
> That ever I was born to set it right!
>
> Shakespeare, *Hamlet* 1.5

The anthropology of time is a notoriously slippery topic, where abstract meta-physical speculation and concrete ethnographic analysis blur into one another with apparently effortless ease, so it is worth taking a moment to define the precise question that I'm interested in.[1] Broadly, this paper follows in the footsteps of Geertz's famous work on 'Person, Time and Conduct in Bali', where he argued that Balinese social interaction was not comprised of individual personalities within durational time, but rather of 'generalized contemporaries' performing socially sanctioned offices. This, for Geertz, implied a 'depersonalized' notion of the person, in which the individuals become instantiated tokens of permanent person-types within a 'motionless present' (Geertz 1973). This sense of a motionless present was derived from the use of non-durational calendrical systems, part of a broader Hindu-influenced cultural tendency to construct personhood in a manner which 'refuses to regard as salient ... the cumulative effects of historical time' (Gell 1992: 72).

Geertz's interpretation has not gone without criticism. Firstly, it has been argued that he veers too close to a monolithic interpretation of 'Balinese time' as non-durational, whereas in reality the Balinese evocation of calendrical systems is varied and multi-faceted (Davis 1976; Gell 1992; Howe 1981); and secondly, that his view of ritual calendars as a homogenous cultural resource mistakes ideology for cognition, thus ignoring the historical exercise of elite ideological power that support, and are supported by, structures of 'ritual time' that are at odds with the comparatively ideology-free 'practical time' of, for example, agricultural production (Bloch 1977).

Whilst both sides of this debate have clear and (varyingly) valid points to make (Gell 1992: Chs. 8–10), one dimension of this problem goes largely unaddressed.

While systems of time-reckoning are indeed ideologies embedded within particular structures of social power (e.g. Tannenbaum 1988), little space is given to the examination of time *as a system of power in itself* – as a means of actively integrating individual experience into social time, or, as Alfred Schutz put it, of unifying inner *durée* and outer (social) 'cosmic time' within a 'vivid present' (Schutz 1971). An analogy here will probably clarify the issue at hand. Medical anthropologists are reasonably *au fait* with the idea that particular medical ideologies serve to support the position of associated medical elites. However, anthropological critique since the 1970s has shown that it is insufficient to discuss such ideological hegemony solely in terms of the degree to which a particular population *accept*, or believe in, a certain ideology (Good 1994: Ch. 1). Rather, medical authority is primarily constructed within the embodied disciplines of the patient-healer relationship, in which a particular medical practitioner not only asserts the truth of a particular medical ideology (which may well be accepted by the patient), but asserts the reality of that truth *within the particular case at hand*. In other words, it is the act of diagnosis and treatment in a *particular* case, referring to *particular* patients which truly embeds those patients within a particular medical ideology, and designates the healer as not simply the peddler of accepted ideologies, but the authoritative *creator* of medical truths in particular social moments.

In much the same way, it is the particular act of *integrating the individual into a general time scheme*, rather than the acceptance of that scheme as a general abstract model, that marks the moment of real ideological hegemony. A simple example of such an act of integration can be seen within the European context of 'national time', an idea most eloquently elaborated by Benedict Anderson in his picture of punctual daily acts of newspaper reading in the European world, a unification of an 'imagined' nation marching together through time (Anderson 1991: 35). Thus, just as when I check my watch against the chimes of Big Ben on the BBC or struggle to be on time for an appointment set according to it, it is not the *validity* of a temporal schema (such as a linear national time) that is in question, but my active, on-going *integration into it* – orientating me towards certain 'sources' of political and temporal authority – that marks true political hegemony on a local scale. This political engagement with 'official' (in this case, governmental) time is also an important part of the emergent construction of personhood: it is part of how I construct and orient a sense of my 'ordinary self' in terms of the world around me (Good 1994: 126; Schutz 1971: 212–22).

'Time anthropology' therefore involves two linked considerations: firstly, a more or less abstract examination of *why people represent time in a particular way* (and who might benefit from them doing so); and secondly, an examination of *the embodied practices by which people do time* – how they orientate themselves towards particular temporal/calendrical ideologies, and thereby integrate themselves into wider ideologically-structured communities.[2] The distinction between these two elements is most clearly seen when social life renders them disjunct: when time becomes, to quote Hamlet, *out of joint.* This dis-articulation of the two components of 'time-ideology' leads to social moments and scenarios in which *official* time is symbolically 'stopped', fractured or rendered null and void. Such moments are more than Bloch's 'non-ritual time', since the values of ritual time are in no sense rejected. Rather, just as the quotidian orientation of the actor towards official time is an essential component of the construction of the 'ordinary self', so the 'fracturing' of time is most usually associated with moments in which the ordinary self is also fractured: moments of social death, radical personal transformation and generational transition. Despite a range of ethnographic possibilities it is difficult to surpass W.H. Auden's rendition of this combination in his poem *Funeral Blues*:

> Stop all the clocks, cut off the telephone,
> Prevent the dog from barking with a juicy bone,
> Silence the pianos and with muffled drum
> Bring out the coffin, let the mourners come.

The British tradition of stopping or covering up clocks upon a death in the family (e.g. Cohen 1985: 315) is perhaps one of the most obvious symbolizations of this kind of understanding, and of the social (and temporal) disempowerment that attends upon the mourning of families. In this case, such temporal disjunction attends upon *families*, a key but increasingly defunct economic unit in modern Britain. It is the argument of this paper that such integrative practices link varying kinds of *embodied agent* into wider 'official' time *as social wholes*. The precise contours of these 'embodied agents' varies from society to society, depending upon the manner in which cultures construct notions of social agency: the individual, the family, even communities as wholes. In what follows, I would like to look at this phenomenon in the context of pollution practices and astrological calendars amongst Tibetan Buddhist communities of Ladakh, North-West India – a society where the *reproductive household* is the primary collective agent of ritual life, and thereby of ritual time.

Calendrical Systems in Buddhist Ladakh

Since the early first millennium, Buddhist communities throughout Asia have used extensive and complex calendars to organize ritual and economic life. Within Tibetan Buddhist areas such as Ladakh, there is a tendency to use combined astrological (*skar-tsis*) and elemental (*jung-tsis*) systems, which link together celestial cycles with geomantic influences, often producing highly localized variants. Like their Thai and Shan counterparts (Davis 1976; Tannenbaum 1988), Ladakhi astrologers use a combined lunar-solar calculation of the year – such that the progression of twelve designated lunar months of thirty designated days is regularly re-adjusted to fit into the progression of the solar year – which is based on the calculation of the auspiciousness (*tashi*) and inauspiciousness (*mi-tashi*) of particular hours, days, months and years for certain kinds of activity. Whilst an analysis of Tibetan astro-elemental divination *per se* is impossible in one short essay, it can simplistically be broken down into two sets of cosmological discussions:

1. Astro-elemental calculations for interpreting the auspiciousness and inauspiciousness of actions *relating to specific individuals of known birth-years and dates* (Cornu 1997; Mumford 1989). These calculations are based on the complex temporal interaction of: cycles of male and female; cycles of animals; elemental cycles; planetary cycles (see below); the transformation of the eight signs of 'life-force' (*sparkha*), symbolized by eight trigrams (familiar from the Chinese *I-Ching*), denoting the auspiciousness of social forces and directions; and finally a numerological system (*sme-ba*), which determines the simple auspiciousness and malevolence of certain dates for certain people. Combined, these systems create a full cycle of either 180 or 360 years of non-identical birth calculations, composed of three lesser cycles of 60 years, to advise on the in/auspicious of certain kinds of activity for certain individuals (e.g. not travelling on business to the North and South-West on a specific day for fear of attack by demonic forces; or re-arranging the rooms in one's house on particular days in order to ensure recovery from illness). One of the most important usages for this system is the 'death horoscope' (Mumford 1989: 201–4), used to determine the cause of death and to look into the possible rebirths for the deceased.

2. More general cycles, indicating the auspiciousness and inauspiciousness of particular kinds of action on particular days throughout the year, month and week, applying as a rule of thumb to everyone (but in principle within the context of their birth calculations). Unlike person-specific calculations (which were made by professional astrologers (*tsispa* and *onpo*), these were widely known and accessible through household calendars. This occurs at three levels: (i) the *yearly* elemental cycle identifies certain months for certain kinds of activity: in spring Wood dominates (and so trees should not be cut), in summer Fire (so waterways can be constructed, because fire dominates water), in autumn Metal (so use of metal implements, such as for tree-cutting, is auspicious), and in winter Water (in its passive, ice mode); (ii) the *monthly* cycle of general tendencies (the waxing of the moon is good for expansive activities such as building, and the waning for destructive ones such as cutting down trees or finishing business); and (iii)

the *weekly* cycle based on the seven planets (Mondays are auspicious days for planting, sowing seeds, expanding the family unit, astrology and divination; Fridays are auspicious for travel, temple-building and medical matters, whilst Sundays were generally inauspicious for these, etc.).

It would be inaccurate, of course, to view these simply as systems of prediction: firstly because, as Mumford points out (1989: 198–202), the interlocking cycles of astrological interpretation often produce conflicting results, requiring mediation by a ritual specialist (either an astrologer or a trained Buddhist monk), who will examine the different interpretations in terms of how clearly they agree with other elements of the specific case; and secondly, because particular influences can be modulated through ritual action. [3] Therefore, the astro-elemental basis for Tibetan systems of divination should not be mistaken for a 'science' in the Western objectivist sense. In the case of elemental (*jung-tsis*) calculations, the elements – both individually and in conjunction – represent 'agents' or 'principles of transformation' (Cornu 1997: 52) that inform certain kinds of action within the world. More explicitly, astrological components are associated with founding Buddhas and deities, and the cycle of twelve animals (those kinds of 'pious' animal blessed by the Buddha at the time of his death) with the mobilization of certain kinds of 'personality' that influence those under their aegis.

In this respect, individuals and groups were felt to 'partake' of agencies already at work within the world, linking together time and socio-ritual agency. Thus, certain dates within the lunar cycle (new moon to new moon) were associated with the mythic *activities* of particular Buddhas or lesser Buddhist divinities: for example, the fifteenth day of the month (full moon) was associated with the acts of the Buddha Sakyamuni, the eighth day with those of the Medicine Buddha, the tenth day with Guru Rinpoche's vanquishing of the local gods, and so forth. On these days, prayers or rites to the commemorated deity are seen as being especially efficacious, and activities based on their 'role' seen to be more effective. The interlocution between time and social agency in such cases was often highly explicit: thus, the eighth day it was normal for village *amchi*s (traditional doctors) to consecrate their medicines, thus rendering them more potent. Trained in the arts of the four medical tantric treatises, the *amchi* would visualize himself as being the Medicine Buddha (into whose lineage the *amchi* would have been ritually initiated) as the ritual basis for the consecration. Similar calculations attend much agricultural and nomadic activity, where the date of the first ploughing, of the movement of livestock to pastures, of going on trading journeys, are all regularly determined by astrological calculation (something which rather militates against Bloch's picture of 'practical' agricultural time). Here then, auspicious agency by social actors is seen as occurring in conjunction with a wider framework of divine and elemental agency within the world. As Roy Dilley argues, it is not so much that events are construed to repeat themselves by virtue of a circular conception of time and history, but rather that 'mythical' pasts and 'mythical' persons become synchronous with the present (Dilley, this volume, p. 236). Time, then, is envisioned not so much as an empty abstract container for social action, but rather a socially-legitimising resource for embodied actions, a legitimation (or auspiciousness) that must be 'sought out' by the ritual practitioner (whether astrologer, monk or farmer) through particular ritual practices and disciplines. In this picture of temporal progression, participation in time is unevenly deriving from relationships with sources of ritual power (called *chinlabs*, or 'blessing'), usually embodied in mythical, divine and semi-divine figures of the past. As Mumford notes: 'Tibetans compare *chinlab* to rain, but the source is the Buddha or the incarnate lama ... *chinlab* can be defined as traces left over from the primal era.'[4]

Ritual relations with sources of blessing in Buddhist Ladakh are mediated through a sacrificial economy organized around the dominant trope of the household (*tr'ongpa*) as both the principal source of the wealth (*yang*) and the principal object of ritual blessing (Mills 2003: 247–8).[5] They are, in Bloch's words, 'the prime social, political and symbolic unit of the society. The house is the source of identity for the people who live in it and they, to a certain extent and in certain contexts, *can be considered as together forming a single social actor*' (Bloch 1992: 70, italics mine; see also Day 1989; Phylactou 1989). Households, and the territorial domains they represent, derive this single legal and social existence as corporate agents from their capacity to sponsor village-wide offering rites to crucial spirits and deities within the calendrical cycle. It is unsurprising therefore that they are the principal objects of concerns over ritual pollution and, I would argue, problems with the 'fragmentation' of ritual time.

Pollution Practices in Buddhist Ladakh

For Tibetan Buddhists of all traditions, the diametric opposite of blessing and auspiciousness is ritual pollution (*dip*), a concept distinct from, but linked to that of negative karma (*mi-gyewa'i-las*). Unlike karma, *dip* is seen as being localized to a single lifetime, curable through direct ritual and medical means, and unrelated to the *intention* of the polluted person (in the manner that karma classically is within Buddhist traditions). The term *dip* itself literally means 'shadow', as in the shade found on the dark northern side of a mountain. The analogy is a commonly used one, evoking images of landscape, light and height that are symbolic commonplaces within Tibetan Buddhist cultures. Sacred objects (such as religious texts) and persons (deity statues, monks, lamas and one's social and genealogical preceptors) are placed higher than oneself, and are seen as 'sources' (*jung-sa*) of blessing (*chinlab*). Here, the term *jung-sa* (place of arising) more colloquially refers to a mountain spring from which a stream runs downwards, but also implied 'sources' of social and religious knowledge and authority.

Much indigenous theorizing about *dip* by monks (for whom it was a topic in the Buddhist monastic curriculum) centred on this understanding of height and social authority. Thus, a monk at one of Ladakh's many monasteries explained that *dip* derived from 'things being upside down': thus, placing your sleeping mattress or your shoes (which should be beneath you) on your head would cause *dip*. At the same time, lack of respect for religious objects and teachers caused *dip*, implying as it did a certain arrogance (*t'oman* – literally, a claim to 'height'). Monks spoke of the inability to see one's religious teacher (*lama*) as a Buddha (one of the injunctions of Mahayana Buddhism) as resulting from 'the *dip* in one's mind'. In this sense, *dip* was caused by a shattering of established hierarchies, and the downwards flow of *chinlab* as the basis for auspicious action. At the same time, pollution was also created by commensality with impure castes and the misplacement of bodily fluids (e.g. saliva touching communal food).

A more powerful image, evoked in the case of birth and death pollution, is that of *severance*, often associated with people's relationship with local water-spirits (*lu*) – earth-bound numina that are seen as the guardians of wealth and the source of human, animal and agricultural fertility, and which are therefore crucial aspects of the ritual elaboration of household life (see also Mills 2003: Ch.8). As with the many numina discussed above, their activity is seen to wax and wane throughout the year (awakening in the spring, being most active in the summer, and returning to sleep during the winter), throughout the lunar month (being most active during the first half, and waning in the second), and the across the week – cycles which are seen as linked to auspicious agricultural activity, and (as we shall see) to the auspiciousness and pollution linked to human reproduction. They are also seen as 'bound' to human activity by the powers of transcendent deities (such as Buddhas), and the acts of ritual practitioners. Disrespect for such water-spirits – such as urinating or defecating near their 'homes' (local springs), or digging up the soil without careful ritual precautions – was identified as the cause of powerful pollution and retribution from these important but capricious spirits.

Such dangers are particularly imminent in the processes of human reproduction. People's relations with *lu* are treated as embodied within the reproductive nexus of the household: father, mother and growing foetus together – even the placenta is often ritually treated as a water-spirit, and subsequent to parturition is placed in the basement of the natal house, where such spirits reside. Indeed, the infant itself is seen – especially in its early stages of foetal growth – as existing more in the realm of the water-spirits than of humans. Parturition, and particularly the severing of the umbilical cord (usually by the husband) is therefore a violent sundering of the previously united nexus of fertility represented by the *lu*. The social agent involved in parturition – in this case, the household and its occupants

– thus become deeply polluting to the water spirits, with whom they have – even if unavoidably – severed their relationship. A similar logic seemed to apply in the case of death pollution, caused by a severance of the individual from the fertile relationship of marriage (celibates such as monks do not incur pollution upon their death, and are seen as immune to its power). Members of households affected by pollution from birth and death were forbidden to enter fields or cross streams for fear of harming the water-spirits responsible for the harvest, and on pain of substantial fines from village councils. It is for this reason that there is a strongly expressed preference for both giving birth and dying in the winter, when the water-spirits sleep and the harvest cannot be harmed.

Ritual Pollution and the Astrological Calendar

As with most forms of ritual pollution, *dip* from such acts was seen as contagious and expansive in the context of ordinary social life. Passing through contact and commensality, it also 'fell' from human bodies to affect the land beneath them. The virulence of *dip* as a social force could be compared with the powerful images of social disempowerment that normatively adhered to the polluted. Here *dip* was seen as an 'obstruction' (*barchad*) to certain kinds of social and ritual action, causing a vulnerability to misfortune. Particularly with birth and death pollution, members of the same household were expected to stay indoors and refrain from cooking, from handling anyone's food but their own, from entering temples and giving offerings to the Three Jewels of Buddhism and local spirits (including the household and hearth gods), and from entering the fields. In effect, pollution undermined the capacity of householders to auspiciously perform all the principal functions of the household as a ritual, social and economic unit: it negated legitimate (or 'auspicious') social agency by disconnecting people from the sources (numinal and social) of that agency. Even in its lesser manifestations, *dip* is said to make people tired, lethargic, to produce an excess of sleepy dust, or in certain cases more serious cases to create unpleasant skin conditions or even paralysis (*tsa-dip* – 'root pollution'). Whatever happens, someone who is badly polluted is regarded as being *confined* in the broadest sense of the word – anything they do is seen as being doomed to failure or worse – better for them and others if they stayed at home.

Severe ritual pollution of this kind was seen to render victims incapable of participating through ritual exchange in the 'ordinary' divine powers embedded within the various astrological cycles; in this sense, it placed them 'outside' normal ritual time. Indeed, rather than their activities being seen as partaking in the blessings of various Buddhas and the good fortune and fertility of local spirits, the polluted (*dipchan*) are seen as embodying *demonic* action (for a comparison in Sri Lanka, see Kapferer 1983). *Dip* is seen as attracting demonic influence (*gnodpa*), such that any actions that the polluted perform are seen in this light, placing them 'outside' the ordinary astrological tempos that organize social life within village communities; moral history and time instead become 'demonic'.[6] During such times, actors become dislocated from ordinary life: in its most severe cases, pollution is seen to cause the life spirit (*la*) to leave the body, especially during twilight, and wander the barren interstices between human habitation, where demons dwell (cf. Tambiah 1970: 242). It also often opens the door to full-scale possession (*lha-zhugs*). This inversion of auspiciousness is a general characteristic of Tibetan understandings of deity. As Sophie Day comments: 'There is little to distinguish [*dip*] from the demonic. When the god is dirty, it causes harm, just like demons. When demons are cleaned and given homes, they cease their malevolence and become gods again' (Day 1989: 141).[7] Certain temporal flows are therefore seen to emerge correctly from socially legitimate sources (Buddhas and local numina); others are not, and become demonic. Clearly then, with regard to Ladakhi Buddhist communities at least, analytical characterizations of pollution practices that ignore either their diachronous nature or their embodied relationship with sources of legitimation/'blessing', are in danger of bracketing out the very contagion and exclusion practices that have rendered the concept meaningful within anthropological discourse.

Time and Pollution in Anthropological Theory

The characterization of *dip* as produced by the movement of social actors to modes of personhood and temporality that are 'out of synch' with established sources of social agency is, of course, reminiscent of Douglas's famous characterization of dirt as 'matter out of place' (Douglas 1966: 56–7). However, despite the unsurprising nature of the ethnography surrounding Ladakhi understandings of *dip* within the wider South Asian context (its association with life cycle transitions, inter-caste relations, patterns of contagion, and its organization around sources of blessing are all features familiar to Hindu and Buddhist ethnographies) at the same time it demonstrates the paucity of synchronic structuralist characterizations of pollution. Douglas's 'category anomalies' are avoided in and of themselves – as inherently anomalous – and therefore have no *emergent* impact upon the world: to take an earlier example, placing a mattress on one's head may well be anomalous action which confuses established categories of social hierarchy (*vide* Douglas), but once removed, the anomaly should – according to Douglas's theory – disappear, presumably taking any associated pollution with it. Ethnographically, this is simply not the case: remove the mattress from one's head and the pollution that has been produced *remains*, requiring subsequent purification.

Merely *undoing* the actions that cause pollution doesn't remove the pollution, because the pollution now exists as a newly emerged generative schema. To extend the 'sources' metaphor used by Ladakhis themselves, placing used eating utensils into a communal cooking pot *creates* a new and emergent arrangement of social categories in which the bodily contamination of the utensils becomes the 'source' of subsequently distributed food, rather than the ideal social source, the hearth-god. Those who eat from the polluted pot must share in the polluter's bodily essences – fine for the owner of the used utensil, all right for close family members (who are seen to share much of that essence already), but certainly no good for guests. Thus pollution lingers, even after its cause (whether a category anomaly or not) has been removed. Pollution is a form of social *memory* (see also Lambek 1992).

This diachronous quality to pollution behaviour – its tempo, in Bourdieu's (1972) terms – is what synchronous structuralist explanations such as Douglas's do not take into account, and thereby do not account for. This is all the more surprising given her famous emphasis on the 'abominations' of Leviticus, which makes persistent reference to the *perduring* qualities of uncleanness associated with contact with forbidden animals. 'And by these ye shall become unclean; whoever touches their carcass shall be unclean *until the evening*: And whoever carries any part of their carcass shall wash his clothes and be unclean *until the evening*' (Leviticus XI: 24–25, quoted in Douglas 1966: 43, italics mine).

Adjusting for this in terms of anthropological theory means asserting that what is 'confused' in pollution are not *objects of knowledge* in a static world, but *processes of socially-acknowledged emergent action* in a world in which time not only marches on, but is the very context within which action is constituted.[8] Specifically, Leviticus structures pollution within the cycle of the Hebrew day, which starts at evening: pollution is therefore removed through a combination of ritual cleansing *and the renewal of the temporal cycle*. Understanding this allows us to address a further question, implied within the ethnography above: if parturition destroys the embodied relationship that the household has with sources of fertility, thus producing pollution, how is it possible for the household group to become *un*-polluted, given that childbirth (and, of course death) are somewhat *one-way* processes?

Purification Practices in Buddhist Ladakh

In Buddhist communities in Ladakh, broadly similar rationales exist for the processes of purifying *dip* as for purifying uncleanness in Leviticus. Here, I shall discuss this in terms of purification practices surrounding birth. Generally, for the first seven days, father, mother and child are polluted (*dipchan*), and are confined to the house. During this period, the house may only be visited by male members of the household's *p'aspun* – a male-centred symbolic kin group comprising one or more nearby households who worship a single *p'alha*, or household god. [9] One lunar week later,[10] the father washes his lower body and monks visit the house to perform a purification ceremony (*trus*) and make offerings (*sangsol*) to the Buddhas, the household god and other local spirits. Following the performance of these rites, the father is free to leave the house, and non-*p'aspun* members can visit, bringing food and gifts (but not eating there). On the thirtieth day (that is, one lunar month later), the monks return to perform another *trus* on behalf of the mother, and a further *sangsol* offering.[11] Thereafter, the house returns to normal functioning: non-*p'aspun* guests can eat there and touch the baby (Norberg-Hodge and Russell 1994); in my own fieldwork site, the child is traditionally taken by the father to be 'shown' to the household and local area gods at their shrines.[12]

Both *trus* and *sangsol* rites involve the evocation of divine figures (principally Buddhas), either to purify existing pollution or to re-establish relations between humans and a variety of local spirits (such as *lu*) following pollution events. In both cases, re-establishing a 'normal' state of affairs is seen as contingent on the ability of the ritual officiant (usually, but not always a member of the monastic community) to evoke the presence of particular Buddhas within the ritual process. *Trus* (literally, 'washing') rites focus on the use of the 'cleansing mirror' (L. *trus melong* – a circular brass plate mirror) and a water vase (L. *bumpa*). The vase is filled with water and consecrated through visualising the retinue and divine mansion of the celestial Buddha Dorje Namjom descending and dissolving into the water. The water is then poured over the face of the mirror as a series of Buddhist divinities are visualized entering a bathing-house (also visualized in the mirror by the officiant) and, being bathed there, further purifying the ritual water, which is then collected in a copper bowl beneath the mirror. Following this, the object or person to be purified is 'washed' again with the same water, thus removing the accumulated pollution. The 'dirty' (*driwa*) water running off the patient is finally collected and added to ground barley, which is then moulded into a *lud*, or ransom-offering; this is then taken out of the house and left at a cross-roads to be consumed by demons (*dre*) and obstructive spirits (*gye*) that would otherwise have plagued the patient. One of the most important aspects of *trus*, which was strongly emphasized by the officiant, was that all present should strongly imagine the officiating monk to be the deity Dorje Namjom, and the patient is conversely instructed to visualize him or herself as Dorje Namjom's faithful disciple. It is only in the context of this 'faith' (*dadpa*) in themselves as the respective embodiment of religious teacher and pupil (*lop-truk*) that the rite is held to have any efficacy, and the 'patient' to be a recipient of the blessings of the Buddhas.

Martin A. Mills

Similar transformations of social role occur in the *sangsol* offering rite, performed to re-establish the patient's relationship with the various divinities and spirits of the local and supra-local cosmos. Such rites have a variety of forms, depending principally upon who is performing them. When performed by laity on their own behalf, they take the form of simple supplications and offerings, entreating the relevant deities to act in the officiants' favour out of compassion, or in return for offerings given to the deities and spirits in question. In many cases, however, monks were employed to perform the rite, due to their tantric training within the various cycles of particular tutelary 'wrathful' Buddhas, whom (in a similar manner to the traditional doctor discussed earlier) they were thereby entitled to 'represent' in rites. Such rites evoked a mythic history of transcendent Buddhas vanquishing errant local spirits (such as *lu*), binding them to accept vegetarian Buddhist offerings and to do the bidding of the officiant. Such an invocation is not merely a summoning, but a reconstruction of the tutelary deity's original moment of magical triumph (Samuel 1993: 185–6), re-establishing a relationship of blessing between deities and the polluted household.

The performance of purificatory rites thus 're-inserts' individuals and households back into a numinal hierarchy from which they have been temporarily dislocated. Moreover, such 're-insertions' are framed within the rhythm of lunar calendrical cycles (one lunar week for the father, one lunar month for the mother). Groups thus resume ritual integration *at the astrological point at which they left off*, in terms of the cycles of shared ritual agency. The implication is that pollution events seem to segment temporal flows, producing a kind of 'shadow' or 'demonic time' that flows in tandem with ordinary social time, but is characterized by an emergent inauspiciousness which normatively disempowers polluted actors and discourages crucial forms of social action.

Conclusion

At the beginning of this analysis I argued that 'time-anthropology' should take note of two linked ideological processes: the intellectual expression of a particular temporal ideology (cyclic, linear or whatever) as a generally valid way of interpreting the world, on the one hand; and those ritualized practices which integrate embodied agents into that schema, on the other. This integration forms a 'vivid present', in Schutz's terms. What unifies these two elements, however, is not a discussion of time *per se*, but a discussion of *legitimate social agency* – a complex series of emergent processes that constitute social personhood. In the Ladakhi case, social and ritual agency is seen as fundamentally derivative, dependent on established ritual relationships between corporate social actors (such as households) and multiple 'sources' of blessing. These relationships cycle through time according to calendrical ideologies of divine agency, rendering specific moments as 'good for' certain kinds of action. In this regard, the mode of integration involved is very much an embodied one, linking the reproductive 'body' of the household to 'sources' of *fertility* (*lu*) and those who can control them (the Buddhas) through sacrificial modes of exchange.

The logical result of this fulcrum of agential time and personhood is that certain moments exist in which the developmental processes of bodies also radically interrupt the established relationship between social agents (whether communal or individual) and sources of blessing. Such events and actions – most obviously, parturition and death – dislocate social agents from the established cycle of sources embedded within astrological and elemental time, generating pollution.[13] The fragmentation of 'ordinary personhood' described above is of course constituted through modes of exchange and symbolism specific to Ladakhi ritual life. It is, however, worth suggesting that such crises are possibilities inherent within the wider phenomenology of embodied experience. Within medical anthropology, Byron Good, recalling Schutz's writings on 'ordinary reality', notes a similar concatenation of alienated personhood and fragmented temporality within the experience of American patients suffering from chronic pain:

> In the everyday world, the self is experienced as the 'author' of its activities, as the 'originator' of on-going actions, and thus as an 'undivided total self'... In contrast, [Patient A] describes his body as having become an object distinct from or even alien to the experiencing and acting self. He articulated several dimensions to this objectification: The pain has agency. It is a demon, a monster lurking within, banging the insides of his body... *For [Patient A], inner and outer time, what Schutz calls durée and cosmic time, seem out of synch. Even more terrifying, time itself seems to break down, to lose its ordering power... Past and present lose their order. Pain slows personal time, while outer time speeds by and is lost.*' (Good 1994: 124–6, italics mine).[14]

Of course, for Good's interlocutor, temporal and social alienation is a distinctly *personal* conundrum and receives little institutional recognition, being precariously expressed within the contours of the individual body (see also Irving's description of the experiences of HIV/AIDS sufferers in this volume). In the ritual economies of Ladakh, this dislocation from the secure bulwarks of social existence follows instead the contours of the household and its associated economic structures, generating emergent *but fractured geographies* of temporal flow within Ladakhi communities.

The dependence of such distinctions on symbolic economy might cause us to reflect on our own complex constructions of political and cultural history. In *Time and the Other*, for example, Johannes Fabian draws polemic attention to the anthropological dichotomies of 'modern progressive time' and 'traditional static time' (Fabian 1983). Fabian sees this distinction as part of an imperialist tendency towards 'allochrony' – an image of fractured time that de-legitimizes the place of disempowered communities by 'removing' them from 'wider' economic and cultural histories. Does such 'allochrony' arise from a tendency to produce *geographies of time* similar in form to those evoked within the Ladakhi Buddhist case, in this case identifying whole *cultures* as agents 'outside' the legitimating historical agencies of Western civilization and economy? If so, then the rituals of time described above imply a politics of experience that is far wider than the intricacies of Tibetan Buddhist ritual, if rarely so precisely articulated. Indeed, while Fabian used his work to rail against the subtle injustices of allochrony in anthropological *theory*, the fracturing of time has often been evoked as an *self*-representation of the very incarceration of the disempowered. Here, we might recall poet Sophia de Mello Breyner's evocation of the peaceful left-wing Carnation Revolution of 1974, *25 de Abril*, when Portugal emerged from forty-eight years of dictatorship and political isolation:

> This is the dawn I was waiting for
> The first day whole and pure
> When we emerged from night and silence
> *Alive into the substance of time.*[15]

More germane to our topic, however: the ethnography of pollution and puri-fication here militates against theoretical interpretations that privilege calendrical and astrological systems as models of or for social action in any directly deter-ministic fashion. The 'fracturing' of corporate social actors from established social time, and the ritualized strategies for re-establishing those hierarchical connections, necessitate a consideration of time-reckoning as an emergent 'social geography' and a consideration of ritual authority in maintaining the hegemonic place of 'cultural time' in particular social instances. As has been observed before, 'time' is rarely a fundamental and irreducible component of human social life, and we should therefore be wary of seeing it as the foundation of 'time-anthropology' itself. We should instead look elsewhere: most saliently, to the construction of agency (corporate or otherwise) within the wider milieu of social existence, or rather, as Good puts it, to 'the making and unmaking of the social world' (Good 1994: 134).

Notes

1. Thanks to Justin Kenrick, Keith Hart, Tim Ingold, Chris Knight, Elizabeth Hallam and Francesca Murphy for comments on this chapter at various stages

of its production, and Olivia Harris, Nigel Rapport and Roy Dilley for a thought-provoking discussion of this topic.

2. This double-articulation of ideological hegemony is similar to Scott's rendition in *Weapons of the Weak* (1985: Ch.8): many people ascribe to power structures (such as taxation) in principle, and seek not to overthrow them through direct conflict; at the same time, they may seek to ensure through various tactics that the power-structure in question does not apply to *them*. However, see also n.12.

3. These two problems highlight the difficulty of seeing astrological systems as being unequivocal laws of cultural time. The significance of individual moments and events, and the consequences in terms of subsequent social action is highly negotiable, bringing together a range of often conflicting claims and interpretations within any one astrological pronouncement. In this regard, 'time' as an object of anthropological discourse has attendant upon it the kind of complexities that dogged the ethnography of kinship: a complex tension between our expectation of cultural *laws*, and our experience of cultural *practice*.

4. Mumford (1989: 97). The clearest example of this are the *terma* (hidden treasure) traditions, wherein prominent religious visionaries 'find' religious treasures such as texts and statues within the landscape (in rivers, rocks and temples), that were hidden by the 'second Buddha' Guru Rinpoche during the 'pure' time of Buddhism's infancy in Tibet (around 767 CE) and in anticipation of the *dus-ngenpa* (evil time) in which religion, morality and the Buddha's teaching would be eclipsed by decay. Those that find these hidden treasures are deemed *tertons* (treasure revealers), seen as reincarnations of Guru Rinpoche's early disciples. Such acts both constitute and contribute to the presence of *chinlab*, or 'blessing' within the present, degenerate world, implying a certain elasticity in local concepts of time. The most substantial such 'traces' can be seen in the *be-yul* tradition – valleys said to have been hidden from history during purer times, which reveal themselves to religious luminaries as sites for renewed religious practice.

5. The 'household' as a trope extends beyond the sphere of village households. It is also used to organize the structure of religious and monastic life, most particularly in the form of temples (*lha-khang*) as divine households (see Mills 2000).

6. Within the Tibetan astrological system, 'demonic time' can affect individuals, households and communities as wholes. The conjunction of certain planets can cause 'demonic' periods with reference to specific people, depending on their birth dates. More generally, certain events, such as solar and lunar eclipses, or the so-called 'day of the nine obstacles' (L. *tsespa'i barchad rgu*) were so profoundly inauspicious (*mi tashi*) that nothing of consequence would be

attempted, since it was bound to end in failure or worse. On the latter occasion, many people simply sat at home, neither visiting others nor being visited, doing nothing; all plans were postponed, and no business was carried out. Depending on the precise astrological cause, such events are generally polluting, and require extensive ritual purification. Indeed, certain traditions – such as the regularly performed *Gya zhi* rite, performed at the new year or on occasions of serious misfortune – are explicitly aimed at ameliorating the darker influences of specific temporal cycles (especially certain baleful planetary influences associated with the days of the week).

7. Intriguingly, Mary Douglas – in her celebrated work *Purity and Danger* – notes the same ambiguity in Old Testament understandings of deity: 'In the Old Testament we find blessing as the source of all good things, and the withdrawal of blessing as the source of all ills. The blessing of God makes the land possible for men to live in… Fertility of women, livestock and fields is promised as a result of the blessing and this is to be obtained by keeping covenant with God and observing all his precepts and ceremonies (Deut. xxviii, 1–4). Where the blessing is withdrawn and the power of the curse unleashed, there is barrenness, pestilence, confusion' (Douglas 1966: 49–50).

8. Death pollution practices are in principle similar, but purification of the living is interwoven with more complex rites given over to guiding the consciousness of the dead (Brauen 1982; Fremantle and Trungpa 1987; Mumford 1989: Ch.10).

9. See Brauen 1980; Phylactou 1989; Mills 2000. The *p'aspun* group dominate most marriage, birth and death ceremonial, and are said to be 'of one bone' (L. *ruspa chig chig*), that is, sharing the same patrilineal substance, although variations in the ritual and organizational structure of *p'aspun* groups in Ladakh and Zangskar are marked.

10. The use of 'lunar week' here refers to a calendrical week as a part of the monthly lunar calendar, which must occasionally be adjusted to link the waxing and waning of the moon to the actual passage of days. This sometimes means that a *lunar* week is longer or shorter than seven days (see Berzin 1991).

11. In certain cases, such as when birth has occurred during the 'sleep' of the water spirits, the month-long seclusion may not be observed.

12. The combination of purification and offerings to divinities – the essential 'mechanism' for the eradication of pollution – is extremely common in Buddhist ritual, often included in ordinary daily rites, and larger consecration ceremonies (Sharpa Tulku and Perrott 1985).

13. This ritual separation from social time-ideologies is neither an opting-out nor a form of resistance, any more than a person who has lost his hands in an

accident is 'opting-out' of, or 'resisting' the social conventions concerning shaking hands at social gatherings.

14. Good later makes explicit parallels between the experience of chronic *physical* pain and the emotional pain associated with grief and mourning rites (Good 1994: 131). Thanks go to Liz Hallam for her comments on this subject.

15. Sophia de Mellow Breyner Andresen (1977), '25 de Abril', from *O nome das coisas,* Trs. Ruth Fainlight in G. Benson et al. (eds), (1999), *Poems on the Underground*, London: Cassell.

References

Anderson, B. (1991 [1983]), *Imagined Communities: Reflections on the Origins and Spread of Nationalism*, London: Verso, 2nd ed.

Bloch, M. (1977), 'The past and the present in the present', *Man* 12: 278–92.

—— (1992), *Prey Into Hunter: The Politics of Religious Experience,* Lewis Henry Morgan Lectures, Cambridge: Cambridge University Press.

Bourdieu, P. (1972), *Outline of a Theory of Practice*, Cambridge: Cambridge University Press.

Brauen, M. (1980), 'The pha-spun of Ladakh', in Aris, M. & A. Suu Kyi, *Tibetan Studies in Honour of Hugh Richardson: Proceedings of the International Seminar on Tibetan Studies,* Oxford 1979.

—— (1982), 'Death Customs in Ladakh', *Kailash* 9(4): 319–32.

Cohen, A.P. (1985), 'Symbolism and social change: matters of life and death in Whalsay, Shetland', *Man* 20:307–24.

Cornu, P. (1997), *Tibetan Astrology,* tr. H. Gregor, London: Shambala Press.

Davis, R. (1976), 'The Northern Thai Calendar and its uses', *Anthropos* 71: 3–32.

Day, S. (1989), 'Embodying Spirits', Ph.D. thesis, University of London.

Douglas, M. (1984 [1966]), *Purity and Danger: An Analysis of the Concepts of Pollution and Taboo*, London: Ark.

Dumont, L. (1960), *Homo Hierarchicus: The Caste System and its Implications,* Chicago: University of Chicago Press.

Fabian, J. (1983), *Time and the Other: How Anthropology Makes its Object,* New York: Columbia University Press.

Fremantle, F. and C. Trungpa (1987), *The Tibetan Book of the Dead*, London: Shambala Press.

Geertz, C. (1973), 'Person, Time and Conduct in Bali', in *The Interpretation of Cultures,* New York: Basic Books.

Gell, A. (1992), *The Anthropology of Time: Cultural Constructions of Temporal Maps and Images*, Oxford: Berg.

Good, B. (1994), *Medicine, Rationality and Experience: An Anthropological Perspective,* Lewis Henry Morgan Lectures, Cambridge: Cambridge University Press.

Howe, L. (1981), 'The social determination of knowledge. Maurice Bloch and Balinese time', *Man* 16: 220–34.

Kapferer, B. (1983), *A Celebration of Demons: Exorcism and the Aesthetics of Healing in Sri Lanka,* Bloomington: Indiana University Press.

Lambek, M. (1992), 'Taboo as cultural practice amongst Malagasy speakers', *Man* 27: 245–66.

Mills, M.A. (2000), '*Vajra* brother, *vajra* sister: renunciation, individualism and the household in Tibetan Buddhist monasticism', *Man* 6: 17–34.

—— (2003), *Identity, Ritual and State in Tibetan Buddhism: The Foundations of Authority in Gelukpa Monasticism,* London: RoutledgeCurzon.

Mumford, S.R. (1989), *Himalayan Dialogue: Tibetan Lamas and Gurung Shamans in Nepal,* Madison: University of Wisconsin Press.

Norberg-Hodge, H. & K. Russell (1994), 'Childrearing in Zangskar', in Crook and Osmaston (eds.) *Himalayan Buddhist Villages,* Bristol: University of Bristol Press.

Phylactou, M. (1989), 'Household organisation and marriage in Ladakh, Indian Himalaya', Ph.D thesis, University of London.

Samuel, G. (1993), *Civilized Shamans: Buddhism in Tibetan Societies,* Washington: Smithsonian Institution Press.

Schutz, A. (1971), 'On multiple realities', in *Collected Papers I: The Problem of Social Reality,* Phenomenologica, The Hague: Martinus Nijhoff.

Scott, J. (1985), *Weapons of the Weak: Everyday Forms of Peasant Resistance,* London: Yale University Press.

Sharpa Tulku & Perrott (1985), The ritual of consecration', *Tibet Journal* 10(2).

Tambiah, S.J. (1970), *Buddhism and the Spirit-Cults of North-East Thailand,* Cambridge: Cambridge University Press.

Tannenbaum, N. (1988), 'The Shan calendrical system and its uses', *Mankind* 18: 14–26.

Index

Adler, H.G. 89.n4
aduŋ (cutting), 268–80 passim
Africa, East, 11, 28, 35, 285, 289, 292
  South 95
  southern 10
  West 23
age-groups (sets),
  in Ethiopia, Oromo, 253–5
  in France 138
  in Kenya, Samburu 269–80 passim
    Meru, 285–98 passim
AIDS, 12, 317–28 passim, 361
Alagwa (Tanzania) 36, 38–43 passim, 48, 50n10
allochronicity, 6, 362
  see also time
ancestors, see spirits
Angola, 331–44 passim
Annales, school of history, 137
Anthropology of Time, 2
archaeology, 20–1, 29
  Dogon and Haya, 23–6
  European, 125–6
  indigenous, 20, 31
  New, 20
  Scientific, 125–6
ark, symbolic (*tabot*) 222–8
art,
  earliest 125
  European, 126
  rock-, 9, 35–53 passim
Art and Agency, 2
artefacts (made objects), 22–31 passim, 84, 125
  as display, 143
  as prestige goods, 88
  as votive offerings, 222, 226, 228, 231
  sacred, 354–5, 364
Association of Social Anthropologists, 1
astrology, 8,13,
  Borana, 256–9, 263
  Buddhist, 351–64 passim

Atacco, Mexico, town, 61–7 passim
Atwood, M., 19, 29
Auden, W.H., 351
ayllu (social group), 187–98 passim
ayyaana (time concept), 251–64 passim

Bali Nyonga Palace, 82–7 passim, 90n11,
  90n13, 90n15
Bandiagra escarpment, 19
bandits, Chinese, 203–15 passim
Bantu, 42, 286, 289, 295
barrenness, *see* infertility
beads
  lomito, 270
  Rangi use, 42–3
  making-,
    Kalahari 126–32 passim
    Kenya 267–80 passim
Blaga, Lucien, 180
blankets, *see* cloth
Bloch, Maurice,
  'practical time', 175, 353–4
  ritual time, 236, 243, 351
  theory of time, 3
  time and meaning, 188
  time and memory, 188
Blombos cave, South Africa, 95
blood
  animal-, 96, 102, 124
  diagnoses, 166, 169n.10
  genealogy of, 238, 246n.5
  in human creation, 343
  menstrual, 109n.15
  ritual, 96, 343
  symbolism, 340, 345n.11
body-painting
  as '*technique du corps*', 126–7
  see also ochre, red
Bolivia, 190–9 passim
Bonaparte, Napoleon I (1769–1821), 139, 143

Index

Mandela, Nelson, 80, 87

marriage
see age-groups; genealogies; sex

Marx, Karl (Marxism), 121, 122, 137, 180

matrilineage, 39, 340

Mau Mau, Kenya, 290, 292

Mauss, Marcel, 3, 6, 126–7, 251, 268, 278, 288

Maya, Mexico, 251, 255, 263

Mbundu, Angola, 333

Mead, Margaret, 278

medicine, 350
in China, 159–60, 162, 165–6
in France 144
in Japan 165
in Kenya 162
in Ladakh (Tibetan) 353

mediumship, *see* possession, spirit

Meheba refugee camp, Zambia, 331–45 passim

memory
and post-socialism, 207
collective, 188
cultural, 31
embedded, 268
embodied, 48, 332–44 passim
inscriptive, 22
political, 142–3
social, 12, 22, 36, 188–9, 207–8, 211, 275, 358

menarche, *see* menstruation

Menelik II Emperor (1844–1913), 219, 220, 226–9

Menstruation, 32, 95–6, 98–112 passim, 124, 340, 341

Meru, Kenya, 12, 285–98 passim

Mexico, 9, 55–67 passim

Miao, West Hunan China, 203–16 passim

Mijikenda, Kenya and Tanzania, 28

millennium, 2, 12, 8, 214, 301–12 passim

millenarianism *see* millennium

missionaries
in CAR, 82–4, 90n15
in Kenya, 269
in Uganda, 308

modernism, 73–80, 139, 165, 171–4

moon-worship, 97–112 passim

MPLA (Popular Movement for the Liberation of Angola, 331, 333

MRTC (Movement for the Restoration of The Ten Commandments), 301–12 passim

Munn, Nancy, 4

musicians
Bolivian, 195–6 passim
djinn-, 40, 44–51 passim

Mwerinde, Ceredonia, 303–12 passim

myth, 7, 10, 119
Khoekhoe, 99–106 passim
Khoisan, 120–5 passim, 132, 208, 214, 236
Meru 296, 297n6
Oromo 254–5

NAGPRA (Native American Graves Protection And Repatriation Act, 36

Namibia, 27, 339

narratives (stories), 30, 119, 120, 124, 126, 189, 208–15 passim, 279n4

Nassiswa, Yudaya, 320–8 passim

Needham, Rodney, 3

New Ireland (Papua New Guinea), 28

Nigeria, 80

Nuer, Sudan, 74

Nyengo magic, 242

ochre, red, 95, 96, 98,102, 109n9, 120, 123, 126–7, 271, 273

Old Gamo Rules (OGR), 219–31 passim

ornamentalism, 89n9

Oromo, East and NE Africa, 251–64 passim, 289

Ottoman Empire, 208

Ovimbundu, Angola, 333

Ozouf, Mona, 138

pastoralists, 42, 96, 98–9 252

patrilineage, 23–4, 27, 30, 39, 254–5, 340
see also genealogies

PLA (People's Liberation Army), 203–6 passim

pollution, ritual, 354–8 passim
see also taboo

Portuguese
as colonial governors 342
as spirit beings, 36
as traders, 342

possession (spirit), 164, 167, 213–14, 216n7
demonic, 357
see also Nyengo

Index

praise-songs, *see* singers
prayers, Muslim, 238–9
presentism, 5–7, 10, 73–80, 87–88
primogeniture, 30, 226
pueblos, definitions of 58–67 passim

Qeso (Ethiopian priests), 220–31 passim
quadripartition, 191–2
  see also animal sacrifice

Radcliffe-Brown, A. R., 6, 7, 76
rainmaking, Bushman, 102
  in Ethiopia, 229
  in Tanzania, 394–7 passim, 50n13, 50n14,
ranchos, definition of, 58–67 passim
Rangi, Tanzania, 36–48 passim, 50n7, 50n14,
  51n51
refugees,
  Angolan, 331–45 passim
reincarnation, 140, 363n4
relativity, theory of, 13
relics, 23
  see also artefacts
religion
  Chinese, 210–12,
  Ethiopian, 219–33 passim
  Khoekhoe Bushman 97–112 passim
  Oromo, 252–64 passim
  see also Christianity, Buddhism, Islam
Rendille, Kenya, 276
Rethinking Anthropology, 3
Revolution,
  Chinese Cultural, 205–6, 209
  French, 138–48 passim
  Portuguese, 362
rock art, *see* art
Rosenthal, Frank, 240
Romania, 171–82 passim
Romanticism, 39

sacrifice
  animal, 42, 44–5, 146, 193–4, 224, 228
  symbolic, 145, 198, 230
Sahlins, M., 4
Samburu, Kenya, 11, 12, 267–80 passim
Sandawe, East Africa, 35, 50n9
SARAP (Southern African Rock Art Project),
  36, 38
Seligman, C. G., 146

serpents (snakes)
  apocalyptic, 306
  snake man guilds, 13
sex
  contemporary practices 293–4
  marital, 98, 107
  mass rape, 12, 294
  -play, 194
  satanic, 306
  -strike, 95–6, 106–8, 109n10, 120
  unmarried, 98
sexuality, 10, 271
Shackleton, Elizabeth, 27
Shilluk, Sudan, 10, 145–7
Simmel, Georg, 77–8, 80
singers
  Ethiopian, 221–5
  Haalpulaaren, 237–47
  Kenyan, 271–9
  Senegalese, 212
  in Zambia, 336, 338–9, 344
skins, (animal), 42, 82–3, 277
snakes, *see* serpents
sorcery, *see* witchcraft
spirits, 35,36,
  ancestor-, 39–48
  Buddhist, 355–65 passim
  Chinese, 210
  djinns, 39, 40, 45, 50n8
  Haalpulaar, 237, 241–2
  mahamba (matrilineal), 341
  Nyabingi (Marian), 307
  Swahili, 167
Steiner, Franz Baermann, 10, 73, 75, 77, 87–8,
  89n4
stories, *see* narratives
synchronicity, 164–5, 168, 240, 242

taboo, 76, 225, 275
  birth, 358–60
  cooking, 101, 356–8
  food, 96n20, 340
  menstrual, 99, 110n19, 110n20
tabot, see ark
Tamil, South India, 29
Tanzania
  Burundians, 344
  Cultural Policy (1997), 35, 47
  Haya, 25

Index

medicine, 159
rituals in, 35
rock art, 35–51 passim
snakesmen guilds, 13
Tapalpa, Mexico, 56–67 passim
TCM (Traditional Chinese Medicine), 159–69 passim
Thompson, E.P, 172
Teleki, Count Samuel, 276, 283
temporality, *see* time
tigers, 81–2, 86, 89, 90n16
time
  as money, 176–7
  chronology of, 24
  'collapsing', 212, 237, 237–45
  continuity of, 322–2
  'demonic' 360, 363n6
  discipline, 172
  étatisation of, 175
  'genealogical', 236–47
  'glacial' 36, 47, 49n3
  historical 77–8, 119, 228, 239, 361
  ideologies 13, 156–68 passim, 349–50, 360,
  individual, 268
  management of, 173–82 passim
  measurement of, 178
  mythic, 212, 214, 354
  'linear', 3, 5, 243, 268, 350, 361,
  ritual, 236, 243, 349
  social, 235
  symbolic, 4
  traditional cyclical', 5, 228, 239, 251–64, 361
    see also allochronicity; clocks' calendars; synchronicity
time-economics, 156
time-measurement, 178
time-punctuation, 238–9
'time-shapes', 12–14, 235–6, 224, 243–4
time-space, 13, 56

timelessness, 224, 231–3
trance, 47, 102, 106, 112n28
tribute (payment) 192–3
trickster figures, 97–9, 101
TRIPS (Agreement on Trade-Related Aspects of Intellectual Property Rights), 36
tun (military colony system), 204, 208
Turner, Victor, 3, 50n8, 79

Uganda, 12, 301–12 passim
UNESCO World Heritage, 9, 35, 37–41, 47–9
UNITA (National Union for Total Independence of Angola), 331–43 passim, 345n3, 345n9
United Nations Universal Declaration of Human Rights (1972), 37
United Nations World Heritage Convention (1972), 49n4
utopias, 138, 140

Veneese (ritual specialists), 39, 40, 45, 49n6
Vickery, Amanda, 27
visions, *see* dreams

Wagogo *see* Bantu
Wales, 21
Wasswa, Francis, 324–8 passim
weavers, 237–42 passim
Wenner-Gren Foundation, 1
West Hunan, 204–15 passim
Williams, Raymond, 55
Whyte, Michael 164, 267–8
Whyte, Susan, 164, 267–8
witchcraft, 27, 47, 290, 297n7, 343
World Heritage *see* UNESCO

Yucatán, 556

Zambia, 12, 331–2, 335
Zoroastrianism, 301